A Short History of Aurangzib

A Short History of Aurangzib

Jadunath Sarkar

Orient BlackSwan

A SHORT HISTORY OF AURANGZEB

ORIENT BLACKSWAN PRIVATE LIMITED

Registered Office
3-6-752 Himayatnagar, Hyderabad 500 029, Telangana, India
Email: centraloffice@orientblackswan.com

Other Offices
Bengaluru, Chennai, Guwahati, Hyderabad, Kolkata,
Mumbai, New Delhi, Noida, Patna

First published 2009
Reprinted 2011, 2012, 2015, 2016, 2017, 2018, 2021, 2022, 2024, 2025

ISBN 978-81-250-3690-6

040909

Typeset in Adobe Garamond 10.5/13 by
InoSoft Systems, Noida

Printed in India at
B.B. Press, Tronica City, Ghaziabad, U.P. 201 103

Published by
Orient Blackswan Private Limited
3-6-752 Himayatnagar, Hyderabad 500 029, Telangana, India
Email: info@orientblackswan.com

Contents

1. Early Life 1618–52 — 1
2. Second Viceroyalty of the Deccan 1652–58 — 21
3. Illness of Shah Jahan and the Rebellion of his Sons — 36
4. War of Succession: Aurangzib Triumphs — 47
5. War of Succession: End of Dara and Shuja — 61
6. The First half of the Reign: A General Sketch — 79
7. Wars on the Frontiers: Assam and Afghanistan — 96
8. Aurangzib's Religious Policy — 117
9. War in Rajputana: Rebellion of Akbar — 134
10. Rise of Maratha Power — 146
11. Shivaji 1670–80 — 173
12. Decline and Fall of Bijapur — 191
13. The Decline and Fall of the Qutb Shahs — 212
14. Reign of Shambhuji, 1680–89 — 227
15. Struggle with the Marathas up to 1700 — 249
16. The Last Phase of Aurangzib's Career — 281
17. Affairs of Northern India — 311
18. Some Provinces during Aurangzib's Reign — 333
19. Aurangzib's Character and the Effect of his Reign — 351
20. The Empire of Aurangzib: Its Resources, Trade and Administrative System — 378

Chronology — 389

Index — 399

1 *Early Life 1618–52*

1.1 Significance of Aurangzib's Reign

The history of Aurangzib is practically the history of India for sixty years. His own reign (1658–1707) covers the second half of the seventeenth century and stands forth as a most important epoch in the annals of our country. Under him the Mughal Empire reached its greatest extent, and the largest single state ever known in India from the dawn of history to the rise of the British power was formed. From Ghazni to Chatgaon, from Kashmir to the Karnatak, the continent of India obeyed one sceptre. Islam made its last onward movement in India in this reign. The empire thus formed, while unprecedented in size, was also one political unit. Its provinces were governed not by the mediation of sub-kings, but directly by servants of the Crown. Herein Aurangzib's Indian empire was vaster than that of Asoka, or Samudragupta or Harshavardhan.

But the reign that saw the formation of the greatest Indian empire of pre-British days, witnessed also unmistakable signs of its commencing decline and disruption. Long before Nadir Shah the Persian or Ahmad Shah the Afghan proved the Padishah to be an impotent shadow of royalty and Delhi the mere memory of past greatness, long before the Maratha confederacy hid beneath its superimposed sway the regular monarchy of the land, even before Aurangzib closed his eyes, the Mughal Empire had turned bankrupt in finance and prestige, the administration had broken down, the imperial power had confessed its failure to maintain order and hold this vast realm together.

The reign of Aurangzib is also marked by the growth of the Maratha nationality out of the ashes of their short-lived kingship, and by the appearance of the Sikh sect in the role of warriors and armed opponents of the ruling power. Thus the dominant factors of Indian history in the eighteenth and early nineteenth centuries owe their origin to Aurangzib's reign and policy.

In the very reign in which the Mughal crescent rounded to fullness and then began to wane visibly, the first glow of a new dawn was distinctly seen in our political sky. The future lords of our country's destiny gained a firm and safe footing on its soil. Madras and Bombay became presidencies of the English East India Company in 1653 and 1687 respectively; Calcutta was founded in 1690. The places of shelter thus gained by the Europeans soon formed a dominion within a dominion.

The end of the seventeenth century reveals the Mughal Empire us rotten at the core. The treasury was empty. The imperial army knew itself beaten and recoiled from its foes. The centrifugal forces were asserting themselves successfully, and the empire was ready for disruption. The moral weakness of the empire was even greater than the material: the Government no longer commanded the awe of its subjects; the public servants had lost honesty and efficiency; ministers and princes alike lacked statesmanship and ability; the army broke down as an instrument of force.

Why was it so? The ruler was free from vice, stupidity and sloth. His intellectual keenness was proverbial, and at the same time he took to the business of governing with all the ardour which men usually display in the pursuit of pleasure. In industry and attention to public affairs he could not be surpassed by any clerk. His patience and perseverance were as remarkable as his love of discipline and order. In private life he was simple and abstemious like a hermit. He faced the privations of a campaign or a forced march as uncomplainingly as the most seasoned private. No terror could daunt his heart, no weakness or pity melt it. Of the wisdom of the ancients which can be gathered from ethical books, he was a master. He had, besides, undergone a long and successful probation in war and diplomacy in his father's reign.

And yet the result of fifty years' rule by such a sovereign was failure and chaos! This political paradox makes his reign an object of supreme interest to the student of political philosophy no less than to the student of Indian history.

1.2 The Tragedy of Aurangzib's Life

The life of Aurangzib was one long tragedy—a story of man battling in vain against an invisible but inexorable Fate, a tale of how the strongest human endeavour was baffled by the forces of the age. A strenuous reign of fifty years ends in colossal failure. And yet this king was one of the greatest rulers of Asia in intelligence, character, and enterprise. This tragedy in history was developed with all the regularity of a perfect drama.

The first forty years of his life were spent in steady and arduous self-training and preparation for the supreme office in the realm. This seed-time was followed by a year of sharp contest for the throne,[1] which put all his powers to the test and rewarded his energy, courage and sagacity with the golden crown of Delhi. Then came twenty-three years of peaceful and prosperous reign and settled residence in the great capitals of northern India.[2] With every enemy removed from his path, the whole empire of India obeying his command, and wealth and culture increasing from the peace and order that his firm and vigilant rule had ensured to the country, Aurangzib seemed now to have attained the summit of human happiness and glory. This was the third Act of his life, and after it began his decline. A pitiless Nemesis, like that of the Greek tragedy, raised against him an enemy in the very bosom of his family. The rebel son of Shah Jahan cannot long enjoy his triumph because he is confronted by the rebellion of his own son Muhammad Akbar (1681).

The flight of the defeated rebel to the Maratha king drew Aurangzib to southern India, where he was destined to spend the last 26 years of his life in tents and wear out the empire's revenue, army, and organized administration as well as his own health in an unending and fruitless struggle. But the irony of Fate at first veiled from his eyes and from the eyes of his contemporaries the futility of his efforts and the impending tragic close of his career. In the fourth Act of his life,[3] all seemed to go well with him—Bijapur and Golkonda were annexed, the Berad chieftain of Sagar was forced to submit, and the troublesome Maratha king was brought to the block and his capital and entire family captured (1689). In this result nothing seemed to be wanting to complete the triumph of Aurangzib. But a few thoughtful observers could already discern ominous

---

[1] For a detailed account see Sir Jadunath Sarkar's *History of Aurangzib*, volume I & II (Orient Longman Ltd., Calcutta, 1973).

[2] For details see Sarkar: *History of Aurangzib*, volume III (Orient Longman Ltd., Calcutta, 1972).

[3] For details see Sarkar: *History of Aurargzib*, volume IV (Orient Longman Ltd., Calcutta, 1972).

signs of the coming doom, peeping out here and there, while others were still blinded as to the future by the brilliance of the empire. The seeds that had been sown in the third stage of his life, unnoticed and in ignorance of their fruits, began to sprout up in the fourth and he had to gather their baneful harvest in the fifth and closing period of his life.

Therefore, the tragedy of Aurangzib is concentrated in the last eighteen years of his life (1689–1707).[4] Slowly, but with increasing clearness does the tragic plot unfold itself, till Aurangzib realizes the true nature of the forces arrayed against him and the real trend of affairs. But he does not abandon the struggle; even when the hopelessness of the contest forces itself on him and his court, his endeavour is as strenuous as before. He tries new remedies; he changes his tactics with changes in the political situation and in the distribution of the enemy forces. At first he sends out his generals, while himself occupying a central position for their control and guidance. His generals fail to achieve a decision; very well, then this old man of eighty-two must go out to conduct the war in person for six years (1699–1705); and he retires to Ahmadnagar only when the first summons of death reach him. Then, and then only, does he mournfully recognize Ahmadnagar as destined to be his 'journey's end' *(khatam-us-safar).*

1.3 Materials for His History

Happily, the materials for a study of his life are abundant in Persian, the literary language of Mughal India. First, we have the official annals—The *Padishahnamah* (in three sections by three writers) and the *Alamgirnamah*—which cover the 41 years lying between the accession of Shah Jahan and the eleventh year of Aurangzib's reign. These works were written to order, on the basis of the State papers preserved in the imperial archives, such as official correspondence, despatches, newsletters, treaties and revenue returns. They are rich in dates and topographical details of the utmost value and accuracy. For the last forty years of Aurangzib's reign we have the concise *Masir-i-Alamgiri,* compiled from the same class of official records, but after his death.

[4] Dealt with in detail in Sarkar: *History of Aurangzib*, volume V (Orient Longman Limited, Calcutta, 1974).

Next come a class of private histories, like those of Masum Aqil Khan, a Rozbhani soldier in Bengal (metrical), and Khafi Khan. These were written by officials, but, not having been meant for the Emperor's eyes, they supply us with many of the facts suppressed in the Court annals, though their dates and names are sometimes inaccurate and their description meagre.

There are even two histories of Aurangzib's reign written by Hindus in the Persian tongue. One is the *Nuskha-i-Dilkasha* by Bhimsen Burhanpuri, the businessman of Aurangzib's general Dalpat Rao Bundela. This author was an active traveller, with a good eye for topographical details, and a careful recorder of all he saw from Mathura to Malabar. His work is of special value for Deccan affairs, because he was brought up and spent nearly all his life there. The other in the *Fatuhat-i-Alamgiri* of Ishwardas Nagar, who long served the Shaikh-ul-Islam and lived at Pattan in Gujrat. This work is of great importance for Rajput affairs.

Besides these general histories of the reign, we have monographs in Persian touching only particular episodes or personages of the time, such as Niamat Khan Ali's account of the siege of Golkonda, Shihab-ud-din Talish's diary of the conquest of Kuch Bihar, Assam, and Chatgaon, the memoirs of Iradat Khan and of some other servants of Bahadur Shah I which start from the closing years of Aurangzib's reign. Of the two Deccani kingdoms, Golkonda and Bijapur, we have separate histories, which throw light on the dealings of the Mughal Government with them. For Assam affairs we have the extremely valuable indigenous annals called *Buranjis.*

Most fortunately, for several portions of Aurangzib's reign I have been able to secure the very raw materials of history—a source of information even more valuable than the contemporary official annals described above. These are the manuscript newsletters of the imperial court *(akhbarat-i-darbar-i-muald)* preserved at Jaipur and in the Royal Asiatic Society's library (London) and the LETTERS of the actors in the political drama of the seventeenth century, of which nearly six thousand, including more than a thousand from Aurangzib himself, are in my possession. In them we see events as they happened day by day, and not as they were dressed up afterwards by writers with a purpose. In them we see the actual hopes and fears, plans and opinions of those who made Indian history.

The European travellers, Tavernier, Bernier, Careri and Manucci, who visited India in this reign, have left long accounts of the country. Their works are of undoubted value as throwing light on the condition of the people, the state of trade and industry, and the history of the Christian churches in India. Moreover, the criticism of Indian manners and institutions by foreign observers has a freshness and weight all its own. But of the political history of India, apart from the few events in which they took part or which they personally witnessed, their report merely reproduced the bazar rumours and the stories current among the populace, and cannot be set against the evidence of contemporary histories and letters in Persian.

1.4 Childhood and Education

Muhi-ud-din Mahammad Aurangzib, who ascended the throne of Delhi as Alamgir I, was the sixth child of Shah Jahan and Mumtaz Mahal. He was born at Dohad[5] in the night of 15th Ziqada, 1027 A.H. (A.D. 24 October, 1618, Old Style).

From 1622 till the end of his father's reign, Shah Jahan was under the old Emperor's disfavour and was driven into rebellion in self-defence. But the prince's efforts were unsuccessful, and he had at last to submit to his father and give up his young sons, Dara and Aurangzib, as hostages. These two reached Jahangir's Court at Lahor in June 1626. Shortly afterwards Jahangir died, Shah Jahan ascended the throne, and the two boys were brought to him at Agra by Asaf Khan (26 February 1628).

Thus, at the age of ten he came to a settled life; and arrangements were evidently now made for his regular education. Mir Muhammad Hashim of Gilan is recorded as his teacher. Bernier speaks of Mulla Salih as his old teacher, but the Persian histories do not bear this statement out.

That Aurangzib had a natural keenness of mind and quickly learnt what he read, we can readily believe. His correspondence proves that he had thoroughly mastered the *Quran* and the *Traditional Sayings of Muhammad (Hadis)*, and was ever ready with apt quotations from them.

[5] Dohad (22.50 N. 74.20 E.) is a sub-division of the Panch Mahal district in the Bombay Presidency, and the town stands just south of the Dohad Station on the B. B. & C. I. Railway, *(Publisher's note:* It now falls in the Panch Mahals district of Gujarat, and is close to the border of Madhya Pradesh.)

He spoke and wrote Arabic and Persian like a scholar. Hindustani was his mother tongue, the language used by the Mughal Court in private life. He had some knowledge of Hindi, too, and could talk and recite popular sayings in that language.

Aurangzib wrote Arabic in vigorous and masterly *naskh* hand. In this he used to copy the *Quran.* Two such manuscripts of his transcription he presented to Mecca and Medina, after richly binding and illuminating them. 'His *nastaliq,* and *shikasta* styles of writing were also excellent,' says Saqi Mustad Khan, and this we can readily believe, for Aurangzib was the author of a vast number of letters, and made it a point to write orders across all petitions in his own hand. He did not like to hear useless poetry, still less laudatory verses. But he made an exception in favour of poems containing good counsels. 'His favourite study was theological works—commentaries on the *Quran,* the traditions of Muhammad, Canon Law, the works of Imam Muhammad Ghazzali, selections from the letters of Shaikh Sharf Yahia of Munir and Shaikh Zain-ud-din Qutb Muhi Shirazi, and other works of that class.'

Painting he never appreciated. Music he banished from his Court, in the outburst of devotion which marked the completion of the tenth year of his reign. Fine chinaware he liked. But he had none of his father's passion for buildings. No masterpiece of architecture, no superb or exquisite mosque,[6] hall, or tomb marks his reign. All that he built were commonplace necessary things, such as the mosques which marked the scenes of his victories, and the numberless *sarais* (resthouses) which he built along the imperial highways running to the south and the west.

1.5 Aurangzib Fights an Elephant

One incident of his boyhood made his fame ring throughout India. On 28 May, 1633, Shah Jahan set two huge elephants, Sudhakar and Surat-sundar by name, to fight a combat on the level bank of the Jamuna at Agra. They ran for some distance and then grappled together just below the balcony of the morning salute in the fort. The Emperor hastened

[6] Except one, the Pearl Mosque in the Delhi palace, which was begun on 10 Dec. 1659 and completed in 5 years at a cost of one lakh and sixty thousand rupees, *(A.N.,* 469). His mosque at Labor is not the best one in that city. The tomb of his wife Dilras Banu at Aurangabad was his grandest building.

there to see the fight, his eldest three sons riding a few paces before him. Aurangzib, intent on seeing the fight, edged his way very close to the elephants.

After a while the brutes let go their grip and each stepped back a little. Sudhakar's spirit was fully roused. Losing sight of his opponent he turned and charged Aurangzib who was standing by. The prince, then only fourteen years old, calmly stood his ground, kept his horse from turning back, and flung his spear at the elephant's head. All was now confusion and alarm. The nobles and the servants ran about shouting, fireworks were let off to scare away the elephant, but all to no effect. The animal came on and felled Aurangzib's horse with a sweep of his long tusk. But the prince jumped up from the ground, drew his sword, and faced the raging beast. His elder brother Shuja, in trying to force his way through the crowd and smoke, was thrown to the ground by his horse rearing. Rajah Jai Singh, too, came up. And then an unlocked for diversion came to the prince's aid. The other elephant, Surat-sundar, ran up to renew the combat, and Sudhakar, daunted by the spear thrusts and fireworks discharged at him, fled from the field with his rival thundering at his heels. The princes were saved. Shah Jahan clasped Aurangzib to his bosom, praised his courage, and gave him the title of *Bahadur* or 'hero'. The courtiers cried out that the boy had inherited his father's reckless courage, and reminded each other how Shah Jahan in his youth had attacked, sword in hand, a wild tiger before the eyes of Jahangir.

On this occasion Aurangzib gave a foretaste of his lofty spirit. When his father lovingly chided him for his rash courage, he replied, 'If the fight had ended fatally for me it would not have been a matter of shame. Death drops the curtain even on Emperors; it is no dishonour.'

On 13 December, 1634, he got his first post in the Mughal peerage, with the rank of a Commander of Ten Thousand Horse. Next September he was sent to the Bundela expedition in order to learn the art of war and the control of men by actual experience.

1.6 The Bundela War 1635

Bir Singh Dev, the Bundela Rajah of Urchha, had risen to great wealth and power through the favour of Jahangir, at whose bidding he had murdered Abul Fazl. His son Jhujhar Singh who succeeded him in 1627, proved refractory in Shah Jahan's reign. He seized the old Gond capital of Chauragarh, slew its Rajah Prem Narayan, and seized his treasure amounting to ten lakhs of rupees. The victim's son appealed to Shah Jahan (1635).

The Emperor sent three armies to converge upon and invade Bundelkhand, with the help of Devi Singh, a descendant of another branch of the Bundela royal family, to whom the throne was now offered. But a supreme commander was needed, whose high position would enforce discipline and ensure unity of plan and cooperation among the three Mughal generals, who were of equal rank. For this purpose Aurangzib was appointed as the nominal head of the expedition. He was to stay in the rear, but the generals were not to act without consulting him.

On 2 October, 1635, a hillock near Urchha was stormed by Devi Singh's men, and on the fourth the Mughals took Urchha itself. Jhujhar had lost heart and fled to Dhamuni and thence, across the Narmada, to Chauragarh. The Mughals, after capturing Dhamuni (18 October), took up the chase of Jhujhar, who was hunted through the Gond countries of Deogarh and Chanda, undergoing terrible privations and fatigue and abandoning his men and property at every step. At last, when sleeping in the heart of the jungle, the fugitive princes were surprised by the Gonds and done to death (December). Such of their wives and daughters as had survived the *jauhar* rite (self-immolation) were dragged into the Mughal harem. Two sons and one grandson of Jhujhar, being of tender age, were made Musalmans; another son and the minister of the late Rajah refused to apostatize and were executed in cold blood. The lofty temple of Bir Singh at Urchha was demolished and a mosque was erected on its site. The fort of Jhansi was taken and the spoils of war including the buried treasure of Bir Singh, amounting to one *crore* of rupees, sent to Delhi.

1.7 Aurangzib's First Viceroyalty of the Deccan 1636–44

Towards the close of Akbar's reign, the Mughal Empire began to expand southwards beyond the Narmada river. Khandesh was annexed in 1599, then Berar and finally in 1600 the city of Ahmadnagar. Its boy, Sultan Nizam Shah was deposed and his kingdom annexed to the Mughal Empire. But the annexation was in name only, as the Mughals could not effectively occupy the new conquest. During Jahangir's feeble reign there was a revival of the Nizam-shahi dynasty and power under the wise and vigorous regency of Malik Ambar, an Abyssinian slave of rare genius and capacity. His wise revenue system made the peasantry happy, while enriching the State. A born leader of men, he conciliated all parties, maintained order, and left a name for justice, vigour and public benefit which has not been yet forgotten. Building up a grand alliance of the Deccani Powers and fully using the Maratha light cavalry, he drove the Mughals back.

Shah Jahan, on his accession in 1627, which just followed Malik Ambar's death, began a vigorous policy in the Deccan. The new Nizam-shahi capital Daulatabad was captured with Husain Shah, the last king of the dynasty (1633). But a fresh complication now arose. The Sultans of Bijapur (Adil Shah) and Golkonda (Qutb Shah) tried to seize the adjoinning parts of the fallen kingdom of Ahmadnagar. Shahji, the father of the famous Shivaji, with Bijapuri help, set up a puppet Nizam Shah and ruled one-fourth of the country in his name.

Shah Jahan made heroic exertions to establish his rights. For more efficient administration, Daulatabad and Ahmadnagar were now separated from the province of Khandesh and placed under another viceroy (November 1634). In February 1636 the Emperor himself arrived in the Deccan to direct the operations. Three Mughal armies, totalling 50,000 men, were held ready to be launched upon Bijapur and Golkonda, while a fourth (8,000 strong) invaded Maharashtra. Qutb Shah immediately submitted in terror, promised an annual tribute of two lakhs of *hun,* and proclaimed the Mughal Emperor as his suzerain.

The king of Bijapur made a stand for his independence. But the three Mughal armies at once entered his kingdom, utterly desolating the fields and villages and enslaving the population. At last in May 1636 a compromise was made. By this treaty, the late Nizam-shahi kingdom was divided between the two powers, the Bijapur Sultan getting Sholapur and Wangi (between the Bhima and the Sina rivers), Bhalki and Chidgupa (in the north-east), the Puna district and North Konkan—in all yielding a revenue of 20 lakhs of *hun* (or 80 lakhs of rupees). The rest of the Ahmadnagar State was annexed to the Mughal Empire. In addition, Adil Shah recognized the overlordship of the Mughal Emperor, promised to be friendly to his fellow-vassal the Sultan of Golkonda (whose boundary was fixed at the Manjera river), and agreed to pay an indemnity of 20 lakhs of rupees, but no annual tribute.

The affairs of the Deccan having been at last settled and the Mughal boundary clearly marked and publicly recognized by the local princes, Shah Jahan returned to northern India, leaving Aurangzib (14 July, 1636) as viceroy of the Deccan, with his seat at Aurangabad. This town, founded by Malik Ambar at the village of Khirki, was allowed by Shah Jahan to be named *Aurangabad* after his third son.

The Mughal conquests in the Deccan were completed by the capture of the forts of Udgir (28 September) and Ausa (19 October), and the crushing defeat of Shahji Bhonsle, who, after a long chase by the Mughal general Khan-i-Zaman and his Bijapuri auxiliary Randaula Khan, had to make a complete surrender at Mahuli (in North Konkan) at the end of October. He gave up to the Mughals his puppet Nizam Shah with his royal property, seven forts, and all his territories in Maharashtra except his small jagirs in the Puna district, which were to be held as a vassal of Bijapur.

Another Mughal general, Khan-i-Dauran, levied heavy contributions from the Gond Rajah of Deogarh and other chiefs. In January 1638, Aurangzib sent an army to conquer Baglana, a small kingdom north of the Chandor range lying on the main route from the Deccan to Gujrat and containing the famous hill-forts of Salhir and Mulhir. Mulhir and Pipla were gained and the entire kingdom annexed by the end of June. Next year (1639) in October, Aurangzib caused the Maratha freebooter Kheloji Bhonsle, a son of Shahji's paternal uncle, to be seized and put to death.

1.8 Aurangzib's Family

Aurangzib had four wives, namely:

1. *Dilras Banu Begam,* a daughter of Shah Nawaz Khan (whose great-grandfather was a younger son of the Persian king Shah Ismail I Safavi). She was married to Aurangzib at Agra on 8 May, 1637, with the most gorgeous ceremonies. She died at Aurangabad on 8 October, 1657, from illness following the birth of her son Muhammad Akbar, and was buried outside that city, with the title of *Rabia-ul-dauaani* or the modern Saint Rabia. Her tomb, popularly called the Deccani Taj Mahal, was repaired by her son Azam under order of Aurangzib. She seems to have been an

imperious lady, proud of bearing the 'Royal blood of Persia,' and her husband stood in awe of her.[7]

2. *Rahmat-un-nisa,* surnamed *Nawab Bai,* was the daughter of Rajah Raju of the Rajauri State in Kashmir, and came of the hill-Rajput blood. But on her son Bahadur Shah's accession to the throne of Delhi, a false pedigree was invented for her in order to give that Emperor the right to call himself a Sayyid. She built a *sarai* at Fardapur, at the foot of the pass, and also founded Baijipura, a suburb of Aurangabad. The misconduct of her sons, Muhammad Sultan and Muazzam, who disobeyed the Emperor under the influence of evil counsellors, embittered her latter life. Her advice and even personal entreaty had no effect on Muazzam, who was at last placed under arrest. Nawab Bai seems to have lost her charms and with them her husband's favour rather early in life, and ended her days in 1691 at Delhi after many years of separation from her husband and sons.
3. *Aurangabadi Mahal,* so named because she entered the prince's harem, in the city Aurangabad. The bubonic plague carried her off at the city of Bijapur in October or November 1688.
4. *Udipuri Mahal,* the mother of Kam Bakhsh. The contemporary Venetian traveller Manucci speaks of her as a Georgian slave-girl of Dara Shukoh's harem who, on the downfall of her first master, became the concubine of his victorious rival. She seems to have been a very young woman at the time, as she first became a mother in 1667. She retained her charms and influence over the Emperor till his death, and was the darling of his old age. Under the spell of her beauty he pardoned the many faults of Kam Bakhsh and overlooked her freaks of drunkenness which must have shocked so pious a Muslim as he.

Beside the above four there was another woman whose supple grace, musical skill, and mastery of blandishments made her the heroine of the only romance in the puritan Emperor's life. *Hira Bai,* surnamed *Zainabadi,* was a young slave-girl in the keeping of Mir Khalil, who had married a

---

[7] Sir Jadunath Sarkar: *Anecdotes of Aurangzib,* No. 27 (to be reprinted shortly by Orient Longman Limited).

sister of Aurangzib's mother. During his viceroyalty of the Deccan, the prince paid a visit to his aunt at Burhanpur. There, while strolling in the park of Zainabad on the other side of the Tapti, he beheld Hira Bai unveiled among his aunt's train. The artful beauty 'on seeing a mango-tree laden with fruits, advanced in mirth and amorous play, jumped up, and plucked a mango, as if unconscious of the prince's presence.' The vision of her matchless charms stormed Aurangzib's heart in a moment; 'with shameless importunity he took her away from his aunt's house and became utterly infatuated with her,' so much so, that one day she offered him a cup of wine and pressed him to drink it. All his entreaties and excuses were disregarded, and the helpless lover was about to taste the forbidden drink when the sly enchantress snatched away the cup from his lips and said, 'My object was only to test your love for me, and not to make you fall into the sin of drinking!' Death cut the story short when she was still in the bloom of youth. Aurangzib bitterly grieved at her loss and buried her close to the big tank at Aurangabad.

Aurangzib had numerous progenies. His principal wife, Dilras Banu Begam, bore him five children:

1. *Zeb-un-nisa,* a daughter, born at Daulatabad, on 15 February, 1638, died at Delhi on 26 May, 1702, buried in the garden of 'thirty Thousand Trees,' outside the Kabul Gate. Her tomb was demolished to make room for a railway. She seems to have inherited her father's keenness of intellect and literary tastes. Her library surpassed all other private collections, and she employed many scholars on liberal salaries to produce literary works at her bidding or to copy manuscripts for her. As Aurangzib disliked poetry, her liberality compensated for the lack of court patronage, and most of the poets of the age sought refuge with her. She wrote Persian odes under the pen-name of *Makhfi* or the Concealed One. But the extant *Diwan-i-Makhfi* was certainly not her work.
2. *Zinat-un-nisa* afterwards surnamed Padishah Begam, "born probably at Aurangabad, on 5 October, 1643. She looked after her old father's household in the Deccan for a quarter of a century till his death, and survived him many years, enjoying the respect of his successors as the living memorial of a great age. Historians speak of her piety and extensive charity. She died at Delhi on 7 May,

1721, and was buried in the Zinat-ul-masajid, a splendid mosque built (1700) at her expense in Delhi.

3. *Zubdat-un-nisa,* born at Multan, 2 September, 1651, married to her first cousin, Sipihr Shukoh (the second son of the ill-fated Dara Shukoh) on 30 January, 1673, died in February, 1707.
4. *Muhammad Azam,* born at Burhanpur on 28 June, 1653, slain at Jajaw, 8 June, 1707, in the war of succession following his father's death.
5. *Muhammad Akbar,* born at Aurangabad, on 11 September, 1657, died an exile in Persia about November, 1704. Buried at Mashhad'.

By Nawab Bai the Emperor had three children:

6. *Muhammad Sultan,* born near Mathura, 19 December, 1639, died in prison, 3 December, 1676. Buried in the enclosure of Khwajah Qutb-ud-din's tomb.
7. *Muhammad Muazzam,* surnamed Shah Alam, who succeeded his father as Bahadur Shah I, born at Burhanpur on 4 October, 1643, died at Lahor on 18 February, 1712.
8. *Badr-un-nisa,* born on 17 November, 1647, died 9 April, 1670.

Aurangabadi Mahal bore Aurangzib only one child:

9. *Mihr-un-nisa,* born on 18 September, 1661, married to her first cousin Izid Bakhsh (a son of the murdered Murad Bakhsh) on 27 November, 1672, died in June, 1706.

Udipuri Mahal was the mother of

10. *Muhammad Kam Bakhsh,* born at Delhi, 24 February, 1667, slain in the war of succession, near Haidarabad on 3 January, 1709.

1.9 AURANGZIB IN DISGRACE

Aurangzib's first viceroyalty of the Deccan ended strangely in his disgrace and dismissal, in 1644.

On the night of 26 March, 1644, the princess Jahanara was coming from her father's chambers to her own in Agra fort, when her skirt brushed against one of the candles lighting the passage. She was so severely burnt that for four months she hovered between life and death.

The Physician Royal of Delhi laboured in vain to cure her burns, but a slave named Arif prepared an ointment which entirely healed her sores. On 25 November, began a most splendid and costly festivity in celebration of her complete recovery. At her request Aurangzib was restored to his father's favour and his former rank and office, which he had lost in the meantime.

Aurangzib had arrived at Agra on 2 May, to see his sister. Here, three weeks afterwards, he had been suddenly dismissed from his post, and deprived of his rank and allowance. From one of his letters we gather that he resigned his post as a protest against Dara's persistent hostility and Shah Jahan's partiality to his eldest son which robbed Aurangzib of the Emperor's confidence and support. He felt that his prestige was lowered in the public eye and he could not govern the Deccan consistently with self-respect or with any chance of doing good service.[8]

At Jahanara's intercession the Emperor restored Aurangzib to his favour, and on 16 February, 1645, sent him off to Gujrat as Governor. His viceroyalty of this province ended in January, 1647, when he was appointed to Balkh. But even in this brief period of less than two years he showed his adminstrative capacity and firmness.

Aurangzib followed an active and firm policy towards the robber tribes and rebels of Gujrat. In order to check them effectually he engaged soldiers in excess of the men whom he was bound to keep by his present rank as a *mansabdar.* He thus established in his father's eyes a reputation for capacity and courage, and it was not long before he was called away to a far-off scene where there was supreme need of these qualities, by being created Governor and Commander-in-Chief of Balkh and Badakhshan (21 January, 1647).

1.10 Aurangzib's Campaigns in Balkh 1647

The provinces of Balkh and Badakhshan, lying immediately beyond the Hindu Kush range north of Kabul, Were dependencies of the Kingdom

[8] A literal interpretation of a Persian phrase *(manzavi)* has given rise in English histories to the myth that young Aurangzib turned hermit in a fit of religious devotion. The fact is that at this time he felt no religious call at all; his motive was political, not spiritual: he merely resigned his office, but did not actually take to a hermit's life. How Aurangzib made a public display of his jealousy towards Dara and was punished by Shah Jahan in consequence, is described in the *Anecdotes of Aurangzib,* No. 2.

of Bukhara. Their king, Nazar Muhammad Khan, was a weak and incompetent ruler, who alienated all classes of his subjects. Within three years of his accession to the throne, rebellions broke out in many parts of his vast kingdom (1645). Shah Jahan seized the opportunity by sending an expedition to conquer Balkh and Badakhshan, 'because these two provinces were the heritage of Babar and also lay in the way to Samarqand, the capital of Timur, who had founded the Mughal dynasty.'

In the month of June in 1646, Prince Murad Bakhsh, with a vast army easily occupied Badakhshan and Balkh. But the prince and his officers alike detested service in the poor, dull and uncongenial land of Central Asia and dreaded any contest with the fierce Uzbeks from beyond the Oxus. In August Murad returned from Balkh, against the Emperor's wishes, leaving his army without a leader! Aurangzib was then sent to retrieve the situation. Leaving Kabul on 7 April, 1647, with Ali Mardan Khan as his right-hand man, he fought his way through the Uzbek hordes step by step and reached the city of Balkh on 25 May.

At the head of the Bukhara national defence stood Abdul Aziz Khan, the able and heroic eldest son of Nazar Muhammad. Under his directions the Uzbek hordes assembled at different places in Balkh and threatened to isolate and invest the Mughal troops. When Aurangzib marched out of the city of Balkh to break up the enemy gathering at Aqcha (40 miles to the northwest), he was daily opposed by the Uzbeks on the way, while another body of them arrived from Bukhara to attack the city of Balkh. The news of it forced Aurangzib to fall back on his capital, fighting every inch of the ground. This march and retreat took up ten days during which the Mughal army was a stranger to repose. Day after day a strenuous fight had to be maintained against the tireless and mobile enemy, while hunger raged in the imperial ranks. The soldiers were ever on the move, and food could be cooked only on the backs of the marching elephants! Bread sold at one rupee or even two rupees a piece and water was equally dear, and there was not enough for all. But in the midst of all this hardship and danger, Aurangzib's firmness and control prevented any slackness or disorder; his watchful eye and active body hastened to the succour of every weak spot, and his wisdom and courage brought the army back to safety.

Aurangzib's grim tenacity had gained its object. Abdul Aziz now desired to make peace. His hope of crushing Aurangzib had failed. He had personally witnessed a striking proof of the prince's cool courage—one day at the hour of evening prayer when the battle was at its hottest, Aurangzib spread his carpet on the field, knelt down and calmly said his prayers, regardless of the strife and din around him. He was then, as during the rest of the campaign, without armour and shield. The Bukhara army gazed on the scene with wonder, and Abdul Aziz, in generous admiration, stopped the fight, crying out, 'To fight with such a man is to court one's own ruin.'

Abdul Aziz proposed that Balkh should be delivered to his younger brother Subhan Quli, as Shah Jahan had publicly offered to restore the country to their father. Aurangzib referred the question to the Emperor, who decided to restore the country to Nazar Muhammad, if the latter saved imperial prestige by begging the Emperor's pardon!

This was done. On 1 October the fort of Balkh was delivered to Nazar Muhammad's agents, and the Mughal army began its retreat to Kabul, undergoing terrible privations and loss of life and treasure in crossing the Hindu Kush passes in the teeth of attacks from the rear and front by Uzbeks and Hazaras. The imperialists lost 5,000 men in this region, besides an equally large number of transport animals. The grain and other provisions and military stores which the Mughals had to abandon were worth several lakhs of rupees. The war cost the Indian treasury four crores of rupees, while not an inch of territory was gained as the result of it.

After the Balkh expedition, Aurangzib acted as governor of Multan and Sindh from March 1648 to July 1652. During this period he was twice called away from his province to lay siege to Qandahar and to try to wrest that fort from the Persians, (January to December 1649 and March to July 1652). His new province contained the wildest and most untractable Afghan and Baluch clans. What Aurangzib could do in that short time was to strike down the most notorious brigand chieftains and secure a nominal profession of allegiance to the Emperor from the border clans.

He also set himself to revive the commerce of the province by affording facilities to the maritime trade. Tatta having ceased to be a port by the accumulation of sand at the river mouth, Aurangzib opened a new port further down the Indus and built there a fort and a dock.

1.11 Aurangzib Besieges Qandahar 1649–52

The fort of Qandahar guards the road to India from the west and to Kabul from the south. Its strategic importance lies in the fact that only 360 miles of level country separate it from Herat, near which the lofty Hindu Kush range sinks down to afford an easy passage to an invading host from Central Asia or Persia. Such an army must pass through Qandahar and must be turned back there, if ever at all. In an age when Kabul was a part of the Delhi Empire, Qandahar was our indispensable first line of defence.

In the seventeenth century, when the Portuguese navy dominated the Indian Ocean and nearly closed the sea-route from India to the Persian Gulf, the commercial importance of Qandahar was no less than its strategic. All west-bound merchandise from India and even the Spice Islands had to follow the land route through Multan, Pishin and Qandahar to Persia and thence to Europe. In 1615, fourteen thousand loaded camels passed into Persia by this route, and the city of Qandahar grew rapidly in wealth and size as a most convenient centre for the exchange of commodities.

Its position naturally made Qandahar a bone of contention between the rulers of Persia and India. In 1522 Babar gained it from its Afghan ruler, but the Persian king conquered it in 1558. Then Akbar bought it from its Persian prince-governor in 1594; but in Jahangir's old age, Shah Abbas the Great took it after a siege of 45 days (1623). In 1638 its Persian governor Ali Mardan Khan, afraid of his master's wrath, delivered the fort to Shah Jahan. But the Persians were not to be denied; in February 1649 they finally wrested it from the Mughals, after a siege of 57 days, while Shah Jahan delayed in sending a relieving force.

Imperial prestige requited that Qandahar should be won back from the Persians, and three costly sieges were undertaken by Shah Jahan's sons, but all to no avail. The first expedition, under Aurangzib and the Wazir Sadullah Khan, 50,000 strong, arrived before Qandahar on 14 May, 1649, and completely invested the fort; but their lack of large cannon made it impossible for them to assault the fort, which was far superior in the calibre and range of its artillery. As the Delhi court historian frankly admits, 'The Persians had grown expert in the capture and defence of forts, by their long wars with the Turks. They were masters of fire-arms and artillery. They held such a strong and well-provisioned fort, with big guns and skilful gunners.... So the imperialists failed with all their efforts.' On 5 September, Aurangzib began his retreat from Qandahar, after having wasted 3 months and 20 days before it. However, in a pitched battle on the bank of the Arghandab, some 24 miles southwest of Qandahar, his generals Qalich Khan and Rustam Khan Deccani signally defeated a large Persian army and pursued it beyond Kushk-i-Nakhud.

Preparations were made on a grander scale for a second attempt to recover Qandahar. Again Aurangzib and Sadullah Khan appeared before the fort and laid siege to it (2 May 1652). Batteries were raised for breaching the walls, and trenches were run towards the ditch of the fort; an attempt was made to drain the ditch dry, and a night attack on the peak of the ridge behind the Forty Steps *(Chihil Zind)* towers was delivered. But all the efforts of the Mughal failed. 'The trenches could not be carried any nearer in face of the severe fire showered from the fort walls.... The enemy issued on three sides, and from sunset to dawn fired their muskets incessantly from loopholes in the fort-walls, so as to give no opportunity to Aurangzib's workmen to make progress.' In fact, the Persian artillery was as excellent as the Mughal was inefficient. The Indian gunners were proverbially bad marksmen and their fire produced no effect on the fort walls.

Within a month of opening the siege, the work of draining the ditch and running mines had to be suspended for lack of materials. The Persians made repeated sorties killing and wounding the Mughals in the trenches and damaging their guns. Even after two months of bombardment the fort walls were unbreached, and it would have been madness to deliver an assault on such a fort. Finally, by Shah Jahan's order, the Mughal army raised the siege and began its retreat from Qandahar on 9 July.

Shah Jahan was very angry with Aurangzib for this ill-success, which he wrongly ascribed to the prince's incapacity. But in truth it is unjust to blame Aurangzib for the failure to take Qandahar. Throughout the siege he was really second in command. The Emperor, from Kabul, directed every movement through Sadullah Khan. His sanction had to be taken for every important step.

Aurangzib's best justification was afforded next year, when a still vaster and costlier expedition against Qandahar led by Dara Shukoh met with an even more humiliating defeat. These three futile sieges cost the Indian treasury over ten crores of rupees, and ruined Mughal prestige in the eyes of all Asia. The Persian king could rightly boast that the rulers of Delhi knew how to steal a fort by means of gold, but not how to conquer it by strength of arms. Naturally the military fame of Persia rose very high. Throughout the rest of the century the rumour of a projected invasion from Persia used to throw the court of Delhi into the greatest alarm. For years afterwards the Persian peril hung like a dark' cloud on the western frontier of India, and the Emperor Aurangzib and his ministers drew their breath more easily when any warlike Shah of Persia died.

2 Second Viceroyalty of the Deccan 1652–58

2.1 Decay and Misery of Moghal Deccan: Financial Difficulties

On his return from Qandahar to Kabul, Aurangzib was appointed subahdar of the Deccan for the second time (1652). After a nine months' halt at Burhanpur on the way, he arrived at his capital, Aurangabad, in November, 1653, and there spent the next four years, leaving it only to invade Golkonda and Bijapur and finally departing on 5 February, 1658, to contest the throne of Delhi.

Since Aurangzib had laid down the viceroyalty of the Deccan in May 1644, the Mughal administration there had not prospered. True, the country enjoyed unwonted repose, but much cultivated soil had lapsed into jungle, the cultivators had declined in number and resources, and the revenue had fallen off greatly. This wretched state of things was the natural result of a succession of short viceroyalties and incompetent viceroys.

The Deccan had long caused a heavy drain on the imperial treasury. The province was large, the country broken, with plenty of jungles, imperfectly settled and organized, and there were two powerful States across the frontier. Therefore, a very large force had to be stationed there. But as the soil was sterile, bad harvests and scarcities were too frequent and standard revenue was never collected. For the four provinces which then constituted Mughal Deccan it stood at three crores and 62 lakhs of rupees a year; but the actual collection in 1652 was only one crore, or less than one-third. Hence, the public income of the Deccan did not balance the expenditure, and the deficit had to be made good by sending money from the older and richer provinces of the empire to support the administration of the South.

On his arrival in the Deccan, Aurangzib was faced with a serious financial difficulty. The actual yield of the *jagirs* was only a fraction of their nominal revenue. The Mughal officers posted in the Deccan would have starved if they had to depend solely on their *jagirs* in that province. Everywhere Aurangzib found signs of maladministration, the work of his predecessors. The actual collection was sometimes only one-tenth of the normal assessment. The new viceroy found it impossible to make both ends meet. At this time the civil and military expenditure of the Deccan, exclusive of the salary derived by the officers from their *jagirs,* produced an annual deficit of Rs 20,36,000, which was made good by drawing on the reserve stored in the treasuries of the Deccan.

Aurangzib shared the difficulty of other *jagirdars* in the Deccan in having to keep up his normal contingent of troops on an income reduced to a fraction of his normal pay. The financial wrangle between father and son dragged on for years. Shah Jahan wished to put a stop to the drain of money to the Deccan, and here was Aurangzib asking for cash from other provinces in the place of *jagirs* in the Deccan!

When appointing him to the Deccan, Shah Jahan had urged Aurangzib to pay special attention to the improvement of the peasantry and the extension of cultivation. Aurangzib had promised to do his best for these objects. He only pleaded for a sufficiently long tenure and the men and money necessary for this purpose, as the depopulation and ravage caused by a generation of warfare followed by ten years of maladministration could not be undone in two or three years. Very soon his viceroyalty was destined to become memorable for ever in the history of land-settlement in the Deccan.

2.2 Murshid Quli Khan: His Character and Revenue System

Murshid Quli Khan was a native of Khurasan who had migrated to India in the train of Ali Mardan Khan, the fugitive Persian governor of Qandahar. He 'combined the valour of a soldier with the administrative capacity of a civil servant.' As *diwan* of Aurangzib in the Deccan, Murshid Quli effected revenue reforms and first achieved success for his new system.

The Deccan hitherto had no revenue system at all. Here, the marking out of plots, the measurement of land by chain survey, the assessment of revenue at so much per *bigha,* or the sharing of the actual produce between the State, landlord and the cultivator were unknown. The peasant in the Deccan cultivated as much land as he could with a plough and a pair of oxen, grew whatever crop he liked, and paid to the State a small amount *per plough*—the rate of revenue varying in different places and being fixed arbitrarily. Thus the peasantry lay open to the caprice and extortion of the petty collectors. The long wars of Mughal aggression and a succession of rainless years completed their ruin. The oppressed *ryots* fled from their homes, the deserted fields lapsed into jungle; many once-flourishing villages became manless wilderness.

The new *diwan's* reform consisted in extending Todar Mal's system to the Deccan. First, he worked hard to gather the scattered *ryots* together and restore the normal life of the villages by giving them their full population and proper chain of officers. Everywhere wise *amins* and honest surveyors were deputed to measure the land, to prepare the record of well marked out holdings *(raqba)*, and to distinguish arable land from rocky soils and water-courses. Where a village had lost its headman *(muqaddam)* he took care to appoint a new headman from the persons whose character gave the best promise of their readiness to promote cultivation and take sympathetic care of the peasantry. The poorer *ryots* were granted loans *(taqavvi)* from the public treasury, for the purchase of cattle, seeds and other needful materials of agriculture, and the advance was recovered at harvest time by instalments.

He had the wisdom to modify his system according to differences of local conditions. Where the peasantry were backward and the population scanty, or where the villages were situated in obscure nooks, he left the old usage of a fixed lump payment per plough undisturbed. In many other places he introduced the system of *metayership* or sharing of the actual produce.

His third method of revenue settlement was the elaborate and complex one of northern India. Here the standard or maximum government share was one-fourth of the total produce, whether grain or pot-herb, fruit or seed. The revenue at the fixed *rate* of so many *rupees per bigha* was assessed and collected after considering the quantity and quality of the crop from seed-time to harvest and its market-price, and actually measuring the sown area. This became the prevalent system in the *subahs* of Mughal Deccan and was known for centuries afterwards as 'the *dhara* of Murshid Quli Khan.' His excellent system, backed by his constant vigilance and personal supervision, led to the improvement of agriculture and increase of the revenue in a few years.

2.3 Improvements made in the Deccan administration by Aurangzib

Immediately on assuming the viceroyalty, Aurangzib tried his best to make the administration efficient. Old and incompetent men were dismissed or removed to minor posts; a number of officers of proved ability were selected by the prince, and to them all situations of trust and importance were given. Keen on securing military efficiency, Aurangzib first of all assured that financial support without which an army cannot be kept up to the mark.

A very able and energetic Inspector-General of Ordnance soon made a clean sweep of the old abuses. He visited every fort, inspected everything, great and small, and supplied every place with the requisite store of food and munitions. Old and useless men who were being borne on the establishment of the artillery were made to undergo an examination in musketry. Those who could not hit the mark even once were dismissed. Old and disabled soldiers were put on pension in consideration of their past services. Thus this officer effected a saving of Rs 50,000 a year, while actually improving the efficiency of the army.

2.4 Causes of Aurangzib's Differences with the Emperor

Aurangzib's second viceroyalty of the Deccan was marked by a series of wrangles with his father. Either Aurangzib's enemies had got hold of the Emperor's ears, or the latter failed to appreciate the prince's difficulties in the South. Aurangzib was misunderstood, suspected, and unjustly reprimanded from the very beginning of his term of office. And the bitterness of feeling thus aroused was one of the reasons why the War of Succession was conducted so heartlessly and unscrupulously.

At the very time of his appointment to the Deccan Aurangzib objected to it, as his *jagirs* there would yield 17 lakhs of rupees less than the fertile fiefs he was holding in Sindh.

His proposal to be given more productive *jagirs* in exchange for the existing ones was the cause of prolonged and acrimonious correspondence with the Emperor.

In some cases the viceroy's recommendations for postings and promotions among his subordinates were not accepted by the Emperor, and the prince wrote indignantly to his father, 'I have been a subahdar since the age of 18 years, and I have never recommended a single man who has proved unfit for his post.' On many other points there were differences between father and son.

Another cause of friction was the charge of diplomatic relations with Bijapur and Golkonda. Aurangzib justly contended that the Mughal envoys at these Courts should take their orders from the viceroy of the Deccan and imperial correspondence with them should pass through his hands. But this power was conceded to him only towards the close of his administration, and even then not fully.

At one time Aurangzib was so disgusted with being constantly misunderstood, censured, and hampered by the Emperor, that he refused to take a most necessary step on his own initiative, but justified his inaction with the bitter remark, 'No wonder that I did not take the responsibility of doing it, seeing that I have been taken to task for acts which I never did. I have now grown more cautious!'

2.5 Minor Expeditions

In the sixteenth and seventeenth centuries much of the modern Central Provinces were under the sway of aboriginal Gond chiefs and was known under the name of Gondwana. The great Gond kingdom of Garh-Mandla had been crippled by a Mughal invasion and the sack of the capital in Akbar's reign and later by Bundela encroachments from the north. But about the middle of the seventeenth century another Gond kingdom, with its capital at Deogarh, rose to greatness, and extended its sway over the districts of Betul, Chindwara and Nagpur, and portions of Seoni, Bhandara and Balaghat. In the southern part of Gondwana stood the town of Chanda, the seat of a third Gond dynasty, the hereditary foe and rival of the Rajah of Deogarh.

In 1637 Khan-i-Dauran had invaded Deogarh and forced the Rajah to promise an annual tribute of 1 1/3 lakhs of rupees to the Emperor. But the tribute fell into arrears, and repeated demands for it produced no effect. So, in 1655, Shah Jahan ordered the country to be invaded. The Gond Rajah, Kasari Singh, made a prompt submission and promised to pay up his arrears.

The little State of Jawhar, lying on a plateau north of Konkan and southwest of Baglana, was ruled by a petty Rajah who did not accept the overlordship of Delhi. Shah Jahan, at Aurangzib's suggestion, sanctioned an invasion of his country, which frightened the Rajah into making his submission and promising an annual tribute (January 1656).

2.6 Golkonda

Golkonda was a very fertile and carefully irrigated country, with a large and industrious population. The capital, Haidarabad, was at this time the centre of the diamond trade, not of Asia alone, but of the whole world. Numbers of foreign traders assembled here and transacted business. The kingdom was famous for several industries and also possessed in Masulipatam the best anchorage in the Bay of Bengal. The forests of the kingdom sheltered large herds of highly prized elephants, which added to the wealth of the king. Tobacco and the palm flourished exceedingly, and the excise on tobacco and toddy juice yielded a large revenue.

Aurangzib had frequent cause to quarrel with the king of Golkonda. The annual tribute of two lakhs of *hun* was always in arrears, and repeated dunning on the part of the Mughal viceroy only met with excuses and petitions for delay.

Next, the exchange value of the *hun* rose from Rs 4 to Rs 4½ in 1636 and finally to Rs 5 in 1654. Qutb Shah had been paying his tribute at the old rate of eight lakhs of rupees a year. The Mughals now demanded that the difference due to changed exchange for *all the past years* should be paid at once, thus forming a new burden of 20 lakhs of rupees.

Then he was rebuked for not having taken his overlord's sanction before conquering the Karnatak. Lastly their was the affair of Mir Jumla which precipitated war.

2.7 Mir Jumla: His History and Position

The treaties of 1636 had clearly marked out the boundary between the Mughal Empire and the two Deccani monarchies. Barred in the north by the strong arm of the Mughals, these two States began to give employment to their troops and a free vent to their ambition by engaging in a career of conquest in other directions. The whole of the Karnatak, from the river Krishna to Tanjore beyond the Cauveri, was covered with a number of petty Hindu principalities, the jarring fragments of the ruined empire of Vijaynagar. These now rapidly fell a prey to Muslim arms. The Golkonda troops advanced conquering to the Bay of Bengal, and occupied the country from the Chilka lake to the Pennar river.

Bijapur advanced conquering southwards and then turned east till it occupied the coast between Jinji and Tanjore. Hemmed in the north and south by the conquests of the two Sultans, as between the two jaws of a monster, lay the kingdom of Chandragiri, the last remnant of the Vijaynagar Empire, with its territory contracted to the region from Nellore to Pondicherry on the east and the Mysore frontier on the west. There was now a race between the Golkonda and Bijapur kings for the absorption of this kingdom; the two jaws began rapidly to close from the north and the south upon the doomed Karnatak. In this work of conquest a most conspicuous part was played by Mir Jumla, the *wazir* of Golkonda.

Muhammad Said, known to history as Mir Jumla, was a Sayyid of Ardistan in Persia, and the son of an oil merchant of Isfahan. Leaving his native country in youth he, like other Shia adventurers, sought his fortune at the Courts of the Deccani Sultans who belonged to his sect (1630). As a diamond merchant he rose to great wealth by his shrewdness and business capacity. His wonderful talents gained him the favour of Abdullah Qutb Shah, who made him his prime minister. Mir Jumla's industry, rapid despatch of business, administrative capacity, military genius, and inborn power of leadership ensured his success in all that he undertook. Great alike in civil government and in war, he soon became the virtual ruler of Golkonda: nothing could reach the Sultan save with his approval. Sent by his master to the Karnatak, he soon effected a complete transformation there. Mir Jumla strenghtened himself by securing a number of European gunners and cannon-founders, raised his army to a high state of discipline and efficiency, and soon wrested the Cuddapa district. His crowning feat was the capture of the rock fortress of Gandikota, hitherto deemed impregnable. Sidhout,[1] east of Cuddapa, was also conquered, and his captains penetrated as far as Chandragiri and Tirupati in the North Afcot district. By looting the rich old temples of

[1] Sidhout is nine miles due east and Gandikota 42 miles n. w. of Cuddapa town. Both are situated on the Pennar river.

the South and hunting out buried treasure, Mir Jumla amassed a vast fortune, till he came to be known as the richest private man in the South and the owner of twenty maunds of diamonds. By his conquests he raised *Tnisjagir* in the Karnatak into a kingdom 300 miles long and 50 miles broad, yielding a revenue of 40 lakhs a year, and possessing several diamond mines. Thus he had made himself fully independent of his master and the virtual king of the Karnatak. Envious courtiers were not wanting to whisper to the Sultan of Golkonda that the absent *wazir's* armed strength was a menace to his own security, and that the servant's wealth overshadowed the grandeur of the master's Court. Qutb Shah, too, naturally wished to have a share of his *wazir's* gains in the Karnatak. Mir Jumla, on the other hand, knowing how weak and worthless his master was, regarded the conquest as entirely his own work and was loath to return to the life of a courtier. Qutb Shah at last openly undertook to crush his disobedient servant.

2.8 Qutb Shah's Rupture with the Mughals 1655

Mir Jumla now looked around for a protector. In addition to making offers of his services to Bijapur, he began to coquet with the Mughal power. Aurangzib, secretly nursing his passionate amibtion of conquering the rich State of Golkonda, was eager to secure such an able helper and counsellor as the prime minister of that kingdom. Through the Mughal envoy at Golkonda the prince opened a secret correspondence with Mir Jumla, promising him boundless favours from the Emperor, if he joined the Mughal service. But Mir Jumla was in no haste to accept the offer; he asked for a year's time, and Aurangzib was disgusted with his duplicity.

Before Qutb Shah could muster either his courage or his forces for the purpose of chastising Mir Jumla, a crisis was precipitated by the conduct of Muhammad Amin, the *wazir's* son. This young man, haughty and reckless, was acting all these years as Mir Jumla's deputy at the Court of Golkonda, and used to treat the Sultan with scant courtesy in the open Darbar. At last, one day Muhammad Amin came to Court reeling with drunkenness, fell asleep on the king's own carpet, and soiled it in crop sickness. The long-suffering king's anger boiled over, and he threw Muhammad Amin and his family into prison and attached their property (21 November, 1655). This was the opportunity for which Aurangzib had so long been waiting.

Aurangzib had received on 18 December the Emperor's letters appointing Mir Jumla and his son to the Mughal service and bidding Qutb Shah not to hinder them in coming to the imperial Court nor to detain their property. He immediately sent the order to Qutb Shah threatening him with war if he delayed or disobeyed. In the meantime he mobilized his troops on the Golkonda frontier. Qutb Shah seemed to have been blind to the coming storm, he disregarded these Mughal letters.

On hearing (24 December) of Muhammad Amin's captivity, Shah Jahan wrote a letter to Qutb Shah to release Mir Jumla's family. He felt sure that his letter alone would effect the purpose. But 'in order to gratify Aurangzib,' he rather reluctantly sanctioned (29 December) the invasion of Golkonda, *in case* Muhammad Amin was still detained. Both these letters reached Aurangzib on 7 January, 1656. He now employed finesse to ruin Golkonda. Without giving Qutb Shah time to receive and follow Shah Jahan's letter of 24 December, which explicity ordered the release of the captives, he declared that the king's refusal to set them free in spite of the Emperor's letter of 3 December amounted to that flat disobedience of impreial orders which had been laid down as a necessary condition for the invasion of Golkonda.

2.9 Aurangzib Invades Golkonda Kingdom 1656

At once, by order of Aurangzib, his eldest son Muhammad Sultan crossed the frontier at Nander (10 January, 1656) and made a dash on Haidarabad with his cavalry. On the twentieth of the month, Aurangzib himself started from Aurangabad and hastened to join his son.

Meanwhile, after Muhammad Sultan had entered his territory, Abdullah got Shah Jahan's stern letter of 24 December and at once sent Muhammad Amin with his family and servants to that prince, together with a humble letter of submission to the Emperor. But Aurangzib had so contrived it that his submission should come too late to save him. Muhammad Amin waited on the prince, 24 miles from Haidarabad (probably on 21 January), but the prince refused to stop hostilities and pressed on to the capital on the plea that Abdullah had not yet restored the property of the captives. Qutb Shah's last hope was gone; the Mughal cavalry had arrived so fast that he had been completely taken by surprise. Confronted with utter ruin, he fled from Haidarabad to the fort of Golkonda on the night of 22 January, abandoning his capital.

This flight saved his life because Aurangzib's secret instructions to Muhammad Sultan breathed deadly animosity:

> Qutb-ul-mulk is a coward and will probably offer no resistance. Immediately on delivering this message, attack him impetuously and if you can manage it, *lighten his neck of the burden of his head.* The best means of achieving this plan are cleverness, promptitude, and lightness of hand.

On 23 January the invaders arrived at the Husain Sagar tank, two miles north of Haidarabad. Confusion reigned in the counsels of Golkonda. Next day the young prince entered Haidarabad. A strong party was posted in the city under Muhammad Beg to prevent plunder and violence. Haidarabad was one of the richest cities of India. This looting of Haidarabad by the Mughal army was the talk of all India in that age. As Aurangzib's equerry, Aqil Khan Razi, wrote in his history, 'Most of the stores and property of Qutb-ul-mulk, such as precious books and other costly things beyond computation, were plundered by Prince M. Sultan.... Much of Qutb-ul-mulk's property—among the rarities of the age—was confiscated by Aurangzib.'

Aurangzib arrived on the scene on 6 February with the bulk of his army. With the vigour and promptitude that marked all his actions, he first made a reconnaissance of the fort of Golkonda and its environs.

Next day the siege of Golkonda began. The west side was unoccupied, but Mughal officers entrenched on the other three sides. The leaguer of Golkonda lasted form 7 February to 30 March, and was conducted very languidly, because, with the materials at his disposal, he could do no injury to such an impregnable fortress. Battles took place with the Golkonda troops hovering round. These skirmishes were varied by the almost daily arrival of presents and offers of peace from the beleaguered king to the invader's camp! But Aurangzib steadily refused to make terms. He coveted the whole kingdom and nothing less. He plied his father with all sorts of arguments to secure his consent to its annexation. But Shah Jahan was loath to ruin a brother king for merely trying to bring his disloyal *wazir* under discipline. Dara, who had been bribed and implored by the Golkonda envoy at Delhi—to the intense disgust and anger of Aurangzib—pleaded hard for Qutb-ul-mulk, and secured peace for him on the payment of an indemnity. The Emperor's letter accepting this settlement reached Aurangzib' on 24 February. Aurangzib suppressed the Emperor's letter of pardon to Qutb-ul-mulk (dated 8 February), lest it should embolden the latter and make him abate his terms.

In the meantime, Abdullah's agent at the Court of Delhi had brought the intercession of Dara Shukoh and Princess Imperial Jahanara [*Guldashta*]. Through them he unfolded to the Emperor the true story of Aurangzib's manoeuvring—how Abdullah had been tricked and almost slain by treachery, how he had not been given a fair chance of carrying out the Emperor's orders, how the imperial *farmans* had been withheld from him, how Shah Jahan's kind intentions towards the suppliant ruler had been thwarted. At this Shah Jahan's righteous indignation boiled over. He wrote a sharp letter of censure to Aurangzib, with orders to raise the siege and quit Golkonda territory *at once*. So, on 30 March, in obedience to the Emperor's peremptory orders, Aurangzib raised the siege and withdrew from the environs of Golkonda. Four days afterwards Muhammad Sultan was married by proxy to the second daughter of Abdullah Qutb Shah. The king of Golkonda, besides paying a war indemnity and arrears of tribute amounting to one crore of rupees, had to cede the district of Ramgir (modern Manikdrug and Chinoor). The Mughal army set out on its retreat on 21 April.

Mir Jumla had come to Aurangzib's camp at Golkonda on 20 March more as a prince than as a noble. Six thousand cavalry, 15,000 infantry, 150 elephants, and a very good train of artillery accompanied him. Summoned immediately to the imperial court, he arrived at Delhi on 7 July and presented the Emperor with articles worth 15 lakhs, including a big diamond weighing 216 *ratis*. He was at once created a Commander of Six Thousand and appointed prime minister in the place of the lately deceased Sadullah Khan.

2.10 Aurangzib's Wrangles with Shah Jahan About the Golkonda Booty

This expedition renewed Aurangzib's wrangles with the Emperor. An exaggerated account of the looting of Haidarabad had reached Delhi. It was also represented to Shah Jahan, probably by the Golkonda envoy, that Aurangzib and his sons had taken costly presents from Qutb Shah, without mentioning the fact in his despatches or setting their price off from the tribute due. Aurangzib, on his part, complained that Shah Jahan had not kept his promise as to sharing the Golkonda indemnity with him; 'the *entire* Golkonda indemnity has been taken by the Emperor and placed in Daulatabad treasury. How can I repay my debt for the war and the arrears of my army, about 20 *lakhs* of Rupees?' The presents received from Golkonda, had, he said, been exaggerated into 'chest-loads of jewels' by malicious, reporters at the imperial Court.

Peace had been made with Golkonda, but one subject of discord remained open. Qutb Shah wanted to keep the Karnatak, and with justice: it had been won by his servant and formed part of his kingdom. But Aurangzib objected, saying that it was Mir Jumla's personal *jagir* and referred the matter to the Emperor, who decided to hold the Karnatak in his own hands as Mir Jumla's *jagir*, and Qutb Shah was ordered to recall his officers from that province. But the Golkonda officers were loath to yield the rich prey. They lingered there and threw every difficulty in the path of the Mughals in occupying and settling the country.

2.11 Aurangzib Invades Bijapur 1657

In the reign of Muhammad Adil Shah (1626–56) the kingdom of Bijapur attained to its highest extent, power and magnificence. His dominion stretched from the Arabian Sea to the Bay of Bengal, across the entire Indian Peninsula. Ever since 1636 Muhammad Adil Shah had lived at peace with the Emperor of Delhi, and we read of friendly exchanges of presents between the two Courts. The Sultan's good name for piety, love of justice, and care for his subjects—which was heightened by a certain simplicity of understanding and ignorance of the world—greatly pleased Shah Jahan. But Mir Jumla's arrival at Delhi (7 July, 1656) secured the triumph of Aurangzib's policy of aggression in the Emperor's council. With Mir Jumla dominating the Emperor's counsels, Aurangzib confidently matured the plan of invading Bijapur on the expected death of its reigning king.

On 4 November, 1656, Muhammad Adil Shah, the seventh of the royal line of Bijapur, died. Through the efforts of his chief minister Khan Muhammad and the Queen Bari Sahiba, the crown was placed on the head of Ali Adil Shah II, a youth of 18 years, and the only son of the late king. Aurangzib immediately wrote to Shah Jahan, urging an invasion on the plea that Ali was not really a son of the deceased Sultan, but a boy of obscure parentage whom Muhammad Adil Shah had brought up in the harem. The death of Muhammad Adil Shah was followed by disorders in the Karnatak; the zamindars recovered much of their former lands. At the capital things were even worse. The Bijapuri nobles quarrelled with one another and with the prime minister Khan Muhammad for the division of power. To aggravate the evil, Aurangzib intrigued with them and succeeded in corrupting several leading men of the Court who promised their adhesion and prepared to desert to the Mughal territory with their troops. Aurangzib hoped to seduce the others with the aid of Mir Jumla.

On 26 November, Shah Jahan sanctioned the invasion and gave Aurangzib a free hand to 'settle the affair of Bijapur in any way he thought fit.' A force of 20,000 troopers, partly from the Court and partly from the *jagirs,* with a large staff of officers and Mir Jumla himself was despatched to reinforce the army of Aurangzib. The war thus sanctioned was wholly unrighteous. Bijapur was not a vassal state but an independent and equal ally of the Mughal Emperor, and the latter had no lawful right to confirm or question the succession at Bijapur. Mir Jumla arrived at Aurangabad on 18 January and that very day, at the auspicious hour chosen by the astrologers, the prince set out with him to invade Bijapur. On 28 February he reached the environs of Bidar, and laid siege to the fort on 2 March. Siddi Marjan offered a stout defence: he made several sorties and falling on the trenches tried to arrest the progress of the siege. But the superior numbers of the Mughals told in the end and Mir Jumla's fine train of artillery did great damage to the fort walls; two towers were demolished and the battlements of the lowermost wall as well as the outer breastworks were levelled to the ground.

The ditch having been filled up, the assault was delivered on 29 March. A spark from a rocket fired by the Mughals fell into a chamber of gunpowder and grenades behind the tower. There was a terrific explosion. Marjan was mortally wounded with two of his sons and many of his followers; the exulting Mughals swarmed out of their trenches and rushed into the city, driving the remnant of the defenders back with fearful slaughter. From his death-bed Siddi Marjan sent his seven sons to Aurangzib with the keys of the fort. Thus, the stronghold of Bidar fell after a siege of only 27 days. Among the spoils of victory were 12 *lakhs* of Rupees in cash, 8 *lakhs* worth of powder, shot, grain and other stores, besides 230 pieces of cannon.

Aurangzib next sent a force of 15,000 well-mounted and experienced troopers under Mahabat Khan, to punish the assembled enemy and ravage the Bijapur territory up to Kaliani in the west and Kulbarga in the south. This Mughal detachment encountered the enemy on 12 April. The Bijapuris, numbering some 20,000, under their famous chiefs Khan Muhammad, Afzal Khan, and the sons of Randaulah and Raihan, began the attack. Mahabat Khan like a good general kept his men well in hand amidst the ring of his enemies and their distracting mode of attack; finally he charged and the Bijapuris fled.

Forty miles west of Bidar, on the old road from the holy shrine of Tuljapur to Golkonda, stands the city of Kaliani, the ancient capital of the Chalukya kings and of the Kanarese country. Aurangzib on 27 April set out with light kit and arrived before Kaliani in a week's time. The place was immediately invested. Day and night the garrison kept up a ceaseless fire from the walls; they made fierce onslaughts on Mir Jumla's trenches, but to no purpose. Once Mahabat Khan himself on escort duty was hemmed round by the enemy at a place 10 miles north-east of Kaliani. The battle raged long and fiercely. The brunt of the fighting fell on the Rajputs. The horsemen of Khan Muhammad burst in vain upon the granite wall of Rao Chhatra Sal and his Hada clansmen. Rajah Rai Singh Sisodia, assaulted by the sons of Bahlol Khan of Bijapur, was wounded and unhorsed in the press of the enemy. Just then relief arrived: a charge by Mahabat Khan broke the enemy's ranks and they fled.

While Aurangzib concentrated his efforts on pressing the siege hard, a Bijapuri army 30,000 strong assembled only four miles from his camp. On 28 May, leaving a screen of tents round the fort, the prince marched with the main body of his troops upon the enemy's position. All divisions of the two armies were engaged with their respective opponents. The fight raged for six hours. The Deccanis kept up a running fight; four times in succession were they broken and as often did they form again and face the advancing Mughals. But at last the repeated charges of the heavily armed northern horsemen prevailed in the close fight; the Mughal army crowded upon the enemy from left and right and scattered them finally; the imperialists pursued them pell-mell to their camp, slaying and capturing all that they could. Everything found in the Bijapuri camp—arms, slave-girls, horses, transport-cattle, and all kinds of property—was plundered. The siege was pressed with vigour, but the defence by the Abyssinian

Dilawwar was equally heroic. The Bijapuris began to assemble again in order to oppose the Mughals. So, on 22 July, Aurangzib sent a large division under his eldest son and Mir Jumla to break up their forces. This Mughal corps advanced forty-eight miles, charged and broke their formation, and pursued them for four miles. The victors proceeded, laying the Bijapuri villages waste, up to Kulbarga.

On 29 July, the imperialists scaled a tower on the other side of the moat of Kaliani. The struggle here was most obstinate. But the assailants swarmed into the fort and held this portion of the defences. On 1 August the keys of the fort were delivered up by Dilawwar, who was given a robe of honour with permission to go to Bijapur.

After the fall of Kaliani, the king of Bijapur opened negotiations for peace. Bijapuri agents intrigued at Delhi and secured the intercession of Dara with the Emperor. It was agreed that Adil Shah would cede to the Mughals the forts of Bidar, Kaliani and Parenda with their dependent territories, as well as a war-indemnity of one *crore* of Rupees. On these terms Shah Jahan ordered Aurangzib to make peace and to return with his army to Bidar, while the reinforcements sent to the Deccan from Malwa and northern India were recalled to their former posts. Thus Aurangzib received a sharp check in the hour of his triumph; he had gained only the northern fringe of the vast Bijapur kingdom when his father cried halt to him. The Bijapuris profited by his distraction and weakened power and delayed and finally refused to surrender Parenda.

To complete the misfortunes of the Mughal cause in the Deccan, Shah Jahan fell ill on 6 September and rumours of his death spread through the empire. Aurangzib, harassed by anxiety and distracted by conflicting plans, began his retreat from Kaliani on 4 October, 1657.

3 *Illness of Shah Jahan and the Rebellion of his Sons*

3.1 Shah Jahan's Eldest Son Dara Shukoh

On 7 March, 1657, Shah Jahan completed three decades of his reign and began the thirty-first year. The reign had been as prosperous as it had been long. The 'wealth of Ind' under this Great Mughal dazzled the eyes of foreign visitors, and on gala days ambassadors from Bukhara and Persia, Turkey and Arabia, as well as travellers from France and Italy, gazed with wonder at the Peacock Throne and the Kohinur and other jewels. The white marble edifices which he loved to build were as costly as they were chaste in design. The nobles of the empire eclipsed the kings of other lands in wealth and pomp. The bounds of the 'protected empire' had been stretched farther than in any preceding reign. Within the country itself a profound peace reigned. The peasantry were carefully cherished; harsh and exacting governors were in many cases dismissed on the complaint of the people. Wealth and prosperity increased on all hands. A kind and yet wise master, Shah Jahan had gathered round himself a band of very able officers, and made his Court the centre of the wit and wisdom of the land. But one by one the great ministers and generals who had contributed to the glory of the reign were being removed by the pitiless hand of Death. And, as the giants of old passed away, the Emperor found no worthy successors to them among the new faces and younger men around him. He had already completed 67 lunar years (24 January 1657). What would happen after him?

Shah Jahan had four sons. All of them were past youth, and all had gained experience as governors of provinces and commanders of armies. But there was no brotherly love among them. The ill-feeling between Dara and Aurangzib in particular was so bitter and had continued to grow bitterer for so many years past that, it was the talk of the whole empire, and peace had been maintained between them only by keening Aurangzib far away from the Court and his eldest brother. Shah Jahan had given clear indications that he wished to leave the crown to Dara, the eldest of his four sons *by the same mother.* In order to train him in the administration of the empire and to smooth the transfer of the supreme authority to him, the Emperor had kept Dara by his side for many years past, and allowed him to govern his viceroyalties by deputies. At the same time the Emperor bestowed on him rank and privileges which raised him to an almost royal position. All had to buy or beg Dara's mediation before they could approach the Emperor.

Dara had just reached forty-two years of age. He had taken after his great-grandfather, Akbar. In his thirst for pantheistic philosophy he had studied the Talmud and the New Testament, the writings of the Muslim Sufis, and the Hindu Vedanta. His aim was to find a meeting-point for Hinduism and Islam in those universal truths which form the common basis of all true religions and which fanatics are too apt to ignore in their zeal for the mere externals of faith. Alike from the Hindu *yogi* Lal-das and the Muslim *faqir* Sarmad, he had imbibed his eclectic philosophy and at the feet of both he had sat as an attentive pupil. But he was no apostate from Islam. He had compiled a biography of Muslim saints, and he had been initiated as a disciple of the Muslim saint Mian Mir, which no *kafir* could have been. The saintly Jahanara also speaks of Dara as her spiritual preceptor. Dara's own words in introducing to the reader his theological works clearly prove that he never discarded the essential dogmas of Islam; he only displayed the eclecticism of the Sufis, a recognized school of Islamic believers. However, his coquetry with Hindu philosophy made it impossible for him, even if he had the inclination, to pose as the champion of orthodox and exclusive Islam, or to summon all Muslims to his banners by proclaiming a holy war against the people beyond the fold of the faith.

His father's excessive love did him a distinct harm. He was always kept at Court and never, except at the third siege of Qandahar, sent to conduct campaigns or administer provinces. Thus, he never acquired experience in the arts of war and government; he never learnt to judge men by the crucial test of danger and difficulty; and he lost touch with the active army. Hence, he was rendered unfit for that war of succession which among the Mughals served as a practical test for the survival of the fittest. His unrivalled wealth and influence were not likely to develop moderation, self-restraint, or foresight in him, while the fulsome flattery which he received from all must have aggravated the natural pride and arrogance of an heir to the throne of Delhi. Evidently he was no judge of character. Men of ability and self-respect must have kept away from such a vain and injudicious master. Dara was a loving husband, a doting father, and a devoted son; but as a ruler of men in troubled times he must have proved a failure. Long continued prosperity had unnerved his character and made him incapable of planning wisely, daring boldly, and achieving strenuously, or, if need be, of wresting victory from the jaws of defeat by desperate effort or heroic endurance. Military organization and tactical combination were beyond his power. And he had never learnt by practice how to guide the varying tides of a battle with the coolness and judgment of a true general. This novice in the art of war was destined to meet a practised veteran as his rival for the throne.

3.2 Shah Jahan Falls Ill, 1657, and Consequent Disorder in the Empire

On 6 September, Shah Jahan suddenly fell ill of strangury and constipation at Delhi. For one week the royal physicians toiled in vain. The malady went on increasing. The daily *darbar* was stopped; the Emperor even ceased to show his face to the public from the balcony. After a week the doctors at last got control over the malady. But the improvement in the Emperor's condition was slight, and so he decided to go to Agra and die there quietly in sight of the tomb of the wife he had loved so well. He entered Agra city on 26 October.

During Shah Jahan's illness Dara constantly watched by his bedside, and tended and nursed him most carefully, and showed no indecent haste to secure the crown for himself. Early in the course of his illness, when Shah Jahan despaired of recovery, he set himself to prepare for the next world. Calling to his presence some confidential courtiers and the chief officers of the State, he made his last will before them and ordered them to obey Dara henceforth as their sovereign. Dara, however, did not assume the crown, but continued to issue orders in his father's name, while attempting to strengthen his own position. He removed Mir Jumla, the confidant and partisan of Aurangzib, from the wazir-ship (end of September) and sent orders to Mir Jumla, Mahabat Khan and other imperial officers to return from the Deccan to the Court with their contingents.

By the middle of November Shah Jahan had recovered sufficiently to be told of important matters which had hitherto been kept from him. One was that Shuja had crowned himself and was advancing from Bengal. With Shah Jahan's consent an army, 22,000 strong, was sent against him (30 November) under Sulaiman Shukoh (the eldest son of Dara) and Mirza Rajah Jai Singh. Soon afterwards equally alarming news arrived from Gujrat. There Murad had crowned himself on 5 December, and formed an alliance with Aurangzib. So, about the end of this month two imperial armies were despatched from Agra into Malwa, one to oppose the advance of Aurangzib from the south and the other to march into Gujrat and oust Murad from that province. The first of these armies was placed under Maharajah Jaswant Singh (of Marwar), who was appointed governor of Malwa *vice* Shaista Khan recalled to Court. Qasim Khan was induced to accept the command of the second army by being created governor of Gujrat. Shah Jahan besought these generals to spare the lives of his younger sons, to try at first to send them back to their provinces by fair words if possible, otherwise by a demonstration of force, and not, except in extreme need, to resort to a deadly battle.

During Shah Jahan's illness Dara at first allowed none but one or two ministers in his confidence to have access to the Emperor. He also watched the ferries and stopped all letters and messengers going to his brothers in Bengal, Gujrat and the Deccan, and kept their agents at the imperial Court under watch lest they should send any report to their masters. But these precautions only wrought greater mischief. The princes and people in the distant provinces naturally concluded from this stoppage of news that Shah Jahan was dead and all the confusion and disorder of a Mughal succession broke out. Everywhere lawless men began to cause tumults, the peasants refused to pay the revenue, the zamindars tried to rob or conquer their rivals, and the frontiers were violated. The local authorities were paralysed by uncertainty and anxiety about the future, and law and order suddenly disappeared from many places.

No doubt letters in Shah Jahan's hand and seal reached the princes assuring them of his recovery, but they maintained that these were really written by Dara, an expert imitator of Shah Jahan's handwriting, and that the late Emperor's seal was necessarily in the possession of the usurper! The three younger brothers, therefore, very plausibly asserted in their letters to the Emperor that their loving minds had been unsettled by these alarming rumours, and they were marching on Agra to see their father with their own eyes and satisfy themselves as to his real condition.

3.3 Murad Bakhsh Crowns Himself in Gujrat

Muhammad Murad Bakhsh, the youngest son of Shah Jahan, was the black sheep of the imperial family. He had been tried in Balkh, the Deccan, and Gujrat, and he had failed everywhere. A foolish, pleasure-loving and impetuous prince, his character had not improved with age; he had not learnt to apply himself to business or to bridle his passions. Worse still, he had not the gift of choosing capable agents. But Murad possessed the reckless valour of a soldier. Place him in the field of combat and the martial spirit of Timur would fire his blood, he would relentlessly force his way to close grips with the enemy, and, amidst the carnage raging round him, forget every other feeling save the fierce delight of slaughter. But his personal valour was a poor compensation for his lack of generalship.

Knowing the prince's incapacity, Shah Jahan had tried to remedy the mischief by sending to him a very capable and honest officer named Ali Naqi as his revenue minister and chief counsellor. Ali Naqi's pure and vigilant administration raised against him a host of enemies among the flatterers and boon companions of the prince. A conspiracy was soon formed by Murad's favourite eunuch against the hated minister. A letter in Ali Naqi's hand and seal, professing adhesion to the cause of Dara, was forged and given to a courier, who contrived to get himself arrested by Murad's road patrol without betraying its real authorship. Murad was revelling in his pleasure-garden when the intercepted letter was brought to him a little before dawn. The prince, who had not slept off his night's debauch, burst into wrath and ordered Ali Naqi to be dragged to his presence. Quivering with pent-up wrath, he ran Ali Naqi through with his spear, shouting, 'Wretch! in spite of all my favours you have turned such a traitor!'

Murad was enlisting troops in large numbers and needed money badly. So he sent a eunuch named Shahbaz Khan with 6,000 troopers and war material to levy contributions from the rich port of Surat. The unwalled city was easily occupied and looted. Under the guidance of some Dutch artificers Shahbaz Khan ran mines under the wall of the fort of Surat, and by exploding one of them forced the place to surrender (20 December). Murad thus gained all the guns and accumulated treasures of Surat, besides taking a forced loan of five *lakhs* of Rupees from two of the richest merchants.

In the meantime, soon after receiving the news of Shah Jahan's serious illness, Murad and Aurangzib had opened a confidential correspondence with each other by means of trusty messengers. They also wrote to Shuja inviting his co-operation against Dara, but the long distance prevented their forming any definite or working agreement. Between Murad and Aurangzib, however, a plan of concerted action was soon matured. From the very beginning Murad placed himself under Aurangzib's guidance. But he was too impetuous. After his success at Surat, he publicly crowned himself as Emperor under the title of Maruwwaj-ud-din (5 December). In letter after letter we find Murad all fire and haste, while Aurangzib is cold and hesitating.

Murad proposed that the brothers should march at once from the south and attack Dara before he had time to consolidate his power and to win over the captains of the imperial army posted far and near. Aurangzib pressed him not to take any compromising step or set up the banner of revolt openly, but to wait, to dissimulate, and to send hollow friendly letters to Dara, till they should know for certain that Shah Jahan was dead. Aurangzib had suggested to Murad that a diversion should be made against Dara by instigating the Persians and Uzbeks to invade Afghanistan, which was then a province of the Mughal Empire. Murad, therefore, wrote to the king of Persia reporting the rumour of Shah Jahan's death and begging armed aid from him. The Shah of Persia wanted to wait and verify the news.

A solemn treaty for the partition of the empire on the following terms was drawn up by Aurangzib, sworn to on the *Quran,* and sent to Murad:

(i) Murad was to hold the Panjab, Afghanistan, Kashmir and Sindh and reign over them as an independent king. The rest of the Mughal dominions were to belong to Aurangzib.

(ii) One-third of the prize of war was to belong to Murad and two-thirds to Aurangzib.[1]

His preparations being now complete, Murad set out from Ahmadabad on 25 February 1658 and effected a junction with Aurangzib's forces at Dipalpur in Malwa on 14 April.

3.4 Aurangzib's Anxieties and Policy on the Eve of the War of Succession

From 4 October 1657, when Aurangzib retired from the war with Bijapur, to 25 January 1658, when he began his march towards Hindustan as a claimant to the throne, he passed through a most anxious and critical time. Events which he could not possibly control were moving fast.

His present position was daily growing more untenable, while the future was ominous. But the difficulties, great and complex, which he overcame, raise to the highest pitch our admiration for his coolness, sagacity, power of managing men, and diplomatic skill.

The news had got out that the Emperor had ordered peace to be made and recalled the additional troops sent to the Deccan. Thus a cruel fate threatened to snatch away from Aurangzib's grasp the fruits of his long and costly war with Bijapur just when he was about to taste them. Aurangzib, therefore, determined to play a game of boldness in order to realize the terms of the treaty before the Bijapuris could recover from their recent defeats or learn of the full extent of the weakness and distraction of the imperial Government.

But this policy of facing round to Bijapur and making military demonstrations in the South had its drawbacks too. The longer Aurangzib delayed in maturing his plans for contesting the throne, proclaiming himself a claimant, and marching on Hindustan, the greater was the time that Dara would gain for recalling the chief captains from the Deccan, winning over officers and men far and near, consolidating his own power, and effectually counteracting Aurangzib's possible designs.

[1] These terms are clearly given in Aurangzib's own letter *(Adab-i-Alamgiri* p. 78), his officer Aquil Khan Razi's history (p. 25), and the *Tazkirat-us-salatin-us-chaghtaia,* thus refuting Bernier's absurd story that Aurangzib promised to give the entire empire to Murad while he himself would go to Mecca as a *darvish* (Hazratji) after overthrowing the infidel Dara.

If, on the other hand, Aurangzib concentrated his forces, made a public claim to the throne, marched northwards and openly broke with the imperial Government by enlisting troops, then he would, no doubt, check Dara in time and secure the adhesion of ambitious adventurers. But at the same time all hope of getting Parenda or the promised indemnity would be gone, and his other enemies in the South would raise their heads; the fruits of the last two years' warfare in the Deccan would be totally lost to him.

Aurangzib's letters, preserved in the *Adab-i-Alamgiri,* tell the story of how the hope of a speedy settlement with Bijapur daily grew fainter and fainter, how he tried diverse means to get the promised territory and money, how he conceded to Bijapur one by one the hard terms wrung out of it by the treaty—till at last, in despair of getting anything from Bijapur, he gave up all thought of the South, and turned his undivided attention and resources to the pursuit of his schemes in northern India.

Leaving Kaliani on 4 October 1657, Aurangzib reached Bidar in five days. This fort was repaired and properly garrisoned and provisioned. On the eighteenth of the month he resumed his retreat march and arrived at Aurangabad on 11 November. As soon as he left Bidar there was the greatest rejoicing in the Deccan kingdoms; here were the Mughals abandoning their late conquests as untenable! He had sent Mir Jumla to the Parenda district (28 Sept.) to get delivery of that fort in terms of the treaty. But the hope of getting Parenda and the Bijapur indemnity grew fainter and fainter, in spite of all the efforts of Mir Jumla, and at last that general returned baffled to Aurangabad (1 January 1658).

As early as 28 October Aurangzib had taken a very necessary precaution by sending a force to seize all the ferries of the Narmada and prevent correspondence between Dara and the imperial officers in the Deccan. But what line of action was he to adopt now? His followers were looking up to him to declare his policy, but a decision at this stage was most difficult to make and beset with dangers. The news from the imperial Court was conflicting, Shah Jahan's exact condition could not be known with certainty and for many weeks Aurangzib lived in the greatest distraction; so did his followers.

Aurangzib had from the first decided not to raise the banner of rebellion before knowing for certain that Shah Jahan was dead. But the quick march of events forced his hand. Dara's plan with regard to the South was now fully unfolded: he had induced the helpless Shah Jahan to remove Murad from the viceroyalty of Gujrat and to transfer the *Subah* of Berar from Aurangzib to Murad, so as to make the two brothers quarrel. Further, Dara had sent two armies against his two brothers in the South (end of December) and recalled Shaista Khan (a strong supporter of Aurangzib) from his province of Malwa to the Court, while Mir Jumla now received an imperial letter of recall from Aurangzib's side which it would have been flat rebellion to disregard. Similar letters reached Aurangzib's officers.

3.5 Aurangzib's Preparations for Contesting the Throne

The time for action had at last arrived if Aurangzib hoped ever to be king or even to live in freedom. His mind was made up early in January 1658, and he took rapid and decisive steps. First, Mir Jumla was arrested by collusion with him, lodged in mock captivity in Daulatabad fort, and all his property and excellent artillery seized by Aurangzib in the name of the State. The prince gave out as the ostensible reason for this act, that Mir Jumla was in secret intrigue with the two Deccani Sultans against the Emperor! He next wrote to Shah Jahan and the new *wazir* Jafar Khan to the effect that his loving heart had been distracted by hearing sad rumours about Shah Jahan, and that like a dutiful son he was going to Agra to see his father in his illness, release him from Dara's control, and thereby save the empire from alarm, confusion and tumult.

Letters were written to Qutb Shah pressing him to pay up the balance of his war indemnity, and the Mughal envoy at the Golkonda Court was ordered to behave gently to that king, and to induce him to do nothing unfriendly to the Mughal interests during Aurangzib's proposed absence from the Deccan. Friendly epistles and presents were sent to the Queen Mother (Bari Sahiba) of Bijapur, urging her to expedite the payment of the promised money and to keep the Bijapuri's quiet during his absence. Still later, a very tempting offer was made to Adil Shah by Aurangzib, as the price of his friendliness: 'Remain loyal and keep your promises.... I agree that (1) the fort of Parenda and its dependent territory, the Konkan, and the *mahal* of Wangi, which have been annexed to the Empire, together with that portion of the Karnatak which had been granted to the late Adil Shah,—should be left to you as before, and (2) out of your promised indemnity of one *crore* of Rupees, thirty lakhs are remitted. Protect this country; improve its administration. Expel Shiva who has sneaked into the possession of some forts of the land. Do you send me at least 10,000 cavalry. I shall grant you all the territory up to the bank of the Wanganga.'

All this time Aurangzib was intriguing actively but in secret with the courtiers in the capital and the high officers in the provinces (especially Malwa). Of all the four sons of Shah Jahan he had the best reputation for capacity and experience. All self-seeking nobles and officers recognized him as the coming man, and hastened to secure their future by doing him friendly turns, or at least by sending him secret assurances of their support.

The enlisting of new soldiers had been going on apace. Large quantities of saltpetre, sulphur and lead were bought for making munitions, while the gunpowder and fuses in the Deccan forts were taken away for the advance on Delhi. In this way Aurangzib's army was swollen to 30,000 picked troopers, besides Mir Jumla's excellent train of cannon served by English and French gunners.

Aurangzib was even stronger in officers than in men and material. During his rule of the Deccan he had gathered round himself a band of very able servants, all attached to him by gratitude and some by personal affection. They did him signal service during the contest for the throne. Such were Murshid Quli Khan, the *diwan,* Shaikh Mir, the warrior and confidential adviser, Aqil Khan Razi, the equerry and personal attendant, Qabil Khan, the facile and trusty secretary, Khan-i-Zaman, the energetic Inspector of Ordnance, Muhammad Tahir, a veteran captain raised to the peerage as Wazir Khan, the faithful envoy Isa Beg (created Mukhlis Khan), the highborn and experienced Shams-ud-din Mukhtar Khan, and above all that jewel of a servant, Mir Jumla, great in war, greater still in counsel. Among his most devoted Hindu followers were Rao Karan of Bikanir, Subh-Karan the Bundela (of Datia), and Rajah Indramani of Dhamdhera.

Before leaving the Deccan Aurangzib took steps to maintain his hold on the country during his absence. Prince Muazzam was left at Aurangabad with two high officers and a strong force to carry on the government, while Aurangzib's harem was placed in the neighbouring fort of Daulatabad.

At last, on 5 February 1658, Aurangzib started from Aurangabad to contest the throne. Burhanpur was reached on the eighteenth, and here a month's halt was made in order to complete the organization of his army and other preparations. Leaving Burhanpur on 20 March, he arrested and put in prison his father-in-law Shah Nawaz Khan, who persisted in his loyalty to Shah Jahan (26 March). The Narmada was crossed at Akbarpur, without the least opposition (3 April), and then while marching northwards to Ujjain, he learnt on the 13th, near Dipalpur (some 26 miles south of Ujjain), that Murad had arrived a few miles west of him. Next day the two brothers joined their forces near the lake of Dipalpur. Jaswant Singh was only one day's march in front of him. In the evening the princes encamped at the village of Dharmat (14 miles s. s. w. of Ujjain), on the western bank of the Gambhiraj, an affluent of the Chambal river. Next day the great War of Mughal Succession began.

4 War of Succession: Aurangzib Triumphs

4.1 Jaswant at Dharmat

Reaching Ujjain with his army at the end of February 1658, Jaswant was quite in the dark about Aurangzib's intentions and movements, so strictly did that prince watch the roads and ferries of the Narmada river. The first news that he got of Aurangzib was that the prince was already in Malwa and rapidly marching on Ujjain.

In utter perplexity Jaswant advanced fourteen miles southwest of Ujjain and encamped opposite Dharmat, to block the path of the enemy coming up from the south. Here another startling news reached him: Murad had joined Aurangzib (14 April) and the two were within a day's march of him.

Jaswant had come to Malwa in the hope that the mere prestige of the imperial banners would send the rebellious princes back to their provinces, and that all that he would have to undertake was a mere demonstration of force. Now, when too late, he realized that his adversaries were in deadly earnest and ready to fight to the bitter end.

Jaswant was severely handicapped by Shah Jahan's instructions to send the two rebellious princes back to their own provinces with as little injury to them as possible, and to fight them only as a last resource. While Aurangzib followed his own judgement only and knew his own mind, Jaswant was hesitating, distracted by the conflict between the instructions from Agra and the exigencies of the actual military situation in Malwa, and entirely dependent for his own line of action on what his opponents would do.

His army, too, was an ill-knit group of discordant elements. The various Rajput clans were often divided from each other by hereditary feuds and quarrels about dignity and precedence. Then, again, there was the standing aloofness between Hindus and Muhammadans. It had been found next to impossible to brigade these creeds together for a campaign under one general. There was no unity of command in the imperial army assembled at Dharmat, because Qasim Khan's orders were to co-operate with Jaswant and not to act as his subordinate. Several of the Muslim officers, moreover, were secretly friendly to Aurangzib; for we find that in the ensuing battle twenty-four Rajput chiefs and only one Muhammadan general were killed on the Emperor's side. Qasim Khan and his men kept themselves out of harm's way in the battle and the full brunt of it fell on the Rajputs.

Finally, Jaswant as a general was no match for Aurangzib; his faulty plan and conduct of the battle proves his inexperience and hot-headedness. He chose his ground badly and so cramped his men that the horsemen could not manoeuvre freely nor gather momentum for a charge; he failed to send timely succour to the divisions that needed it most, and, the battle once begun, he lost control over his forces as if he were a mere divisional leader and not the supreme commander of all. Lastly, he made the fatal mistake of despising artillery.

Evidently Jaswant's plan was to skirt the enemy's artillery and come to close quarters with their troops, disregarding the gun-fire during the first few minutes of the wild gallop. But when the battle began, the Rajputs were penned within a narrow space with ditches and entrenchments on their flanks, and subjected to deadly fire before they could spread out for a charge. Secondly, after they had passed by the enemy's artillery and engaged Aurangzib's troops, the French and English gunners of the prince quickly turned their guns sideways and began to mow down the Rajputs in their new position. It was truly a contest between swords and gunpowder, and artillery triumphed over cavalry.

4.2 Battle of Dharmat

The two armies were almost equally matched and numbered a little over 35,000 men each, though Aurangzib's force was immensely superior in cohesion and artillery.

Two hours after sunrise on the fifteenth of April, the rival hosts sighted each other. Aurangzib's army advanced slowly upon the imperialist position, keeping its regular formation, and began to shoot down the

Rajputs, densely packed in columns without space to manoeuvre freely. The Rajput losses began to mount up every minute. Then their vanguard, led by Mukund Singh Hada, Ratan Singh Rathor, Dayal Singh Jhala, Arjun Singh Gaur, Sujan Singh Sisodia and others, with their choicest clansmen, galloped forward. Shouting their war-cry of *Ram! Ram!* 'they fell on the enemy like tigers, casting away all plan.' The flood of Rajput charge first burst on Aurangzib's artillery. The guns and muskets fired at point-blank range, woefully thinned their ranks, but so impetuous was their onset that it bore down all opposition. Murshid Quli Khan, the Chief of Artillery, was slain after a heroic resistance and his division was shaken; but the guns were not damaged. The artillerymen probably fled before the storm, and returned as soon as it passed away. Victorious over the artillery guard, the assailants fell on the front part of Aurangzib's vanguard. Here an obstinate hand-to-hand combat raged for some time. The Rajputs, flushed with success, swept onward and pierced into the heart of Aurangzib's vanguard. This was the most critical moment of the day; if the Rajput charge were not checked, all would be over with Aurangzib.

But this front division of the prince's army was composed of his most picked troops, 8,000 mail-clad warriors, and their generals were reliable men, who, seated on their elephants, kept their ground firmly like hills while the flood of Rajput charge raged round and round them in eddies. Here the most stubborn and decisive fighting of the day took place, and 'the ground was dyed crimson with blood like a tulip bed.' The force of Rajput impact was divided and weakened when it struck the dense mass of Aurangzib's vanguard.

Only a few men from Jaswant's centre and advanced reserve had moved up to support their brethren thus struggling in front; the Mughal troops under Qasim Khan rendered no assistance. Thus, the charge of Jaswant's vanguard was not followed up; Aurangzib's troops, who had parted before the rushing tide, closed again behind them, and cut off their retreat. By this time the watchful eye of Aurangzib had taken the situation in, his advance reserve had been pushed up to reinforce the van, and he himself moved forward with the centre to form a wall of support and refuge close behind them. Above all, Shaikh Mir and Saif Shikan Khan, with the right and left wings of the centre, struck the Rajputs in the waist from the two flanks, while they were engaged with Aurangzib's van in front. All the six Rajput chieftains engaged in the charge were slain. Hopelessly out-numbered now, assailed in front, right, and left, and cut off from their rear, the Rajputs were slaughtered after performing frantic deeds of valour.

Meanwhile the action had become general. Recovering from the shock of Mukund Singh's charge as soon as the Rajput cavalcade swept on to another point, Aurangzib's gunners, with their pieces mounted on high ground, concentrated their fire on the enemy's centre under Jaswant himself.

The imperialists crowded together on a narrow ground and flanked with impassable ditches and swamps, could not manoeuvre freely, and 'sacrificed their lives like moths in the flame of war.' At the sight of the annihilation of their brave vanguard and a triumphant forward movement on the part of Aurangzib, Rai Singh Sisodia from the right flank of Jaswant's centre, and Sujan Singh Bundela and Amar Singh Chandrawat from his van, left the field with their clansmen and returned home.

Meantime, Murad Bakhsh with his division had fallen on Jaswant's camp close to the field, secured the submission of one of its defenders, Devi Singh Bundela, and driven off the rest. Then advancing into the field itself, Murad fell on the left wing of the imperial army, and it soon ceased to exist, after losing its commander Iftikhar Khan.

4.3 Flight of Jaswant and His Troops

Rai Singh's flight had already uncovered Jaswant's right flank; the fall of Iftikhar Khan exposed his left. Meanwhile his van had almost entirely melted away; the Musalmans, under Qasim Khan, who had kept aloof from the fighting, prepared to run away as they saw Aurangzib's host advancing on them. And now Aurangzib from the front, Murad from the left, and Saif Shikan Khan from the right, were converging on Jaswant like a tumultuous flood, to envelop his small remnant of clansmen. The Maharajah, who had received two wounds, wanted to drive his horse into the advancing enemy's ranks and get slain. But his generals and ministers seized his bridle and dragged his horse out of the field, and took the road to Jodhpur. The battle had been already lost, and after the flight of the Rathors there was a general rout. But there was no pursuit; victor and vanquished alike were worn out by the strife, and there was a rich prize at hand. The entire camp of the two imperial generals, with all their artillery, tents, elephants and treasure, became the victorious princes' spoil, while their soldiers looted the baggage and equipment of the vanquished army.

But far greater than all these material gains was the moral prestige secured by Aurangzib. Dharmat became the omen of his future success. At one blow he had brought Dara down from a position of immense superiority to one of equality with his own, or even lower. Waverers hesitated no longer; they now knew beyond a moment's doubt which of the four brothers was the chosen favourite of Fortune.

No sooner had Jaswant and Qasim Khan turned their backs than Aurangzib's band struck up the notes of victory: Aurangzib knelt down on the field and with folded arms rendered thanks to the Giver of Victory.

On the imperial side nearly six thousand men fell in this battle, and the main portion of the loss was borne by the Rajputs. Every clan of Rajasthan contributed its share to the band of heroes who sacrified their lives in their master's service (*swami-dharma*). To Ratan Singh Rathor (the progenitor of the houses of Rutlam, Sailana and Sitamau) a noble stone monument was raised by his descendants on the spot where his corpse was burnt.

4.4 Aurangzib Advances to Agra

The day after the victory the two princes reached Ujjain and marching thence arrived at Gwalior on 21 May. It was here learnt that Dara had come to Dholpur with a vast army and seized all the well-known and frequented fords over the Chambal river. His entrenchments frowned on the crossing places; his artillery crowned the opposite bank; and everywhere strong parties of his troops were on the alert for the enemy's arrival. To cross the river with its steep rocky banks and wide ravine-intersected approaches, in the face of such opposition, would have led to a heavy loss of life. So Aurangzib secured the help of a local zamindar and learnt that at Bhadaoli, 40 miles east of Dholpur, there was an obscure ford with only knee-deep water, which Dara had omitted to guard.

No time was to be lost. In the very evening after their arrival near Gwalior (21 May), while the main army halted, a strong division under three generals and some artillery made a forced march all night, reached the ford next morning, and crossed safely to the other bank. That day Aurangzib himself set out from Gwalior, covered the interval in two long marches and crossed the river at the same place with the rest of his army (23 May). 'The path was rough, the soldiers underwent much hardship before arriving at the ford; and on the way nearly 5,000 men died of thirst.' The military advantage of the movement was immense. By one stroke he had turned the enemy's position and rendered Dara's elaborate trenches and batteries useless. The road to Agra now lay open before him. It was now Dara's turn to abandon the line of the Chambal and fall back on the capital. He had to leave many of his heavier guns on the river bank, and thus weakened himself in artillery in the next battle. From the Chambal the victors marched north and in three days came in touch with the enemy near Samugarh, about ten miles east of Agra.

4.5 Dara's Movements After Dharmat

The news of the defeat at Dharmat reached the imperial Court, then at Baluchpur, ten days after the battle. Dara now raised a new army in all haste. It looked formidable in appearance only, being 60,000 troopers in number. But it was composed of a miscellaneous host of diverse classes and localities, hastily got together, and not properly co-ordinated nor trained in concerted action. Moreover, many of its commanders were carpet-knights of the Court, having neither the courage nor the experience of the veterans from the Deccan. Dara had made the fatal mistake of sending away his trustiest adherents and ablest lieutenants with Sulaiman Shukoh to oppose Shuja and now felt a sore need of such efficient instruments. The foreign Muslim soldiers in the imperial service resented Dara's reliance on the Rajputs and left him to his fate. And he was also hampered by Shah Jahan. Even now the Emperor urged him to avoid war; he still fondly hoped that the quarrel among his sons could be peacefully ended by diplomatic messages.

On 18 May, Dara left with his troops for the bank of the Chambal, after a most pathetic leave-taking from his aged father in the Diwan-i-am of Agra fort. He reached Dholpur on the twentysecond of the month, and seized all the fords over the Chambal in the neighbourhood. His aim was to retard Aurangzib's advance without precipitating a battle and thus gain time for Sulaiman Shukoh's army to join him. But he soon learnt to his consternation that Aurangzib had crossed the river forty miles east of Dholpur, on the twentythird. So, he fell back towards Agra and encamped outside that city near Samugarh, where Aurangzib arrived on the twentyeighth.

That day Dara, on hearing of Aurangzib's approach, drew up his troops and rode out as if to fight. But after sighting the enemy he halted, waiting to see what his rivals would do. At sunset he returned to his camp. It was a most unwise step; Aurangzib was numerically inferior and his troops were worn out by a ten mile march in the sun over a waterless dusty plain, while Dara's army was fresh. Dara's soldiers and their horses and elephants were prostrated by the extreme heat in which they stood hour after hour doing nothing, while the prudent Aurangzib rested his men all that evening and night for the morrow's contest.

4.6 Battle of Samugarh, 29 May, 1658

Next morning, 29 May, Dara marshalled his ranks on a wide plain two miles in front of his camp. His forces numbered about 50,000. Its backbone was composed of the Rajput contingent and Dara's own retainers, all devoted to his interests. But nearly half of his army belonged to the Emperor's service, and these men could not be relied on; several of their chiefs, notably Khalilullah Khan had been corrupted by Aurangzib. All the artillery of Dara was drawn up in one row along his entire front; behind it stood his foot musketeers, next the elephants, and last of all dense masses of cavalry. Dara's artillery was less mobile and more inefficiently served than Aurangzib's, and his horses and transport animals were out of condition.

In opposition to this host stood Aurangzib's hard-bitten troops, seasoned veterans on seasoned horses, and his excellent train of field-pieces handled by the European gunners of Mir Jumla and well supplied with munitions. There was absolute unity of command in his army, and all the officers had been taught to obey without hesitation or question the master's will.

The battle joined about noon. Dara at once took up the offensive and discharged all his artillery, making a fearful noise but doing little damage to the enemy at that long range; Aurangzib wisely reserved his powder and shot.

An hour passed in this kind of cannonade, and then Dara ordered a charge. His left wing was led by Rustam Khan. Filing out through the spaces between his guns, it formed a mass and attacked the opposing artillery with flashing blades and wild battle-cries. Aurangzib's chief of artillery, Saif Shikan Khan, and the musketeers behind his guns stood their ground well and received the charge with one deadly volley from the guns and a shower of bullets, arrows, and javelins. The flood of onset could not reach and overwhelm the guns; its speed slackened as the cannon balls ploughed up its ranks. So Rustam Khan swerved to his right in search of an easier prey, and galloped towards Aurangzib's van, leaving a cloud of dust behind. But Bahadur Khan with the right flank of Aurangzib's centre had hurried up to the front into the gap between the van and the artillery, and barred the path of Rustam Khan. A close hand to hand combat now ensued; Bahadur Khan fell down wounded, and his division seemed at the point of being routed, when Islam Khan came to its aid from the right wing and Shaikh Mir with the advance reserve. It was now the turn of Rustam Khan to be outnumbered and borne down. Mortally wounded in his arm, with a dozen other desperate men he hewed his way to the centre of the enemy's ranks and there fell amidst a heap of the slain. The small remnant of Dara's left wing now fled back under Sipihr Shukoh.

At the same time a more terrible fight was being waged on Aurangzib's left. There the Rajputs of the imperial vanguard under Chhatra Sal Hada slipped through the interval between Zulfiqar's artillery and Murad's division and fell upon that prince with fierce vigour, thus driving a wedge which separated Murad from Aurangzib's army. Rajah Ram Singh Rathor, wearing the gay yellow robe of *Holi* and with a string of priceless pearls tied to his turban, fell on Murad's elephant, crying out in derision, '*You* want to wrest the throne from Dara!' Shouting to the driver to make the elephant kneel down if he valued his life, the Rajah flung his spear at Murad, but it missed the aim, and the prince shot him dead with an arrow. Other Rajputs fell as 'they swarmed round Murad's elephant, and with their robes 'made the ground look yellow like a field of saffron!' The Rajput horsemen could not reach the prince on this lofty elephant; but Murad received three wounds in his face; his driver was killed and the *hawda* of his elephant bristled with arrows like the back of a porcupine; he was borne backwards by this onslaught.

The victorious Rajputs pressed on to the centre and fell on Aurangzib, who was hastening to the aid of Murad on hearing of the disaster on his left. The clash between these two powerful forces was terrible. The Rajputs forced their way to Aurangzib himself, but that prince's guards offered an opposition equally heroic, and being themselves fresh they prevailed over the Rajputs who were worn out and thinned in number by the struggle with Murad. Yet the Rajputs fought on against overwhelming odds 'in utter contempt of life.' But one by one all their leaders fell—Chhatra Sal Hada, Ram Singh Rathor, Bhim Singh Gaur and Shivaram Gaur. But the remnant only made a more frantic struggle, 'like ravening dogs', as a European eye-witness describes the scene. Rajah Rup Singh Rathor in reckless audacity jumped down from his horse, with his drawn blade hewed a way to the elephant of Aurangzib, and tried to cut the girths of the *hawda* in the hope of hurling the prince down to the ground. He slashed the beast's leg, but was himself cut to pieces by the bodyguard. The rest of the Rajputs perished. Thus both the left and right wings of Dara had been annihilated by this time.

4.7 Dara's own Movements at Samugarh; The End

At the very beginning of the battle, as soon as Rustam Khan and Chhatra Sal had charged with his left wing and van, Dara quitted his position in the centre, rode through his artillery, and went towards Aurangzib's right wing in order to support Rustam Khan. No more fatal mistake could have been committed. Dara could no longer survey the whole field and control his troops as their supreme leader; and at once everything fell into confusion. Secondly, by advancing in front of his artillery he obstructed its fire, while Aurangzib's guns continued to mow down his ranks without any chance of reply. This mistake ruined Dara more than all other causes put together. Dara now turned to the right in order to avoid the enemy's artillery in front of him, and fell upon Shaikh Mir's division.

Just then Aurangzib was left without any guards. If Dara could now have forced his way to his rival's side, the victory would have been his. 'But he made a short halt, owing to the difficulties of the ground and to the fatigue that overcame him.' His force lost its growing momentum, and the vigour of its onslaught greatly slackened, and the golden chance was lost for ever. For, in the meantime Aurangzib had dressed his ranks and made new disposition, and Dara was soon afterwards called upon to abandon his forward movement straight on his rival's elephant and to turn aside towards his own right wing in order to back the troops of Chhatra Sal. Thus Dara made a long movement across his entire front from the extreme left to near the extreme right. The frightful heat struck down his men, and horses during this unprofitable manoeuvre, while the artillery stationed in the enemy's front fired volleys straight into his left flank. The men with him were exhausted by this long and toilsome march over loose burning sand, amidst suffocating dust, and under a blazing sun which made their armour blister the skin, while not a drop of water could be had to quench their thirst.

Meanwhile, Aurangzib's vanguard, in obedience to his rigid discipline, had kept its proper position. But now seeing Dara's two wings and van overthrown and his centre in disorder and out of its proper place, Prince Muhammad Sultan, at the head of his father's van, sprang forward to attack Dara. At the same time Aurangzib's victorious right wing wheeled round to envelop Dara's division, while the batteries from the right and left alike assailed it. This was really the end of the fight. Dara had learnt of the death of his best generals, and now Aurangzib's, troops, 'like the waves of the sea, approached him with countless guns in front of them.' Their heavy and well-directed fire mowed down the troops still around him every minute. Dara's own elephant now became 'a target for the enemy's balls,' which began to carry off his personal attendants. The wretched prince had no help but to get down from this elephant and take to a horse.[1] At once all was over with him. His remaining troops all over the field, finding his *hawda* empty, concluded that their master had fallen. Already they were half dead with fatigue and thirst, and now a desolating hot wind sprang up and struck Dara's fainting troops in the face. Many of them died of thirst, without strength to use their arms. What still remained of the imperial army had been only waiting

[1] Dara dismounted from his elephant at a time of extreme danger, when he had lost all hope of victory, is asserted by *A.N.* (104), Aquil (48), Masum (63*b*) and Kambu (15a). These contemporary and first-rate authorities refute the bazar gossip reproduced by Manucci and Bernier that Dara changed his elephant for a horse at the treacherous advice of Khalilullah Khan at a time when he had almost completely defeated Aurangzib, and that this act on the part of Dara turned his assured victory into a rout. (*Storia*, *i.* 281–282; Bernier, 53–54, also Ishwardas, 24*a*–25*b*.)

for a decent pretext for flight, and the sudden disappearance of Dara from the back of his elephant gave them the wished for opportunity. At once the whole army broke and fled in the utmost disorder. Dara stood almost alone, deserted by all save a few hereditary followers. They took him out of the field to Agra.

The last trace of resistance now vanished; but there was no pursuit. Nor was any pursuit needed, for no victory could be more complete. On the side of the vanquished ten thousand men had fallen, besides horses and transport animals beyond count. Among the slain imperial commanders of high rank, nine Rajputs and nineteen Muslims are mentioned by name.

Bravest among so many brave men was Rao Chhatra Ṣal Hada, the chieftain of Bundi and the hero of fifty-two fights. 'With his Hadas clad in their saffron robes, the ensigns of death or victory, the Bundi prince formed the vanguard of Dara. Cheering on his men, he mounted his elephant, but whilst encouraging them by his voice and example, a cannon-ball hitting his elephant, the animal turned and fled. Chhatra Sal leaped from its back and called for his steed, exclaiming "My elephant may turn his back on the enemy, but never shall his master." Mounting his horse, and forming his men into a dense mass, he led them to the charge against Prince Murad whom he singled out, and had his lance balanced for the issue, when a ball pierced his forehead.' In the two battles of Dharmat and Samugarh no less than twelve princes of the blood, together with the head of every Hada clan, gave up their lives.

The most renowned victim of the day, however, was Rustam Khan, surnamed Firuz Jang, the hero of the Uzbak and Persian wars.

The army of Aurangzib lost only one chief of the first rank, Azam Khan, who died of the excessive heat.

4.8 Events at Agra and Captivity of Shah Jahan, June 1658

From the fatal field of Samugarh, Dara reached Agra with a few attendants at about 9 o'clock at night, and shut himself up in his house in the city. There was universal alarm and lamentation in the royal family. Shah Jahan sent word to Dara to come to the fort and see him; but Dara was utterly broken down in body and spirit, and declined saying,

'I cannot show my face to your Majesty in my present wretched plight. Permit me to go away with your farewell blessing on the long journey that is before me.'

The miserable prince, with his wife, children and a dozen servants, set off from Agra towards Delhi at 3 o'clock in the morning. Mules laden with gold coins from the palace treasury were sent with him by order of Shah Jahan, and he took away as much of his own jewels and cash as he could transport in that hurry. For the next two days small groups of his followers began to join him on the way, so that his force was raised to 5,000 men by the time he reached Delhi.

After the Battle of Samugarh, Aurangzib went to Murad, and congratulated him, saying that the victory was due entirely to his younger brother's heroism and that Murad's reign would date from that day. He even nursed the wounded Murad affectionately.

In two marches from the battle-field the victors arrived in the garden of Nur Manzil or Dhara outside Agra (1 June). Here they stayed for ten days. Every day large numbers of courtiers, nobles and officers deserted the imperial side and joined them, and so did the former officers of Dara.

The day after Samugarh, Aurangzib wrote to Shah Jahan directly, excusing his late actions as forced upon him by his enemies. On reaching Nur Manzil he received a reply in Shah Jahan's own hand, inviting him to an interview. This, after some hesitation, Aurangzib declined to do, at the advice of some of his friends (especially Shaista Khan and Khalilullah) who told him that Shah Jahan had formed a plot to get Aurangzib murdered by his Tartar guard-women as soon as he would enter Agra fort.

The mask was at last thrown away, and on the fifth of June the prince began the siege of Agra fort, after sending his eldest son Muhammad Sultan to occupy Agra city (3 June) and maintain order there. Shah Jahan had shut the gates of Agra fort, prepared to stand a siege there. It was one of the strongest forts of that age, and Aurangzib's artillery was quite ineffective on its defences. Success by breaching and assault was therefore out of the question. A regular investment would have detained the victorious brothers there for months and even years and thus given Dara time to raise a new army.

So, Aurangzib sent his men to make a sudden rush and seize the outside of the water gate (*Khiziri*) of the fort which opens on the Jamuna. Thus the water-supply of the garrison was cut off and they began to suffer the horrors of thirst in midsummer. The few old and long disused wells within the fort yielded only a bitter water unfit for drinking. At this, many of the Emperor's officers, pampered idlers of the Court, slipped out of the fort.

For three days Shah Jahan held out under these conditions. He had made a pathetic personal appeal to Aurangzib entreating him not to kill a living father by thirst, but to that letter Aurangzib had replied, 'It is your own doing.' Then, amidst raging thirst, with only despair and treason around him, the aged Emperor decided to yield. On 8 June he opened the gates of the fort to Aurangzib's officers and became a prisoner within the harem of the palace, being confined to the quarters behind the Hall of Public Audience. He was deprived of all power; a strong force was posted in and around the fort to prevent rescue, and careful watch was kept on his eunuchs lest they should carry letters from him outside. The vast treasures of Agra fort—the accumulations of three generations of prosperous rulers of India, passed into Aurangzib's possession.

On 10 June Princess Jahanara visited Aurangzib to try the effect of her personal influence and sisterly persuasion. She proposed, in Shah Jahan's name, a partition of the empire among the four brothers. Aurangzib naturally declined.

4.9 Murad Bakhsh's Captivity and Death

On 13 June Aurangzib set out from Agra city towards Delhi in pursuit of Dara. But on the way, at Mathura, he had to halt because an alarming situation had arisen on account of Murad's jealous and wilful conduct. This prince's courtiers were telling him how power was daily slipping out of his grasp and Aurangzib was becoming all in all. He was keen on reigning as king, but Aurangzib seemed to be putting off the fulfilment of that desire to a more and more distant future. Therefore, Murad must assert himself, if he was not to be made a cat's paw and then thrown away by Aurangzib.

Led on by such counsellors, Murad began to act openly in opposition to Aurangzib: he increased his army, seduced from Aurangzib's side many of the recently joined imperial troops by promises of higher pay and greater licence, and conferred titles. Lastly he gave up visiting Aurangzib as beneath his dignity. Thus, an open opposition to Aurangzib was set up in the allied camp.

The situation was very critical. But Aurangzib's plan was quickly formed and skilfully carried out. He first lulled Murad's suspicion to sleep by presenting him with 20 lakhs of Rupees and 233 horses, and invited him to a feast for celebrating his complete recovery from his wounds and for maturing a plan of campaign against the fugitive Dara. Lastly, Aurangzib heavily bribed and won over to his side Murad's favourite body-servant Nur-ud-din Khawas, who induced Murad to accept his brother's invitation and enter Aurangzib's camp when returning from a hunt (25 June).

Murad was cordially received by Aurangzib, well fed, plied with wine, and when asleep deprived of his arms and made a prisoner. At midnight the captive was sent in a covered ladies' *hawda,* under a strong cavalry escort to Salimgarh and thence to the State-prison of Gwalior. This 'excellent stratagem' had been carried out so smoothly that Murad's followers did not hear of his fate till it was too late. Next morning his leaderless soldiery were taken into Aurangzib's service, and even his devoted officers had no course left open to them but to submit to this new master. The entire establishment and property of Murad passed into Aurangzib's possession.

Murad lived for three years in the fortress of Gwalior, but an attempt at escape which his friends outside had planned and which narrowly missed success through Murad's own thoughtlessness, determined Aurangzib to get rid of him. At the Emperor's instigation, the second son of Ali Naqi demanded retaliation in blood from Murad for the murder of his father at Ahmadabad in 1657. This, under the Islamic law, the judges were bound to grant. So, on 4 December, 1661, the luckless aspirant to the throne of Delhi was beheaded by two slaves in the prison cell of Gwalior and his corpse was buried within that fort.

5 *War of Succession: End of Dara and Shuja*

5.1 Pursuit of Dara After Samugarh

Dara reached Delhi on 5 June 1658 and tried to raise and equip a new army by appropriating the Government property in the capital. But a week afterwards he left Delhi for Lahor, on learning that the fall of Agra fort had set Aurangzib free to pursue him. The Panjab was strongly attached to Dara; the province had long been his viceroyalty and was now held by his faithful deputy Sayyid Ghairat Khan. Leaving Delhi at the head of 10,000 men, Dara reached Lahor on 3 July, and spent a month and a half there in completing his war preparations. Seizing the imperial treasure there, he assembled an army of 20,000 men and sent off strong detachments to guard the ferries over the Sutlej at Taiwan and Rupar.

In the meantime, Aurangzib had deputed Khan-i-Dauran to wrest Allahabad from Dara's men and Bahadur Khan to take up the pursuit of Dara, and then pushed on to Delhi on 6 July. At this capital he stayed three weeks, constructing a new administration in the place of the old one, and finally he crowned himself Emperor under the title of *Alamgir Ghazi* on 21 July. Khalilullah Khan was appointed governor of the Panjab and sent to reinforce the pursuit of Dara.

In the night of 5 August, Bahadur Khan crossed the Sutlej by surprise at Rupar, and Dara's generals fell back from that river to Govindwal on the Beas. But when Aurangzib from Delhi reached the Sutlej, Dara fled from Lahor (18 August) to Multan, with his family and treasure, by boat. Once more Dara's genius quailed before that of Aurangzib: he despaired of success, and his despair infected his troops.

Aurangzib's forces set off from Lahor on 30 August at the heels of Dara, and the Emperor himself joined the pursuers on 17 September. But Dara again fled, from Multan (13 September) to Sakkar (13 October). From the environs of Multan, Aurangzib turned back (30 September) for Delhi to meet Shuja's invasion, but the chase of Dara was relentlessly continued by Saif Shikan Khan and Shaikh Mir at the head of two strong columns, totalling 15,000 men, following the two banks of the Indus.

At Sakkar the imperialists learnt (23 October) that Dara had left much of his property and his big guns in the fort of Bhakkar in charge of his eunuch Basant, with many European gunners under Nicholas Manucci, and himself fled towards Sehwan, deserted by all his troops except 3,000 men. Even the trusty Daud Khan was at last driven to leave his unjustly suspicious master. At Sehwan the imperialists came up with Dara by forced marches (31 October) and occupied both banks of the Indus, hoping to intercept him. But they were very weak in boats, and Dara who was stronger in that respect dashed through the broad river (2 November) in safety and reached Tatta (13 November). The imperialists made forced marches after him to Tatta (18), but learnt that Dara had fled further south of Badin (24) and was marching over the gulf of Cutch towards Gujrat.

The pursuers were now recalled to Court; the pursuit which they had carried on with such unflagging vigour and amazing endurance for three months since Dara left Lahor, had missed success, when almost within their grasp, solely through their lack of boats.

5.2 Dara in Rajputana: Battle of Deorai

After leaving Badin, 55 miles (approx. 90 km.) east of Tatta, Dara crossed the *Rann* or salt lagoon (end of November), suffering unspeakable hardship through lack of water. At Bhuj, the capital of the island of Cutch, he was welcomed and given every help by the Rajah, as also by the Jam of Nawanagar in Kathiawad. Thus he arrived at Ahmadabad at the head of 3,000 men. Here Shah Nawaz Khan, the new governor of the province, joined him and opened the royal treasury to him (9 January, 1659). Dara now raised his army to 22,000 men, brought away the 5 artillery of Surat, and learning that Shuja had advanced beyond Allahabad to attack Aurangzib, he made a dash towards Agra at the same time. On the way he received an invitation to Ajmir from Jaswant Singh, who promised to join him with the Rathors and other Rajputs.

But, in the meantime, Aurangzib, after crushing Shuja at Khajwa (5 January), had won over Jaswant with the help of Mirza Rajah Jai Singh by means of mingled threats of invasion and hopes of promotion. Dara had no help but to fight, for Aurangzib had arrived near him. He wisely changed his plan. Instead of fighting a pitched battle in an open plain, he decided to hold the pass of Deorai, four miles south of Ajmir, in the narrow breadth of which a small host can keep a superior force of assailants back. His two flanks were protected by the hills of Bithli and Gokla; while behind him lay the rich city of Ajmir, whence he could easily draw his supplies. He ran a low wall south of his position, from hill to hill across the valley, with trenches in front and redoubts at different points.

Aurangzib approached this position from the south, and began a bombardment of it from the sunset of 12 March, 1659, to the night following the thirteenth. Dara's artillery and muskets, from their high and sheltered position, showered death on Aurangzib's unprotected gunners and infantry, while the latter could not fire back with effect. The enemy's trenches were impregnable. So, on the fourteenth Aurangzib held a council of war and adopted a new plan of attack, viz. to make a concentrated attack of overwhelming strength on the enemy's left wing under Shah Nawaz Khan, while the right wing was to be kept in play by the imperial division opposite it; but the success of the scheme was to depend not on this frontal attack but on a secret movement to turn the enemy's left rear (the Gokla Hill), which was to be scaled from behind by Rajah Rajrup of the Jammu hills and his clansmen expert in mountaineering, who had discovered a path to its top.

Towards the evening of the fourteenth, the imperial army, massed in front of the enemy's left, delivered their assault upon Shah Nawaz Khan's trenches. Their artillery reopened fire with great rapidity and prevented the other divisions of Dara's army from leaving their trenches and marching across the front to aid their hard-pressed brethren on the left. The hardest fight raged in this part of the field. Dara's men obstinately defended their lines. Wave after wave of the imperialists swarmed up to the charge; and at last they pushed back all the enemy out of the plain and won the ground to the edge of the trenches.

By this time Rajrup's men had toiled up the back of the Gokla Hill, while the enemy were absorbed in the severe contest in their front. They planted their banners on the top and raised a shout. Dara's left wing was seized with despair at their rear being thus turned, but many of his men still fought with courage. To overcome this last opposition, Shaikh Mir drove his elephant forward, but was killed by a bullet. At last, these trenches were stormed. Shah Nawaz Khan, while cheering his men even after all was over, was blown away by cannon-ball. The rank and file broke and fled away under the cover of darkness.

True, only one of the four entrenchments had so far been carried; but it was enough: Dara's lines had been fatally pierced and rendered untenable by the turning of the Gokla Hill. Accompanied by his son Sipihr Shukoh and only a dozen of his men, Dara fled from the field in headlong haste towards Gujrat. The country round Ajmir became a wild scene of plunder; thousands of Rajputs had assembled in the neighbourhood at the call of Jaswant and were hovering round like vultures for their expected prey. They now looted the property and transport animals of the vanquished army.

5.3 Flight and Capture of Dara

During the Battle of Deorai, Dara's harem and treasure had been left on the bank of the Anasagar Lake (at Ajmir), on elephants, camels and mules, in charge of the faithful eunuch Khwajah Maqbul and an escort of troops, ready for flight. These fled from the place in the night of the fourteenth and joined Dara near Mairta in the afternoon of the fifteenth. But Aurangzib had already detached a strong force under Jai Singh and Bahadur Khan in pursuit of them, and therefore Dara could not rest anywhere but had to resume his march with the same haste as before. Only 2,000 troopers accompanied him when he left Mairta. Covering thirty miles or even more a day in their rush to Gujrat, they underwent extreme misery from heat and dust and want of tents and transport animals. Their few horses and camels perished from heat and overwork.

Everywhere Dara found Aurangzib's letters had preceded him and the local officers were ready to seize him. His last hope was gone when his messenger returned from Ahmadabad with the dismal news that he would be resisted if he tried to enter that city. At this destruction of their last hope of refuge the party was 'overwhelmed with confusion and dismay,... and the shrieks of the females drew tears from every eye.' Dr. Bernier who was attending on Dara's sick wife, gives a heartrending picture of their misery and suffering at this time. 'Reduced to the poorest and sorriest dress,... accompanied by one horse, one bullock-cart, five camels for his ladies, and a few other camels for transport, his retinue shrunk to a few men,' the chosen heir to the richest throne in Asia crossed the terrible *Rann* once again, and reached the southern coast of Sindh (beginning of May).

Here, too, he found his path to lower Sindh closed by the forethought of Aurangzib, who had sent down Khalilullah Khan from Lahor to Bhakkar. Aurangzib's local officers and Jai Singh's advanced detachments were converging on their prey from north, east and south-east. Only one path of escape remained open: Dara turned to the north-west, crossed the Indus and entered Siwistan, intending to flee to Persia by way of Qandahar.

In the meantime Jai Singh from Ajmir had been pushing on behind Dara, covering 16 to 20 miles a day (approx. 30 km.), in spite of scarcity of water, want of fodder, and exhaustion of his horses and transport animals. Following Dara's tracks he crossed the lesser and the greater *Rann* and the island of Cutch, suffering frightful privations on the way. 'At places grain sold at a seer per Rupee, at others no food at all could be procured.' But he pursued his course with grim tenacity and reached the Indus on the border of Siwistan on 11 June, 1659, though more than three-fourths of his troop horses perished during the journey. Then, learning that Dara had gone out of Mughal India, he began his return march to Hindustan up the Indus.

But Dara's family were utterly opposed to the idea of migrating to Persia. His beloved wife, Nadira Banu, was seriously ill and the privations of a journey through the desolate Bolan Pass and the inhospitable region of Qandahar would have killed her. Dara, therefore, changed his mind and looked about for a chieftain in that neighbourhood who would give him a safe shelter and the services of his clansmen. Such a friend he hoped to find in Malik Jiwan, the zamindar of Dadar, a place nine miles east of the Indian end of the Bolan Pass. Years ago this Afghan chief had been sentenced by Shah Jahan to be trampled to death by an elephant. Dara, then at the height of his father's favour, had successfully begged the condemned man's life and liberty from the Emperor. He now looked for Jiwan's gratitude, and reached Dadar, where the chief took him to his house, showing him every respect and care (probably 6 June).

On the way to Dadar, Nadira Banu succumbed to hardship and want of medicine and rest. Dara was frantic with grief at losing his life's companion. 'The world grew dark in his eyes. He was utterly bewildered. His judgment and prudence were entirely gone.' He sent her corpse to Lahor for burial in the graveyard of the saint Mian Mir (his own spiritual guide), under escort of all the 70 troopers still left at his side and his most devoted officer, Gul Muhammad. He offered his companions a free choice between returning to their homes and accompanying him to Persia. Thus it happened that not a single devoted follower now remained with Dara, and he became utterly helpless and dependent upon his host's fidelity.

Cupidity overcame the Afghan's gratitude and fidelity to plighted word. He treacherously arrested Dara and his younger son and two daughters (9 June) and delivered them to Bahadur Khan.

5.4 Humiliation and Murder of Dara

When these prisoners arrived at Delhi they were paraded through the streets of the capital, in disgrace (29 August). Dara was seated in an uncovered *hawda* on the back of a small female elephant covered with dirt. By his side was his second son, Sipihr Shukoh, a lad of fourteen; and behind them with a naked sword sat their ferocious gaoler, the slave Nazar Beg. The heir to the richest throne in the world was now clad in a travel-tainted dress of the coarsest cloth, with a dark dingy-coloured turban, such as only the poorest wore, on his head, and no necklace or jewel adorning his person. His feet were chained, though his hands were free. Exposed to the full blaze of an August sun, he was taken in this guise through the scenes of his former glory and splendour. In the bitterness of disgrace he did not raise his head, nor cast his glance on any side, but sat 'like a crushed twig.'

The pity of the citizens swept every other feeling away. The crowd assembled was immense, and everywhere, Bernier observed, the people were weeping and lamenting the fate of Dara.

That evening Aurangzib held a private consultation with his ministers about Dara's fate. Danishmand Khan (Bernier's patron) pleaded for his life, but Shaista Khan, Muhammad Amin Khan, Bahadur Khan, and the Princess Raushanara from the harem demanded his death for the good of Church and State. The pliant theologians in the Emperor's pay signed a decree stating that Dara deserved death on the ground of his deviation from Islam.

A riot by the citizens of Delhi against the traitor Malik Jiwan (recently created a hazari with the title of Bakhtiyar Khan), when on his way to the Court, on the 30th, precipitated the end of Dara. That very night Nazar Beg and some other slaves visited Dara's prison in Khawaspura, tore away Sipihr Shukoh from his father's arms and hacked Dara to pieces. By Aurangzib's order the corpse was placed on an elephant, paraded through the streets of the city a second time, and then buried in a vault under the dome of the tomb of Humayun.

5.5 End of Sulaiman Shukoh

We shall now trace the fate of Dara's eldest son, Sulaiman Shukoh. After his victory over Shuja near Benares, he had pursued his defeated uncle through Bihar to Mungir, when early in May 1658, he received a summons from his father to return quickly to his side as Aurangzib had triumphed at Dharmat. So, he hurriedly patched up a peace with Shuja and set out *on* his return. On 2 June, when 105 miles west of Allahabad, he received news of his father's ruin at Samugarh. His soldiers were distracted; Jai Singh and Dilir Khan, his greatest generals, as well as all the other imperial officers left him for Aurangzib. Only 6,000 men, less than one-third of Sulaiman's army, accompanied him in his retreat to Allahabad (4 June), where he wasted a precious week in distraction not knowing what to do with his cumbrous and costly furniture and plate and vast harem of women. At last, at the advice of his chief followers the Sayyids of Barha, he decided to make a wide loop round Delhi, march by the northern side of the Ganga, through their home the Middle Doab, and then cross the rivers at the foot of the hills, in order to reach his father in the Panjab without fear of interception.

Sulaiman rapidly moved by way of Nagina to Chandi, on the bank of the Ganga opposite to Hardwar. Numbers of soldiers deserted him daily, and strong enemy forces pushed up from Delhi barred his path everywhere in the south, east and west. So, Sulaiman fled to the Srinagar hills for asylum, his Sayyid followers of Barha refusing to accompany him there. Prithwi Singh, the Rajah of Srinagar (in Garhwal) admitted him on condition of his being accompanied by his family and seventeen servants only but none of his soldiers. The Rajah was all kindness and attention to his princely guest in distress, and Sulaiman enjoyed peace in his rude but safe refuge for a year.

But when Aurangzib was at last triumphant over all his brothers, he turned against Sulaiman. On 27 July, 1659, he sent Rajah Rajrup to secure the surrender of Sulaiman from the Rajah of Srinagar; but for a year and a half his efforts were futile. Aurangzib next employed Jai Singh, who wrote to Prithwi Singh not to destroy his kingdom by disobeying the Emperor's order. The Garhwal Rajah was old and refused to undertake the sin and shame of betraying an accepted refugee. But his son and heir, Medini Singh, was more worldly-minded; the hope of rewards from Delhi conquered his scruples. There was also the fear of losing his kingdom, as Aurangzib was instigating the neighbouring and rival hill-Rajahs to invade and annex Garhwal. On hearing of this decision of his host, Sulaiman tried to escape over the snow to Ladak, but was pursued, captured wounded, delivered to Aurangzib's agent, and brought to Delhi on 2 January, 1661.

On 5 January the prisoner was placed before his dreaded uncle in the Hall of Private Audience of the Delhi palace. His youth, extreme beauty, martial fame, and present misery deeply interested the courtiers and even the ladies of the imperial harem in his fate. Aurangzib spoke to him with apparent kindness. 'Be comforted; no harm shall befall you. You shall be treated with tenderness.' The prince made the *salam* or sign of grateful acknowledgment.... He then told the Emperor, with much self-possession, that if it were intended to give him the *pousta*[1] to drink, he begged that he might be immediately put to death. Aurangzib promised in a solemn manner, and in a loud voice, that this drink should most certainly not be administered.

The captive was sent to Gwalior and in that dismal state-prison Aurangzib, in violation of his 'solemn promise', caused the death of the unhappy Sulaiman Shukoh (May 1662) by overdoses of opium.

---

[1] The *pousta* is a drink made of poppy-heads crushed and soaked in water for a night. This was the potion generally given to princes confined in the fortress of Gwalior, whose heads the Emperor was deterred by public shame from taking off. A large cup of this beverage was brought to them early in the morning, and they were not given anything to eat until it was swallowed. This drink emaciated the wretched victims, who lost their strength and intellect by slow degrees, became torpid and senseless, and at length died.

5.6 Battle of Bahadurpur

Prince Muhammad Shuja, the second son of Shah Jahan and governor of Bengal, was a man of great intelligence, elegant taste, and amiable disposition. But his constant devotion to pleasure, the easy administration of Bengal, and his 17 years' residence in that enervating country, had made him weak, indolent and negligent, incapable of arduous toil, sustained effort, vigilant caution, or profound combination. He had allowed his administration to drift, his army to grow inefficient, and all his departments to fall into a slack and sleepy condition. His mental powers were as keen as before: but they required great emergencies to call them forth, and shone only by flashes; he was still capable of vigorous action, but only fitfully.

The story of Shah Jahan's illness, with the usual exaggeration, reached Shuja at Rajmahal, then the capital of Bengal, and he immediately crowned himself Emperor with the title of Abul Fauz Nasir-ud-din Muhammad, Timur III, Alexander II, Shah Shuja Ghazi.

Starting with a large army, an excellent park of artillery, and the highly useful war-boats *(nawwara)* of Bengal he reached Benares about 24 January, 1658. Meanwhile Dara had despatched against him an army of 22,000 men under his eldest son Sulaiman Shukoh, assisted by the able and experienced Mirza Rajah Jai Singh and Dilir Khan Ruhela.

Early in the morning of 14 February, Sulaiman suddenly attacked Shuja's camp, at Bahadurpur, 5 miles (8 km.) north-east of Benares. The surprise was so complete that the sleeping Bengal soldiers and their leader had no time to put on their tunics, but fled away leaving everything behind. With great difficulty Shuja mounted on an elephant, forced his way out of the ring of his enemies and found safety in his war-boats, whose gun-fire kept the enemy away from the bank. His entire camp and property, estimated at fifty lakhs of Rupees, were seized by the victors; even the humblest soldier had to abandon his all.

The panic-stricken army fled by the land route through Saseram to Patna, robbed by the villagers on the way. But hearing of the approach of the pursuing imperialists, Shuja fled to Mungir and blocked the road with his trenches and batteries. This brought Sulaiman sharply to a halt at Surajgarh, 15 miles (25 km.) south-west of Mungir, and he wasted precious months here without being able to advance. But the news of Dharmat forced him to make a hurried peace with Shuja, leaving Bengal, eastern Bihar and Orissa to that prince (7 May), and set out on his return to Agra.

Aurangzib, after crowning himself at Delhi (21 July), wrote a friendly letter to Shuja, adding the entire province of Bihar to his viceroyalty and promising him other favours.

The news of Aurangzib's absence in the far off Punjab at the heels of Dara revived Shuja's ambition. Now was the time to conquer the undefended country up to Agra and release Shah Jahan. So, at the end of October, 1658, Shuja started from Patna with 25,000 cavalry and artillery and boats, and reached Khajwa, three days' march beyond Allahabad on 30 December. Here he found Sultan Muhammad barring his path. In the meantime, Aurangzib after abandoning the pursuit of Dara at Multan (30 September), had hastened back to Delhi by forced marches (20 November), and strongly reinforced his army near Allahabad with men and money. Shuja's open road to Agra was now blocked, and on 2 January, 1659, the Emperor himself joined his son near Kora, eight miles (13 km.) west of Shuja's position. Mir Jumla, too, arrived there from the Deccan on the same day.

5.7 Khajwa: Jaswant's Treachery

On 4 January, Aurangzib marched his army in perfect order till he arrived one mile (1½ km.) in front of the enemy's camp. Here he halted, his soldiers maintained their exact positions, each man sleeping on the gound with his armour on and his saddled horse standing at his head. That night Mir Jumla, with a born general's instinct, seized a mound midway between the two armies and by hard labour dragged 40 guns to it, which commanded the enemy's camp. Careful vigil was kept by his officers throughout the night.

A few hours before the dawn of the 5th of January, the day fixed for the battle a confused noise arose in the vanguard of Aurangzib's army; the alarm and disorder rapidly spread through the entire camp. The air was filled with the yells of the assailants, the cries of the fugitives, and the tramp of horsemen recklessly galloping away. The darkness heightened the confusion. The .root of all this trouble was Maharaja Jaswant Singh, the commander of the imperial right wing, who had brooded over some fancied slight or neglect and matured a deep plan of vengeance. He had, it was said, sent a secret message to Shuja saying that he would attack the imperial camp behind the field at the close of the night, and that while the Emperor would hasten to the rear to repel him Shuja should swiftly fall on the disordered army and crush it between two adversaries. So, shortly after midnight he got his 14,000 Rajputs ready, turned his back to the field, rushed the camp of Prince Muhammad Sultan which lay in the path of his flight, and there carried off everything that the Rajputs could lay their hands on. Much of the Emperor's own camp suffered the same fate. The Rajputs took the road to Agra, but in the darkness and surprise the confusion spread to the army at the front.

But the situation was saved by Aurangzih's wonderful coolness and Shuja's hesitation. Shuja received Jaswant's message, heard of the tumult but did not leave his own camp at night, fearing it might be a mere *ruse* contrived between Aurangzib and Jaswant to lure him on to his destruction!

The Emperor was at his *tahajjud* prayer in his field-tent, when the news of Jaswant's attack and desertion reached him. Without uttering a word, he merely waved his hand as if to say, 'If he is gone, let him go!' After deliberately finishing the prayer, he issued from the tent, mounted a *takht-i-rawan* (portable chair), and addressed his officers, 'This incident is a mercy vouchsafed to us by God. If the infidel had played the'traitor in the midst of the battle, all would have been lost. His flight (now) is good for us.'

So Aurangzib firmly kept his own position, and prevented the confusion from spreading to his division. Orderlies were sent off to urge the leaders of the various corps not to stir from, their own places, but to rally the fugitives. With the return of daylight many faithful officers who had been swept far away by the tide of flight hastened to rejoin the imperial banners, round which more than 50,000 soldiers were now assembled as against Shuja's 23,000.

5.8 Battle of Khajwa

Shuja knew that he could not adopt the customary plan of battle, making his force correspond, division for division, to the enemy's dispositions. His small force would then have been overlapped and swallowed up by the vastly extended front of an enemy who outnumbered him as three to one. So, with great judgement he made a new formation today: all his army was drawn up in one long line, behind the artillery. With true generalship Shuja decided to assume the offensive, and make up for the smallness of his number by the moral superiority which the attacking party always has.

The battle began at 8 a.m. with a furious discharge of cannon, rockets and muskets; then the two vans closed together and plied their bows. Sayyid Alam, at the head of Shuja's right wing, charged the imperial left wing, driving in front three infuriated elephants, each brandishing a two *maund* iron chain in its trunk. Neither man nor beast could stand their impetuous onset. The imperial left, which had no prince or great general to command it, broke and fled. The panic spread even to the centre; the soldiers ran about in confusion. To make matters worse, a false report of the Emperor's death suddenly spread through the ranks and many fled away. The enemy, after clearing the left wing, pushed on towards the centre, where only 2,000 troopers now remained to guard the Emperor. But his two reserves flung themselves forward and barred the enemy's path. The Emperor with the centre turned his elephant's head to the left, in order to support that wing. Sayyid Alam was repelled and fled back by the same path that he had come.

But the three elephants continued to advance wildly, their wounds having made them fiercer than before. One of them came up to Aurangzib's elephant. It was the critical moment of the battle. If the Emperor had given ground or turned back, his whole army would have fled. But he stood like a rock, chaining legs of his elephant to prevent its flight. At his order one of his matchlockmen, Jalal Khan, shot down the *mahut* of the attacking elephant, a brave royal *mahut* nimbly leaped on its back and brought the riderless beast under control. The Emperor now got breathing time, and turned to succour his right, which had been hard-pressed by a charge of the enemy's vanguard and left wing under Prince Buland Akhtar. In spite of their small number, their gallant charge dislodged their opponents; many of the imperialists fled away. Freed from the danger on his left, Aurangzib now looked at his right and found three signs of confusion and flight. But even in the greatest difficulty and danger, his coolness and presence of mind did not desert him. It at once struck him that, as his own front had hitherto been turned towards the left, if he were now to turn round suddenly und march to the right, the rest of the army would interpret this *volte face* as flight. So, he first sent orderlies to the van to tell the generals of his real object and to urge them to fight on without fear.

Then he wheeled the centre round and joined his hardpressed right wing. The succour came not a minute too soon. This was the decisive move of the day. The tide of battle now rolled restlessly against Shuja. The imperial right, newly strengthened, made a counter-charge and swept away the enemy from before them, with great carnage.

Meantime the imperial van, under Zulfiqr Khan and Sultan Muhammad, had beaten back the attack on it, advanced, and shaken the enemy's front line. So thick was the shower of cannon-balls, rockets and bullets from Aurangzib's army that no man could stand it. There was now a general advance of the whole imperial army, right, centre, and left. 'Like masses of dark clouds, they surrounded Shuja's own division (the centre), his two flanks having been scattered already. The cannon-balls flew about his own head and killed many of his personal attendants.' Therefore, he left the dangerous prominence of the elephant's back and took to horse.[2]

This was the end of the struggle. All was now lost, as his soldiers believed that their master was dead. In a moment all that still remained of the Bengal army broke and fled. Shuja galloped away from the field with his sons, his general Sayyid Alam and a small body of troops. His entire camp and baggage were plundered by the imperialists. 114 pieces of cannon and 11 of the celebrated elephants of Bengal became the victor's prize.

5.9 Pursuit of Shuja and the War in Bihar

In the afternoon following the victory of Khajwa, Aurangzib sent a pursuing column under Muhammad Sultan after Shuja. Reinforcements under Mir Jumla soon raised this force to 30,000 men. Shuja fled through Benares and Patna to Mungir, where he made a fortnight's stand (19 February–6 March). The city of Mungir stands in a narrow plain, two and a half miles broad, between the Ganga river and the Khargpur Hills. Along this plain runs the most convenient road from Patna to Bengal. Shuja had blocked the road by means of a wall and a ditch running from the river

---

[2] Bernier's statement, copied by Steward, that Shuja was on the point of gaining the victory when he lost all by dismounting from his elephant, merely gives the bazar gossip. None of the contemporary authorities on whom my account of the battle is based, supports such an idea, which is also naturally improbable. Indeed, the battle had been already lost and Shuja was in imminent risk of being captured, when he took to horse.

to the hill, with raised bastions at every thirty yards' distance, defended with large guns landed from his boats and manned by his soldiers.

Early in March Mir Jumla arrived before Mungir, and finding the main road barred, bribed Rajah Bihroz of Khargpur and under his guidance carried the imperial Army through the hills and jungles south-east of Mungir fort, thus turning Shuja's rear. That prince now fled from Mungir (6 March) to Sahibganj, where he blocked the narrow pass with a wall (10–24 March). But the imperialists won over Khwajah Kamal Afghan, the zamindar of Birbhum and Chatnagar, and with his help and guidance made a detour round the south-east of the Mungir district and reached Suri on 28 March.

But a false rumour that Dara had triumphed near Ajmir and was wreaking vengeance on the Rajput States now induced the Rajput contingent under Mir Jumla (especially the troops of Ram Singh, the eldest son of Jai Singh) to desert and return to their distant homes. Thus the pursuing force lost 4,000 men (30 March), but was still twice as strong as Shuja's army.

In the meantime, Shuja had evacuated Sahibganj (27 March) for Rajmahal; but finding even Rajmahal unsafe, he retreated (4 April) to the Malda district. His chief noble Alawardi Khan, who had planned to desert to Mir Jumla with many other officers, was beheaded (2 April), on the detection of his plot. The imperialists occupied Rajmahal on 13 April, and thus the whole country west of the Ganga passed out of Shuja's hands.

The war that now ensued between the two sides was a curious contest like that between a tiger and a crocodile. Shuja's regular troops had by now been reduced to five thousand men, while Mir Jumla's army was five times as large and, man for man, superior in fighting capacity. Shuja was, therefore, hopelessly inferior on land. But Mir Jumla's army was a purely land force. He had not at first a single boat of his own for campaigning in this land of water-ways, and his guns were fewer and smaller than his enemy's. On the other hand, Shuja had an artillery of big pieces admirably served by European and half-breed gunners. He had the entire flotilla *(nawwara)* of Bengal at his disposal for crossing rivers, transporting his troops, or cannonading the imperial defences and camp on the river-bank wherever he liked. This gave Shuja wonderful mobility and multiplied the effective strength of his small army, while the lack of boats paralysed Mir Jumla's efforts and neutralized his superiority on land.

Shuja, making Tanda (four miles (6½ km.) west of the fort of Gaur) his base, entrenched various places on the eastern bank of the Ganga to prevent Mir Jumla from crossing over. But his plans were foiled by Mir Jumla's wonderful activity in procuring boats from remote places and Aurangzib's clever strategic move in sending another army, under the governor of Patna, to make a diversion on the left bank of the Ganga and turn Shuja's right flank.

From his headquarters at Dogachi, thirteen miles (21 km.) south of Rajmahal, Mir Jumla struck two successful blows at Shuja. He wrested from the enemy, by a night surprise, an island in midstream, opposite Dogachi, where a detachment of Shuja's men was posted, and he held it against repeated attempts to recover it. Later, the imperialists surprised and destroyed a battery of eight guns which the enemy had erected on the eastern bank facing Suti.

The imperial army was distributed along the entire western bank: Muhammad Murad Beg was left in command at Rajmahal in the extreme north; the prince with Zulfiqar Khan, Islam Khan, and the bulk of the army, remained at Dogachi, 13 miles (21 km.) southwards, facing Shuja. At Dunapur, some 8 miles (13 km.) further south, Ali Quli Khan was posted, while Mir Jumla himself with six or seven thousand troops occupied Suti, the southernmost point of the Mughal lines, 28 miles (46 km.) south of Rajmahal.

But a third *coup* planned by Mir Jumla failed with heavy loss, because this time Shuja was on the alert and had prepared an ambush. On May 3, 1659, when only the first party of the expedition sent by the Mughal general had landed, the men and their boats were attacked by a superior enemy force which had been waiting for them in hiding. The imperial detachment sacrificed in this vain attempt four high officers and many hundred soldiers, besides the 500 taken as prisoners. No succour could be sent by Mir Jumla from the western bank, as his boats were afraid to face the Bengal flotilla.

Late in the night of 8 June, Prince Muhammad Sultan fled from his post of Dogachi to Shuja. He had long been chafing under the tutelage of Mir Jumla, and aspired to reign independently! Shuja secretly offered him the hands of his daughter Gulrukh Banu, and his help in gaining the throne, and thus won the thoughtless prince over. On hearing the news, Mir Jumla at Suti firmly kept his own men quiet, and the morning, after the flight rode to the prince's camp at Dogachi, harangued the leaderless troops, put heart and hope into them, and restored order and discipline. A council of war was held; all the other generals agreed to obey him as their sole head. Thus the army weathered the storm; 'it lost only one man—the prince.'

Soon afterwards, the torrential rains of Bengal suspended military operations. Mir Jumla, with about 15,000 men, took post at Masuma-bazar, while the rest of the imperial army, under Zulfiqar Khan, stayed at Rajmahal, the two divisions being separated by 60 miles (100 km.) of road impassable in that season.

The rains converted the neighbourhood of Rajmahal into one marshy lake. The city's food supply from the Majwa Hills (in the north-west) was cut off by Shuja's bribing, its Rajah; the water-route was commanded by Shuja's flotilla; and so scarcity of grain reached its extreme among the Mughal garrison in Rajmahal. In this situation, Shuja made a sudden attack with his flotilla and captured the city on 22 August, with all the property of the Mughals.

5.10 The War in Bengal

At the beginning of December 1659 Shuja marched from Rajmahal with 8,000 men, against Mir Jumla who was encamped near Belghata (42 miles (70 km.) southwards, and opposite Jangipur in the Murshidabad district). Here he twice attacked the imperialists and did them such damage, on account of their marked inferiority in artillery, that Mir Jumla fell back on Murshidabad, while Shuja marched parallel to him to Nashipur. But in the meantime, Daud Khan the governor of Bihar, with a second army had forced a passage across the Kushi river, swept away the Shujaite forces on the north bank of the Ganga and was in full march on Tanda. On hearing this news Shuja left Nashipur (26 December) and hastened towards Tanda via Suti. Mir Jumla immediately gave him chase, Shuja crossed the Ganga at Rajmahal and the imperialists recovered that city on 11 January, 1660. Thus, the whole country west of the Ganga was finally lost to Shuja.

This year Mir Jumla's plan of campaign was brilliantly novel: he would attack the enemy from an unexpected quarter, the north-east. Shuja's position now was a long line, stretching north-west to southeast from Samda island (opposite Rajmahal) to Tanda, with his headquarters about the middle of the line at Chauki Mirdadpur. Mir Jumla's plan was to make a wide detour in a semi-circle north of this position, by way of Rajmahal, Akbarpur and Malda, then turn sharply south and swoop down upon Tanda from the east. With the help of the 160 boats brought from Patna, he carried his army over the Ganga, 16 km. (10 miles) north of Rajmahal, and joined Daud Khan.

Shuja was hopelessly outnumbered from the first, and now (February 1660) found his only line of retreat, in the south,, threatened. At this time, Prince Muhammad Sultan deserted him and sneaked back to the Mughal camp at Dogachi (8 February). He was doomed to pass the rest of his life in prison.

On 6 March Mir Jumla reached Malda and worked hard for a month to complete his preparations for his crowning stroke which would crush Shuja in one move. From his headquarters: at Mahmudabad (a few miles below Malda town), he started on 5 April, and after a march of 16 km. (10 miles) surprised the small enemy patrol at an obscure ford of the Mahananda river. Without a moment's delay, the imperialists plunged into the water; all order was gone and in the confusion the shallow ford was missed; vast numbers went below their depth on both sides of the track, and more than a thousand soldiers were drowned, including a son of Dilir Khan.

But it was the decisive move of the campaign. All was now over with Shuja. He must immediately flee to Dacca, before the enemy's net could completely close round him. He hastened to Tanda at dawn of 6 April and ordered his Begams to come away at once 'without waiting even to change their dress.' His treasure and a selection from his other property were loaded in four large boats and sent down the stream. In the afternoon he himself embarked. His two younger sons, (Buland Akhtar and Zain-ul-abidin), his chiefs, Mirza Jan Beg, Sayyid Alam of Barha, Sayyid Quli Uzbak,and Mirza Beg, a few soldiers, servants, and eunuchs,—300 men in all,—accompanied him in 60 boats (*kosas*). This was the sole remnant of the splendid court amidst which he had ruled three provinces, and the vast army with which he had twice contested the throne of Delhi!

Wild terror and confusion now reigned in his camp at Tanda. His unguarded property was plundered. Next day (7 April) Mir Jumla occupied the city and restored order. He seized for the Government all the property he found or could recover from the plunderers; the women left behind by Shuja were properly guarded and taken care of. At Tartipur 400 loaded boats of Shuja's flotilla were seized, besides the two treasure-laden *ghurabs*. His army now came over to Mir Jumla (9 April). Then the general set off from Tanda (19 April) for Dacca.

5.11 Shuja Abandons Bengal; His End

On 12 April, Shuja reached Dacca, the second capital of Bengal, a bankrupt in fame and fortune. But it was to be no asylum to him. The *zamindars* were all up against him and he was too weak either to subdue them or to face Mir Jumla who was hastening behind him. So, on 6 May he left Dacca and glided down the river towards the sea. At every stage soldiers and boatmen deserted him in large numbers. He had already begged help from the king of Arracan, and two days after leaving Dacca he was met by 51 ships sent by that king's governor of Chatgaon. All hope of maintaining a hold on Bengal was given up and he steeled his heart to banish himself to the land of the savage Maghs.

The news spread consternation among his family and followers. The piracy of the Arracanese of Chatgaon in the rivers of East Bengal had made them too well known to the people. Whole districts in Noakhali and Baqarganj had been depopulated through their ravages. Their daring attacks, ferocious cruelty, uncouth appearance, barbarous manners, lack of religion and caste, and practice of eating unclean animals,—all caused them to be regarded by the people of East Bengal, Hindus and Muslims alike, with a mixture of terror and loathing.

But there was no help for it, if Shuja wanted to avoid the fate of Dara Shukoh and Murad Bakhsh at the hands of Aurangzib. So, on 12 May 1660, he finally left the home of his ancestors and the province which he had ruled for twenty years, and sailed for Arracan with his family and less than forty followers; ten of these were Sayyids of Barha, famous throughout India for their valour and devotion to their master.

Shuja was not happy in his new home. His unquiet ambition brought down a tragic end upon him. 'Many dwellers in Arracan, Mughal and Pathan,... showed themselves inclined towards him. He planned an outbreak intending to slay the king and take his kingdom, and then advance once more to test his fortune in Bengal.' The king of Arracan heard of the plot and 'planned the assassination of Shah Shuja. Shah Shuja with a few men fled into the jungle. The Maghs.... pursued the poor prince,... cutting his body into pieces.' (Dutch report, February, 1661).

6 The First half of the Reign: A General Sketch

6.1 The Contrast Between the Two Halves of Aurangzib's Reign

The reign of Aurangzib is naturally divided into two equal parts of about 25 years each, the first of which he passed in northern India and the second in the Deccan. During the earlier of these two periods the centre of interest lies unmistakably in the North, not because the Emperor lived there, but because the most important developments, civil and military, concerned this region, while the South figured as a far off and negligible factor. In the second half of the reign the situation is reversed: all the resources of the empire are concentrated in the Deccan; the Emperor, his court and family, the bulk of the army, and all his best officers live there for a quarter century, and Hindustan sinks back to a place of secondary importance. The generals and soldiers in their enforced exile in the Deccan sigh for a return to their northern homes; one homesick noble offers the Emperor a lakh of Rupees for leave to spend only one year at Delhi; the Rajput soldiery complain that their breed is dying out by reason of their lifelong stay in the Deccan away from home and family. During this period, practically extending over one human generation, the administration in northern India naturally falls into decay at the withdrawal of the master's eye and the ablest officers; the people grow poorer; the upper classes decline in morals, intelligence and useful activity: finally lawlessness breaks out in most parts.

During the first half of the reign the centre of interest in northern India shifts with startling rapidity and range. The imperial banners march from Kabul in the extreme west to the Namrup hills in the extreme east of India, from Tibet beyond our northern limits to Bijapur across the southern boundary of the empire. Many operations on a smaller scale are carried out against lawless peasants and chiefs in several widely separated districts. We see the Emperor's religious intolerance fully unmasked during this period.

After his grand coronation at the commencement of the second year of his reign (which began on 13 May, 1659), Aurangzib mostly lived at Delhi, guiding the State from the capital. At the capital he received (1661–67) the grand embassies sent from all parts of the outer Muslim world to wish him well on his accession. For the benefits of these foreign guests he made that lavish display of his wealth and power which 'dazzled even eyes which were accustomed to the pomp of Versailles.' In the fifth year of his reign, Aurangzib made a trip to Kashmir, leaving Delhi on 8 December 1662 and returning to that city on 18 January 1664. In February 1666 his father's death took him to Agra. So long as Shah Jahan lived in captivity, Aurangzib had naturally avoided Agra and held his Court at Delhi.

In 1674 the seriousness of the Afridi rising forced the Emperor to go to Hasan Abal, to be near enough to Pashawar to direct the operations of his armies. Here he lived from 26 June 1674 to 23 December 1675, returning to Delhi on 27 March 1676. Early in 1679, the death of Maharajah Jaswant Singh and the opportunity it presented of annexing the Jodhpur State drew him to Ajmir. In Rajputana he spent the next two years and then, early in the twentyfifth year of his reign, he started for the Deccan where he finally exhausted his life and empire after 25 years of strenuous but unavailing toil.

Aurangzib first *sat on the throne* on 1st Ziqada, year 1068 of the Hijera era (21 July 1658); but his second or grand coronation took place on 24th Ramzan, 1069 (5 June 1659). In the second year it was ordered that in official documents *every year of the reign* should be *calculated from 1st Ramzan.*

But it was found inconvenient to feast and rejoice in a season of religious fasting and prayer, and so, from the fourth year onwards the Emperor sat on the throne immediately at the end of the month of Ramzan i.e., on the day of the Id-ul-fitr, (sometimes a day later), and the celebration ran on for 10 days from that date. In the twenty first year (1677) he abolished the celebrations, the making of presents to him by the nobles, and all kinds of display at Court on the occasion of the coronation anniversary.

6.2 Aurangzib's Illness 1662

Early in the fifth year of his reign, Aurangzib had a severe illness, which was aggravated by his obstinate devotion to work and religious austerities. The days of Ramzan (10 April–9 May, 1662) were extremely hot and long, and overwork and lack of sleep and proper nourishment during this entire month of fasting in the daytime in the frightful heat of a Delhi summer, greatly weakened him. At last on 12 May, a fever seized him; the doctors bled him so much that he became extremely weak; at times he fell into fits of insensibility and a deadly pallor spread over his face. The greatest anxiety and distraction reigned in the palace and the capital, and the evil was aggravated by the rival movements of his sons to gain adherents and secure their own succession.

Up to the fifth day, his fever and weakness continued without abatement. But such was Aurangzib's strength of mind that he showed his face in the Audience Hall for a moment that evening and the next, leaning on a mace and receiving the presentation of the royal standards. The illness continued for a month more, but there was no longer any cause for public alarm or disorder. On Friday the 23rd and 30th he went to the Jama Mosque in a litter to pray in public. His complete recovery was celebrated on 24 June. The absolute peace that was: maintained throughout the empire during 'this critical month and a half is the highest tribute to the strength of Aurangzib's; character[1] and the stability of the rule he had founded.

On his recovery, Aurangzib was advised to regain his strength and refresh his spirits by a visit to the pleasant valley of Kashmir,, then known as the 'Earthly Paradise.' Early in May 1663 he started from Lahor for Kashmir, entering the valley through the Pir Panjal Pass at Bhimbar. The Court passed two and a half months most happily at Srinagar. On the return journey Lahor was reached on 29 Septembeer 1663, and Delhi on 18 January next.

During these early years passed at Delhi, when there was no cloud on the horizon of the frontiers, Aurangzib often devoted himself to the pleasures of the chase in the neighbourhood of the capital or in the

---

[1] Bernier's *Agha* (Danishmand Khan) on hearing of Aurangzib's fortitude during this illness, exclaimed, 'What strength of mind! What invincible courage! Heaven preserve thee, Aurangzib, for greater achievements! Thou art not yet destined to die!' (p. 125).

Doab, though in old age he condemned *shikar* as the business of the idle (*bekar*).

6.3 Lawless Risings in the Provinces

Many minor conquests took place in the outskirts of the empire during the first quarter-century of Aurangzib's reign; such as Palamau (south of Bihar), Assam and Kuch Bihar (both abandoned), Idar, Chatgaon, and Tibet (in 1665, amounting only to the acknowledgment of the Emperor's suzerainty by the Buddhist ruler of that country. This Tibet was evidently Ladak or Little Tibet).

The disturbances of internal peace in Aurangzib's reign were of three classes: (*a*) The outbreaks inevitable during a succession dispute among the princes, when the collapse of civil authority tempts plunderers and ambitious chiefs to enrich themselves by lawless acts without fear of punishment, (*b*) Hindu risings against the policy of temple destruction which began to be enforced throughout the empire in the twelfth year, (*c*) Revolts of vassal princes. We have also a few sporadic cases of defiance of imperial authority by petty chieftains in out-of-the-way or jungly places.

The Hindu revolts provoked by Aurangzib's bigotry, as well as his dealings with the Sikhs, will be treated in detail in a subsequent chapter.

Some local disturbances were also caused by pretenders setting up for his dead brothers or nephews. A false Dara Shukoh appeared in Gujrat in August 1663, a false Shuja in the Morang hills (west of Kuch Bihar) in May 1669, a second in the Yusufzai country in 1674, and a third in Kamraj (Kashmir) as late as 1707; a bogus Buland Akhtar (second son of Shuja) in the Allahabad province in July 1699, and a counterfeit of the rebel prince Akbar in the Deccan in March of the same year.

Rao Karan of the Bhurtiya clan, the chieftain of Bikanir, had served in the Mughal army of the Deccan in the last .year of Shah Jahan's reign, but had come back to northern India at Dara's instigation without taking Aurangzib's leave. Afterwards he had put off paying the customary visit of respect to the new Emperor. So, in August 1660, an army 9,000 strong, was sent under Amir Khan to bring him to reason. Rao Karan was cowed into submission, waited on the Emperor (27 November) and received his pardon.

The next lawless Rajah to feel Aurangzib's heavy hand was Champat Rai Bundela. After the war of 1635 the family of Bir Singh Dev was dispossessed and the throne of Urchha given to Devi Singh, a descendant of his eldest brother. But a family sprung from a younger brother of Bir Singh's father ruled as the lords of Mahewa in Eastern Bundelkhand. Their leader was Champat Rai. When Aurangzib reached Ujjain after his victory over Jaswant, Champat Rai joined him. But when Shuja was advancing to Khajwa and the wildest rumours spread through the empire, Champat deserted, and returning home took to his old game of robbery. The Emperor sent an army under Subhkaran Bundela and other Rajput officers against the rebel (10 February 1659). A contingent under Rajah Devi Singh Bundela and the jagirdars and local troops of Malwa were ordered to assist him. Everybody's hands were now turned against Champat, who fled from place to place closely followed by the imperialists.

At last about the middle of October 1661, Champat Rai finding capture by his false friends imminent, and unable to defend himself in the extreme agony of fever and weakness, stabbed himself to death, and so also did his constant companion in life, Rani Kali Kumari. But his son Chhattra Sal lived to be long a thorn in the sides of the Mughals and finally to found a new kingdom, Panna, in Eastern Bundelkhand.

6.4 Conquest of Palamau

Beyond the southern limits of Bihar lies the district of Palamau as a sort of rugged step leading to the plateau of Chota Nagpur on the south-east and the Central Provinces on the south-west. It is a wild country, broken up by spurs and peaks, with many rainy-weather rivers unfit for navigation and yielding no assured supply of water for irrigation. The southern part of the district is extremely rocky barren and jungly; in the northern part the valleys are a little wider and more fertile; but 'nowhere in the district is it possible to get more than 10 or 11 km. (6 or 7 miles) from a well-defined hill. There are no level plains, and the general appearance of the district is that of a confused mass of rocky hills, mostly covered by a dense growth of jungle. From the summit of a ridge or hill, the country appears covered by a waving sheet of low forest, with all signs of human habitation concealed from view, except perhaps a glimpse here and there of a low red tiled roof, a distant grove of trees, or an occasional herd of cattle.' The population is scanty, living in small and scattered villages embosomed in the hollows among the hills.

The dominant clan of the district in the seventeenth and eighteenth centuries were the Cheros, a Dravidian people, said to have branched off from the Rajbhant tribe. In 1643, the Mughals taking advantage of family disputes, reduced Rajah Pratap Chero to the status of Mughal *mansabdar,* and turned his ancestral kingdom into a fief, subject to an annual tribute of one lakh of Rupees. The tribute was exorbitant in amount, and beyond the power of the Rajah to pay regularly. It naturally fell into arrears, while additional provocation was given by the cattle-raids of the Cheros across the Bihar frontier every year.

By order of the Emperor, Daud Khan, the governor of Bihar, invaded Palamau in April 1661. He easily occupied the forts of Kuthi, Kunda, and Deogan which guarded the northern frontier of that kingdom, and advanced cutting the jungle and making a road towards the capital. On 7 December he attacked the enemy's trenches 3 km. (2 miles) before Palamau, and after a severe fight for three days put the Chero army to flight. Then a path was cleared with great labour through the remaining 3 km. (2 miles) of the jungle, and the Mughals attacked the Rajah's trenches before his capital on the thirteenth. After a stubborn fight for six hours, the enemy fled into the city, which was immediately stormed by the exultant Mughals. At night the Rajah escaped from his fort, which was seized by the Mughals next day. Palamau was annexed to the *subah* of Bihar.

In 1662, a disputed succession in Nawanagar, the capital of the State of Halar in north-western Kathiawad, led to the Mughal suzerain's intervention. The faujdar of Junagarh, after a stubborn fight with the usurper in which the imperialists lost 611 men in killed and wounded (13 February 1663), slew the usurper and restored the rightful heir to the throne. But the peninsula long continued unsettled.

In 1664 two forces were sent from Darbhanga and Gorakhpur to co-operate in chastising the rebel Rajah of Morang (a hill country west of Kuch Bihar and north of the Purnea district). Early in 1676 we read of Morang being conquered anew.

A punitive expedition visited the Kumaun hills, the dominion of Rajah Bahadur Chand, in 1665. After a long contest, the Rajah secured his pardon in 1673.

6.5 The Emperor's Islamic Ordinances

Immediately after his second enthronement, Aurangzib took two measures which had become pressing necessities. During the War of Succession the economic ruin of many parts of northern India was complete, and grain was selling at famine prices. The evil was aggravated by the inland transit duties; at every ford, ferry, hill pass or provincial boundary, *rahdari* or toll of one-tenth of the value of the goods was taken on the passing merchandise as wages for guarding the roads. In the larger towns, like Agra, Delhi, Lahor, and Burhanpur, a duty (called *pandari)* was levied on all articles of food and drink brought from outside for sale. Aurangzib abolished both the *rahdari* and the *pandari* in the Crownlands and requested the jagirdars and zamindars to do the same in their estates. This was done, and there was a free flow of corn to every place affected by scarcity, and the price of grain fell appreciably. A large number of cesses (*abwabs*), many of them trivial and vexatious, were abolished by Aurangzib in 1673. [See my *Mughal Administration,* Ch. 5.] The *octroi* duty on tobacco was abolished in 1666.

Aurangzib had claimed the throne as the champion of pure Islam against the heretical practices and principles of Dara Shukoh. Soon after his second coronation (June 1659) he issued the following ordinances to restore the rules of orthodox Islam and to bring the lives of the people into closer accord with the teaching of the *Quran.*

(1) The Mughal emperors before him used to stamp the Muhammadan confession of faith *(kalima)* on their coins. Aurangzib forbade it.

(2) The aritient kings of Persia, and following them the Muslim rulers of that country as well as the Mughal sovereigns of India, used to observe the day when the Sun enters the Aries as an occasion of general rejoicing and carnival at Court because it was the New Year's Day (*nauroz*) of the Zoroastrian calendar (1st of Farwardin). Aurangzib forbade the keeping of the day and transferred the customary Nauroz rejoicings of the Court to the coronation festivity following the month of Ramzan,

(3) A Censor of Morals (*muhtasib*) was appointed to enforce the Prophet's laws and put down the practices forbidden by him, such as drinking distilled spirits or fermented beer, *bhang* and other liquid intoxicants, gambling, and the illicit commerce of the sexes. Opium and *ganja,*

however, were not interdicted. The punishment of heretical opinions, blasphemy and omission of prayer and fast by Muslims also lay within the province of this Inquisitor. A party of *mansabdars* and *ahadis* was posted under him to enforce his orders.

(4) An imperial circular, dated 13 May 1659, was sent to all the provinces, forbidding the cultivation of *bhang*.

(5) All the old mosques and monasteries, many of which had become mere ruins, were repaired, and *imams, muazzins, khatibs* and attendants were appointed in them with regular salaries.

His puritanical rigour grew with age. We may conveniently note here his measures for enforcing his own ideas of the morose seriousness of life:

(6) At the commencement of the eleventh year of his reign, he forbade the Court musicians to perform before him. 'Gradually music was totally forbidden at Court.'

The sons of the Muses took their revenge by turning the public laughter against their crowned foe. About one thousand of the musicians of Delhi assembled on a Friday when Aurangzib was going to the mosque. They came out with over twenty highly ornamented biers, as is the custom of the country, crying, aloud with great grief. From afar Aurangzib saw this multitude and heard their great weeping and lamentation, and wondering, sent to know the cause of so much sorrow. The musicians replied with sobs that the king's orders had killed Music, therefore they were bearing her to the grave. The king grimly remarked that they should see that she was thoroughly well buried

(7) The ceremony of weighing the Emperor against gold and silver on his two birthdays (according to the lunar and solar calendars) was stopped.

(8) In 1668, the two stone elephants placed by Jahangir on the two side-pillars of the Hatipul gate of Agra fort, were removed by the Emperor.

(9) In April 1670, the courtiers were ordered to give up the Hindu practice of saluting each other by raising the hand to the head and to confine themselves to the cry 'Peace be on you!' (*salam alekum*).

(10) In March 1670 he forbade the festivities which used to be held on his birthday; henceforth the royal band was to play for three hours only instead of the whole day. Early in the twentyfirst year of his reign (November 1677) the customary rejoicings on the anniversary of his coronation were abolished.

(11) It had formerly been the practice of the emperors to apply a spot of paint (*tika*) with their own fingers to the foreheads of great Rajahs when investing them. In May 1679 the ceremony was altogether abolished as savouring of Hinduism.

(12) Aurangzib gave up the ceremony of *darshan* or appearing every morning at a balcony on the wall of the palace to receive the salute of the people assembled on the ground outside—which Akbar had introduced and his successors had hitherto practised. It was akin to the Hindu practice of having a look at one's tutelary idol before beginning the day's work.

(13) The roofing over of buildings containing tombs, the lime-washing of sepulchres, and the pilgrimage of women to the graveyards of saints, were forbidden, as opposed to the Quranic law.

But his attempt to elevate mankind by one leap failed, and the administration made itself ridiculous by violently enforcing for a time, then relaxing, and finally abandoning a code of puritanical morals opposed to the feelings of the entire population, without first trying to educate them to a higher level of thought. As Manucci noticed, 'It was so common to drink spirits when Aurangzib ascended the throne, that one day he said in a passion that in all Hindustan no more than two men could be found who did not drink, namely himself and the Chief Qazi. The regulations were strict at first, but little by little they were relaxed,... there being few who do not drink secretly.... The ministers themselves drank and loved to get drunk.' So, too, in the case of the order against music.

Notorious instances of gambling were punished by the Emperor. Manucci mentions that he ordered all the public women and dancing-girls to marry or leave the realm; but the same writer's narrative shows that this rule was a dead letter. His prohibition of the *holi* celebration in the streets, when obscene songs were sung and faggot was extorted from all people for bonfires, was clearly a police regulation. So, also, was the order putting a stop to Muharram processions in future, after a deadly fight between rival processionists at Burhanpur in 1669.

In 1664 Aurangzib issued an order forbidding the burning of Hindu widows with their husbands' corpses. But Government was powerless to enforce the prohibition everywhere. The inhuman practice of castrating children with a view to selling them as harem slaves, was ordered to be suppressed (1668), throughout the empire.

6.6 Persecution of Dara's Favourite Theologians and of Heretics

The enforcement of Islamic orthodoxy gave Aurangzib an opportunity for punishing those liberal holy men of his creed whom Dara had favoured. One such was Shah Muhammad Badakhshi, a disciple of Mian Mir and a facile composer of mystic poetry. Dara had greatly honoured and cherished him; after Aurangzib's accession he was summoned to the imperial presence. But on the way he died at Lahor in 1661.

But the most notable victim of this class was Sarmad, a Sufi? of the highest celebrity in India. This man was born of Jewish parents at Kashan in Persia and made himself a *rabbi* (theological scholar) by his mastery of the Hebrew Scriptures. Then he embraced Islam under the name of Muhammad Said, and after coming to India as a trader, met at Tatta a Hindu lad named Abhay Chand, with whom he was so infatuated that he became a naked *faqir* and induced Abhay Chand to be his disciple. At Delhi, he was made much of by Dara Shukoh and even introduced to Shah Jahan.

Sarmad was a pantheist, and his smooth flowing verses breathe not only the mystic fervour of the Sufi, but also a lofty spirit of catholicity which rises above the wrangle of sects and adores the truth inherent in all creeds. His attitude to Muhammad was one of deep respect: but on several points of Muslim theology and tradition his opinions were unorthodox. 'God,' he held, 'is a *material* substance ... and his materiality is symbolized by a human figure and body.... The reward of good deeds and the punishment of sins take place in *this* world. A man's soul is born again after a period of sleep exactly as long as his last life.'

Sarmad used to go about stark naked. As an uncompromising Monist, he denied the existence of Matter and felt no shame about anything pertaining to his body.

A bench of Muslim theologians sat in judgment over Sarmad and sentenced him to death on account of heresy. The real reason was political, as he is said to have assured Dara of success in contesting the throne.

In 1672, a Shia officer (*diwan*) named Muhammad Tahir was beheaded for cursing the first three Khalifs. In 1667, a Portuguese friar who had embraced Islam and then reverted to his former faith, was killed at Aurangabad for apostacy. The spiritual guide of the Bohra sect, Sayyid Qutb-ud-din of Ahmadabad, is said to have been put to death with 700 of his followers, by order of Aurangzib.

6.7 Aurangzib's Relations with the Outer Muslim World

After he was firmly seated on the throne, Aurangzib received a succession of embassies from all the Muhammadan States which had trade relations with India', to congratulate him on his accession.

After the War of Succession, he planned to drown in a shower of gold any scruples which the headmen and theologians of the Holy City might have felt in acknowledging as lawful sovereign the usurper of a loving father's throne. In November 1659, shortly after his grand coronation, he despatched Sayyid Mir Ibrahim, with six lakhs and sixty thousand rupees for distribution among the Sayyids, recluses, servitors of the mosques and shrines, and devotees at Mecca and Medina. Thereafter agents of the Sharif used to visit the Delhi Court every year and levy contributions in the name of the Prophet. But at last the Sharif's greed made Aurangzib turn against him. In the last decade of his reign he wrote to his *wazir*, 'The Sharif of Mecca, having heard of the great wealth of India, sends an envoy every year for making his own gain. The money that I send there is meant for the poor and not for *him*.'

After Aurangzib had made himself the undisputed master of the throne, Shah Abbas II, sent a grand embassy under. Budaq Beg, the captain of his musketeers, to congratulate him (1661).

The Persians have been rightly called the Frenchmen of Asia. Their country has been the spring-head of the culture, thought and fashion of the entire Islamic world. Persian influence has moulded the poetry of all Muslim lands, and Persian manners and taste have been laboriously, if sometimes clumsily, imitated by all Muhammadan Courts from Cordova and Constantinople to Delhi and Seringapatam. Kings have dreaded the sharpness of a Persian satirist's pen more than their enemies' swords. The news that a Persian mission was coming caused a flutter in the Mughal Court. Every one from the Emperor down to the meanest guardsman felt that he and his country were on trial. His manners and conduct would be judged by the masters of social decorum in all Asia, and if he was found wanting in correctness of taste and proper dignity in the least praticular, he would be made the laughing-stock of the entire Muslim world.

The presents from the Shah were worth Rs 4,22,000. On 27 July 1661 the envoy was given leave to depart. On him and his entourage the Emperor conferred gifts worth Rs 5,35,000. A return embassy charged with a reply to Shah Abbas's letter, was sent under Tarbiyat Khan, the governor of Multan, on 2 November 1663, with presents worth more than seven lakhs of rupees, and a letter in which Aurangzib thanked the Shah for his friendly views, but declared in a lofty tone that he needed no man's help as he depended solely on God's favour; his astonishing victories were a proof of God's abounding grace on him. Then he naturally glided into a long and exultant narrative of his triumphs over his brothers. The Mughal envoy had audience of the Shah at Isfahan, but he was very rudely treated and subjected to much humiliation and suffering. The Persian king often uttered threats of invading India in his presence. It was probably at this time that he sent Aurangzib a long letter composed by Mirza Tahir Wahid, vigorously defending the Shia religion, glorifying the Persian royal house, sneering at Aurangzib, and bragging of his own success as a ruler and defender of the true faith!

At last after a year's stay in Persia, Tarbiyat Khan was given *conge* (1666) and entrusted with a taunting letter for Aurangzib. In it Shah Abbas writes, 'I learn that most of the zamindars of India are in rebellion because their ruler is weak, incompetent and without resources. The chief of them is the impious *kafir Shiva,* who had long lived in such obscurity that none knew his very name; but now, taking advantage of your lack of means and the retreat of your troops, he has made himself visible like the peak of a mountain, seized many forts, slain or captured many of your soldiers, occupied much of that country, plundered and wasted many of your ports, cities and villages, and finally wants to come to grips with you. You style yourself a World conqueror (*Alamgir*) while you have only conquered your father and have gained composure of mind by the murder of your brothers. It is beyond your power to repress lawless men. My ancestors have been the refuge of the kings of the world,—witness how we restored to their thrones Humayun and Nazar Muhammad Khan. Now that you, the successor of Humayun, are in distress, it is my royal aim to go personally to India with my multitudinous army, meet you (which has long been my desire), give you every help and extinguish the fire of disorder.' Aurangzib vented his impotent rage on the innocent envoy, accused him of having failed in his duty, denied him audience, and degraded him in rank.

This Shah died in August 1667, and the threatened Persian invasion of India ended in words, though Aurangzib kept a vigilant eye on his Persian frontier to the end of his life. Other embassies to Aurangzib came from Balkh and Bukhara (1661 and again in 1667), Kashghar (1664), Urganj (Khiva), Constantinople (1690), and Abyssina (1665 and again in 1671). The Delhi Government had also friendly intercourse with several petty chiefs of Arabia and Central Asia, as well as the Turkish governors of Basra.

In the space of less than seven years (1661–67), Aurangzib spent over 21 lakhs of rupees in receiving and sending out these embassies, besides the 11 lakhs given to Abdullah Khan, the ex-King of Kashghar, who took refuge in India in 1668, and the seven lakhs presented to the Sharif of Mecca.

6.8 Shah Jahan's Life in Captivity at Agra Fort

When Shah Jahan opened the gates of Agra fort to his victorious son, he became a prisoner for the rest of his life. To the 'King of Kings' the change was very bitter indeed, and it was only after many a struggle that he accepted it. The letters that he wrote to Dara and Shuja were intercepted by Aurangzib's men and the eunuchs who tried to smuggle them out of Agra fort were severely punished. The result of these futile attempts was; to tighten the bonds of his captivity. Shah Jahan was now completely ringed round by enemies. No one could interview him. Every remark made by the captive was promptly reported to Aurangzib by official spies. Even writing materials were withheld from the ex-Emperor.

The fall of the most magnificent of the Great Mughals was robbed of dignity by Aurangzib's insatiable cupidity, which led to many sordid wrangles between father and son for the possession of the crown jewels worn by Shah Jahan or kept in Agra fort. The captive Emperor could never forget that he was their lawful owner and that his son was an usurper without any moral right to State property. To this argument Aurangzib replied, 'The royal property and treasures exist for the good of the community, because these pay no tithe.... The king is only God's chosen custodian and the trustee of God's money for the benefit of the people.' All the crown property in Agra fort, therefore, belonged to him as the reigning sovereign.

Dara at the time of his flight had deposited 27 lakhs of rupees worth of jewels, belonging to his wives and daughters, in Agra fort. Aurangzib demanded their surrender. Shah Jahan long resisted, but at last he yielded them up. Again, Aurangzib demanded that Dara's women singers should be sent to him. Immediately after the capitulation of Agra fort (8 June 1658), Aurangzib had sealed up all the rooms of royal apparel, furniture, plates, jewels and treasure. All this property was ordered to be 'attached strictly and with every possible care.'

On the departure of Muhammad Sultan, the eunuch Mutamad became all in all and treated Shah Jahan with great harshness and neglect. 'He sometimes allowed it to be seen that he treated Shah Jahan as a miserable slave.'

During the first year of his captivity a very acrimonious correspondence passed between father and son. Throughout the controversy Aurangzib poses as the champion of Islam and good government, as the humble instrument of God in the work of reform and popular beneficence; he condemns his father's incompetence and unjust rule, and defends his own conduct with all the mingled self-righteousness and affected humility of a Pharisee. To the charge of being an unnatural son and a rebel, he replies thus:

> So long as you held the reins of govenment, I never did anything without your permission, nor did I ever step beyond my jurisdiction. During your illness Dara usurped all power, girt up his loins to promote Hinduism and destroy Islam, and acted as king, totally setting you aside. The government fell into disorder.... My march on Agra was not due to a rebellious spirit, but to a desire to put an end to Dara's usurpation, his lapse from Islam, and his exaltation of idolatry throughout the empire.... I was compelled, out of regard for the next world, to take up the perilous load of the crown, from sheer necessity and not from free choice,—for restoring peace and the rules of Islam in the realm.

His own idea of the king's position and duty is high, even stoical: 'Kingship means the protection of the realm and the guardianship (of the people), and not the enjoyment of bodily repose or the lusts of the flesh.'

He points exultantly to his own success against heavy odds, as a proof of God's favour to him and of the righteousness of his cause. Shah Jahan, therefore, as a wise man must submit to the divine dispensation and accept Aurangzib's triumph as the best thing that could have happened to him!

In utter scorn for such hypocrisy, Shah Jahan taunted Aurangzib with being a robber of other people's property, while professing to be a true Mussalman. The prince defended his conduct in a lofty strain of idealism: 'You have written that it is contrary to the Muslim faith to seize another's property. Know that the royal property and treasures exist for the good of the people.... A kingdom is not hereditary private property. The king is merely God's elected custodian and the trustee of his money for the good of the subjects.'

Next, Shah Jahan warned his cruel son to remember that *his* sons might treat him as he had treated his own father. Aurangzib's reply breathes the confident self-righteousnes of the Pharisee: 'Well, nothing happens without God's will. The fate that you have mentioned overtook (my) elders also. How can I escape from the dispensations of Providence? Every one gets from God a return according to his own intentions, and as my intentions are good, I believe that I shall not get anything but good [from my sons].'

But Shah Jahan was a truer prophet than his boastful son. The Nemesis of Aurangzib came in the person of his fourth son Muhammad Akbar. When that prince rebelled in 1618, he addressed a bitter and taunting letter to his father, which bears a striking similarity to Aurangzib's present letters to Shah Jahan. In it Aurangzib is taxed with administrative failure and advised to pass his old age in religious meditation as an atonement for the sin of having deposed his father and murdered two of his brothers. And finally, Aurangzib is asked, with what propriety he could tax Akbar with being an unnatural son when he himself had rebelled against his own father!

The correspondence between Shah Jahan and his son became intolerably bitter. At last the old monarch bowed to the inevitable and like a child that cries itself to sleep, he ceased to complain.

Blow after blow fell on his stricken heart. First Dara Shukoh, then Murad Bakhsh, then Sulaiman Shukoh, were done to death by Aurangzib. Shuja and all his children were driven to destruction among the unknown horrors of the land of the Maghs. 'But in spite of these calamities, he never lost patience or thankfulness to God; to the last day his heart was the home of endurance and steadiness.'

Religion gave him solace. His constant companion now was Sayyid Muhammad of Qanauj. This pious man officiated as his chaplain, lector and almoner. 'All the ex-Emperor's time was divided between (professing) obedience to God, prayer, performance of the obligatory religious services with all the *sunun,* reading the *Quran,* or listening to the histories of the great men of the past.'

Another no less saintly but more tender comforter he had in his daughter Jahanara, whose loving care atoned for the cruelty of all his other offsprings. This princess, a disciple of the saint Mian Mir, now practically led the life of a nun in the harem of Agra fort, nursing her aged and forlorn father with the devotion of a mother and daughter in one, while she also looked after the orphan daughters of Dara and Murad whom she had gathered under her protective wings. In such spiritual company, Shah Jahan prepared himself for the better land. Death lost its terrors in his eyes, and even appeared as a welcome release from misery.

6.9 Shah Jahan's Last Days

That deliverance, so wistfully desired but so calmly waited for, came in January 1666. On the seventh of that month, Shah Jahan was seized with a fever. Soon other complications appeared. He had now completed 74 solar years of age and had gone through much hardship before his accession to the throne. The intense cold of midwinter lowered his vitality.

Early, in the night of Monday, 22 January, his condition was declared hopeless and the end was expected any moment. At the news that death was near, Shah Jahan thanked God for all the gifts and favours received in life and proclaimed his resignation to the will of his Maker. With perfect composure, he gave directions for his funeral, offered consolation to his surviving wives, Akbarabadi Mahal and Fathpuri Mahal, his eldest daughter Jahanara, and the other ladies of the harem, who were weeping around his bed, and charged Jahanara to look after her half-sister Purhunar

Banu and other women whom his death would leave helpless. Next, he made his will, took leave of his family and servants, giving them his last presents and keepsakes, and ordered the *Quran* to be read. Finally, while the sacred verses were being solemnly intoned, amidst the wail of the women and the sobs of his attendants, Shah Jahan, retaining full consciousness to the last and gazing on the resting-place of his beloved and long-lost Mumtaz Mahal, repeated the Muslim confession of faith, and murmured the prayer,

> O God! make my condition good in this world and the next, and save me from the torments of hell-fire!

A moment later he sank peacefully into eternal rest. It was a quarter past seven in the evening.

The body lay in the octagonal tower (Musamman Burj) where life had departed, in full view of the Taj Mahal, where he wished his mortal remains to mingle with those of his queen.

The officers in the fort broke open the door at the base of the staircase of the tower, which had been walled up during Shah Jahan's captivity, and took the coffin out.

Then, conveying the coffin over the Jamuna in a boat, they reached the Taj Mahal, and buried him by the side of all that remained on earth of his consort Mumtaz Mahal.

The public grief at the death of Shah Jahan was universal and sincere. All his virtues were told over again and his few faults forgotten.

Nearly a month after the event Aurangzib came to Agra and visited Jahanara, whom he showed every courtesy and favour. During the last days of Shah Jahan, her entreaties had conquered his just resentment and he had at last signed, after many previous refusals, a pardon to Aurangzib for the wrongs he had done to his father.

Aurangzib's treatment of his father outraged not only the moral sense of his contemporaries but also the social decorum of the age.

7 *Wars on the Frontiers: Assam and Afghanistan*

7.1 Mughal Relations with Kuch Bihar and Assam before 1658

Early in the sixteenth century, a Mongoloid soldier of fortune named Vishwa Singh (ruled 1515–40) founded a dynasty which still rules over Kuch Bihar. He adopted the Hindu religion and Hindu culture and ably organized his administration and army. His eldest son and successor Nara Narayan (ruled 1540–84) was a saintly recluse; but Raghudev, the son of this king's younger brother, forced him to instal him as king over Kamrup on the eastern Kuch country, lying between the rivers Sankosh and Bar Nadi, which the Muslim historians call the province of Kuch Hajo and which now forms the Goalpara and Kamrup districts of Western Assam. Raghudev's son Parikshit attacked Lakshmi Narayan, the successor of Nara Narayan, who sought the aid of the Mughal governor of Bengal. The Muslim army conquered and annexed Kuch Hajo (1612), and thus the imperial frontier was carried up to the Bar Nadi on the north-east, and the Mughal Government came into contact with the Ahom kings who ruled over central and eastern Assam across that stream.

The Ahoms were a branch of the Shan race, whose cradle was the hilly region lying north and east of Upper Burma. In the thirteenth century a prince of their ancient kingdom of Pong established himself in the south-east corner of the Barhmaputra valley. He then advanced westwards, conquering the tribes on the way. The Ahoms were a hardy race of demon-worshippers, eating beef and fowl and drinking spirituous liquor, with the Burmese expertness in building stockades and bamboo-bridges, plying boats and making night attacks. They were feudally organized under a number of noblemen (called *Gohains*, *Baruas*, and

Phukans). The nobles cultivated their estates by slave labour. The entire adult male population was liable to military service. Their army consisted entirely of foot-soldiers, stiffened by elephants.

The king was the patriarch of the clan, and was venerated as a semi-divine being and the custodian of the tutelary god of the tribe (*Somdeo*). Ahom punishments were draconic, men being put to death with torture for the slightest fault.

But in the course of their stay in Assam, the Ahoms began to change under the influence of Indian civilization and the Hindu religion. Hindu priests and artisans had entered Assam in the train of the queens of the Kuch race. Victory in wars with the Pathan Sultans of Bengal had led to the Ahoms learning the use of fire-arms, and to the settlement of large numbers of captive Bengalis (mostly Muhammadans) in the country. Lastly, the Vaishnav religion was preached by Shankardev and other saints, and it made great progress in the land.

The weak point of the Ahom kingdom was its diversity of population. The dominant race was the Ahoms. The middle stratum of the population was composed of the Assamese proper,—plainsmen with many Bengal affinities, defective in physical strength, endurance and martial spirit. At the bottom of society lay a vast body of slaves, some being Mongoloid serfs, but most being Bengali prisoners of war. These last were unwilling dwellers in the land.

Early in the seventeenth century, the Mughals, after annexing Kuch Hajo (1612), had a long war with the Ahoms, who had harboured a prince of the deposed dynasty. At last in 1638 a peace was made, by which the Muhammadans were allowed to retain the country west of the Bar Nadi in the north Brahmaputra valley, and west of the Asurar Ali in the region south of that great river. This peace lasted for 20 years.

7.2 Ahom Conquest of Kamrup 1658

When in 1657 Shuja set out with most of the troops of Bengal to contest his father's throne, Pran Narayan, the Rajah of Kuch Bihar, took advantage of the defenceless state of the province, and sent an army under his *wazir* Bhabanath to arrest an obnoxious vassal who had fled to Mughal territory (Hajo). At the same time the Ahom viceroy of the west was making preparations for entering Mughal Kamrup. Mir Lutfullah Shirazi, the *faujdar* of Gauhati, fearing an attack from two sides and knowing help from Bengal to be impossible, fled by boat to Dacca. The Assamese occupied Gauhati, the capital of Kamrup without a blow, and plundered all the movable and immovable things in it.

This happened early in 1658. But by June 1660 the civil war was finally over, and Mir Jumla was appointed viceroy of Bengal with orders to 'punish the lawless zamindars of the province, especially those of Assam and Magh (Arracan).'

7.3 Mir Jumla Conquers Kuch Bihar and Assam

On 1 November 1661, the viceroy started from Dacca with an army of 12,000 horse, and 30,000 foot. A vast flotilla of war-vessels (at least 323 boats of all kinds) accompanied him, —the most powerful of them being *ghurabs* or floating batteries, each towed by four long row-boats (called *kosas*) and carrying 14 guns and a crew of 60 men.

Mir Jumla made his way into Kuch Bihar by an obscure and neglected highway. In six days the Mughal army reached the capital (19 December), which had been deserted by the Rajah and his people in terror. The name of the town was changed to Alamgirnagar; a mosque was built by demolishing the principal temple, and the whole kingdom was annexed to the Mughal Cmpire.

After a 16 days' stay the general left Kuch Bihar (4 January 1662), and invaded Assam. 'On account of the jungles and numerous *nalas* the daily progress did not exceed 7 or 8 km (4 or 5 miles).' His men had to go through unspeakable fatigue. The Ahom army, devastated by cholera, offered a feeble resistance, always retreating before the invaders or being routed with heavy slaughter. The Muslims advanced victoriously up the Brahmaputra, carrying all the stockades, trenches and holes full of bamboo spikes on the way. Fort after fort was occupied,—Jogigupha at the mouth of the Monas river (20 January), Gauhati, Srighat at the mouth of the Bar Nadi (5 February), Pandu, Beltala, Kajali at the mouth of the Kallang, Samdhara at the mouth of the Bharali river and Simlagarh opposite to it on the south bank of the Brahmaputra, (25 February). The Ahom fleet tried its fortune against the Mughal navy in the night of 3 March, when Mir Jumla annihilated the enemy's naval power and seized 300 boats.

The invaders reached Garhgaon on 17 March. Its Rajah Jayadhwaj had fled away, abandoning his capital and all his property. The spoils taken in Assam were enormous—82 elephants, 3 lakhs of rupees in cash, 675 pieces of artillery, 1345 camel-swivels, 1200 *Ramchangis*, 6750 matchlocks, 340 maunds of gunpowder, a thousand and odd boats, and 173 storehouses of paddy, each containing from 10 to 1,000 maunds of grain.

Mir Jumla now made his arrangements for going into cantonments and keeping hold of the conquered country during the coming rainy season. Owing to the shallowness of the river near the capital, the Mughal fleet could not sail up to that town, but had to halt some 28 km. (18 miles) north-west of it at Lakhau. The general with the main army went into quarters at Mathurapur, a village lying on a high ground, 11 km. (7 miles) south-east of Garhgaon (31 March). The Ahom capital, containing all the artillery, elephants, stores and property of the Mughal army, was held by a strong garrison under Mir Murtaza. Many outposts were set up.

The enemy's forces were thus distributed: the Bar Gohain occupied the mountains south of Garhgaon, most of the other nobles with their followers lived in the huge island of Majuli, formed by the fork of the Brahmaputra and the Dihing, while the Rajah fled to Namrup, the easternmost province of his dominion.

7.4 Constant Fighting with Ahoms

There was, however, no repose in the Mughal outposts even from the first. The Ahoms soon resumed the offensive, making night attacks on the outposts. Even Garhgaon was assaulted; but the attempts failed. Early in May, the rains came down in torrents, the rivers rose in flood, the movement of troops by land became impossible, and the imperial outposts were isolated. In fact, during the whole rainy season, from the beginning of May to near the end of October, the Mughal army in Assam lived in a state of siege. Each of its posts stood like an island surrounded by water, and no provision could come from the fleet at Lakhau because the river of Garhgaon was not deep-enough for the large armed boats, while the small trading vessels could not safely ply on it so long as the Ahom entrenchments on its banks were not won over.

For lack of proper food, cavalry horses and draught cattle perished by the thousand. No supplies of any kind, not even news, could come from the outside world.

On 10 May the Mughal outpost at Gajpur fell, the Ahoms thus cutting off communications between the Mughal army and navy. At Garhgaon, too, the enemy concentrated and kept the garrison in perpetual alarm. Mir Jumla, therefore, withdrew all his *thanas.* The Ahom king recovered all his country east of Lakhau. The Mughals held only Garhgaon and Mathurapur.

The vigour of Ahom attack was now redoubled. The minor encounters that took place almost daily are beyond count. The well-bred cavaliers of Delhi fought without heeding how they were blistered by the sun, or soaked in water and bespattered with mud,—but ever vigilant and ever ready to repel the enemy.

After almost daily attacks and alarms; an assault in force was delivered on Garhgaon in the night of 8 July. The Ahoms broke down the bamboo railing on the north side of the palace enclosure, routed the Buxari matchlock-men posted there, and seized half the enclosure, which was the citadel of Garhgaon. Finally, by the exertion of every man in the garrison the fort was completely recovered, and the night of crisis passed away. The grandest of all the assaults was delivered on 12 July by the entire Ahom army in four divisions from four sides at the same time; but all failed, and never again was the enclosure penetrated by the enemy.

In August a terrible epidemic broke out in the Mughal camp at Mathurapur; fever and flux carried off hundreds daily. Dilir Khan's corps was reduced from 1,500 troopers to about 450. The whole of Assam was infected, and two lakhs and thirty thousand of its people died of disease that year. In the Mughal camp no suitable diet or comfort was available for the sick; all had to live on coarse rice; no wheat, no pulse, no *ghee*, no sugar, and no opium or tobacco except a little at fabulous prices. A pipe of tobacco sold at Rs 3, a *tola* of opium at a gold *mohar*, a seer of *mung-dal* at Rs 10, and salt also at the same rate as the last. The Hindustani and Turki soldiers languished for want of wheaten bread; the horses perished from eating rice.

At last life at Mathurapur became unbearable, and on 17 August the army returned to Garhgaon; many of the sick were left behind for want of transport.

The exultant Ahoms renewed their attacks on Garhgaon and there was fighting every night outside the fort. The pestilence now reached its extreme, as the refugees from Mathurapur had infected the garrison of Garhgaon. Mir Jumla lived and ate like the common soldiers.

By the third week of September, the worst was over. The rain bagan to decrease, the flood went down, the roads re-appeared.

7.5 Mir Jumla Resumes the Offensive

Through all these dark months the Mughal navy, posted at Lakhau under admiral Ibn Husain, saved itself and thus saved the army. His boats plied up and down river and kept constant touch with Gauhati and through it with Dacca and Delhi. Then he landed and made reprisals against the Ahom nobles sheltering in the Majuli island. And finally, when the rains began to decrease he co-operated from the north to open the road to Garhgaon. From Lakhau large quantities of provisions were now sent by land and water under escort, and arrived at Garhgaon on 24 and 31 October respectively. Plenty now took the place of famine.

The land having dried, the Mughal cavalry was again irresistible, and Jayadhwaj and his nobles fled to the hills of Namrup a second time. Mir Jumla now resumed the offensive, and marched by way of Solaguri to Tipam, (18 December). This was destined to be the farthest point of his advance. On 20 November he had a fainting fit. 'This was the beginning of the disease of which he was to die.' But he clung tenaciously to his purpose. On 30 November Baduli Phukan came over to the Mughal side, and was highly rewarded and made the Emperor's viceroy for Eastern Assam. More Ahom notables followed his profitable example of desertion, and Jayadhwaj was left helpless and alone in the pestilential hills of Namrup.

On 10 December, Mir Jumla had a severe attack of illness; a burning fever seized him, to which pleurisy was soon added. The entire Mughal army refused to enter the pestilential and unexplored hills of Namrup and plotted to desert their general and return home.

7.6 Treaty of Peace with Assam

Through Dilir Khan's mediation a treaty was signed with the Ahom king, on the following terms:

(i) Jayadhwaj would send his daughter and the sons of the Tipam Rajah to the Mughal Court.

(ii) The Ahom king would deliver immediately a war indemnity of 20,000 *tolas* of gold, 1,20,000 *tolas* of silver, and 20 elephants to the Emperor (besides 15 and 5 elephants for Mir Jumla and Dilir Khan respectively).

(iii) During the next 12 months he would deliver 3 lakhs of *tolas* of silver and 90 elephants in three equal instalments, as the balance of the indemnity.

(iv) Thereafter he would pay an annual tribute of 20 elephants.

(v) Pending the full payment of the indemnity, the sons of the Burha Gohain, the Bar Gohain, the Garhgaonia Phukan, and the Bar Patra Phukan, were to be held by the Nawab as hostages.

(vi) Assam, west of the Bharali river on the north bank of the Brahmaputra and west of the Kallang river on the south bank, was to be annexed to the empire. Thus the Mughals were to get more than half of the province of Darrang, rich in elephants.

(vii) The captives carried off by the Ahoms from the Mughal dominions (especially Kamrup) were to be released, as also the wife and children of Baduli Phukan whom the king had thrown into prison.

On 5 January 1663, the Ahom king's daughter, hostages, and some gold, silver and elephants, as part of the indemnity, reached the Mughal camp, and five days later Mir Jumla began his return march. At last, yielding to medical advice he embarked on a boat and glided down the river towards Dacca, dying on the way on 31 March 1663.

7.7 Greatness of Mir Jumla's Character

Judged as a military exploit, Mir Jumla's invasion of Assam was a success. He forced the Rajah to make a humiliating treaty, realized a large indemnity, and secured the promise of a large cession of territory and further payments. If its political consequences were not permanent, if the ceded districts were lost and even Gauhati was wrested from the Mughal grasp only four years after his death, the fault was not his.

Though Mir Jumla's expedition ended in a heavy loss of men, his own death from disease and exhaustion, and the speedy loss of his acquisitions in Kuch Bihar and Assam, yet his character shone with supreme radiance in this enterprise. No other general of that age conducted war with so much humanity and justice, or kept his soldiers, privates and captains alike, under such discipline; no other general could have retained to the last the confidence and even affection of his subordinates amidst such appalling sufferings and dangers. The owner of 20 maunds of diamonds, viceroy of the rich province of Bengal he shared with the meanest soldier the privations of the march and brought premature death on himself by scorning delights and living laborious days. He issued strict orders forbidding plunder, rape and oppression on- the people, and saw to it that his orders were obeyed. The stern punishment which he meted out to the first few offenders had a salutary effect. We realize Mir Jumla's peculiar excellence more clearly by contrast with others. With a hero like Mir Jumla, the rhetoric of the historian Talish ceases to be extravagance; his eulogy of the general is not fulsome flattery but homage deservedly paid to a born king of men.

7.8 Mughals Lose Kamrup 1667–81

The Mughals continued to hold Mir Jumla's gains in Assam till 1667. The Ahoms paid the war-indemnity in full, but in five years. Their new king Chakradhwaj (accession in November 1663) determined on war and made preparations for it. In August 1667 he sent two armies under his nobles down the two banks of the Brahmaputra. The Mughal forts on the way fell in rapid succession, and finally Gauhati itself was captured early in November. Immense quantities of arms, horses, and other spoils fell into the hands of the victors, and large numbers of Muslims, including several officers, were taken prisoner and massacred. At one blow the Mughal frontier was pushed back to the Monas river. Gauhati became the seat of an Ahom viceroy.

The Mughals tried to reconquer the lost territory, but a long desultory and finally fruitless warfare followed. In February 1669, Ram Singh (the son and successor of Mirza Rajah Jai Singh) arrived at Rangamati from the Court to take charge of the war. But from the first his task was hopeless. He had only 8,000 troopers round his standards and his losses were seldom replenished. The Ahoms, being a nation in arms, mustered one hundred thousand when mobilized. Unlike the time of Mir Jumla's invasion, the mastery of the water now belonged to the Ahoms, and the Mughals could do little with their 40 war-vessels on the Brahmaputra.

Nor had Ram Singh his heart in the work, as he knew that he had been sent to Assam to die of fever as a punishment for his having assisted in the escape of Shivaji from Agra in 1666. Soon after his arrival on the scene, Ram Singh laid siege to Gauhati, but all his attempts to take it failed. In March 1671 he fell back on Rangamati and stayed there for some years, doing nothing. Finally in 1676 he was permitted to return to Court.

After the death of Chakradhwaj (1670), the Ahom monarchy was greatly weakened by internal troubles. From 1670 to 1681 'in the short space of eleven years there were no less than seven kings, not one of whom died a natural death;' ambitious and unscrupulous nobles usurped the supreme power, fought each other for selfish gain, made and unmade kings. In February, 1679, the Bar Phukan, in fear of his rival the Burha Gohain, betrayed Gauhati into the hands of the Mughals.

But in 1681 Gadadhar Singh ascended the Ahom throne and soon retrieved the glory of his house. He easily captured Gauhati with a vast amount of booty. Thus, Kamrup was finally lost to Bengal.

While Mir Jumla was besieged in Garhgaon (1662), Kuch Bihar had been recovered by its Rajah and the Mughal garrison expelled. In March 1664, Shaista Khan, the new governor of Bengal, reached Rajmahal, and the Kuch Rajah immediately made his submission in fear of the Mughal arms, and paid an indemnity of five and a half lakhs of rupees. This Rajah, Pran Narayan, died in 1666, and thereafter, for nearly half a century, his

State was paralysed by civil wars, royal oppression and internal - disorder. The Mughals took advantage of it to extend their sway over the southern and eastern portions of the kingdom, conquering much of the present districts of Rangpur and Western Kamrup, and forcing the Rajah in 1711 to confirm these gains by treaty.

7.9 Pirates of Chatgaon and their Ravages in Bengal

The district of Chatgaon was for many centuries a debatable land between the Muslim rulers of Bengal and the Mongoloid chiefs of Arrakan. Early in the seventeenth century the Feni river was fixed as the boundary between the two powers, but during the next half century the Magh ascendency in the rivers and creeks of East Bengal became complete in consequence of Jahangir's supine administration, the rebellion of his heir Shah Jahan, and the increase of the Arrakanese naval power by the infusion of a foreign element, viz. the Feringi or Portuguese adventurers and their half-caste offsprings, who lived in Chatgaon as the obedient instruments of the local Rajah.

'The Arrakan pirates, both Magh and Feringi, used constantly to come by the water-route and plunder Bengal. They carried off the Hindus and Muslims that they could seize. On reaching home the pirates employed some of the hardy men that had survived the voyage in tillage and other degrading pursuits. The others were sold to the Dutch, English and French merchants at the ports of the Deccan. As they continually practised raid for a long time, Bengal daily became more and more desolate and less and less able to resist them. The district of Bakla (i.e. Baqarganj and part of Dacca), which formerly abounded in houses and cultivated fields and yielded a large revenue as duty on betel-nuts, was swept so clean with their broom of plunder and abduction that none was left to tenant any house or kindle a light in that region.'

'The sailors of the Bengal flotilla were inspired with such fear of the pirates that whenever a hundred war-boats of the former sighted only four of the latter, the Bengal crew thought themselves lucky if they could save their lives by flight.'

'The Feringi pirates used to give half of their booty to the Rajah of Arrakan and keep the other half. They were popularly known as the *Harmad* (a corruption of the Portuguese word *Armada* or fleet) and owned a hundred swift galleys full of war-material.' Manucci knew them as 'men hard of heart, accustomed to kill even little children without a regret.'

A heavy loss was caused to the imperial revenue by the depopulation of the riverside areas of East Bengal. Imperial prestige was even more grievously affected. The safety of the province demanded that the nest of pirates at Chatgaon should be conquered.

Shaista Khan was ordered to undertake this unfinished work of Mir Jumla. At first sight his task seemed to be utterly hopeless. The Mughal flotilla (*nawwara*) stationed in Bengal, for the maintenance of which 14 lakhs of rupees a year was provided by means of land grants, had greatly deteriorated owing to Prince Shuja's slack administration and the peculation of the officers. What remained of it was ruined during Mir Jumla's invasion of Assam. In short, the Bengal navy had now practically ceased to exist and Shaista Khan's first task was to create one anew.

This he now did. His spirit and energy overcame every obstacle. At the dockyards of Dacca, Hughli, Jessore, Baleshwar, Karibari, etc. new ships were built, and in a little over a year's time a new navy of 300 boats was built and manned and equipped for war. At Dhapa, six miles southeast of Dacca town, a hundred war-vessels were stationed and 200 more at Sangramgarh 30 miles further south, the two posts being connected by a military road raised above the flood level. The island of Sondip is a very convenient half-way house between Sangramgarh and Chatgaon, being only six hours' sail from the latter town. Its present master was Dilawwar, a runaway captain of the Mughal navy,' but a warrior and ruler of remarkable ability.

In November 1665, the cruising admiral Abul Hasan attacked and captured Sondip; Dilawwar who had fought most heroically, though he was now an old man of eighty, was wounded and taken in chains to Dacca, and a Mughal garrison was put in the island.

Shaista Khan now won the Feringis over with tempting offers of service under the Mughals. His work was made easier by a murderous quarrel between these men and their Arrakanese masters. The whole Feringi colony of Chatgaon hurriedly fled with their families and property to Mughal territory (December 1665). Their leaders were enrolled in the imperial navy on liberal salaries.

'The coming over of the Feringis gave composure to the hearts of the people of Bengal.'

7.10 Mughal Conquest of Chatgaon

On 24 December 1665, the expeditionary force, 6,500 strong, left Dacca under the command of Buzurg Ummed Khan, a son of Shaista Khan. The imperial fleet numbered 288 vessels of all kinds; the Feringis, with about 40 vessels of their own, acted as auxiliaries. The plan of campaign was that the fleet: under Ibn Husain should creep along the coast, while the army should march parallel to it, cutting the jungle along the sea-shore stage by stage and making a way, each branch supporting the other. Farhad Khan, leading the vanguard, crossed the Feni river on 14 January 1666, and entered the Arrakanese territory.

On the 23rd, the Mughal admiral sailed out of the Kumaria creek and encountered the enemy's fleet, consisting of 10 *ghurabs* and 45 *jalias*, which had come out of the Kathalia creek to give battle. The Feringis led the Mughal van, and their onset decided the day. The Maghs in the *ghurabs* jumped overboard giving their ships up to capture, while *the jalias* fled away.

But this was only the light squadron of the enemy's fleet. Their larger ships, which carried more guns, now came out of the Hurla creek into the open sea.

The second and greater victory was won next morning (24 January), when the Muslims flying their victorious banners, advanced upon the enemy firing their guns. The Arrakanese fleet retreated into the Karnafuli river, firing on the advancing Mughals. Entering the mouth of the river at 3 p.m., they drew up their ships in line of battle between Chatgaon and an island in midstream. On the opposite bank, close to the village of Feringi-bandar, they had erected three bamboo stockades. But Ibn Husain sent most of his ships up the river and also made an attack by land, and took the stockades.

Then the Mughals, flushed with victory, dashed themselves upon the enemy's ships. A great battle was fought. The fort of Chatgaon also opened fire on the Mughals. At last the enemy were vanquished; many of their sailors jumped overboard and escaped by swimming, a few being drowned; the rest were slain or taken prisoner. One hundred and thirtyfive vessels became the prize of the victors. Next day (25 January), the fort of Chatgaon was besieged. Early in the morning of the 26th the fort capitulated to Ibn Husain; but the disorderly followers of the zamindar Munawwar Khan who entered first with a view to plundering, set fire to the houses and much of the town, including two State elephants, was burnt. The Arrakanese also fled from the fort on the other bank of the Karnafuli river, but the fugitives were attacked and plundered by their former slaves, the kidnapped Muslims of Bengal who had been settled here as peasants.

Meanwhile, ever since hearing the news of the advance of the fleet on the 23rd, the army under Farhad Khan had been making strenuous efforts to force a way through the dense jungle towards Chatgaon. At his approach the Maghs abandoned their outposts on the way. The Commander-in-Chief himself arrived at Chatgaon on the 26th and made his triumphal entry into the fort the next day. The prize taken was of little monetary value. It consisted of three elephants, 1,026 pieces of cannon made of brass and iron (mostly small pieces, carrying ½ kg or smaller shot), many matchlocks and camel-swivels (*zamburaks*), and much ammunition. But the most glorious result of the victory was the release and restoration to home of thousands of Bengal peasants who had been kidnapped by the pirates and held in serfdom; and its greatest benefit was the increase of cultivation in deltaic Bengal. Chatgaon was made the seat of a Mughal faujdar and the name of the town was changed to *Islamabad.*

7.11 The Afghans and their Relations with the Mughal Empire

In the valleys leading from India to Kashmir and Afghanistan, and in the encompassing hills, live numberless Turko-Iranian clans, called Pathans in the north and Baluches in the south. Even after conversion to Islam, they have retained their old speech, their old tribal organization, and their immemorial profession of brigandage.

Brave and hardy as these people are above all the races of the plains, they are torn by the feud of clan against clan and often of family against family. In all their history they have failed to establish any large and compact State, or even any enduring confederacy of tribes.

They have never formed a nation, but always clans. Within the clans even, the strict discipline of the Rajput tribal system is wanting; the Yusufzai or Afridi follows his chieftain only when it is in his interest or pleasure to do so. These ever-forming ever-dissolving groups of families are the only effective forces of an Afghan clan for offence or defence; the nominal chieftain merely governs on the sufferance of his followers. The family and not the clan is the true unit of Afghan society.

This was the state of affairs even in the Mughal times. Highway robbery was then the hereditary profession of these hardy savages, as cunning as they were bold. Their lands yielded too scanty a sustenance for their fast-growing numbers; and the peaceful gains of agriculture were too poor and slow a reward in comparison with the plunder of their more industrious neighbours and of the rich traders passing within easy reach of them. The right of the hillmen—Afridis, Shinwaris, Yusufzais and Khataks—to levy toll on the traffic between India and Kabul, had been practically admitted by the Mughal Government, which had found by long experience that it was cheaper to bribe the clansmen than to coerce them, as a means of preserving order in that region and keeping the roads open. But even political pensions of six lakhs a year were not always effective in securing their obedience. A leader would spring up among them, pretending sanctity or princely descent, organize a band of young men by feeding them for some time at his own cost, and then swoop down upon the fields of rival clans or the imperial territory below, for plunder. The gang held together as long as the stream of booty did not fail; but when it ran dry, or the least inequality in its division was suspected, these natural democrats turned their arms against one another, and the league broke up.[1]

A strong Mughal emperor would resolve to enforce his authority and protect his subjects; armies would be poured into the valleys of the clansmen, and after heavy losses their organized resistance would be beaten down, their houses demolished, the level country held by means of a chain of military posts, their crops cut down and the Afghan population thinned by the sword.

But every now and then they would cut off a weak garrison; the Mughal outposts would have to be withdrawn in winter and the work of pacification renewed in spring.

In a few years the growth of population would more than fill the void caused by the Mughal sword; and the hungry hordes would again begin to swarm into the neighbouring districts or plunder trade caravans.

The first disaster to the Mughal arms here took place in February 1586, when an army of 8,000 men under Rajah Birbal was cut off in a Swat defile. The Emperor had finally to patch up a peace by pensioning the tribal leaders and overlooking their depredations. Under Jahangir and Shah Jahan, the same state of things continued.

7.12 Yusufzai Rising of 1667

Early in 1667 began another movement for expansion among the Yusufzais, whose home lies in the Swat and Bajaur valleys and the plain of north Peshawar. One of their great men, named Bhagu, drew the heads of other families into his scheme, crowned a pretended scion of their ancient kings as Muhammad Shah, and secured religious prestige to

[1] 'A famous saint among the Yusufzais is said to have left his tribe a blessing and a curse, "That they should always be free, but that they should never be united".' (Elphinstone, 338.)

his banners by association with Mulla Chalak, who enjoyed a great local reputation for sanctity. Bhagu, as *wazir* and virtual king, organized an expeditionary force of 5,000 clansmen, crossed the Indus above Attock and invaded Pakhli, a plain lying east of that river in the Hazara district, through which ran the principal road to Kashmir. Here they captured the fort of Shadman, the local chieftain, and leavied rent from the peasants. The number of invaders daily increased and more Mughal outposts were attacked, Other Yusufzai bands began to plunder the imperial territory in the western Peshawar and Attock districts.

The Emperor took strong measures of defence, and ordered the rebel country to be invaded by three columns. The enemy anticipated the invasion by coming over to the south side of the ferry of Harun across the Indus and holding it in force, so as to prevent the Mughals from crossing into their country. On 1 April 1667, they were attacked here by Kamil Khan (the faujdar of Attock). After a stubborn fight, the enemy broke and were driven into the river; two thousand of them were slain, many wounded, and many more drowned, The imperial territory on this side of the Indus was cleared of the enemy.

In May, Shamshir Khan, at the head of a large detachment from Afghanistan, took over the supreme command and crossed the Indus into the Yusufzai country.

Shamshir fought many a battle with them and gained many a success. Entrenching his camp at Und, he occupied the level country of Mandaur where the Yusufzais used to grow their food crops, and destroyed all their farms and homesteads in the lowlands. On 4 June, he marched out of Und to attack Bhagu in his present position. Several villages were taken after hard fighting against heavy odds and with considerable losses; the houses were burnt down, the property looted and no vestige of cultivation left. The enemy's trenches at Mansur on the Panjshir river were carried (28 June 1667). At the end of August, Muhammad Amin Khan, one of the highest grandees of the realm, arrived with a large force and took over the supreme command from Shamshir. The villages near Shahbazgarhi and in the valley of Karahmar were plundered, while in the Swat valley the village of Hijas was destroyed (October). The Yusufzais seem to have been quieted by these hard blows; and there was no general rising of the frontier tribes till 1672.

7.13 Afridi and Khatak Risings of 1672; Disasters to Mughal Generals

In 1672, the tactless action of the *faujdar* of Jalalabad bred discontent among the Khaibar clans. The Afridis rose under their chieftain Acmal Khan, a born general, who crowned himself king, struck coins in his own name, and proclaiming war against the Mughals, summoned all the Pathan clans to join the national movement and closed the Khaibar Pass.

In the spring of 1672, Muhammad Amin Khan, now viceroy of Afghanistan, started from Peshawar for Kabul with his army, which was accompanied by families and household property. At Jamrud he learnt that the Afghans had blocked the way ahead. But intoxicated with wealth and power, and despising the Afghans' prowess, he rushed blindly on to his doom. Advancing to Ali Masjid (21 April) he entrenched. At night the Afridis descended from the hillside and cut him off from the stream whence he drew his water-supply. Next day men and beasts in the imperial army began to perish of thirst from the heat of the sun. The Afghans assailed the Mughals with a storm of missiles. From the lofty peak of Tartara, stones were rolled down on the doomed men crowded in the narrow gorge below. The leaders were soon killed, and disorder seized the Mughal army. 'Horses, elephants and men were mixed up in confusion.' The Afghans now charged down the hillside, slaying and plundering the entire Mughal camp.

Muhammad Amin Khan and some of his high officers, succeeded in escaping to Peshawar with their bare lives; but everything else was lost. 'Ten thousand men fell under the enemy's sword in the field, and above two krores of rupees in cash and kind were looted by the enemy. They captured twenty thousand men and women and sent them to Central Asia for sale.' The viceroy's family—his mother, wife and daughter—had been made captives, and he had to secure their release by paying a huge ransom. This signal victory increased the fame and resources of the Afridi leader. The tale of his rich booty went round of the hills and lured recruits to his banners.

The Khataks are a large and warlike clan occupying the southern part of the Peshawar district and much of Kohat and Banu. They were the hereditary enemies of the Yusufzais, because the boundaries of these two clans met in the middle of the Peshawar district. Their chieftain Khushhal Khan was a great poet. Years ago he had inspired defiance of the imperial government among his clansmen. But he had been treacherously arrested and kept in Hindustan for three years as a prisoner. In 1667 he had joined the Mughal force that invaded the Yusufzai country. But now joining Acmal, he became the leading spirit of the national opposition, inspiring the tribesmen with his pen no less than his sword, and winning many a victory over the Mughals.

The danger to the empire was very great: the rising was a national one, affecting the whole Pathan land 'from Qandahar to Attock,' and its leaders were also men who had served in the Mughal army in Hindustan and the Deccan, and knew the organizational efficiency and tactics of the imperialists. The two sides had the same arms, and except that the Afghans lacked heavy artillery, the superiority lay with them, as they were hardy hillmen fighting in their own rugged country, while the Indian troops have always had a horror of mountain war and an aversion to facing privation and cold.

The Emperor, immediately on hearing of the disaster, took strong measures to guard Peshawar against any Afghan incursion; Muhammad Amin Khan was degraded; Mahabat Khan, who had governed Afghanistan thrice before and achieved success in dealing with these people, was recalled from the Deccan and sent to Kabul as viceroy for the fourth time. But the new governor shrank from risking the fate of his predecessor. He avoided any energetic action against the exultant Afghans, and made a secret arrangement with them, each side promising not to molest the other. Next spring he went to Kabul by the Karapa Pass after bribing the Afghans on the way not to oppose him. But the Khaibar route remained closed as before. The Emperor was highly displeased and sent Shujaet Khan in independent command of a large force with abundant war-material and artillery, to punish the Afghans (14 November 1673). Jaswant Singh was to co-operate with him.

Shujaet Khan was a man of humble origins who had risen to high rank and the Emperor's favour by his success in quelling the Satnami rising. He was therefore regarded with jealousy and contempt by high-born officers like Mahabat Khan and Maharajah Jaswant Singh. Shujaet, on his part, proud of his master's favour and of his own past triumphs, despised the advice of Jaswant, and took his own line of action. This lack of co-operation among the Mughal leaders caused the disaster of 1674.

Shujaet Khan tried to push on to Kabul. After crossing the Gandab, he ascended the saddle (*kotal*) of the Karapa Pass (21 February). That night there was a heavy fall of rain and snow and everyone in the Indian camp was brought to death's door by the extreme cold and wet. The Afghans, from the heights on the two sides, began to harass the suffering army. The imperialists were benumbed with cold. At dawn the Afghans charged the miserable army from all sides. Shujaet Khan, forgetful of his duty as a general, sought and found a soldier's death in the front rank. His leaderless troops were hemmed round; but a band of 500 Rathors, wisely sent by Jaswant, larrived with guns, broke the enemy's cordon, and brought the remnant of the army back to camp. Three hundred of the Rajputs sacrified themselves in this heroic exploit. Of Shujaet's followers thousands had fallen earlier.

To restore imperial prestige, Aurangzib himself went to Hasan Abdal, between Rawalpindi and Peshawar (26 June 1674), and stayed there for a year and a half directing the operations. A vast army accompanied him with a large stock of artillery. Strong and well-equipped columns with plenty of material were sent into the enemy's country. Aghar Khan, a Turkish noble, who had often distinguished himself in fighting the Afghans, was hurriedly recalled from the Deccan and deputed to clear the way in the Khaibar region (July). Mahabat Khan was removed from his post as viceroy on suspicion of having connived at the destruction of Shujaet Khan.

With Aurangzib's arrival on the scene, imperial diplomacy, no less than imperial arms, began to have effect. Many clans were won over by the grant of presents, pensions, *jagirs*, and posts in the Mughal army for their headmen. As for the irreconcilables, their valleys were penetrated by detachments from Peshawar. Thus, in a short time, the Ghorai, Ghilzai, Shirrani and Yusufzai clans were defeated and ousted from their villages. Dariya Khan Afridi's followers promised to bring the head of Acmal, the Afridi pretender, if their past misdeeds were forgiven (end of August).

Meanwhile, great deeds were being done by Aghar Khan, west of Peshawar. First, he foiled a night attack of the Mohmands and their allies and retaliated by slaying 300 of them, ravaging their homes and bringing away 2,000 captives and much booty. Then he tried to open the Khaibar Pass, but after a long contest near Ali Masjid in which both sides lost heavily and Aghar Khan was severely wounded, the attempt was abandoned. The jealousy of his colleagues, especially of the Hindustani nobles, added to the difficulties of Aghar Khan and his brother Turks. Next, with a force of 5,000 friendly Rajputs and Afghans, he occupied Nangrahar and tried to keep the roads open. The Ghilzais who had seized the Jagdalak Pass were repeatedly defeated and expelled from it. Of all the Mughal generals he alone was uniformly victorious over the frontier tribes, and the Afghan mothers, it is said, used to hush their babies to sleep with his dreaded name.

In the spring of 1675, when Fidai Khan set out on his return from Kabul to Peshawar, the Afghans attacked him in the Jagdalak Pass. His van was defeated, its Arab commander was slain, and many of the elephants, artillery, baggage and women of this division were carried off by the enemy. But the viceroy's courage and steadiness saved the centre. Aghar Khan, then at the *thana* of Gandamak, on hearing of his critical situation, came to the rescue by rapid marches, and forced the Jagdalak Pass, routing the enemy from the hilltops.

Early in June, however, 'a great defeat befell the imperial army.' Mukarram Khan with a large force was operating against the Afghans near the saddle (*kotal*) of Khapush in the Bajaur country, where one day he was lured into an ambush, hopelessly outnumbered, and lost heavily.

Retributory measures were taken immediately, and all the Mughal positions in Afghanistan were strengthened.

At the end of August came the news of two reverses, though on a small scale; Hizbar Khan, the *thanadar* of Jagdalak, was slain with his son and other Mughal soldiers; Abdullah, the *thanadar* of Barangab and Surkhab, was driven out of his post, after losing many of his troops. But on the whole, the imperialists held their own by means of outposts and forts at strategic points in the Pathan country. By the end of the year 1675 the situation had sufficiently improved to enable the Emperor to leave Hasan Abdal and return to Delhi.

7.14 Amir Khan Ably Governs Afghanistan 1778–98

Mir Khan, the son of Khalilullah, had previously distinguished himself by punishing the Yusufzais of Shahbazgarhi and suppressing two rebellious Afghan chiefs in Bihar. In 1675 he was given the title of Amir Khan, and on 19 March 1677 appointed viceroy of Kabul. He arrived at his post on 8 June 1678 and continued to govern Afghanistan with signal ability till his death twenty years later. He set himself to win the hearts of the Afghans and enter into social relations with them, with such success that the chiefs of the clans 'left their shy and unsocial manners and began to visit him without any suspicion.' They became very friendly to him, and every one of them looked up to him for advice in conducting his domestic affairs. Under his astute management, they ceased to trouble the imperial Government and spent their energies in internecine quarrels. Once he broke up the confederacy under Acmal by secretly instigating that chieftain's followers to ask him to divide the conquered territory among them. Acmal declined the proposal, saying, 'How can a small territory be divided among so many men?' The disappointed hillmen threw up his service and began to return home in anger. Acmal had at last to make a division of the land; but as he naturally showed greater consideration to his own clansmen and kinsfolk, his other followers were disgusted and left his camp. Much of Amir Khan's administrative success was due to the wise counsel, tact and energy of his wife, Sahibji, a daughter of Ali Mardan Khan.

The Emperor triumphed in Afghanistan by following the policy of paying subsidies[2] and setting clan against clan or, to use his own metaphor, 'breaking two bones by knocking them together.' The imperial dominions were no longer invaded from beyond the border. The Khaibar route was kept open by paying regular pensions to the hillmen. Amir Khan's diplomacy broke up the following of Acmal. And when that self-styled king died, the Afridis made terms with the Empire.

The struggle was, however, continued for many years afterwards by the stern and unbending independent Khush-hal Khan Khatak. The Bangashes and Yusufzais—his very son Ashraf—were fighting against him in the Mughal ranks; but neither age, nor a growing sense of the hopelessness

---

[2] In *Kalimat,* 16*b*, Aurangzib described the deceased Amir Khan's administrative methods,.... how he was a just governor, possessed of practical skill and tact in dealing with all men; how he used to make savings in the budgeted expenditure of the province and keep the passes open to traffic; and how he kept many of the hillmen usefully empolyed by enlisting them in the imperial service, and profusely bribed the clans out of the imperial coffers, his own income and his illegal exactions. Also 11*d*. On 25 October 1681 Aurangzib received a despatch from Amir Khan stating, 'Six lakhs of rupees were allotted by Government to be paid to the Afghans for guarding the roads. I have spent one and a half lakhs for this purpose and saved the remainder to the State.'

of his cause, could tame his bitterness of feeling and obduracy of spirit. Alone he kept the flag of Pathan freedom flying, till his own son betrayed him into the enemy's hands. An exile from his country, a captive in his enemy's fortress, he could still boast:

> I am he who has sorely wounded Aurang's heart. Khaibar's pass have I made to the Mughals their dearest purchase.

This Afghan war made the employment of Afghans in the ensuing Rajput war impossible. Moreover, it relieved the pressure on Shivaji by draining the Deccan of the best Mughal troops for service on the north-western frontier. The Maratha chief took advantage of this diversion of his enemy's strength to sweep in a dazzling succession of triumphs through Golkonda to the Karnatak and back again through Mysore and Bijapur to Raigarh, during the fifteen months following December 1676. It was the climax of his career; but the Afridis and Khataks made its unbroken success possible.

8 *Aurangzib's Religious Policy*

8.1 The Muslim State: Its Theory and Character

By the theory of its origin the Muslim State is a theocracy. Its true king is God, and earthly rulers are merely His agents bound to enforce His law on all. The civil authorities exist solely to spread and enforce the true faith. In such a State infidelity is logically equivalent to treason, because the infidel repudiates the authority of the true king and pays homage to his rivals, the false gods and goddesses. Therefore, the toleration of any sect outside the fold of orthodox Islam is no better than compounding with sin. And the worst form of sin is polytheism, the belief that the one true God has partners in the form of other deities. Islamic theology, therefore, tells the true believer that his highest duty is to make 'exertion (*jihad*) in the path of God'[1] by waging war against infidel lands (*dar-ul-harb*) till they become a part of the realm of Islam (*dar-ul-Islam*) and their populations are converted into true believers. After conquest the entire infidel population becomes theoretically reduced to the status of slaves of the conquering army.

The conversion of the entire population to Islam and the extinction of every form of dissent, is the ideal of the Muslim State. If any infidel is suffered to exist in the community, it is as a necessary evil, and for a transitional period only. Political and social disabilities must be imposed

[1] *Jihad fi sabil ullah* (*Quran,* ix. 29). For *jihad* see Hughes, 243–248, 710; *Encyclopaedia of Islam,* i, 1041. 'And when the sacred months are passed, kill those who join other deities with God, wherever ye shall find them....But if they shall convert.... then let them go their way.' (*Quran,* ix. 5, 6.) 'Say to the infidels, if they desist from their unbelief, what is now past shall be forgiven them, But if they return to it,... fight then against them till strife be at an end, and the religion be all of it God's' (viii. 39–42).

on him, and bribes offered to him from the public funds, to hasten the day of his spiritual enlightenment and the addition of his name to the roll of true believers.[2]

8.2 Political Disabilities of Non-Muslims

A non-Muslim, therefore, cannot be a citizen of the State; he is a member of a depressed class; his status is a modified form of slavery. He lives under a contract (*zimma*) with the State: for the life and property that are grudgingly spared to him by the Commander of the Faithful he must undergo political and social disabilities, and pay a commutation-money (*jiziya*).

He must pay a tax for his land (*kharaj*), from which the early Muslims were exempt; he must pay other exactions for the maintenance of the army, in which he cannot enlist even if he offers to render personal service instead of paying the poll-tax; and he must show by humility of dress and behaviour that he belongs to a subject class. No non-Muslim (*zimmi*) can wear fine dresses, ride on horseback or carry arms; he must behave respectfully and submissively to every member of the dominant sect.[3]

As the learned Qazi Mughis-ud-din declared to Ala-ud-din Khalji, in accordance with the teaching of the books on Canon Law: 'By these acts of degradation are shown the extreme obedience of the *zimmi*, the

[2] 'With regard to the idolaters of a non-Arabic country, Shafi maintains that destruction is incurred by them also; but other learned doctors agree that it is lawful to reduce them to slavery, thus allowing them, as it were, a respite during which it may please God to direct them into the right path, but making, at the same time, their persons and substance subservient to the cause of Islam.' (Hughes, 710). *Encyclopaedia Islam,* i. 917 (*dar-ul-harb*).

[3] For *zimmis* or protected non-Muslims, Hughes 710–713; *Encyclopaedia of Islam,* i. 958, 1051; Muir's *Caliphate,* 3rd ed., 149–158. 'Each adult, male, free, sane Zimmi must pay a poll-tax, *jiziya.* His real estate either becomes a *waqf* for the whole body of Muslims, but of which he continues to have the use, or he holds it still as his own. In either event he pays on it and its crops a land-tax, *kharaj,* which on the owner being a Muslim falls. He is liable also to other exactions for the maintenance of the Muslim armies. He must distinguish himself from believers by dress, not riding on horseback or carrying weapons, and by a generally respectful attitude towards Muslims. He is also under certain legal disabilities with regard to testimony in law courts, protection under criminal law and in marriage.... Nor in the exercise of their worship may they (the *zimmis*) use an offensive publicity. *They are not citizens of the Muslim State.*' (*Encyclopaedia. Islam,* i. 958–959.)

glorification of the true faith of Islam, and the abasement of false faith. The Prophet has commanded us to slay them, plunder them, and make them captive.... No other religious authority except the great Imam [Hanifa] whose faith we follow, has sanctioned the imposition of the *jiziya* on Hindus. According to all other theologians, the rule for Hindus is "Either Islam or death".'

The *zimmi* is under certain legal disabilities with regard to testimony in the lawcourts, protection under the criminal law, and marriage. The State, as the other party to the contract (*zimma*), guarantees to him security of life and property and a modified, protection in the exercise of his religion; he cannot erect new temples, and has to avoid any offensive publicity in the exercise of his faith.

The early Arab conquerors, notably in Sindh, followed the wise and profitable policy of leaving the shrines and religious practices of the non-Muslim population practically undisturbed. There was at first no wanton or systematic iconoclasm. With the growth of the Muslim population, however, the long enjoyment of unchallenged power bred in them a spirit of intolerance and a love of persecution.[4] Every device short of massacre in cold blood was resorted to in order to convert heathen subjects. In addition to the poll-tax and public degradation on dress and demeanour imposed on them, the non-Muslims were subjected to various hopes and fears. Rewards in the form of money and public employment were offered to apostates from Hinduism. The leaders of Hindu religion and society were systematically repressed, to deprive the sect of spiritual instruction, and their religious gatherings and processions were forbidden in order to prevent the growth of solidarity and a sense of communal strength among them. No new temple was allowed to be built nor any old one to be repaired, so that the total disappearance of all places of Hindu worship was to be merely a question of time. But many of the more

[4] Elliot, i. 469. The *zimmis* 'may repair and even rebuild existing churches but not erect new ones on new sites.' (*Encyclopaedia*, i. 959). 'The construction of places of worship in the Muslim territory is unlawful for them, unless within their own houses, but if churches and synagogues originally belonging to Christians and Jews be destroyed or fall to decay, they are at liberty to rebuild and repair them.' (Hughes 711.) 'It has been settled according to Canon Law that no long-standing temple should be demolished nor any new one allowed to be built.' (Aurangzib's Benares *farman*, *J.A. SOB.*, 1911, 689).

fiery spirits of Islam tried to anticipate the destructive hand of Time and forcibly pulled down temples.

In this later age, particularly among the Turks, the old Arab toleration of false faiths appeared sinful. Outside their own realms, the destruction of temples and the slaughter of Hindus sanctified every war of aggression. Thus a frame of mind was produced in the Muslim community which habitually regarded plunder and homicide as the purest of human acts, as 'exertion (*jihad*) in the path of God.' The murder of infidels (*kafir-kushi*) is counted a merit in a Muslim. It is not necessary that he should tame his own passions or mortify his flesh; it is not necessary for him to grow a rich growth of spirituality. He has only to slay a certain class of his fellow-beings or plunder their lands and wealth, and this act in itself would raise his soul to heaven.[5]

A creed whose followers are taught to regard robbery and murder as a religious duty, is incompatible with the progress of mankind or with the peace of the world. Nor has it been conducive to the true interests of its followers.

8.3 Influence of Quranic Political Ideals on the Muslim Population and the Subject Creeds

Muslim polity formed 'the faithful' into a body with no other profession than war. As long as there were any fresh lands to conquer and any rich *kafirs* to plunder, all went well with the State.[6] The dominant body prospered and multiplied rapidly; even arts and industries, literature and painting of a certain type were fostered. But when the tide of Muslim

[5] When, in 1910, Boutros Pasha was murdered by an Egyptian Muhammadan for no personal provoction but for the political reason that he had presided over the court that sentenced the Denshawai villagers, and the guilt of the murderer was conclusively proved by evidence, the Chief Qazi of Egypt pronounced the judgement that according to Islam it is no crime for a Muslim to slay an unbeliever. This is the opinion held by the highest exponent of Islamic law in a modern civilized country.

[6] 'The Arabs lived on the fat of the conquered provinces, and subject peoples served them. Of booty taken in war four-fifths were distributed to the army on the field.... And there arose, also, new sources of revenue in the land assessment and poll-tax of conquered countries, the surplus of which, after defraying civil and military charges, became equally with spoils of war, patrimony of the Arab nation.' (Muir's *Caliphate*, 158). Elliot, i. 461.

expansion reached its farthest limit and broke in vain on the hills of Assam and Chatgaon, or the arid rocks of Maharashtra, there was nothing, to avert a rapid downfall. The State had no economic basis, and was not able to stand a time of peace. The cruel kindness of the Government had made the dominant people unfit for the avocations of peace and the silent but deady struggly for existence. War is the only trade they have a natural aptitude for, and peace means to them 'unemployment,' vice and downfall.

The settled principle of Islam ended by making the Muslims a privileged class, nourished on State bounties, naturally prone to indolence in peace time and unable to stand on their own legs in the arena of life. Public office came to be regarded as the birthright of the faithful, and so every inducement to display superior ability or exertion was taken away from them. The vast sums spent by the State in maintaining pauper houses and in scattering alms during Ramzan and other holy days and joyous ceremonies, were a direct premium on laziness. Thus a lazy and pampered class was created in the empire, who sapped its strength and was the first to suffer when its prosperity was arrested. Wealth bred indolence and love of ease; these soon led to vice; and vice finally brought about poverty and ruin.

At the same time, the treatment of the subject people prevented the full development of the resources of the State by them. When a class of men is publicly depressed and harassed by law and executive caprice alike, it merely contents itself with dragging on an animal existence. The Hindus could not be expected to produce the utmost of which they were capable; their lot was to be hewers of wood and drawers of water to their masters, to bring grist to the fiscal mill, to develop a low cunning and flattery as the only means of saving what they could out of the fruits of their own labour. Amidst such social conditions, the human hand and the human mind cannot achieve their best; the human soul cannot soar to its highest pitch. The barrenness of the Hindu intellect and the meanness of spirit of the Hindu upper classes are the greatest condemnation of Muhammadan rule in India. The Islamic political tree, judged by its fruit, was an utter failure.

As a widely travelled and profound modern philosopher writes, 'Islam is a religion of absolute surrender and submissiveness to God—but to a God of a certain character—a War-Lord.... The ritual of this belief embodies the idea of discipline.... This military basis of Islam explains all the essential virtues of the Musalman. It also explains his fundamental defects—his unprogressiveness, his incapacity to adapt himself, his lack of initiative and invention. The soldier has simply to obey orders. All the rest is the affair of Allah.' (H. Keyserling)

When public offices are distributed in consideration of race or creed and not of merit, the non-Mulsim populations are thereby driven to conclude that they have no lot or part in such a State. The Islamic theocracy when set up over a composite population has the worst vices of oligarchy and of alien rule combined.

In Mughal India it was, in addition, the domination of a small minority. And this minority differed from the politically depressed majority not in racial qualities, physical or mental, but in creed only. It was rightly felt by all persons outside the fold of the dominant creed that the power and resources of the community, entrusted to the Government for the public good, were being misused by being applied to the propaganda of a Church which aimed at their extinction. Such a State had no right to be called national; it did not rest on the love and devotion of the people.

8.4 No Toleration under Islam

Such was the ideal of the State as conceived by orthodox Islam. No doubt, common sense often triumphed over logic and statesmanship over theology; or the weakness of human nature made it impossible for every kind and every officer to enforce the intolerant system everywhere or in its entirety. Thus it happened that under Muslim rule there were periods when the Hindus enjoyed toleration and security of property, or when an enlightened and liberal king encouraged them to make progress in literature and art, wealth and public service, and his State grew in strength and material resources.

But such indulgence of infidelity was by its very nature precarious and exceptional. The Muslim world regarded it as a deplorable falling off from the orthodox ideal, and a wicked neglect of royal duty. The Muslim soldiery, on whose sword depends the king's power, would regard the liberal Sultan as an apostate, unworthy to rule over them.

Therefore, the growth and progress of non-Muslims, even their continued existence, is incompatible with the basic principles of a Muslim State. The political community is in a condition of unstable equilibrium, till either the dissenters are wiped out or the sceptre passes out of Muslim hands. Thus a chronic antagonism between the rulers and the ruled is set up, which has in the end broken up every Islamic State with a composite population. And the reign of Aurangzib was to illustrate this truth.

8.5 Aurangzib's Bigotry and Temple Destruction

Aurangzib began his attack on Hinduism in an insidious way. In the first year of his reign, in a charter granted to a priest of Benares, he avowed that his religion *forbade* him to allow *the building of new temples*, but did not enjoin the destruction of old ones. During his viceroyalty of Gujrat, 1644, he had desecrated the recently built Hindu temple of Chintaman in Ahmadabad by killing a cow in it and then turned the building into a mosque. He had at that time also demolished many other Hindu temples in the province. An order was issued early in his reign in which the local officers in every town and village of Orissa from Cuttack to Midnapore were called upon to pull down all temples, including even clay huts, built during the last 10 or 12 years, and to allow *no old temple to be repaired.*

Next, on 9 April 1669, he issued a general order 'to demolish all the schools and temples[7] of the infidels and to put down their religious teaching and practices.' His destroying hand now fell on the great shrines that commanded the veneration of the Hindus all over India—such as the second temple of Somnath, the Vishwanath temple of Benares, and the Keshav Rai temple of Mathura.

The holy city of Mathura has always been the special victim of Muslim bigotry. It stood on the king's highway between Agra and Delhi. Aurangzib appointed a 'religious man', Abdun Nabi, as *faujdar* of Mathura, to repress the Hindus.

On 14 October 1666, learning that there was a stone railing in the temple of Keshav Rai, which Dara Shukoh had presented to it, Aurangzib ordered it to be removed. And finally in January 1670, he sent forth commands to destroy this temple altogether and to change the name of the city to *Islamabad.* The destruction of Hindu places of worship was one of the chief duties of the *Muhtasibs* or Censors of Morals who

[7] For a list of the temples destroyed by him with quotations from authorities, see J. Sarkar's *History of Aurangzib*, Vol. III, Appendix V.

were appointed in all the sub-divisions and cities of the empire. In June 1680, the temples of Amber, the capital of the loyal State of Jaipur, were broken down.

In 1674 he confiscated all the lands held by Hindus as religious grants (*wazifa*) in Gujrat.

8.6 Jiziya or Poll-Tax on Non-Muslims

For permission to live in an Islamic State the unbeliever has to pay a tax called *Jiziya*, which means *substitute money*, i.e. the price of indulgence. It was first imposed by Muhammad, who bade his followers 'fight those who do not profess the true faith, till they pay *jiziya* with the hand in humility.' (*Quran*, ix. 29). The last two words of this command have been taken by the Muslim commentators to mean that the tax should be levied in a manner humiliating to the taxpayers: the taxed person must come on foot and make the payment standing, while the receiver should be seated. Women, children below fourteen, and slaves were exempted from the tax; blind men, cripples and lunatics paid only when they were wealthy; monks were untaxed if they were poor, but if they belonged to rich monasteries the heads of these religious houses had to pay. The impost was not proportioned to a man's actual income, but the assessees were roughly divided into three classes according as their property was estimated at not more than 200 *dirhams* ('the poor'), between 200 and ten thousand *dirhams* ('the middle class'), and above ten thousand ('the rich'). Money-changers, cloth-dealers, landowners, and physicians were placed in the highest class, while artisans—such as tailors, dyers, cobblers, and shoe-makers were counted as 'poor'. This last class paid only when their professional income left a margin above the cost of maintaining themselves and their families. Beggars and paupers naturally escaped the tax.

The rates of taxation were fixed at 12, 24 and 48 *dirhams* a year for the three classes respectively—or Rs 3 1/3, Rs 6 2/3 and Rs 13 1/3. On the poor, therefore, the incidence of the tax was at least 6 per cent of their gross income; on the middle class it ranged from 6 to ¼ per cent, and on the rich it was always lighter than even 2 ½ per thousand. In violation of modern canons of taxation, the *jiziya* hit the poorest portion of the population hardest, and annually took away from the poor man the full value of one year's food as the price of religious indulgence. Akbar had abolished the tax and removed an invidious badge of degradation from the majority of his subjects (1564). Aurangzib reversed this policy.

By imperial orders the *jiziya* was reimposed on the 'unbelievers' in all parts of the empire from 2 April 1679 in order, as the official historian records, to 'spread Islam and put down the practice of infidelity.' The Hindus of Delhi and its environs gathered together and piteously cried for the withdrawal of the impost. But the Emperor turned a deaf ear to them. Next Friday, the whole road from the gate of the Fort to the Jama Mosque was blocked by a crowd of Hindu supplicants. They did not disperse in spite of warning; and the Emperor, after waiting vainly for an hour to go to the public prayer, ordered elephants to be driven through the mass of men, trampling them down and clearing a way for him. A temperate and reasoned letter from Shivaji urging the impolicy of the new impost and appealing to Aurangzib to think of the common Father of mankind and the equality of all sincere beliefs in God's eyes, met with no better success. (*Vide* Appendix VI of Vol. Ill of my *History of Aurangzib* or *Shivaji*, ch. 13).

The tax yielded a very large sum. In the province of Gujrat, for instance, it was 5 lakhs of rupees a year; and we shall not be far wrong in holding that *the jiziya* meant for the Hindus an addition of fully one-third to every subject's *direct* contribution to the State. To be a Muslim was to be free from this extra taxation.

The officially avowed policy in reimposing the *jiziya* was to increase the number of Muslims by putting pressure on the Hindus.[8] As the contemporary observer Manucci noticed, 'Many Hindus who were unable to pay turned Muhammadan, to obtain relief from the insults of the collectors.... Aurangzib rejoices.'

---

[8] As the official history, written from State Papers at the instance of his favourite secretary, puts it, 'All the aims of the religious Emperor being directed to the the spread of the law of Islam and overthrow of infidel practices, he issued orders that from 1st Rabi-ul-awwal (2 April 1679), *jiziya* should be levied from the *zimmis* in accordance with the Quranic injunction 'till they pay compensation out of their hands in humility'.' *(M.A.* 174). The *Mirat-i-Ahmadi,* 313, another history based upon official papers ascribes the same motive to the Emperor. The theory of some modern writers that the *jiziya* was only commutation money paid for exemption from military service is not born out by history, for it was *as late as 10 May 1855*, that 'the *jiziya* as a tax on the free exercise of religion was replaced by a tax for exemption from military service' even in European Turkey. *(Encyclo-Islam.* i. 1052).

8.7 Repressive Measures Against the Hindus

By an ordinance issued on 10 April 1665 the *mahsul* or custom duty on all commodities brought in for sale was fixed at 2 ½ percent of the *value* in the case of Muslims and 5 per cent in that of Hindu vendors.

On 9 May 1667 the Emperor abolished the custom duty altogether in the case of Muslim traders, while that on the Hindus was retained at the old level. The real loss to the State was likely to be still greater as the Hindu traders had now a strong temptation to pass their goods off as the property of Muslims, in collusion with the latter.

A third instrument of the policy of putting economic pressure on unbelievers, was the granting of rewards to converts and the offering of posts in the public service, liberation from prison, or succession to disputed property, on condition of turning Muslim.

In 1671 an ordinance was issued that the rent collectors of the Crownlands must be Muslims, and all viceroys and *taltiqdars* were ordered to dismiss their Hindu head clerks (*peshkars*) and accountants (*diwanian*) and replace them by Muslims. It was found impossible to run the administration after dismissing the Hindu *peshkars* of the provincial governors, but in some places Muslims replaced Hindu *kroris* (direct rent-collectors). Later on, the Emperor yielded so far to necessity as to allow half the *peshkars* of the revenue minister and paymaster's departments to be Hindus and the other half Muhammadans. Under Aurangzib, 'qanungoship on condition of turning Muslim' became a proverbial expression; and several families in the Panjab still preserve his letters patent in which this condition of office is unblushingly laid down.

Some of the converts were, by the Emperor's orders, placed on elephants and carried in procession through the city to the accompaniment of a band and flags. Others got daily stipends, four annas at the lowest.

In March 1695 all Hindus, with the exception of the Rajputs, were forbidden to ride *palkis*, elephants or thoroughbred horses, or to carry arms.

On certain days of the calendar, the Hindus all over India hold fairs near their holy places. Men, women and children in vast numbers gather together; booths are set up and packs opened by the traders. Here the village women meet their distant friends and kinsfolk, and enjoy the show. Aurangzib in 1668 forbade such fairs throughout his dominions.

The Hindu festival of lamps (*diwali*) and spring carnival (*holi*) were ordered to be held only outside bazars and under some restraints.

8.8 Hindus of Mathura District Oppressed: Peasant Uprisings

Such open attacks on Hinduism by all the forces of Government naturally produced great discontent among the persecuted sect. Some frantic attempts were made on the Emperor's life but they were childish and ended in failure. Early in 1669 a most formidable popular rising took place in the Mathura district.

Abdun Nabi Khan, who was faujdar of Mathura from August 1660 to May 1669, entered heartily into his master's policy of 'rooting out idolatry.' Soon after joining his post he built a Jama Masjid in the heart of the city of Mathura (1661–62) on the ruins of a Hindu temple. Later, in 1666, he forcibly removed the carved stone railing presented by Dara Shukoh to Keshav Rai's temple. When in 1669 the Jat peasantry rose under the leadership of Gokla, the zamindar of Tilpat, Abdun Nabi marched out to attack them in the village of Bashra, but was shot dead during the encounter (about 10 May). Gokla, flushed with victory, looted the pargana of Sadabad, and the disorder spread to the adjacent Agra district.

At this Aurangzib sent strong forces under high officers to quell the rebellion. Throughout the year 1669 lawlessness reigned in the Mathura district. On 4 December Hasan Ali Khan attacked some rebel villagers. They fought till noon when, being unable to resist any longer, many of them slaughtered their women and rushed upon the swords of the Mughals, fighting with the recklessness of despair.

Next month Hasan Ali Khan defeated Gokla. The rebels, who mustered 20,000 strong, mostly Jat and other stalwart peasants, encountered the imperial forces at a place 33 km (20 miles) from Tilpat. But after a very long and bloody contest they gave way before the superior discipline and artillery of the Mughals, and fled to Tilpat, which was besieged for three days and at last stormed at the point of the sword. The havoc was terrible. On the victors' side 4,000 men fell and on the rebels' 5,000, while 7,000 persons, including Gokla and his family, were taken prisoner. The Jat leader's limbs were hacked off one by one on the platform of the police office of Agra, and his family was forcibly converted to Islam.

Hasan Ali's strong measures had the desired effect, and peace was soon restored to the district, but for a time only. In 1686 the second Jat rising began, under the leadership of Rajaram, which will be described later.

8.9 The Satnami Sect: Their Rising in 1672

The *Satnamis* who rose against Aurangzib were really *Sadhus*, who employ the name Satnami among themselves. They are a Unitarian community, founded in 1543 by Birbhan of Bijesar, near Narnol, and may be looked upon as an offshoot of the Rai Dasis. The people nicknamed them *Mundiyas* or Shavelings from their practice of shaving off all the hair, even the eye-brows, from their heads. Their stronghold in the seventeenth century was the district of Narnol, 125 km (75 miles) south-west of Delhi.

Khafi Khan gives them a good character as an honest and manly brotherhood, saying, 'Though they dress like faqirs, most of them follow agriculture or trade on a small capital. Following the path of their own faith, they wish to live with a good name and never attempt to obtain money by any dishonest or unlawful means.'

These people came into conflict with the forces of Government from a purely temporal cause. 'One day a Satnami cultivator near Narnol had a hot dispute with a foot-soldier *[piada]* who was watching a field, and the soldier broke the peasant's head with his thick stick. A party of Satnamis beat the assailant till he seemed dead. The *Shiqdar* [petty revenue collector], hearing of it, sent a body of *piadas* to arrest the men; but the Satnamis assembled in force, beat the *piadas*, wounded some of them, and snatched away their arms. Their number and tumult increased every hour.'

The quarrel soon took on a religious colour and assumed the form of a war for the liberation of the Hindus by an attack on Aurangzib himself. An old prophetess appeared among them and declared that her spells would render the Satnamis fighting under her banner invulnerable to the enemy's weapons, and that if one of them fell eighty others would spring up in his place. The movement spread like wildfire and the Government was completely taken by surprise. Soon some five thousand Satnamis were up in arms. The local officers underrated the danger and sent out troops in small parties which were successively defeated. These initial victories only raised the confidence of the rebels and confirmed the tale of their magical powers. The faujdar of Narnol was routed with heavy loss and that town seized by them. The victorious rebels plundered Narnol, demolished its mosques, and established their own administration in the district, holding it by means of outposts and collecting the revenue from the peasants. The noise of their tumult reached Delhi, where the grain supply became scanty and the citizens were greatly alarmed and distracted. Superstitious terror of their magical powers demoralized the imperial army.

Aurangzib was now fully roused. On 15 March he sent a large force, 10,000 strong, under Radandaz Khan and many other high officers with artillery and a detachment from the Emperor's body-guards against the rebels. To counteract the spells of the Satnamis, the Emperor, who had the reputation of being a living saint (*Alamgir zinda pir*), wrote out prayers and magical figures with his own hand and ordered the papers to be sewed on the banners of his army and displayed before the enemy. The encounter was terrible. After a most obstinate battle, two thousand of the Satnamis fell on the field, while many more were slain during the pursuit. 'Very few of them escaped; and that tract of country was cleared of the infidels.'

8.10 Changes in the Sikh Religion

Towards the close of the fifteenth century, there arose in the Punjab a Hindu reformer named Baba Nanak, who called upon the people to prefer the essence to the form of religion, a living faith to a dead mechanical ritual, and the spirit to the letter of their scriptures; he insisted on the unity of the Godhead underlying the multitude of the idols of popular worship, invited earnest believers to his fold without distinction of caste or creed, and tried to form a brotherhood of the elect. The aims of Nanak were abandoned by his sect when his successors in the leadership of the Sikhs set up a temporal dominion for themselves and made military drill take the place of moral self-reform and spiritual growth. 'Today there is no spirit of progress among the Sikhs. They have crystallized into a small sect. Centuries have failed to produce a new spiritual teacher from among them.' [Rabindranath Tagore]

Nanak, a Hindu of the Khatri or trader caste, was born in 1459 at Talwandi (now Nanakana), 58 km (35 miles) south-west of Labor. The essence of his creed was belief in the one true living God, and the shaping of every man's conduct in such a way as to realize that God.

As he said, repeating the words of Kabir, 'God can be obtained by humility and prayer, self-restraint, searching of the heart, and fixed gaze on Him.' Nanak (who lived till 1538) drew round himself a band of earnest worshippers, and in time they solidified into a sect.

The Sikh gurus throughout the sixteenth century, from Nanak to Arjun the fifth guru, won the reverence of the Mughal emperors by their saintly lives, and they had no quarrel either with Islam or the State.

Before the reign of Aurangzib the Sikhs were never persecuted on *religious* grounds, and their collision with the Mughal Government, which began in Jahangir's time, was due entirely to *secular* causes, and the change in the character of the gurus was solely responsible for it.

Under Arjun, the fifth guru (1581–1606), the number of Sikh converts greatly increased, and with them the guru's wealth. He organized a permanent source of income. A band of agents were stationed in every city from Kabul to Dacca where there was a Sikh, to collect the tithes and offerings of the faithful; and this spiritual tribute, so far as it escaped peculation by the agents, reached the central treasury at Amritsar. The guru was treated as a temporal king and girt round by a body of courtiers and ministers called *masands*, which is the Hindi corruption of the title *masand-i-ala* borne by nobles under the Pathan Sultans of Delhi. In a weak moment Arjun blessed the banners of Khusrau, the rival of Jahangir for the Mughal throne, and even gave monetary help to that prince. On the defeat of the pretender, Jahangir fined the guru two lakhs of rupees for his disloyalty to the king *de jure*. The guru refused to pay the fine and stoically endured imprisonment and torture, which were the usual punishments of revenue defaulters in those days. Worn out by being forced to sit in the burning sand of Lahor, he died in June 1606.

With his son Har Govind (1606–45), a new era began. 'Unlike his father, Har Govind constantly trained himself in martial exercises and systematically turned his attention to the chase.' He increased his body-guard of 52 warriors till it became a small army. As he told a follower, 'In the guru's house religion *and worldly enjoyment* shall be combined.' Soon after Shah Jahan's accession, when that Emperor was hawking near Amirtsar, the guru entered the same area in pursuit of game, and his Sikhs quarrelled with the servants of the imperial hunt about a bird. The two parties came to blows, and in the end the imperialists were beaten off with slaughter. An army was sent against the audacious rebel, but it was routed with heavy loss at Sangrana near Amritsar in 1628. The victor's fame spread far and wide. 'Many men came to enlist under the guru's banner. They said , that no one else had power to contend with the Emperor.' Such an open defiance of imperial authority could not be tolerated *so* near Lahor. Larger and larger armies were sent against the guru, and though he gained some successes at first, his house and property at Amritsar were, in the end, seized, and he was forced to take refuge at Kiratpur in the Kashmir hills beyond the reach of Mughal arms. Here he died in 1645.

On the death of guru Har Kishan in 1664, a scene of disorder and rapacity broke out among the Sikhs. 'Twenty-two [men] of Bakala claimed the right to succeed him. These self-made gurus forcibly took the offerings of the Sikhs.' After a time Tegh Bahadur, the youngest son of Har Govind, succeeded in being recognized as the guru by most of the Sikhs.

While residing in Anandpur he was roused to action by the sight of his creed being wantonly attacked and its holy places desecrated. He encouraged the resistance of the Hindus of Kashmir to forcible conversion to Islam and openly defied the Emperor. Taken to Delhi, he was cast into prison and called upon to embrace Islam, and on his refusal was tortured for five days and then beheaded on a warrant from the Emperor (December 1675).

Now at last open war broke out between the Sikhs and Islam. Soon a leader appeared among the Sikhs who organized the sect into the most efficient and implacable enemy of the Mughal Empire and the Muslim faith. Govind Rai (1676–1708), the tenth and last guru and the only son of Tegh Bahadur, was a man of whom it had been prophesied before his birth that 'he would convert jackals into tigers and sparrows into hawks.'

We may here pause to consider what causes made the success of Guru Govind possible. The first was the gradual elevation of the guru to a superhuman position. The Sikhs were taught to obey their guru with blind unquestioning devotion. This implicit faith in a common superior knit the Sikhs together like the soldiers of a regiment. The Sikhs were famous in the seventeenth century for their sense of brotherhood and love for each other. They felt themselves to be a chosen people, the Lord's elect. In the language of Bhai Gurudas: 'Where there are two Sikhs, there is a company of saints; where there are five Sikhs, there is God!' The unity due to sameness of religion was further cemented by the abolition of caste distinctions under orders of Govind. All restrictions about food and drink, so prevalent in Hindu society, had already been discarded. If Cromwell's Ironsides could have been inspired with the Jesuits unquestioning acceptance of their Superior's decisions on moral and spiritual questions, the result would have equalled Guru Govind's Sikhs as a fighting machine.

8.11. Guru Govind: His Ideal and Career

Govind steadily drilled his followers, gave them a distinctive dress and a new oath of baptism, and began a policy of open hostility to Islam. He harangued the Hindus to rise against Muslim persecution, and imposed a fine of Rs 125 on his followers for saluting any Muhammadan saint's tomb. His aims were frankly material. 'Mother dear, I have been considering how I may *confer empire* on the Khalsa.' He lived in princely state.

In the hills of north Punjab, Govind passed most of his life, constantly fighting with the hill-Rajahs from Jammu to Srinagar in Garhwal, who were disgusted with his followers' violence and scared by his own ambition. Large imperial forces were sent from Sarhind to co-operate with the quotas of the hill-Rajahs and suppress the guru; but they were usually worsted. His army went on increasing, as recruits from the Panjab *doabs* flocked to him and received baptism. Even Muslims were enlisted. Anandpur was five times invested. After the last attack, the guru evacuated the fort, and closely pursued by the Mughals, passed through many adventures and hairbreadth escapes, changing his place of shelter repeatedly like a hunted animal. His four sons perished. Then Govind with his few but faithful guards undertook a journey to southern India. In 1707 the new Emperor Bahadur Shah I induced him to accompany him on the march to Rajputana and the Deccan. The guru reached Nander on the Godavari, 250 km (150 miles) north-west of Haidarabad in August 1707 at the head of some infantry and 2 to 3 hundred cavalry, and there after a stay of more than a year he was stabbed to death by an Afghan (1708). With him the line of gurus ended.

Thus we see that the Mughal Government under Aurangzib did succeed in breaking up the guru's power. It robbed the Sikhs of a common leader and a rallying centre. Thereafter the Sikhs continued to disturb the public peace, but only in isolated bands. They were no longer an army fighting under one chief, with a definite political aim, but merely moving bodies of brigands—extremely brave, enthusiastic, and hardy, but essentially plunderers uninspired by any ambition to build up an organized government in the land. If Ranjit Singh had not risen, there would have been no large and united State under Sikh dominion, but a number of petty principalities in the Punjab with a ruling aristocracy of Sikh soldiers, sending their organized marauders every year to raid and lay the country waste.

The worst consequence of Aurangzib's bigotry, however, was the war that he provoked with the two greatest Rajput clans.

9 *War in Rajputana: Rebellion of Akbar*

9.1 Aurangzib Seizes Marwar 1679

Marwar is a desert land, but in Mughal times its strategic importance lay in the fact that the shortest and easiest trade-route from the Mughal capital to the rich manufacturing city of Ahmadabad and the busy port of Cambay lay through its limits. From Agra the western road through the loyal State of Jaipur up to the imperial city of Ajmir was safe and well-frequented. Thereafter it crossed a gap in the Aravali barrier and ran level through the Marwar cities of Pali and Jhalor to Ahmadabad. If such a province could be annexed to the imperial dominions, the proud lord of Udaipur would be taken in flank, and a long wedge of Muslim territory would be driven right across Rajputana, cleaving it into two isolated halves which could be crushed in detail. Marwar was the foremost Hindu State of northern India at this time. Its chieftain was Jaswant Singh, who enjoyed the unrivalled tank of a Maharajah and whom the death of Jai Singh eleven years ago had left as the leading Hindu peer of the Mughal Court. The success of Aurangzib's plan of the forcible conversion of the Hindus required that Jaswant's State should sink into a quiescent dependency or a regular province of the empire. Hindu resistance to the policy of religious persecution must be deprived of a possible efficient head.

On 10 December 1678, Maharajah Jaswant Singh died at Jamrud[1] when commanding the Mughal posts in the Khaibar Pass. Immediately on hearing of Jaswant's death Aurangzib took steps to seize his kingdom and place it under direct Mughal rule. On 9 January 1679 the Emperor

---

[1] He was never viceroy of Afghanistan or even governor of Kabul city, but merely *thanadar* of Jamrud.

himself set out for Ajmir, in order to be close enough to Jodhpur to overawe opposition.

The death of Jaswant had thrown the Rathors into confusion and dismay. Their State was without a head, Jaswant's highest officers and best troops were absent in Afghanistan. At first no resistance could be offered to the vast and well-directed Mughal armies that poured into the land.

Aurangzib had learnt (on 26 February) that two of Jaswant's widows had given birth to two posthumous sons at Labor. But the Emperor was not to be moved from his policy of annexing Marwar by any regard for the law of legitimate succession. He returned from Ajmir to Delhi (2 April). On that day the invidious poll-tax on the Hindus was imposed again after a century of abeyance.

Indra Singh Rathor, the chieftain of Nagor and grand nephew of Jaswant, was invested as Rajah of Jodhpur in return for a succession fee of 36 lakhs of rupees (26 May), and sent to Marwar. But the Mughal administrators and generals in occupation of the country were retained there, evidently to help the new Rajah in taking possession of his State.

9.2 How Durgadas Saved Ajit Singh

On reaching Labor two of the widowed Ranis of Jaswant gave birth to two sons (February 1679), one of whom died in a few weeks, while the other, Ajit Singh, lived to mount the throne of Jodhpur after a most eventful and romantic career. At the end of June the Maharajah's family reached Delhi, and the rights of Ajit were again urged before Aurangzib; but he only ordered that the child should be brought up in his harem, with a promise to give him a rank in the Mughal peerage and investiture as Rajah when he would come of age. One contemporary historian says that the throne of Jodhpur was offered to Ajit on condition of his turning Muslim.

The loyal Rathors were seized with consternation at Aurangzib's proposal. They vowed to die to a man to save their chieftain's heir. Their leader and guiding genius was Durgadas, the flower of Rathor chivalry, and son of Jaswant's Minister Askaran, the baron of Drunera. But for Durgadas's twenty-five years of unflagging exertion and wise contrivance, Ajit Singh could not have secured his father's throne. Fighting against terrible odds and a host of enemies on every side, with distrust and wavering among his own countrymen, he kept the cause of his chieftain triumphant. Mughal gold could not seduce, Mughal arms could not daunt that constant heart. Almost alone among the Rathors he displayed the rare combination of the dash and reckless valour of a Rajput soldier with the tact, diplomacy and organizing power of a Mughal minister of State.

On 15 July the Emperor sent a strong force under the provost of Delhi city and the captain of the imperial guards to seize the Ranis and Ajit and lodge them in the prison fortress of Nurgarh. The Rathor plan was to ensure the escape of Ajit by offering desperate resistance and sacrificing their own lives freely in a series of rear-guard actions. Raghunath, a Bhatti noble of Jodhpur, with a hundred devoted troopers made a sortie from one side of the mansion. Before their wild charge the imperialists quailed, and seizing this momentary confusion Durgadas slipped out with Ajit and the Ranis dressed in male attire, and rode away direct for Marwar. For an hour and a half Raghunath dyed the streets of Delhi with blood, but at last he fell. The Mughals now set off in pursuit, but Durgadas had covered nine miles by the time he was overtaken. It was now Ranchhordas Jodha's turn to face round with a small band and gain precious time by barring the enemy's path. This happened thrice; in the evening the Mughals, worn out by the three murderous conflicts, abandoned the pursuit, and Ajit was safely conducted to Marwar (13 July). His name became the rallying cry of the Rathor legitimists. Aurangzib's policy in Marwar seemed to have been wrecked. But his statecraft struck a shrewd blow to counter the action of Durgadas: he brought up a milkman's infant in his harem as the true Ajit Singh and proclaimed Durgadas's protege to be a bogus prince. At the same time he dethroned Indra Singh, the two months' Rajah of Marwar, for his manifest incapacity to rule.

A strong Mughal force was sent into Marwar for the reconquest of the State. Anarchy and slaughter were let loose on the doomed province.

The Emperor took up his headquarters at Ajmir on 25 September 1679; his army advanced fighting under his son Muhammad Akbar. The Mughal van was led by Tahawwur Khan, the *faujdar* of Ajmir. The Mairtia clan of Rathors, under one Raj Singh, barred his path in front of the temple of the Boar near the sacred lake of Pushkar, and a three days' continuous battle ended only with the extinction of the brave defenders. Thereafter the Rajputs always carried on a guerrilla warfare from their lurking places in the hills and desert. The Emperor now divided Marwar into districts over each of which a Mughal officer was placed as *faujdar* (end of October). No resistance could stand against such heavy odds, and the whole country was soon occupied by the foe. 'Jodhpur and all the great towns in the plain fell and were pillaged; the temples were thrown down and mosques erected on their sites.'

9.3 Mughal War with Maharana of Udaipur

The annexation of Marwar was but the preliminary to an easy conquest of Mewar. On the revival of the *jiziya* tax, a demand for its enforcement throughout his State had been sent to the Maharana. If the Sisodias did not stand by the Rathors now, the two clans would be crushed piecemeal, and the whole of Rajasthan would lie helpless under the tyrant's feet. So thought Maharana Raj Singh, and so thought his clansmen. The mother of Ajit Singh was a Mewar princess, and Raj Singh could not, either as a kinsman or as a knight, reject her appeal to defend the orphan's rights.

Raj Singh began his preparations for war. Aurangzib with his usual promptitude struck the first blow. Seven thousand picked soldiers under Hasan Ali Khan marched in advance from Pur, ravaging the Rana's territory and clearing the way for the main Mughal army. The Rajputs had nothing that could make a stand against the excellent Mughal artillery served by European gunners. Hence the Rana had prepared for the invasion by abandoning the low country and retiring with all his subjects to the hills, whither the Mughals durst not penetrate. Even the capital Udaipur was found evacuated. The Mughals took possession of it and destroyed its great temple, and also three temples on the Udai-sagar lake.

Hasan Ali Khan entered the hills north-west of Udaipur in search of the Rajput army; on being reinforced and freshly provisioned, he inflicted a defeat on the Maharana (22 January), capturing his camp and property and much gram on the way, and destroying 173 temples in the environs of Udaipar. Chitor had been already occupied by the Mughals, and 63 temples of the place were destroyed when Aurangzib visited it at the end of February. The Emperor left Udaipur and returned to Ajmir (on 22 March), while a strong force under Prince Akbar held the Chitor district as a base. But the imperial outposts were too far scattered to be defended easily, while the whole of the Rajput land was seething with hostility. The Mughal positions in Mewar and Marwar were isolated from each other by the wedge of the Aravali range, whose crest the Rana held in force, and from which he could make sudden descents and deal crushing blows on the east or on the west as he pleased, while the Mughals in transferring troops from Chitor to southern Marwar had to make a long and toilsome detour through the Bednor, Beawar, and Sojat districts.

The rough circle formed by the massed hills of Mewar and stretching from Udaipur westwards to Kamalmir and from the Rajsamudra lake southwards to Salumbra, resembled a vast impregnable fort with three gates, opening east, north and west, viz. Deobari, Rajsamudra, and Deosuri, through which the garrison could sally out in full force and crush any isolated mughal outpost. The Mughals, on the other hand, could effect a concentration only by moving along a long arc of which the Rana held the short base.

Prince Akbar had been left at Chitor in charge of all the Mughal posts east of the Aravali and south of Ajmir. But his force was too small for the effective defence of this vast region. The Rajputs, fighting in their homeland, knew every nook of the ground and were helped by a friendly peasantry. The Mughals were strangers in that wild broken country and marched among a hostile population.

A marked increase of Rajput activity began with the Emperor's retirement to Ajmir (in March). They made raids, cut off supply trains and stragglers, and made the Mughal outposts extremely unsafe, thus creating a terror of their prowess. The command of Mughal outposts went abegging, captain after captain declining the dangerous honour; the Mughal troops refused to enter any pass; detachments sat down only a short distance from their base and refused to advance further.

About the middle of next May Akbar's camp near Chitor was surprised at night and some slaughter done by the Rajputs who had entered it by a ruse. The Maharana descended from the hills and roamed the Bednor district, threatening Akbar's communications with Ajmir. At the end of this month (May), a terrible reverse befell the Mughal arms: Akbar was surprised by the Rana and evidently suffered a heavy loss. A few days later, the Rajputs carried off a convoy of *Banjaras* with 10,000 pack-oxen bringing grain to the prince's army from Malwa. One of the Rana's armies under his son Bhim Singh ranged the country, striking swift and sudden blows at weak points. 'Our army is motionless through fear,' so Akbar complained.

At these signal instances of Akbar's failure, the Emperor in high wrath sent him off to Marwar and placed the command of Chitor in the hands of another son, Prince Azam (26 June).

The imperial plan henceforth was to penetrate the Mewar hills in three columns,—from the Chitor or eastern side Prince Azam would advance by way of the Deobari pass and Udaipur, from the north Prince Muazzam by way of the lake Rajsamudra, and from the west Akbar through the Deosuri pass. The first two failed to achieve their tasks.

9.4 Prince Akbar's Campaign in Marwar

Prince Akbar, on transfer from Chitor, took post at Sojat in Marwar on 18 July 1680. But in Marwar he met with no better success than in Mewar. The Rathor bands spread over the country, closing the trade routes and keeping the land in perpetual turmoil. Akbar's instructions were to make the central position at Sojat secure, then occupy Nadol, the chief town of the Godwar district, and from this new base to send his vanguard under Tahawwur Khan to advance eastwards into Mewar by the city of Narlai, force the Deosuri pass and invade the Kamalmir region, where the Maharana and the defeated Rathors had taken refuge. But so great was the terror inspired by the 'death-loving' Rajputs that Tahawwur's troops sat down in fear and inactivity.

Akbar left Sojat on 21 Setember, and reached Nadol at the end of the month. But Tahawwur Khan refused to enter the hills, and Akbar had to use compulsion towards his timid lieutenant. On 27 September the Khan advanced towards the mouth of the pass to reconnoitre. When he had yielded to Rajput seduction and decided to play the traitor, we do not know, but from September 1680 we notice a suspicious slackening of his activity.

At last the Emperor's patience was worn out. He sent to Akbar the imperial Bakhshi with orders to enforce a forward movement of the division. Further delay could not be excused. So, Akbar advanced his base from Nadol to Deosuri (19 November), and from the latter village sent Tahawwur Khan on to force the Jhilwara pass; the Mughals advanced to Jhilwara, fighting and carrying the barricades across the path, and the Khan, from his station at Jhilwara, began to ravage the neighbouring country freely.

The advance to Jhilwara was made on 22 November. The next step would have been to push on 13 km (8 miles) south to Kamalmir, the last refuge of the Rana. But during the next five weeks we have again the same suspicious inactivity on Tahawwur Khan's part. In truth, the prince's treasonable plot was fully hatched during this period. On 1 January 1681 he united with the Rajput rebels, issued a manifesto deposing his father, and crowned himself Emperor; and the next day he set out for Ajmir to wrest the Mughal crown from Aurangzib's brows.

9.5 Prince Akbar Proclaims Himself Emperor, 1681

Sultan Muhammad Akbar, the fourth son of Aurangzib, was only 23 years of age at this time. In his campaign in Mewar he had given signal proofs of slackness and incapacity, for which the Emperor had sharply censured him. In Marwar, where he was sent next, he failed either to crush the roving Rathor bands or to penetrate into Mewar by the Deosuri pass as planned by his father. Smarting under disgrace for these repeated failures, he lent a ready ear to the tempting invitation of the Rajputs to seize his father's throne with their help.

Tahawwur Khan, his chief officer, was the intermediary of these treasonable negotiations. The Maharana Raj Singh and Durgadas, the Rathor leader, told Akbar how his father's bigoted attempt to root out the Rajputs was threatening the stability of the Mughal Empire, and urged him to seize the throne and restore the wise policy of his forefathers if he wished to save his heritage from destruction. They promised to back him with the armed strength of the two greatest Rajput clans, the Sisodias and the Rathors.

Everything had been arranged for a march against Aurangzib at Ajmir, when the Maharana died (22 October 1680), and during the month of mourning that followed, his successor Jai Singh naturally remained inactive. Thereafter, Tahawwur Khan having reached the Jhilwara pass, not far from the Rajput headquarters at Kamalmir, the negotiations were easily resumed and quickly concluded. The Rana agreed to send half his army, both foot and horse, under his son or brother to fight the prince's battles. The second of January 1681 was fixed as the day when Akbar would begin his march on Ajmir to contest the imperial throne.

Two days before this date he wrote a false letter to his father to disarm his suspicion: 'The brother and son of the new Rana, under the guidance of Tahawwur Khan, have descended from the hills and come to me. The Rathor leaders also have come here to make terms through the mediation of the Khan. They urge that unless I myself conduct them to your Majesty and personally beg pardon on their behalf, they cannot compose their minds for coming over to our side. I am therefore, starting [with them] for your Presence.'

Then Akbar threw off the mask. Four theologians in his pay issued a decree under their seals, declaring that Aurangzib had forfeited the throne by his violation of the Islamic Canon Law. Akbar crowned himself Emperor (1 January), and created Tahawwur Khan his Premier Noble. Most of the imperial officers with him were powerless to resist or to escape, and feigned adhesion to his cause.

The Emperor's situation at Ajmir was critical. The two main divisions of his army which were untainted by treason, were quartered far away. His immediate retinue consisted merely of unserviceable soldiers, with his personal attendants, clerks and eunuchs, while rumour swelled the rebel army to 70,000 men, including the best blades of Rajputana.

Everyone expected a rapid advance of Akbar's troops, the rout of the small imperial body-guard, and a change of sovereigns. But Akbar began to spend his days and nights in indolence and pleasure. He took a fortnight (2–15 January) in covering the 200 km (120 miles) which separated him from his father, when every hour's delay told in Aurangzib's favour.

For, meantime, couriers had galloped off on all sides to recall the scattered Mughal detachments to the Presence. Loyal captains were straining every nerve and marching day and night to join the Emperor in time, Shihab-ud-din Khan, the father of the first Nizam, reached Ajmir (9 January) with his troops after a forced march from Sirohi, in which he covered 200 km (120 miles) in two days. Some other officers were equally quick. Thus the acute stage of the crisis was soon over. The palace at Ajmir was put in a posture of defence; entrenchments were dug around the camp; the passes leading to the city were held in force; on 14 January, the Emperor issued forth into the open, and encamped 9 km (6 miles) south of Ajmir on the historic field of Deorai. But despair and defection raged in the camp of Akbar. As he came nearer, increasing numbers of Mughal officers began to desert him and escape to the imperial camp. The thirty thousand Rajputs, however, remained true to him.

The crisis came on 15 January. The Emperor advanced 6 km (4 miles) further south and waited at Do-rahah.

In the evening, Prince Muazzam, after a forced march through rain and wind and the bitter cold of midwinter, joined the Emperor, doubling his strength. On the other side, Akbar arrived 4 km (3 miles) from his father's camp, halted there for the.night, and fixed the next morning for the decisive battle.

9.6 Murder of Tahawwur Khan, Failure of Akbar

But during the night Aurangzib's cunning diplomacy secured the completest victory without resort to arms. Tahawwur Khan, the right-hand man of Akbar, had married a daughter of Inayet Khan, a high officer then in the imperial camp. Aurangzib made Inayet write to Tahawwur Khan urging him to come to the Emperor, with a promise of pardon for the past, and a threat that if he declined 'his women would be publicly outraged and his sons sold into slavery at the price of dogs.'

The letter bewildered Tahawwur Khan. After putting on a coat of scale armour under his robe, as a precaution against treachery, he secretly left his tent without informing Akbar or Durgadas, arrived at the imperial camp a little before midnight, and demanded audience, but refused to put up with the indignity of being ushered into the Presence unarmed like a captive. The dispute became loud. At last the crowd of royal attendants, attracted to the spot by the noise, rained down blows on him with their maces. The hidden cuirass saved him for a time, but at last some one cut his throat and 'silenced his uproar.'

Meanwhile, Aurangzib had written a false letter to Akbar. In it the prince was praised for the success he had hitherto gained in carrying out his father's stratagem of luring all the Rajput fighters into a snare and bringing them within easy reach of the Emperor; and he was now instructed to crown his achievement by placing them in his van in next morning's battle, so that they might be crushed when attacked by Aurangzib from the front and Akbar from the rear. As contrived by Aurangzib, the letter fell into Durgadas's hands, who read it and went to Akbar's tent for an explanation. The prince was asleep and his eunuchs had strict orders not to wake him. Durgadas next sent men to call Tahawwur Khan. Then the Rajputs discovered that the soul of the whole enterprise had stolen away to the imperial camp some hours ago; the intercepted letter was believed to have been verified by these facts. No time was to be lost if the Rajputs were to escape from the treacherous plot they had discovered by good luck. Three hours before dawn they took horse, robbed what they could of Akbar's property, and galloped off to Marwar. Profiting by this chance, the imperial troopers whom Akbar had forced to march under his banners and the loyal captains whom he had placed under arrest, escaped towards the camp of Aurangzib. Tahawwur Khan had been the connecting link between the Rajputs and Akbar; he had been the new Emperor's commander-in-chief and prime minister in one, and his flight dissolved the confederacy.

In the morning Akbar woke to find himself deserted by all. His vast army had melted away in a single night, as if by magic, and only his faithful old retainers, a band of 350 horse, were left with him. Mounting his ladies on horses and loading what treasure he could on camels, he rode away for dear life in the track of the Rajputs.

The remnant of Akbar's property which had escaped plunder was seized, and his deserted family,—consisting of one wife, two sons, and three daughters,—was brought away to the Emperor's camp. Relentless punishment was meted out to his followers. The Princess Zeb-un-nisa, whose secret correspondence with Akbar was discovered, was deprived of her allowance of four lakhs of rupees and her landed property, and confined in the Salimgarh fortress.

A well-appointed army under Prince Muazzam was next sent into Marwar to hunt Akbar down. During the second night after Akbar's flight, Durgadas having discovered the fraud played by Aurangzib, turned back and took Akbar under his protection. Rajput honour demanded that the refugee should be defended at all costs. Akbar with his protectors roamed through Marwar, never passing twenty-four hours at the same place; but the Mughal officers in Gujrat were on the alert and headed the rebel off. Then Durgadas most chivalrously undertook to conduct Akbar to the Maratha Court, the only Power in India that had successfully defied Mughal arms. Every known ferry and pass was guarded by imperial pickets; but the Rathor leader with the greatest skill evaded-them and misled his pursuers as to his real objective, crossed the Narmada (9 May) near the ferry of Akbarpur, and appeared within a short distance of Burhanpur on the Tapti (15 May). But here, too, his path was barred by imperial officers, and he marched due west through Khandesh and Baglana, finally reaching Shambhuji's protection in Konkan (1 June).

9.7 Partial Peace in Rajasthan

Akbar's rebellion disconcerted the Mughal plan of war at a time when their net was being drawn closer round Mewar, and it gave automatic relief to this State. It was probably at this time that the Sisodias seized the opportunity of making reprisals, under the gallant prince Bhim Singh and the Maharana's finance minister Dayaldas, ravaging Gujrat and Malwa.

The Rajput war was a drawn game as far as the actual fighting was concerned, but its material consequences were disastrous to the Maharana's subjects; their corn-fields in the plains were ravaged by the enemy; they could stave off defeat but not starvation. So both sides desired peace. Maharana Jai Singh personally visited Prince Muhammad Azam (14 June 1681), and made peace with the Empire on the following terms:

1. The Rana ceded to the empire the *parganas* of Mandal, Pur and Bednor in lieu of the *jiziya* demanded from his kingdom.
2. The Mughals withdrew from Mewar, which was restored to Jai Singh with the title of Rana and the rank of a Commander of Five Thousand.

Thus Mewar at last recovered peace and freedom. Not so Marwar. That unhappy theatre of war was turned into a wilderness during the truceless conflict which constitutes Jodhpur history for the next thirty years. 'The sword and pestilence united to clear the land.' Akbar's junction with Shambhuji raised a more formidable danger to the Empire and Aurangzib had to concentrate all his forces in the Deccan and even to be present there in person. The Mughal hold on Marwar was consequently relaxed. This was the salvation of the Rathors. Throughout the succeeding generation we find the Mughal hold on Marwar pulsating with the military situation in the Deccan.

The Rathor system of warfare, under Durgadas's able guidance, anticipated the Maratha method and its success by harassing and exhausting the imperialists and even by driving the helpless Mughal commanders to buy a secret forbearance by paying *chauth* to the Rathors. Thus the war went on with varying fortunes, but without cessation for 30 years, till August 1709, when Ajit Singh entered Jodhpur in triumph for the last time and his lordship of Marwar was formally and finally acknowledged by the Emperor of Delhi.

In the height of political unwisdom, Aurangzib only provoked rebellion in Rajputana, while the Afghans on the frontier were still far from being pacified. With the two leading Rajputs clans openly hostile to him, his army lost its finest and most loyal recruits. Nor was the trouble confined to Marwar and Mewar. It spread by sympathy among the Hada and Gaur clans. The elements of lawlessness thus set moving overflowed fitfully into Malwa and endangered the vitally important Mughal road through Malwa to the Deccan.

10 *Rise of Maratha Power*

10.1 Keynote of Deccan History in Seventeenth century

In the middle of the fourteenth century the foundation of the Bahmani kingdom created an independent centre of Muslim power in southern India, and Indian Islam started on a new career of expansion in the south and repeated the work of the Delhi Sultanate in North India by crushing out the great Hindu kingdoms of the Deccan which had hitherto retained their independence. This process went on throughout the fifteenth century. Even when, at the end of the first quarter of the next century, the great house of Bahmani fell, its heritage passed into the worthy hands of Nizam Shah and Adil Shah. Ahmadnagar and Bijapur now became centres which fully kept up the traditions of Islamic dominion and Islamic culture founded by the Sultans of Kulbarga. The first quarter of the seventeenth century saw the final extinction of the Nizam Shahs. Bijapur now rushed in to fill the leadership vacated by Ahmadnagar.

But with the commencement of the seventeenth century a new combatant had entered the southern arena. The Mughal Emperor was now free to conquer the Deccan, and this fact dominated the whole history of southern India throughout the seventeenth century. Adil Shah (the ruler of Bijapur) found that he must give up the dream of winning the hegemony of the Deccan, as the heir of the Bahmanis and the Nizam Shahs, and that he must find an outlet for his ambition eastwards and southwards only, so as not to cross the path of the dreaded Mughals in the north. By the partition-treaty of 1636, the southern boundary of Mughal Deccan had been clearly marked out, and during the following twenty years Bijapur had risen to the pinnacle of her greatness by stretching her sway from sea to sea across the Indian peninsula, while the capital city had become the mother of arts and letters, of theology and science. But the warrior-kings of an earlier, poorer and ruder generation were now followed by successors who preferred the harem and the *darbar* to the tented field and the saddle. The climax of the Adil Shahi power was also the beginning of its rapid decline and dismemberment.

A feudal State cannot be governed by *a. faineant* king nor by a constitutional prime minister. When the king is no longer a hero, the military viceroys of the provinces will not obey him. Therefore, after the death of the last great Adil Shah (in November 1656), the dissolution of the remaining Muslim kingdoms of the Deccan and their absorption into the Mughal Empire would have taken place as an inevitable, speedy and almost silent operation of Nature, but for the entracne of a new factor into Deccan politics.

These were the Marathas. They dominated Deccan history for the century and a half that followed the accession of Aurangzib, and North Indian history for the last fifty years of the eighteenth century. The Maratha *people* had been there from time out of mind, but since the eighteenth century they had lived dispersed through many States, as the subjects of aliens on the land of their birth, without any political organization or status of their own. A genius was needed to gather these scattered units together into a *nation* and drive them like a solid wedge into the Mughal Empire, shattering it to bits. That genius was Shivaji, the contemporary and antagonist of Aurangzib.

From the day when Emperor Akbar launched forth into a policy of conquest south of the Vindhyas to the day 94 years later, when Aurangzib rode in triumph into the fallen capital of the last of the Qutb Shahs, the Sultans of Bijapur and Golkonda could never for a moment forget that the sleepless aim of the Mughal Emperor was their final extinction and the annexation of all their territories. They found in the genius of Shivaji and the reckless audacity of Shambhuji their only shield in the hour of supreme danger. A union of hearts between Bijapur or Golkonda and the Mughal Empire against the Marathas was a psychological impossibility.

European historians maintain that it would have been wiser for Aurangzib to have left Bijapur and Golkonda in independence to serve as the police of the Deccan against the growing Maratha lawlessness which finally proved too strong for the Mughals. This view is based upon ignorance of the true condition of the Deccan. By the time that Shivaji had succeeded in forming a national State as a nucleus round which the Maratha chiefs hitherto in Muslim pay might cluster, the kingdoms of Bijapur and Golkonda had arrived at the last stage of decline. Their kings were mere puppets sunk in pleasure, their capitals ran blood during the frequent faction-fights for the office of *wazir,* the administration had utterly broken down, law and order had disappeared, the provincial governors had become independent, the generals were selling themselves to the highest bidder. Such governments could not be expected to tame Shambhuji and chastise Shanta Ghorpare more effectually than Aurangzib himself could do.

Briefly put, the grouping of Powers in the Deccan was this: The dread of Mughal aggression drove the Sultan of Golkonda whole-heartedly, and that of Bijapur distrustfully and intermittently, into the arms of Shivaji. Bijapur's leagues with Shivaji were formed only when Mughal invasion was an insistent fact and the situation of Adil Shah was desperate; and these leagues were soon dissolved by the growing fear that Shivaji was trying to enrich himself by treacherously seizing its forts and lands. Of the three Deccani Powers, Qutb Shah may be left out of our account, as he never sought a rupture with the Mughals during this period. The Bijapur Goverment fell into a hopeless decline[1] after 1666, when Ali Adil Shah II gave himself up entirely to wine, while rival nobles began to fight for the wazirship and the control over the capital and *the faineant* king. Matters grew worse when the boy-king Sikandar succeeded in 1672, and the history of Bijapur became in effect the history of its regents. Utter disorder prevailed in the administration. This was the opportunity which made Shivaji's rise to independent power possible.

Shivaji could never for a moment be sure of the Delhi Government's pacific disposition or fidelity to treaty promises. Hence, he lost no chance of robbing Mughal territory in the Deccan. With Bijapur his relations were somewhat different. He could rise his head or expand his dominion only at the expense of Bijapur. But when, about 1662, an understanding with him was effected by the Adil Shahi ministers, he gave up molesting the heart of the Bijapur kingdom. With the Bijapuri nobles whose fiefs lay close to his dominions and across the path of his natural expansion (e.g. Kolhapur, Kanara and Kopal), he could not be at peace, though he did not wish to challenge the central government of Bijapur.

[1] The downward course had begun much earlier, in 1646, when Muhammad Adil Shah was prostrated by a severe and lingering illness.

10.2 Causes of Mughal Weakness in the Deccan

From January 1658, when Aurangzib left the Deccan to contest his father's throne, till March 1682 when he returned to the south to wear out the last quarter century of his life in ceaseless warfare, a period of 24 years intervened, during which there were five viceroys of the Mughal province of the Deccan, among whom Prince Shah Alam held the office for eleven years, Bahadur Khan for six years, Shaista Khan for four, Jai Singh for nearly two, and Dilir Khan for one year. During these twenty-four years the Mughals pursued a vigorous forward policy against Bijapur only under Jai Singh (1666), Bahadur Khan (1676–77), and Dilir Khan (1679–80). Military operations against the Marathas were actively carried on by Shaista Khan (1660–62), Jai Singh (1665), Mahabat Khan (1671–72), Bahadur Khan (1673–75), and by Dilir Khan for a short while in 1678–79. A state of war between Shivaji and the Mughals existed for a much longer period, but during most of it the imperial generals acted languidly, so as to hoodwink their distant master, while maintaining a secret understanding with Shivaji (and later, with Shambhuji) and accepting bribes from him.

Only a few clear successes but no decisive result was achieved by the Mughal arms in the Deccan during these 24 years. The cause of this failure was partly personal and partly political. Shah Alam was a timid, unenterprising prince, inclined by nature to peace with his neighbours and the pleasures of the harem or the chase. Besides, his chief lieutenant Dilir Khan's open definace of his authority often made the viceregal camp in the Deccan as powerless as a country torn by civil war. Shah Alam and Dilir always worked at cross purposes and thus ensured Mughal failure in the Deccan.

Secondly, the imperial officers were heartily sick of the ceaseless war with Shivaji. The Hindu officers in Mughal pay secretly fraternized with the Deccani champion of Hinduism, while several of the Muslim generals were glad to bribe him to let them live in peace. Above all, no Mughal governor of the Deccan was supplied with men and money even half adequate to the task of defeating Bijapur and the Marathas.

The rebellion of Prince Akbar and his flight to Shambhuji (1681) raised a danger to the throne of Delhi which could be met only by Aurangzib's personal appearance in the south. Thus a complete change was forced on the imperial policy in that quarter. The first task of Aurangzib now was to crush the power of Shambhuji and render Akbar impotent for mischief.

10.3 Maharashtra: The Land and its People

The home of the Maratha people is made up of three clearly marked regional divisions. Between the Western Ghats and the Indian Ocean lies a long narrow strip of land of varying breadth, called *konkan* (between Bombay and Goa) and Kanara (south of Goa). It is an area of certain and heavy rainfall,—from 254 to 305 cm (100 to 120 inches) in the year,—with rice as the predominant crop, and dense mango-groves, plantain orchards and coconut-palms. Then, after crossing the Ghats eastwards we have a belt of land, some 32 km (20 miles) in breadth, called Maval. 'It is extremely rugged, a series of table-lands cut on every side by deep winding valleys.' Going further towards the east, the spurs of the Western Ghats sink, the river valleys widen out and form *Desh* or the vast rolling black-soil plain of the central Deccan.

This land, almost locked among the hills and open only in the east, is the cradle of the Maratha kingdom. East of the Ghats the rainfall decreases rapidly, and is uncertain and insufficient for agriculture, while the soil is naturally sterile and broken up by low ranges of bare rocky hills. 'The Deccan, generally speaking, yields to much labour a bare measure of subsistence.'

In such a country, where Nature enforces a Spartan simplicity, there can be no luxury, no learned leisure (except among the priests), no aesthetic development, no polished manners even. But such a country and climate have their compensating advantages. They develop self-reliance, courage, perseverance, a stern simplicity, a rough straight-forwardness, a sense of social equality and consequently pride in the dignity of man as man. In the seventh century, the Chinese pilgrim Yuan Chwang noted the Marathas for being 'proud-spirited and warlike, grateful for favours and revengeful for wrongs.' In the course of the next ten centuries they became more cunning and less chivalrous; but the basis of their character remained the same,—activity, self-reliance, self-respect and love of equality.

Social distinctions were fewer and much less sharp among the sixteenth century Marathas than among richer and more civilized communities. The same sense of equality was fostered by religion. Their popular saints of the 15th and 16th centuries taught the the sanctity of conduct rather than that of mere birth, and the oneness of all true believers before God.

The simplicity and uniformity of early Maratha society were also reflected in their language and literature, which were poor, undeveloped, and essentially popular. Nature provided them with many ready-made and easily defensible forts close at hand, where they could quickly flee for refuge and whence they could offer a tenacious resistance. 'The whole of the Ghats often terminate towards the top in a wall of smooth rock, the highest points of which, as well as detached portions on isolated hills, form natural fortresses ... (with) a level space on the summit.... In many of them there are springs of the finest water.' Thus a remarkable community of language, creed and life was attained in Maharashtra in the seventeenth century, even before political unity was conferred by Shivaji.

The backbone of Shivaji's army was composed of the peasantry belonging to the *Maratha* and *Kunbi* castes,—a simple, frank, independent, manly and hardy race. With the Muslim conquest of the Deccan and the extinction of the last Hindu kingdom in Maharashtra in the 14th century, the fighting classes among the natives gathered round their own leaders in small bands and hired out their swords to the new rulers of the land. Many Maratha families rose to wealth, power and distinction as captains of mercenary troops in the service of the Muslim States in their neighbourhood.

10.4 Shahji Bhonsle: His Career

One such family, bearing the name of Bhonsle, originally lived in the Patas sub-division of the Puna district, as the headmen (*patil*) of two villages. They followed agriculture and gained much local credit by their sober honest character and religious benefactions. Some buried treasure that they discovered in their fields enabled them to buy arms and horses and develop into captains of mercenaries under the Nizam Shahi dynasty at the close of the sixteenth century. Such was Shahji Bhonsle, the eldest son of Maloji. Born in 1594, he was married when a child to Jija Bai, the daughter of the high-born Lakhji Yadav Rao, baron of Sindhkhed and one of the greatest Hindu nobles of Ahmadnagar. Shahji first saw service probably as the commander of the small contingent of his family during the rule of Malik Ambar, the regent of Nizam Shah.

On the death of Malik Ambar in May 1626, the State fell into rapid decay; there were frequent assassinations at Court. During these troubled times, Shahji first followed the Nizam Shahi Government, then joined the Mughals, deserted them, fought against the Bijapuris, went over to their side afterwards, and finally set up a puppet Nizam Shah (1633) in one of the hill-forts of the Sahyadri range. He seized one quarter of the Nizam Shahi dominion from Puna and Chakan to Balaghat and the neighbourhood of Junnar, Ahmadnagar, Sangamner, Trimbak and Nasik, and for three years (1633–36) carried on the government in this Sultan's name. He made Junnar his capital. But in 1636 a grand campaign was opened by the imperialists against Shahji, in which he was completely defeated and forced to give up eight of his forts, enter the service of Bijapur, and leave Maharashtra.

10.5 Childhood, Education, and Character of Shivaji

Shivaji, the second son of Shahji and Jija Bai, was born in the hill-fort of Shivner, which overlooks the town of Junnar, on 10 April 1627. After entering Bijapur service towards the end of 1636, Shahji was sent away to the Tungabhadra region and the Mysore plateau, and later on to the Madras coast to conquer fresh territories for his new master and jagirs for himself. But here his favourite wife Tuka Bai and her son Vyankoji accompanied him, while Jija Bai and Shivaji were sent to live at Puna, in charge of his land-steward Dadaji Kond-dev.

Her husband's neglect drove the mind of Jija Bai inwards and deepened her natural religious spirit, which she imparted to her son. Shivaji grew up in solitude, a mateless child, without brother, sister or father. The isolation of their lives drew mother and son very close together and intensified his love for her till it became almost an adoration for a deity. From a very early age, he was thrown on his own resources, and learnt to carry out his own ideas unaided and to take the initiative without referring to any higher authority. Such education as he received was eminently practical; he became skilled in fighting, riding and other manly accomplishments; but he mastered the contents of the great Hindu epics by listening to recitations and story-tellings and thus learnt their political lessons and moral maxims. He loved for distraction, religious readings and songs (*kirtan*) and sought the society of Hindu and Muslim saints wherever he went.

The *Mavals* or western belt of the Puna district, stretching along the rugged forest-clad side and foot of the Sahyadri range, were the homes of a sturdy, healthy, and brave race of peasants called *Mavles*. From them Shivaji drew his earliest comrades, his most devoted followers, and his best soldiers. In the company of Mavle chieftains of his own age, young Shivaji wandered over the hills and forests of the Sahyadri range, and along the mazes of the river valleys, thus hardening himself to a life of privation and strenuous exertion. A stoical earnestness mingled with religious fervour was very early imparted to the character of Shivaji. He began to love independence and loathe a life of servile luxury in the pay of some Muslim king.

Dadaji Kond-dev died on 7 March 1647, and Shivaji became his own master at the age of twenty. He had already been trained in martial exercises and civil administration; he had familiarized himself with the troops of his father's western jagir, and the people he would have to govern. Initiative and power of command had been freely developed in him.

10.6 Early Conquest of Shivaji

The year 1646 marks a crisis in the history of Bijapur. The king fell seriously ill, and lingered on for ten years more, but during these years no serious business could be attended to by him. This was Shivaji's opportunity. He occupied Torna fort by tricking its Bijapuri commandant. Here he seized Government treasure amounting to 2 lakhs of *hun*. 8 km (5 miles) east of it, on the crest of the same spur of hills, he built a new fort named Rajgarh. Later he took Kondana (Singhgarh) from a Bijapur agent. After the death of Dadaji, Shivaji set himself to bring all parts of Shahji's western jagir under his own control, so as to form one compact State ruled by one authority.

On 25 July 1648, Shahji was arrested and all his property and contingent attached by the Bijapuri commander-in-chief, Mustafa Khan, then investing Jinji in the South Arcot district.

Shahji was brought in chains to Bijapur, and kept under guard until he submitted to his sovereign.

Shivaji was in a terrible dilemma: he appealed to Prince Murad Bakhsh, the Mughal viceroy of the Deccan, entreating him to secure the Emperor's pardon for Shahji's past conduct and protection for him and his sons in future, and offering to come and join the Mughal service. Shah Jahan, however, did not put any pressure on Adil Shah to release Shahji. Shahji was set at liberty through the mediation of the Bijapuri noble Ahmad Khan and in return for the surrender of three forts (Bangalore, Kondana and Kandarpi) to the Sultan, (in May 1649). As the release of Shahji had been conditional, Shivaji kept comparatively quiet during the six years from 1649 to 1655, instead of giving the Bijapur Government any new provocation. His chief acquisition at this time was the hill-fort of Purandar, gained by treachery to its Maratha Brahman owners.

At the extreme north-western corner of the Satara district lies the village of Javli, which was then the centre of a fairly large principality, including nearly the whole of that district, owned by a Maratha family named More, the head of which bore the hereditary title of Chandra Rao. They kept 12,000 infantry, mostly sturdy hillmen of the same class as the Mavles.

The State of Javli, by its situation, barred the path of Shivaji's ambition in the south and south-west. So he sent his agent Raghunath Ballal Korde to murder Chandra Rao, during pretended negotiations for a marriage between Shivaji and the late Chandra Rao's daughter. Immediately on hearing of the murder, Shivaji advanced and assaulted Javli (15 January 1656). The leaderless garrison defended themselves for six hours and were then overcome. The whole kingdom of Javli now passed into Shivaji's possession 3 km (2 miles) west of Javli he built a new fort named Pratapgarh, and here he set up an image of his patron goddess Bhavani. In the April following he captured Raigarh, his future capital, from the Mores.

10.7 Shivaji's First War with the Mughals, 1657

On the death of Muhammad Adil Shah (4 November 1656), Aurangzib began active preparations for the invasion of Bijapur, and tried to seduce as many Adil Shahi nobles and vassals as he could. Shivaji's envoy Sonaji reached the prince's siege-camp before Bidar (in March 1657) and was assured that the Mughal Government would grant all the prayers of the Maratha chief, namely (*i*) a formal recognition of his right to all the Bijapuri forts and villages actually in his possession and (*ii*) the annexation of the port of Dabhol and the territory appertaining to it. A reply in these terms was also written to Shivaji by Aurangzib on 23 April, 1657. But Shivaji had already decided on the different policy of fighting for his own hand. He considered it more profitable to make a diversion in favour of Bijapur by raiding the south-western corner of Mughal Deccan.

Two Maratha captains, Minaji Bhonsle at the head of 3,000 horse and Kashi, crossed the Bhima and plundered the Mughal villages in the Chamargunda and Raisin subdivisions respectively. They carried devastation and alarm to the very gates of Ahmadnagar, the chief city of Mughal Deccan, (end of April 1657). A Maratha attempt to loot the city (*peth*) which nestled under shelter of the fort of Ahmadnagar was defeated by a timely sortie of the garrison. At the same time, Shivaji was busy looting the Junnar sub-division in the north. In the dark night of 30 April,he silently scaled the walls of Junnar city with rope-ladders and after slaughtering the guards, carried off 300,000 *hun* in cash, 200 horses, and much costly clothing and jewellery. Aurangzib, on hearing of these disturbances, poured reinforcements into the Ahmadnagar district. Nasiri Khan, Iraj Khan, and some other officers at the head of 3,000 cavalry were ordered there. Meanwhile, Multafat Khan had issued from the fort of Ahmadnagar and relieved the beleaguered outpost at Chamargunda by defeating Minaji, (28 April).

But when the Mughal pressure in the north Puna region became too great, Shivaji slipped away to the Ahmadnagar district and began to plunder it. By this time (end of May), however, Nasiri Khan had reached the scene. By a forced march he surprised Shivaji's army and nearly encircled it. Many of the Marathas were slain, many wounded, and the rest put to flight, (4 June). Aurangzib ordered his officers to make reprisals by entering Shivaji's land from all sides, 'wasting the villages, slaying the people without pity, and plundering them to the extreme.' His new dispositions for guarding his south-western frontier showed excellent combination and judgment. The rains now set in with the full violence of the monsoons, and the campaign had to be suspended during June, July and August.

When in September his liege-lord, the king of Bijapur, made peace, Shivaji found it useless and even ruinous to himself to continue the war with the Mughal Empire single-handed. He sent his envoy Raghunath Pant to Aurangzib. The prince was just then starting on his march to northern India (25 January 1658) and wrote to Shivaji in reply,' 'Though your offences do not deserve pardon, I forgive you as you have repented.'

But Aurangzib's mind was not really composed; he felt convinced that the young Maratha chief was a raider whose daring was only equalled by his cunning, and an ambitious adventurer who would place self-interest above fidelity to his plighted word.

In the last quarter of the year 1657, the northward retreat of Prince Aurangzib, the likelihood of a civil war for the throne of Delhi, and the wrangles among the Bijapuri nobles about responsibility for their ill-success in the recent war with the Mughals (which culminated in the murder of the *wazir* Khan Muhammad),—all combined to remove the only checks on Shivaji's ambition. Crossing the Western Ghats he burst into Konkan. The northern part of this coast-strip formed the Kalian (modern Thana) district and was then governed by an Arab named Mulla Ahmad of the Navaiyat (emigrant) clan, one of the leading nobles of Bijapur. Shivaji easily seized the rich towns of Kalian and Bhivandi (24 October 1657), which were then without walls, and there took much wealth and costly merchandise. The fort of Mahuli, which had once been the last refuge of Shahji, was next captured (8 January 1658). Kalian and Bhivandi were immediately turned into naval bases and dockyards by Shivaji.

By the year 1659 he had extended his dominions in the uplands or *Desh* to the southern limit of the Satara district, and in North Konkan from Mahuli to near Mahad.

10.8 Shivaji Slays Afzal Khan of Bijapur, 1659

In 1659, the Bijapur Government being freed for the time being from the constant menace of the Mughals on the frontier, began to call its refractory vassals to account. The command of the expedition against Shivaji was given to Abdullah Bhatari, surnamed Afzal Khan, a noble of the first rank, who had fought with conspicuous bravery and skill in the Karnatak expeditions and the more recent war with the Mughals. But only 10,000 cavalry could be spared to accompany Afzal, while popular report had raised the strength of Shivaji's Mavle infantry to 60,000 men. Afzal Khan was therefore instructed by the Dowager Queen to effect the capture or murder of Shivaji by 'pretending friendship' with him and offering to secure his pardon from Adil Shah.[2] From his camp

[2] Against Shivaji the Queen this year sent Abdullah Khan with an army of 10,000 horse and foot, and because she knew with that strength he was not able to resist

at Wai, Afzal sent his land-steward Krishnaji Bhaskar to Shivaji with a very alluring message, saying, 'Your father has long been a great friend of mine, and you are, therefore, no stranger to me. Come and see me, and I shall use my influence to make Adil Shah confirm your possession of Konkan and the forts you now hold.'

Shivaji treated Afzal's envoy, Krishnaji Bhaskar with respect, and at night met him in secrecy and solemnly appealed to him as a Hindu and a priest to tell him of the Khan's real intentions. It was well known that when Afzal was besieging the fort of Sera, he had put to death Kasturi Ranga, the Rajah of the place, who had come to his camp to make his submission. Krishnaji yielded so far as to hint that the Khan seemed to harbour some plan of mischief. Shivaji then sent the envoy back with Pantaji Gopinath, his own agent, who learnt from Afzal's officers by a liberal use of bribes that 'the Khan had so arranged matters that Shivaji would be arrested at the interview, as he was too cunning to be caught by open fight.'

The place chosen for their interview was the crest of an eminence, below the fort of Pratapgarh, and overlooking the valley of the Koyna, where a richly decorated tent had been pitched for the purpose. On each side four men were present within the tent,—the principal, two armed retainers and an envoy. But Shivaji was seemingly unarmed, like a rebel who had come to surrender, while the Khan had his sword at his side. But concealed in Shivaji's left hand was a set of steel claws (*baghnakh*) fastened to the fingers by a pair of rings, and up his right sleeves lay hidden a thin sharp dagger called the scorpion (*bichwa*).

The attendants stood below. Shivaji mounted the raised platform and bowed to Afzal. The Khan rose from his seat, advanced a few steps and opened his arms to receive him in his embrace. The short slim Maratha only came up to the shoulders of his opponent. Suddenly Afzal tightened his clasp, and held Shivaji's neck in his left arm with an iron grip, while with his right hand he drew his long straight-bladed dagger and struck at the side of Shivaji. The hidden armour beneath Shivaji's coat rendered the blow harmless. He groaned in agony as he felt himself being

Shivaji, she counselled him to *pretend friendship* with bis enemy, *which he did.* And the other [i.e., Shivaji], whether through intelligence or suspicion it is not known, dissembled his love toward him &c.' (Revington at Rajapur to Company, 10 December 1659, *F.R.* Rajapur.)

strangled. But in a moment he recovered from the surprise, passed his left arm round the Khan's waist and tore his bowels open with a blow of the steel claws. Then with the right hand he drove the *bichwa* into Afzal's side. The wounded man relaxed his hold, and Shivaji wresting himself free, jumped down from the platform and ran towards his own men outside.

The Khan cried out, 'Treachery! Murder! Help! Help!' The attendants ran up from both sides. Sayyid Banda, an expert swordsman attending on Afzal, faced Shivaji with his long straight sword and cut his turban in twain, making a deep dint in the steel cap beneath. But Jiv Mahala hacked off the right arm of the Sayyid, and then killed him. Shambhuji Kayji cut off Afzal's head, which he carried in triumph to Shivaji.

Freed from danger, Shivaji and his two comrades then made their way to the summit of Pratapgarh, and fired a cannon. This was the signal for which his troops were waiting in their ambush in the valleys below. At once the armies of Moro Trimbak and Netaji Palkar and the thousands of Mavles rushed on the Bijapuri camp from four sides. Afzal's officers and soldiers alike were panic-stricken at the news of their chief's death and this unexpected attack in that unknown region, where every bush seemed to be alive with enemies. The carnage in the Bijapuri army was terrible.

The booty taken was immense: all the artillery, wagons, ammunition, treasure, tents and equipage, transport cattle and baggage of an entire army, fell into the victor's hands. Among them were 65 elephants, 4,000 horses, 1,200 camels, 2,000 bundles of clothing, and 10 *lakhs* of rupees in cash and jewellery.

Flushed with their victory over Afzal Khan (10 November 1659) and the destruction of his army, the Marathas poured into South Konkan and the Kolhapur district, capturing the fort of Panhala, defeating another Bijapuri army, and making extensive conquests (December 1659–February 1660).

10.9 Shivaji Besieged in Panhala

Early in 1660, Ali Adil Shah II sent his Abyssinian slave Siddi Jauhar (created Salabat Khan) with an army to put down Shiva. Jauhar drove Shivaji into Panhala (2 March 1660), which he invested with a force of

15,000 men. But Shivaji corrupted Jauhar, so that the siege was conducted for mere show. Fazl Khan, the son of the slain Afzal, however attacked the Marathas with relentless vigour and by seizing a neighbouring hillock threatened to make Panhala untenable. So, one dark night (15 July) Shivaji slipped out of the fort with half his forces, and though pursued by a Bijapuri army, made his escape to Vishalgarh, 43 km (27 miles) to the west. His success was due to the desperate resistance of his rear-guard, under Baji Prabhu (who was slain with most of his men) at the pass of Gajpur. The men he had left in Panhala surrendered it on 22 September.

10.10 Shaista Khan Occupies Puna and Chakan

Early in 1660, Shaista Khan, the new Mughal viceroy of the Deccan, opened the campaign against Shivaji from the north, after arranging for an attack upon the Maratha dominions by the Bijapuris from the south at the same time. Leaving Ahmadnagar with a vast army on 25 February, the Khan marched southwards along the eastern side of the Puna district, methodically capturing and garrisoning all the strongholds that guarded the approaches to Puna on the east and south. The Marathas at first retreated before him without risking a battle, till near Purandar. The Mughals were victorious in fight and Shaista Khan entered Puna on 9 May.

Leaving Puna on 19 June, the Khan arrived on the vicinity of Chakan (29 km i.e. 18 miles northwards) on the 21st, reconnoitred the fort and began to run trenches towards the fort's walls. After 54 days of hard labour a mine was carried from his own position in the north to under the tower at the north-eastern corner, and it was exploded at 3 p.m. on 14 August 1660. The work and its defenders were blown away; the Mughals rushed to the assault. Next day the citadel capitulated. But the imperialists had to purchase their victory at a heavy price, with 268 killed and 600 wounded. Shaista Khan, on his return to Puna (end of August 1660) after the capture of Chakan, spent the rainy season there in enforced inactivity. He employed his time more usefully in inducing Ghalib, the Bijapuri commandant of Parenda, to surrender that fort to Aurangzib for a high price (20 November).

At the beginning of next year (1661), Shaista Khan turned his attention to the Kalian district or North Konkan. Here a small Mughal force, only

3,000 strong, under Ismail, had been operating since April last and had occupied a part of the country, though the important cities and forts (like Kalian) remained unconquered. In January 1661, a strong Mughal force from Puna under Kar Talb Khan descended into Konkan. At Umbarkhind (about 24 km i.e. 15 miles due east of Pen), Shivaji by secret and rapid marches came up with them and cut off their lines of advance and retreat alike. Kar Talb's army seemed doomed to perish from thirst, without the power to move. In despair he gave up all the property in his camp and paid a large ransom to Shivaji and thus bought a safe retreat for his army (3 February 1661). The Kalian district having been thus freed from the new enemies, Shivaji left it alone, and marched southwards, easily capturing city after city, till all the coast-strip from Danda-Rajpuri to Kharepatan was commanded by him. But these successes were chequered by a great defeat. In May 1661 the Mughals wrested Kalian from the Marathas and kept hold of it for nine years more. The net result of the operations of these two years was that the Mughals kept their grip on the extreme north of Konkan, while Shivaji remained master of the southern part. In March 1663, the Mughals gave a long and vigorous chase to Netaji, the Master of the Horse in Shivaji's army. Netaji got away, though not without the loss of 300 horse and himself wounded.

10.11 Shivaji's Night-attack on Shaista Khan

But within a month of meeting with this reverse to his arms Shivaji dealt a masterly blow at the Mughals. He surprised and wounded the Mughal viceroy of the Deccan in the heart of his camp, in his very bed-chamber, within the inner ring of his bodyguards and slaves.

Shaista Khan was residing at Puna in the Lal Mahal or the unpretentious home of Shivaji's childhood. His harem was with him, and around his mansion lay the quarters of his guards and attendants, the band-room and offices. Further off, across the road leading southwards to Singhgarh lay the camp of his lieutenant, Maharajah Jaswant Singh, and his contingent of 10,000 men. To surprise him here was an enterprise that required no less agility and cunning than bravery and dash. Shivaji directed two supporting divisions of one thousand each, under Netaji Palkar and Moro Pant the *Peshwa, to* take post on the two flanks of the vast Mughal encampment, at a kilometre's distance from its outer side. After nightfall (Sunday,

5 April 1663), with 400 picked men he himself entered the limits of Puna, replying to the challenge of the Mughal guards that they were Deccani soldiers of the imperial army going to take up their appointed posts. After resting for a few hours in some obscure corner of the camp, the party arrived near the Khan's quarters at midnight. Shivaji knew the ins and outs of the city and every nook and corner of the house where he had passed his boyhood and youth.

It was the sixth day of *Ramzan*, the month of fasting for Muslims. The servants of the Nawab's household, had mostly fallen asleep after their day's abstinence followed by the heavy meal at night. Some cooks who had risen from bed to make a fire and prepare the meal which is taken a little before dawn throughout the month of *Ramzan*, were despatched by the Marathas without any noise. The wall dividing this outer kitchen from the body-servants' room within the harem once had a small door in it, but the opening had been closed with brick and mud to complete the seclusion of the harem. The Marathas took the bricks out and made an opening there. Shivaji, with his trusty lieutenant Chimanji Bapuji, was the first to enter the harem, and was followed by 200 of his men. When he reached the bedroom of the Khan, the frightened women roused the Nawab, but before he could use his weapons Shivaji was upon him and severed the thumb with one stroke of his sword. It was evidently at this time that the lamps in the room were put out by some wise woman. In the darkness two of the Marathas tumbled into a cistern of water; and the confusion that followed was used by Shaista Khan's slave-girls to carry him away to a place of safety. The Marathas continued their work of slaughter in the darkness for some time.

Meanwhile the other half of Shivaji's force, (200 men), who had been left outside the harem, had rushed the main guard, slaying the sleepers and the awake and crying out in derision, 'Is it thus that you keep watch?' They next entered the band-room and ordered the bandsmen, as if from the Khan, to play. The loud noise of the kettle-drums drowned all voices, and the yells of the enemy swelled the confusion.

Abul Fath, a son of Shaista Khan, had been the first to hasten to his father's rescue without waiting for others; but the brave youth was slain after he had struck down two or three Marathas.

Shivaji, finding his enemies fully awakened and arming, delayed no longer, but promptly left the harem, called his men together, and withdrew from the camp by the direct route, unmolested and unpursued. During the surprise the Marathas lost only six men killed and forty wounded, while they slew a son and a captain of Shaista Khan, forty of his attendants and six of his wives and slave-girls, besides wounding two other sons, eight other women and Shaista Khan himself. The public throughout the Deccan ascribed Shivaji's exploit to the connivance of Jaswant Singh.

The daring and cunning of the Maratha hero were rewarded by an immense increase of his prestige. He was taken to be an incarnation of Satan; no place was believed to be proof against his entrance and no feat impossible for him. The Emperor heard of the disaster and ascribed it to the viceroy's negligence and incapacity. As a mark of his displeasure, he transferred Shaista Khan to the government of Bengal (1 December 1663), which was then regarded as a penal province. The Khan left the Deccan about the middle of January 1664, on being relieved by Prince Muazzam.

10.12 Shivaji's First Sack of Surat

While this change of governors was going on at Aurangabad, Shivaji performed a feat of even greater audacity than he had ever displayed before. From 6 to 10 January he looted the city of Surat, the richest port of the Mughal Empire. It had, at that time, no wall to protect it. Its wealth was boundless. The imperial customs alone yielded a revenue of 12 *lakhs* of rupees a year.

The city of Surat covered nearly seven square kilometres, including gardens and open spaces, and had a population of two lakhs souls. The streets were narrow and crooked; but the town was mainly composed of poor men's huts built of wooden posts and bamboo walls and with floors plastered with mud. 'In the greater part of the town scarcely two or three brick-houses were to be seen in a street, and in some part ... not one for many streets together.'

Early in the morning of Tuesday, 5 January 1664, Surat was suddenly alarmed by the news that Shivaji had arrived with an army at Gandavi, 44 km (28 miles) southwards, and was advancing to plunder the town. At once the people were seized with a panic, and began to flee away with their wives and children, mostly across the river, to save their lives. Rich men found shelter in the fort by bribing its commandant. Inayet Khan, the governor of the town—who was quite distinct from the commandant of the fort,—himself fled to the fort, leaving the town at the enemy's mercy. He used to draw from the Treasury the pay of 500 soldiers but had so long appropriated the money without maintaining a proper force. His cowardice also prevented him from organizing a defence or even from dying at his post. The English and Dutch merchants resolved to defend their own factories at all costs, though these were open houses, not built to stand an attack.

At 11 o'clock in the morning of Wednesday, 6 January 1664, Shivaji arrived at Surat and pitched his tent in a garden, half a kilometre outside the Burhanpur or eastern gate. The Maratha horsemen immediately afterwards entered the defenceless and almost deserted city, and after sacking the houses began to set fire to them. Throughout Wednesday, Thursday, Friday, and Saturday, this work of devastation was continued, every day new fires being raised, so that thousands of houses were consumed to ashes and two-thirds of the town destroyed. Near the Dutch factory stood the grand mansion of Baharji Borah, then 'reputed the richest merchant in the world,' his property having been estimated at 80 *lakhs* of rupees. The Marathas plundered it at leisure day and night till Friday evening, when having ransacked it and dug up its floor, they set fire to it. Close to the English factory were the lofty residence and extensive warehouses of another very rich merchant, Haji Said Beg, who, too, had fled away to the fort, leaving his property without a defender. All the afternoon and night of Wednesday and till past the noon of Thursday, the Marathas continued to break open his doors and chests and carry off as much money as they could. But in the afternoon of Thursday the brigands left it in a hurry, on being scared by a sortie which the English had made into the street. The English merchants next day put a guard of their own in the house of Said Beg and thus he suffered no further loss. The plunder of Surat yielded above a *krore* of rupees.

The cowardly governor Inayet Khan, who had run into the fort on Tuesday night, formed an infamous plot from his safe refuge. On Thursday he sent a young follower of his to Shivaji with pretended terms of peace but really to murder him at the interview. A Maratha body-guard that stood before the Rajah with a drawn sword, struck off the assassin's hand with one blow. But so great was the force of the desperado's rush that he did not stop but drove the bloody stump of his arm on Shivaji's person and the two rolled on the ground together. At ten o'clock in the morning of Sunday 10, Shivaji suddenly departed from Surat with his army, on hearing that a Mughal force was coming to the relief of the town.

The Emperor showed his sympathy with the afflicted citizens by excusing the custom duties for one year in the case of all the merchants of Surat, and he rewarded the valour of the English and the Dutch traders by granting them a reduction of one per cent from the normal import duties on their merchandise in future.

The year 1664 that lay between the departure of Shaista Khan and the arrival of Jai Singh, was not marked by any Mughal success. The new viceroy, Prince Muazzam, lived at Aurangabad, caring only for pleasure and hunting.

10.13 Jai Singh Against Shivaji: Capture of Purandar

The failure of Shaista Khan and the sack of Surat caused bitter mortification to Aurangzib and his Court, and he decided to send his ablest Hindu and Muhammadan generals, Jai Singh and Dilir Khan, to put down Shivaji.

Jai Singh had fought under the imperial banner in every part of the Empire,—from Balkh in Central Asia to Bijapur in the Deccan, from Qandahar in the west to Mungir in the east. Hardly a year had passed during the long reign of Shah Jahan when this Rajput chieftain had not seen active service somewhere, received some promotion for conspicuous merit. In diplomacy he had attained to a success surpassing even his victories in the field. Wherever there was a difficult or delicate work to be done, the Emperor had only to turn to Jai Singh. A man of infinite tact and patience, an adept in a ceremonious courtesy of the Muslims, a master of Turki and Persian, besides Urdu and the Rajput dialect, he was an ideal leader of the composite army of Afghans and Turks, Rajputs and Hindustanis, that followed the crescent banner of the sovereign of Delhi. His foresight and political cunning, his smoothness of tongue and cool calculating policy, were in striking contrast with the impulsive generosity, reckless daring, blunt straightforwardness, and impolitic chivalry which we are apt to associate with the Rajput character.

Jai Singh played skilfully upon the hopes and fears of the Sultan of Bijapur, holding forth the chance of reduction of tribute and removal of the Emperor's displeasure, if Adil Shah aided the Mughals and thus clearly proved his want of connection with Shivaji. He also arranged to combine against Shivaji all his enemies and distract his attention by attacks from all possible quarters. Money and promises of high rank in the Mughal service were lavishly employed on Shivaji's officers to corrupt their loyalty, and with some success. Above all, Jai Singh concentrated all authority in his own hands, as an indispensable condition of success in war. He rightly insisted that in war there should be only one head, and that the 'man on the spot' should be given full authority, or else the work would suffer. The Emperor yielded to the argument and Jai Singh gained absolute civil and military authority alike.

Jai Singh, with a true general's eye for the ground, made Saswad his base. Puna was strongly garrisoned. An outpost was established opposite Lohgarh to observe and blockade it and guard the road leading north to the Mughal frontier near Junnar. A flying column was organized to ravage the Maratha villages embosomed among the hills to the west and south-west of Saswad.

On 31 March, Jai Singh took up a permanent base, between Saswad and Purandar, only 7 km (4 miles) from the latter place. There he laid siege to the fort of Purandar.

Ten kilometres (six miles) south of Saswad rises the stupendous mountain mass of Purandar, the highest point of which towers 1370 m (4,564 feet) above sea level and more than 750 m (2,500 feet) above the plain at its foot. It is really a double fort, with an independent and very strong sister- enclosure, named Vajragarh, on a ridge running out east of it. Purandar consists of an upper fort or citadel with percipitous sides all around, and a lower fort or *machi*, 90m (300 feet) or more below it. The latter is a ledge running round the waist of the hill with many a winding, the entire circuit being 7 km (four miles). On the north side the ledge widens out into a broad terrace, containing the barracks and offices of the garrison. This terrace is bounded on the east by the high spur named Bhairav Khind, which starts from the base of the steep overhanging north-eastern tower (called *Khad-kala* or the sky-scraper) of the upper fort, and runs for about 1.5 km (1 mile) eastwards in a narrow ridge, ending in a small table-land (1090 m i.e. 3618 feet above sea-level), crowned with the fort of Rudramal (now called Vajragarh). This Vajragarh commands the *machi* or lower fort of Purandar on its northern and most important face, as the garrison has to live here. Jai Singh, like a true general, decided to attack Vajragarh first.

The incessant bombardment by the Mughals demolished the bases of the tower in front of Vajragarh. At midnight, 13 April, Dilir Khan's division stormed the tower and drove the enemy into an enclosure behind it. Next day, the victorious Mughals pushed on to the inner enclosure and the garrison, oppressed by their fire, capitulated in the evening (14 April).

The possession of Vajragarh was the stepping-stone to the capture of Purandar. Dilir Khan now turned to the latter fort, while Jai Singh organized raids into the Maratha country, in order, as he wrote to the Emperor, to convince Shivaji and the Sultan of Bijapur that the Mughal army was large enough to be able to spare troops from the siege, and also to prevent any concentration of forces round Shivaji by creating constant terror and disturbance in various parts of his kingdom. There was also a secret reason for thus sending away some generals from the siege-camp. He had some disloyal officers under him, whose presence was worse than useless. Daud Khan Qureshi was posted to watch the postern gate (*khirki*) of the fort; but after a few days it became known that a party of Marathas had entered the fort by that gate, without being opposed by him. 'Subh-Karn Bundela did not at all give his heart to the work, but preferred above everything else to favour Shiva!'

The Maratha efforts to raise the siege were many, but on the whole they failed to shake Jai Singh.

After the capture of Vajragarh Dilir Khan advanced along the *machi* or lower fort of Purandar. His trenches approached the tower of Khadkala at the north-eastern angle of the fort.

When, in the course of May, the Mughal trenches reached the foot of the two White Towers, which had been dismantled by bombardment, the garrison began to throw down lighted naptha oil, leather bags full of gunpowder, bombs and heavy stones which effectually stopped the further advance of the Mughals. Jai Singh ordered a high wooden platform of logs and planks to be made, on which guns were to be mounted and parties of gunners and musketeers placed, to command the enemy's position. On 30 May, with only two hours of daylight remaining, some Ruhela soldiers, without informing Dilir Khan, stormed the White Tower. After an obstinate struggle at close quarters, the Marathas lost heavily and retreated to behind the Black Tower, which they were forced to evacuate after two days. Thus five towers and one stockade of the lower fort fell into the hands of the Mughals. Purandar now seemed doomed.

Early in the siege, the gallant qiladar Murar Baji Prabhu, with seven hundred select men had made a sortie on Dilir Khan, who was trying to climb the hill with 5,000 Afghans and some more troops of other races. Murar Baji with his Mavles slew 500 Pathans besides many *Bahlia* infantrymen, and at the head of sixty desperate followers cut his way to Dilir Khan. The Khan, in admiration of his matchless courage, called upon him to yield and promised him his life and a high post under him. Murar indignantly refused, and was going to strike Dilir when the latter shot him down with an arrow. Three hundred Mavles fell with him, and the rest retreated to the fort.

The Mughal victory of 2 June, and the impending fall of the lower fort decided Shivaji. The families of the Maratha officers were sheltered in Purandar, and its capture would mean their captivity and dishonour. He resolved to interview Jai Singh and make peace with the imperialists.

10.14 Treaty of Purandar, 1665

On 11 June at 9 o'clock in the morning, while Jai Singh was holding court in his tent at the foot of Purandar, Shivaji came to him and was welcomed with every honour.

Up to midnight the two sides haggled for the terms of a permanent peace. 'Gradually, after much discussion, we came to this agreement: (*i*) That 23 of the forts,[3] the lands of which yielded 4 *lakhs* of *hun* as annual revenue should be annexed to the Empire; and (*ii*) that 12 of his forts, including Rajgarh, with an annual revenue of 1 *lakh* of *hun,* should be left to Shiva, on condition of service and loyalty to the imperial throne.' Shivaji, however, begged to be excused from attending the Emperor's Court like other nobles and Rajahs, and proposed to send his son, as his

[3] The Maratha forts surrendered to the Emperor by the treaty of Purandar (*A. N.* 905) were: *in the Deccan:* 1. Rudramala or Vajragarh, (2) Purandar, (3) Kondana, (4) Rohira, (5) Lohgarh, (6) Isagarh, (7) Tanki, (8) Tikona, (9) Khad-kala near Kondana, *in Konkan:* (10) Mahuli, (11) Muranjan, (12) Khidurg, (13) Bhandardurg, (14) Tulsikhul, (15) Nardurg, (16) Khaigarh or Ankola, (17) Marg-garh or Atra, (18) Kohaj, (19) Basant, (20) Nang, (21) Karnala, (22) Songarh, and (23) Mangarh.

representative, with a contingent of 5,000 horse, (to be paid by means of a jagir), for regular attendance and service under the Emperor or the Mughal governor of the Deccan.

In addition to the above terms, Shivaji made another and a conditional engagement with the Mughals: 'If lands yielding: 4 *lakhs* of *hun* a year in the lowlands of Konkan and 5 *lakhs* of *hun* a year in the uplands (Balaghat Bijapuri) are granted to me by the Emperor and I am assured by an imperial *farman* that the possession of these lands will be confirmed to me after the expected Mughal conquest of Bijapur, then I agree to pay to the Emperor 40 *lakhs* of *hun* in 13 yearly instalments.' He was expected to wrest these lands from the Bijapuri officers by means of his own troops. Here we detect the shrewdness of Jai Singh's policy in throwing a bone of perpetual contention between Shivaji and the Sultan of Bijapur. Next day (12 June), according to the agreement, 7,000 men and women, (of whom 4,000 were combatants), left Purandar, and the Mughals entered into possession of it; all the stores, weapons, artillery, and other property found within were attached by the Government. Mughal officers were sent with Shivaji's men to take charge of five other forts surrendered by the Marathas.

10.15 Shivaji Visits Aurangzib at Agra

Jai Singh at the end of his Bijapur campaign, had undertaken to send Shivaji to the imperial Court. He plied Shivaji with hopes of high reward and 'used a thousand devices' to induce him to go to Agra. In spite of these temptations, Shivaji hesitated long. Both he and his friends were as much alarmed at the idea of his going to the Mughal Court as at the prospect of his interview with Afzal Khan. But Jai Singh took the most solemn oaths possible for a Hindu that Shivaji would not be harmed during his visit. Shivaji's arrangements for the administration of his kingdom during his expected absence in northern India, were a masterpiece of forethought and organization. His plan was to make his local representatives absolutely independent of any need for his orders or guidance during his absence. His mother Jija Bai was left as Regent. He began his journey to northern India on 5 March, 1666 with his eldest son Shambhuji, seven trusty chief officers, and 250 troopers. On 11 May he arrived at the outskirts of Agra, where the Emperor was then holding Court.

The 12th of the month was appointed as the day of his audience. It was the 50th lunar birthday of the Emperor. The Hall of Public Audience in Agra Fort was splendidly decorated for the birthday *darbar*, and Shivaji was to have been presented to the Emperor here along with other vassal chiefs. But due to the blundering of Kumar Ram Singh (the eldest son of Jai Singh and Shivaji's host in Agra) there was so much delay in the Maratha King reaching Agra city, that it was already high noon and the Emperor had withdrawn from the Public Darbar to the smaller Diwan-i-Khas or Hall of Select Audience in the inner part of the palace. Ram Singh hurriedly conducted Shivaji there without having the time to instruct him in Court etiquette. The Assistant Paymaster General presented the Maratha chief to the Emperor, and placed before the throne his offering of 1,000 gold mohars and Rs 2,000 as present (*nazar*) and Rs 5,000 as propitiatory gift (*nisar*). Aurangzib spoke not one word of welcome or recognition in return; Shivaji was then led back from the throne and placed standing in the line of 5-*hazaris* or third-grade nobles, the work of the *darbar* proceeded, and Shivaji seemed to have been forgotten.

This was not the kind of reception he had so long been picturing to himself and expecting as almost a certainty from his many conversations with Jai Singh. He learnt from Ram Singh that he was among the commanders of 5,000. 'What!' he exclaimed, 'my little son of seven years was created a 5-*hazari* without having had to come to the Emperor's presence. My servant Netaji is a 5-*hazari*. And am I, after rendering all these services and coming all the way to the Court, to get the same low rank?' Then he asked, who the noble standing in front of him was. Ram Singh replied that it was Maharajah Jaswant Singh. At this Shivaji cried out, 'Jaswant, whose back my soldiers have seen! I to stand behind him? What does it mean?'

Next, robes of honour were given to the princes, the Grand Wazir, and Jaswant Singh, but none to Shiva. Deeply mortified he protested to Ram Singh in a high tone against this public humiliation. Saying, 'I cast off the *mansab* given to me. Kill me if you like, but I am not going to the Emperor's presence again'—he turned his back to the throne and walking away to a corner behind the pillars, sat down in nervous agitation. This disturbance was explained away to the Emperor as due to the rustic Maratha chief having suddenly taken ill in the unaccustomed heat of an imperial *darbar*. Aurangzib ordered Ram Singh to take Shiva back to his quarters and there soothe him without waiting for the close of the *darbar.*

On returning from the Court, Shivaji openly taxed the Emperor with breach of faith towards him. Ram Singh was ordered to lodge him in the Jaipur camp outside the city walls, and be responsible for his custody. Shivaji was forbidden the Court, and he found himself a prisoner in fact. His appeals to the Emperor and the prime minister for release only met with evasive replies, like 'Wait a little and I shall do what you ask for.' At the same time his position became worse than before. Fulad Khan, the police chief of Agra, by imperial order placed a large guard with artillery round Shivaji's mansion and he now became a prisoner in appearance as well as in reality. The courtiers envious of Jai Singh, the relatives of Shaista Khan in the imperial harem, and the partisans of Jaswant Singh, all combined to urge the Emperor to kill Shivaji or at least to keep him in prison for life. But the Emperor held his hand back from such open violence in view of the solemn assurance of safety given to Shivaji by Jai Singh, though he planned to send him on the Afghan expedition, where he might be easily killed on the way.

Jai Singh was placed in a dilemma by this unexpected result of Shivaji's visit to the Court. He continued to write to his Court agent, Ram Singh, to see to it that Shivaji's life was safe and the solemn assurances of the Rajput father and son remained inviolate.

10.16 Shivaji's Escape from Agra

Shivaji turned to his own inner resources to effect his liberation. He succeeded in getting permission for his Maratha escort to return to the Deccan. Being thus freed from anxiety about his followers, Shivaji set about devising plans for his own escape. He feigned illness and began to send out of his house every evening sweetmeats for Brahmans, religious mendicants and courtiers. These were carried in huge baskets slung from a pole which was borne by two men on their shoulders. The guards searched the baskets for some days and then allowed them to pass out unchallenged. This was the opportunity for which Shivaji had been waiting. In the afternoon of 19 August, he sent word to his guards that he was very ill and had taken to his bed and that they should not disturb him. His half-brother Hiraji Farzand, who looked somewhat like him, lay down on his cot, with a quilt covering all his body except the outstretched right arm adorned with Shivaji's gold wristlet,—while Shivaji and his son crouched down in two baskets, which were safely sent out shortly after sunset through the line of unsuspecting guards, being preceded and followed by baskets of real sweets.

The baskets were deposited at a lonely spot outside the city; the porters were dismissed; and then Shivaji and his son issued forth and made their way to a village 10 km (6 miles) from Agra, where the trusty Niraji Raoji (his Chief Justice) was waiting for them with horses. After a hurried consultation in a jungle the party divided; Shivaji with his son and three officers, Niraji Raoji, Datta Trimbak and Raghu-mitra, a low caste Maratha, smeared themselves with ashes like Hindu ascetics, and hastened towards Mathura, while the others took their own way homewards.

Meanwhile, at Agra, Hiraji lay in bed all that night and well into the forenoon of the next day. The guards who peeped in in the morning were satisfied when they saw Shivaji's gold bracelet on the sleeper's wrist, and a servant sitting on the floor massaging the patient's feet. About 8 a.m. Hiraji quietly walked out of the house with the servant, warning the sentries at the gate, 'Make less noise; Shivaji is ill and under treatment.' Gradually the guards' suspicion was aroused; the house seemed strangely deserted; no crowd of visitors came to see Shivaji as usual; and there was no sound, no stir in the house. They entered his room and found that the bird had flown away! They at once ran with the astounding news to their chief Fulad Khan, who reported it to the Emperor, ascribing Shivaji's flight to witchcraft and saving himself from all blame. But by this time Shivaji had had fourteen hours' clear start over his pursuers. The Emperor suspected that Shivaji had fled with the connivance of Ram Singh. The Rajput prince was punished, first by being forbidden the Court and then by being deprived of his rank and pay.

With consummate cunning Shivaji threw his pursuers off the scent, by following a route exactly opposite to that which leads to Maharashtra. Instead of moving due south-west from Agra, through Malwa and Khandesh or Gujrat, he travelled *eastwards* to Mathura and Bundelkhand, and then south-westwards though Gondwana and Golkonda. After making many hairbreadth escapes, Shivaji reached Rajgarh on 12 September, 1666.

On returning home from Agra Shivaji found the political situation in the Deccan entirely changed. The Mughal viceroy, Jai Singh, was no longer in a position to repeat his former success over the Marathas. Worn out by age, toil, disappointment and domestic anxieties, discredited in his master's eyes by the failure of his invasion of Bijapur, Mirza Rajah Jai Singh died at Burhanpur on 28 August 1667, after having been relieved of the viceroyalty by Prince Muazzam in the preceding May.

The return of the weak and indolent Muazzam and the friendly Jaswant to power in the Deccan (May 1667) relieved Shivaji of all fear from the Mughal side. It is true that Dilir Khan returned to the side of Prince Muazzam in October 1667, but the coming of this famous warrior brought no accession of strength to the imperialists. The prince was jealous of Dilir's influence and prestige at his father's Court, resented his insubordinate spirit, and regarded him as a spy on behalf of the Emperor. The proud Ruhela general, on his part, publicly slighted Maharajah Jaswant Singh, the right-hand man and trusted confidant of the prince, so that for some time to come a civil war raged in the Mughal camp in the Deccan, and no step could be taken against Shivaji. But even if the viceroy of the Deccan had been a man of greater spirit and enterprise, it would have been impossible for him for some years from this time to get adequate men and money for an attempt to crush Shivaji. The resources of the Empire had to be concentrated elsewhere to meet more pressing dangers: in March 1667, the Yusufzai rising in Peshawar broke out, which taxed the imperial strength for more than a year afterwards.

The Maratha chief, on his part, was not eager for a war with the imperialists. For three years after his return home from Agra, he lived very quietly, and avoided giving any fresh provocation to the Mughals. He wanted peace for a time to organize his government, repair and provision his forts, and consolidate and extend his power on the western coast at the expense of Bijapur and the Siddis of Janjira. He entreated Jaswant Singh to be his intermediary in making peace with the Empire. He wrote to the Maharajah, 'Mirza Rajah, my patron, is dead. If through your intercession I am pardoned, I shall send Shambhu to wait on the prince and serve as a *mansabdar* at the head of my followers wherever ordered.'

Jaswant Singh and Prince Muazzam jumped at the offer and recommended Shivaji to Aurangzib, who accepted the proposal. The Emperor recognized Shivaji's title of Rajah (early in 1668), but did not restore any of his forts except Chakan. Thus a peace was made which lasted for two years.

11 *Shivaji 1670–80*

11.1 Shivaji's Rupture with the Mughals and Recovery of Forts

In terms of his new agreement with the Mughals, Shivaji sent a Maratha contingent to Aurangabad under Pratap Rao and Niraji Raoji (August 1668). Shambhuji was created a Commander of Five Thousand again and presented with an elephant and a jewelled sword. Jagirs were assigned to him in Berar. During 1667, 1668 and 1669, Shivaji remained very quiet, as a vassal of the Mughal Government. His relations with Bijapur were also pacific. In fact, during these three years (1667–69), he was busy framing a set of very wise regulations, which laid the foundations of his Government broad and deep.

But the peace was essentially a hollow truce on both sides. Aurangzib, ever suspicious of his sons, looked upon Muazzam's friendship with Shivaji as a possible menace to his throne, and he secretly planned to entrap Shivaji a second time, or at least to seize his son and general as hostages. Another ill-judged measure of imperial parsimony was to attach a part of Shivaji's new jagir in Berar in order to recover the *lakh* of rupees advanced to him in 1666 for his journey to the Court. The news of it reached Shivaji and he broke with the Mughals at the end of the year 1669.

Shivaji opened his offensive with great vigour and immediate success. His roving bands looted Mughal territory, and he recovered several of the forts which he had ceded to Aurangzib by the Treaty of Purandar. His most conspicuous success was the capture of Kondana from Udai-bhan, its Rajput *qiladar*, (4 February 1670). Assisted by some Koli guides who knew the place well, one dark night, Tanaji Malusare, with 300 picked

Mavle infantrymen, scaled the less abrupt hillside near the Kalian gate by means of rope-ladders. The garrison fought desperately, but the Mavles with their war cry of *Hara! Hara! Mahadev!* carried havoc into their ranks. The two chiefs challenged each other and both fell down dead, after a single combat. Twelve hundred Rajputs were slain, and many others perished in trying to escape down the hillside. Shivaji named the fort *Singhgarh* after the lion-heart that had won it.

Ludi Khan, the *faujdar* of Konkan, was wounded in a battle with the Maratha forces, defeated in a second encounter and expelled from his district. The Mughal *faujdar* of Nander fled away, deserting his post. The only officer who made an attempt to uphold the imperial prestige in the Deccan was Daud Khan Qureshi, who successfully held Parnir and Junnar.

By the end of April 1670, Shivaji had looted 51 villages near Ahmadnagar, Junnar and Parenda.

11.2 Quarrel Between Muazzam and Dilir

The Mughal administration of the Deccan was, during half of the year 1670, passing through a civil war between the viceroy Shah Alam and his general Dilir Khan. The latter refused to wait on the prince, fearing that he might be treacherously killed or imprisoned by his chief! At this act of insubordination, the prince and his favourite lieutenant Jaswant wrote to the Emperor accusing Dilir Khan of rebellion. The Khan had already denounced the prince to the Emperor, saying that he was in collusion with Shivaji. Aurangzib was at this time filled with serious anxiety at Muazzam's wilful conduct, neglect of the imperial business, and failure to carry out orders. Popular voice in the Deccan could account for the open audacity and easy success of Shivaji's raids and the prince's inactivity, only by ascribing to Muazzam a treasonable design of seizing his father's throne in alliance with the Marathas.

So, at the end of March 1670, the Emperor had sent his Chamberlain *(Khan-i-saman),* Iftikhar Khan, to Aurangabad to investigate how matters really stood,—whether Muazzam was really bent on treason and what his relations with Shivaji were. This officer was now instructed to inquire into the prince's charges against Dilir Khan.

Dilir, finding his position in the Deccan intolerable, wanted to go back to the imperial Court without waiting for Shah Alam's permission;

but the prince ascribed this course to a wicked desire of creating disorder in northern India. Imperial orders reached him to force Dilir Khan back to the path of obedience. Though it was the height of the rainy season (August), the rivers swollen and the roads miry, Dilir burnt his tents and stores and fled northwards to Ujjain with his army. As soon as he started from the south, Prince Muazzam and Jaswant gave him chase with all the available Mughal troops. But on the frontier of Khandesh a letter came from the Emperor ordering Muazzam back to Aurangabad (September). For, in the meantime, Bahadur Khan, the governor of Gujrat, had taken Dilir Khan under his protection and written to the Emperor praising Dilir's loyalty and past services, and recommending that Dilir might be permitted to serve under him as *faujdar* of Kathiawad. The Emperor agreed. Muazzam promptly obeyed his father's order and returned to Aurangabad at the end of September 1670.

These internal troubles paralysed the Mughal arms, and Shivaji made the most of this golden opportunity. In March the English factors at Surat wrote, 'Shivaji marches now not as before as a thief, but in gross with an army of 30,000 men conquering as he goes, and is not disturbed though the prince (Shah Alam) lies near him.' On 3 October Shivaji plundered Surat for the second time.

11.3 Second Loot of Surat

On 2 October came successive reports of Shivaji's arrival with 15,000 horse and foot within 32 kilometers (20 miles) of Surat. All the Indian merchants of the city, and even the officers of Government had fled away in the course of the preceding day and night. On the 3rd, Shivaji attacked the city, which had recently been walled round by order of Aurangzib. After a slight resistance the defenders fled to the fort, and the Marathas possessed themselves of the whole town except only the English, Dutch and French factories, the large *New Serai* of the Persian and Turkish merchants and the *Tartar Serai* midway between the English and French houses, which was occupied by Abdullah Khan, ex-king of Kashghar, just returned from a pilgrimage to Mecca. The French bought off the raiders by means of 'valuable presents.' The English factory, though it was an open house, was defended by Streynsham Master with 50 sailors.

The Tartars made a stout resistance all the day, but finding the post untenable they fled with their king to the fort at night, giving up to plunder their house with its valuable property. The Turks in the *New Serai* successfully defended themselves, inflicting some loss on the raiders. The Marathas plundered the large houses of the city at leisure, and burnt down nearly half the town, retreating on the fifth.

An official inquiry ascertained that Shivaji had carried off 66 *lakhs* of rupees worth of booty from Surat. But the real loss of Surat was not to be estimated by the plunder which the Marathas carried off. The trade of this, the richest port of India, was practically destroyed. For several years after Shivaji's withdrawal from it, the town used to throb with panic every now and then, whenever any Maratha force came within a few days' march of it, or even at false alarms of their coming. On every such occasion the merchants would quickly remove their goods to ships, the citizens would flee to the villages, and the Europeans would hasten to Swally. Business was effectually scared away from Surat.

11.4 Shivaji Defeats Daud Khan at Dindori, October 1670; Raids Berar

After this second sack of Surat, Shivaji entered Baglana and plundered the villages at the foot of Mulhir fort. Daud Khan, who had been called away from Burhanpur to go against the Maratha raiders, reached the town of Chandor, where the road from Baglana to Nasik crosses the hill range. At the midnight following 16 October, his spies reported that Shivaji had already issued from the pass and was rapidly following the road to Nasik with half his forces, while the other half of his army was holding the pass to pick up stragglers. Daud Khan at once resumed his march. Ikhlas Khan Miana, leading the Mughal vanguard, sighted the enemy in the early morning, and without waiting for his troops to come up, recklessly charged the enemy. The Maratha rear-guard, which had faced about, was 10,000 strong and commanded by distinguished generals like Pratap Rao Gujar the Master of the Horse, Vyankoji Datto, and Makaji Anand Rao (a natural son of Shahji Bhonsle). Ikhlas Khan was very soon wounded and unhorsed. After a tune Daud arrived and reinforced his van. For hours together an obstinate and bloody battle raged. The Marathas, 'like the *Bargis* of the Deccan, fought hovering round the imperialists.' But the Bundela infantry of the Mughal army with their abundant firearms kept the enemy back. There was a lull in the fight at noon. In the evening the Marathas charged again, but were driven back, evidently by the artillery. At night the Mughals bivouacked under the autumn sky, their camp was entrenched, and they engaged in burying the dead and tending the wounded. The Marathas retreated to Konkan without further opposition. About a week later the Peshwa captured the fort of Trimbak (Nasik district). This battle neutralised the Mughal power for more than a month afterwards. The day after the fight, Daud Khan marched with the broken remnant of his army to Nasik, and halted there for one month, evidently to recoup his strength. Late in November, he removed to Ahmadnagar. Early in December a Maratha force under Pratap Rao made a raid into Khandesh, after capturing Ahivant and three other forts in Baglana on the way. Advancing by rapid marches, he plundered Bahadurpura, a village three kilometres (two miles) from Burhanpur. Passing into Berar, he fell, when least expected, upon the rich and flourishing city of Karinja, and looted it completely. Four thousand oxen and donkeys were loaded with the booty—consisting of fine cloth, silver and gold, to the value of a *krore* of rupees, captured here. All the rich men of the place were carried off for ransom. The other towns also yielded vast sums of money. That rich province, with its accumulated wealth of more than half a century of peace and prosperity, afforded a virgin soil to the plunderers in this their first raid.

While Pratap Rao had been sacking Karinja in Berar, another Maratha band under Moro Trimbak Pingle had been looting West Khandesh and Baglana, and now these two divisions united in the neighbourhood of Salhir, and laid siege to that fort. Daud Khan arrived near Mulhir at about 8 p.m., but could advance no further as most of his camp and army were lagging behind. And so he could not come to the relief of Salhir promptly.

Shivaji had invested Salhir with a force of 20,000 horse and foot, and one day finding the garrison off their guard he scaled the wall by means of rope-ladders. The *qiladar* Fathullah Khan fell fighting, and his wife's brother then gave up the fort to the enemy (*c.* 5 January 1671). The success of the Marathas continued. Their roving bands cut off the grain supply of Neknam Khan, the faujdar of Baglana.

11.5 Campaigns of Mughal Generals, 1671–72

These reverses roused Aurangzib to a sense of the gravity of the situation. He appointed Mahabat Khan to the supreme command in the Deccan. Reinforcements in men, money and provisions were poured into Baglana (January 1671).

Late in January 1671, Mahabat Khan joined Daud Khan near Chandor and the two laid siege to Ahivant, which Shivaji had recently taken. After a month the garrison capitulated. Leaving a force to hold Ahivant, Mahabat spent three months at Nasik and then went to Parnir (32 km i.e. 20 miles west of Ahmadnagar) to pass the rainy season (June to September) there.

The Emperor was dissatisfied with Mahabat Khan for the poor result of his campaign and his long spell of inactivity afterwards, and suspected him of having formed a secret understanding with Shivaji. So, he sent Bahadur Khan and Dilir Khan to the Deccan next winter. They marched from Gujrat into Baglana, laid siege to Salhir (now in Maratha hands), and leaving Ikhlas Khan Miana, Rao Amar Singh Chandawat and some other oificers to continue the siege, proceeded towards Ahmadnagar. Dilir Khan with a flying column recovered Puna massacring all the inhabitants above the age of 9 years, (end of December 1671). But the division left to besiege Salhir was attacked by a large force of Marathas under Pratap Rao, Anand Rao and the Peshwa. After an obstinate battle, Ikhlas Khan and Muhakam Singh (the son of Rao Amar Singh Chandawat) were wounded and captured, with 30 of their principal officers, while Rao Amar Singh and many other commanders as well as several thousand common soldiers were slain, and the entire siege-camp was taken by the enemy. Shortly afterwards Moro Pant captured Mulhir. This took place at the end of January and the first week of February, 1672. Shivaji's prestige and confidence in his own power were immensely increased by these successes.

About the middle of 1672, Mahabat and Shah Alam were recalled to Hindustan, and Bahadur Khan was appointed commander-in-chief and acting viceroy of the Deccan, in the place of these two, becoming substantive *subahdar* in January 1673 and holding that office till August 1677.

11.6 Maratha Occupation of the Koli Country and Demand of Chauth from Surat, 1672

On 5 June, a large Maratha army under Moro Trimbak Pingle captured Jawhar from its Koli Rajah, Vikram Shah, and seized there treasure amounting to 17 *lakhs* of rupees. Advancing further north, he took the other Koli State of Ramnagar in the first week of July.

The annexation of Jawhar and Ramnagar gave the Marathas a short, safe and easy route from Kalian up Northern Konkan to Surat, and laid that port helplessly open to invasion from the Marathas.

From the neighbourhood of Ramnagar, Moro Trimbak Pingle sent three successive letters on behalf of his master to the governor and leading traders of Surat demanding four *lakhs* of rupees as blackmail, and threatening a visit to the city in the event of their refusal.

From their base in the Koli country, a Maratha force under Moro Trimbak easily crossed the Western Ghats into the Nasik district (middle of July 1672) and plundered it, defeating Jadav Rao and Siddi Halal, the Mughal *thanadars* in charge of the southern and northern sub-divisions of the district. For this failure, these two officers were sharply censured by Bahadur Khan and they went over to the Marathas in anger!

11.7 Maratha Activities during 1673

In November next Shivaji sent his cavalry to make a lightning raid into Berar and Telingana. The Mughal general was baffled in his attempt to come up with them. The Marathas from Ramgir divided into two bodies, one escaping south into the Golkonda State and the other turning northwards to Chanda and thence westwards into Berar. The first division was headed off into Bijapur territory by Dilir Khan who captured much of their booty. The second band was opposed by Bahadur Khan near Antur (61 km i.e. 38 miles north of Aurangabad) and much plunder was recovered from them and restored to the owners. Another battle was fought 10 km (6 miles) from Aurangabad, in which the Marathas were repulsed, with a loss of 400 dead, by the Bundelas under Subh-Karn (December).

This Maratha raid into Khandesh and Berar, unlike their first incursion in December 1670, was completely foiled by the commendable activity of the Mughals.

In 1673 Bahadur Khan encamped at Pedgaon, on the north bank of the Bhima, 13 km (8 miles) due south of Chamargunda. This place became the residence of his army for many years afterwards, and here a fort and town grew up from their cantonment, which the Emperor permitted him to name Bahadurgarh.

Pedgaon occupies a position of great strategic importance. It stands on the plain just clear of the long mountain spur running eastwards from Puna. From this place the Mughal general could at will move westwards along the north of the range to protect the valleys of the Mula and the Bhima (the North Puna district), or along the south of it to guard the valleys of the Nira and the Baramati (the southern portion of the district). Northwards he could communicate with his great depot of arms and provisions at Ahmadnagar, without having to cross any river (except at the foot of that fort); and southwards he could easily invade Bijapur through the Sholapur district.

This year Shivaji's attempt to gain Shivner (the fort of Junnar) ty bribery was foiled by Abdul Aziz Khan, the Mughal governor of the fort, who was a Brahman convert to Islam and one of the most faithful and valued servants of Aurangzib. He accepted Shivaji's bribe, but at the same time secretly informed Bahadur Khan of the plot; the Maratha army fell into an ambuscade planned by the Mughals, and retired in disappointment with heavy loss.

Ali Adil Shah II died on 24 November 1672, and in a few months the government of Bijapur (with a body of four on the throne) fell into disorder and weakness. This was Shivaji's opportunity. On 6 March 1673, he got possession of Panhala a second time, by bribery, and on 27 July he secured the hill-fort of Satara by the same means. In May his men under Pratap Rao Gujar burst into the inland parts of Bijapur Kanara, looting Hubli and many other rich cities. But they received a great check from the Bijapuri general Bahlol Khan.

On *Dasahara* day (10 October 1673), an army 25,000 strong, led by Shivaji in person, burst into Bijapuri territory, plundering many rich towns, and then passed into Kanara for more plunder. Here they remained busy till the middle of December.

Late in January 1674, a Mughal army tried to descend into Konkan and cause a diversion in that quarter simultaneoulsy with the Bijapuri invasion of the Panhala region. But Shivaji stopped the paths by breaking the roads and mountain passes and keeping a constant guard at various points where the route was most difficult; and the Mughals had to return baffled.

Soon afterwards, the Mughal power in the Deccan was crippled. The rising of the Khaibar Afghans became so serious that Aurangzib had to leave Delhi (7 April) for Hasan Abdal, in order to direct the war from the rear, and next month Dilir Khan was called to the north-western frontier. Bahadur Khan was left alone in the Deccan with a greatly weakened force. This lull in the war was utilized by Shivaji to crown himself with the greatest pomp and ceremony, on 6 June 1674, at Raigarh.

11.8 Loot of Bahadur Khan's Camp and Extensive Contest with the Mughals, 1674

The coronation exhausted Shivaji's treasury and he was in need of money to pay his troops. Towards the middle of July, a body of 2,000 Maratha light cavalry, made a false demonstration and lured Bahadur Khan some 80 km (50 miles) away from his cantonments at Pedgaon, when Shivaji himself with another division, 7,000 strong, swooped down by another route on his defenceless camp, carried away a *krore* of rupees in booty and 200 fine horses. Late in October, a large army commanded by Shivaji in person crossed the Ghats into the Deccan plateau, skirted Bahadur Khan's camp, which was 'hotly alarmed,' looted several towns near Aurangabad, and then burst into Baglana and Khandesh, where they continued for more than a month (November to middle of December). Among other places they pillaged and burnt Dharangaon, 16 km (10 miles) north of Erandol, and its English factory.

Shivaji next opened delusive peace negotiations with Bahadur Khan, and for nearly three months (March–May) kept the Mughals in play, by feeding false hopes of a peace. But by the time (July 1675) that Phonda was captured, Shivaji threw off the mask and dismissed the Mughal envoys with taunts.

In January 1676 Shivaji was taken severely ill, and passed the next three months on the sick-bed at Satara. The civil war that had broken out between the Deccani and Afghan parties at Bijapur on the usurpation of the regency by Bahlol Khan (end of 1675) was Shivaji's opportunity. 'He ranged up and down, plundered and robbed without any hindrance or danger.' On 31 May Bahadur Khan opened a vigorous and long campaign against Bijapur, the consequence of which was to drive the new regent Bahlol Khan into the arms of Shivaji.

11.9 Shivaji's Preparations for his Karnatak Expedition

In January next (1677), the Maratha king set out on the greatest expedition of his life, the invasion of the Eastern Karnatak. The political situation in the neighbouring countries was eminently favourable to Shivaji's design. The Emperor's best troops were still engaged in controlling the revolted hillmen of the Afghan frontier. At Bijapur the Mughal viceroy openly took the side of the Deccani party and on 31 May opened a campaign against Bijapur which was to continue for more than a year. Shivaji's clever diplomacy won a complete triumph over Bahadur Khan, who had already coquetted with the Maratha king for a friendly understanding. And now, on the eve of opening the Mughal campaign against Bijapur (May 1676), it was as much his interest to make friends with the Marathas on his right flank as it was Shivaji's to secure Mughal neutrality in his rear during his invasion of'the Karanatak. Shivaji sent his Chief Justice, Niraji Raoji, to Bahadur Khan, with costly presents and induced him to promise neutrality during his projected absence in the Karnatak, the conquest of which was expected to take one year.

With Golkonda close friendship and co-operation were secured. Madanna Pandit, the all-powerful wazir of Abul Hasan Qutb Shah, had already made a subsidiary alliance with Shivaji, promising him an annual tribute of one *lakh* of *hun* for the defence of the realm. Prahlad Niraji, a shrewd diplomat, had been posted at Haidarabad as Maratha envoy. Shivaji decided to get from Golkonda the expenses of the campaign and the assistance of an auxiliary force, by promising to Qutb Shah a share of his conquests.

11.10 Shivaji's Alliance with Golkonda and Conquest of the Karnatak

Shivaji started from Raigarh at the beginning of January 1677, and advanced due east by regular marches, at the head of 50,000 armed men, arriving at Haidarabad early in February. On entering the Qutb

Shahi territory he had issued strict orders to his men not to rob or molest any inhabitant of the country, and had enforced obedience by severe punishment.

The city of Haidarabad was gaily decorated by the people to give a royal welcome to the great friend and protector of its king. The Maratha army marched through the streets in perfect order and halted before the Dad Mahal palace, while Shivaji with five of his officers went upstairs and had a friendly conversation with the Sultan for three hours. Abul Hasan, being very favourably impressed by Shivaji's personal charm, character and ability, and the strength and discipline of his army, bade his wazir grant him whatever he wanted. After some discussion a secret compact was made regarding the coming campaign. The Sultan was to pay Shivaji a subsidy of 3,000 *hun* a day, or four and a half *lakhs* of rupees a month, and send an army of 5,000 men in charge of one of his generals *(sar-i-lashkar),* Mirza Muhammad Amin, to co-operate in the conquest of the Karnatak. In return for this aid, Shivaji promised his ally such parts of his conquest in the Karnatak as had not belonged to his father Shahji. The defensive alliance against the Mughals was strengthened anew with solemn oaths. Qutb Shah promised to pay his annual subsidy of one *lakh* of *hun* regularly and to keep a Maratha ambassador at his Court, as the price of his protection against the Mughals.

The dominions of the vassals of the fallen Vijaynagar Empire had been mostly seized by Adil Shah and Qutb Shah. Bijapur now possessed northern and eastern Mysore and the Madras plain (or Karnatak lowlands) from the Palar river southwards to the Kolerun (branch of the Kaveri), i.e., the country from Vellore to near Tanjore, while Golkonda had annexed the region north of the Palar, namely from Chicacole to Sadras. In the Karnatak plain the local governors of Bijapur were Nasir Muhammad Khan (a son of the ex-wazir Khan Muhammad) with his seat at Jinji, and south of him Sher Khan Lodi (an Afghan *protege* of Bahlol Khan) with his capital at Vali-kanda-puram (in the north of the Trichinopoly district). Further south were the Hindu kingdoms of Tanjore (conquered by Shivaji's half-brother Vyankaji in 1675) and Madura. All these powers were ever bent on fighting with and annexing one another's territories. Taking advantage of these internal dissensions, the Qutb-Shahi minister Madanna planned to reconquer Bijapuri Karnatak with the help of Shivaji and restore Hindu rule there.

Leaving Haidarabad after a month, Shivaji hastened southwards by way of Karnul, Shri Shailam, Anantpur, Tirupati, Kalahastri and Peddapolam (11 km i.e. 7 miles west of Madras) in the first week of May. He then took the strong fort of Jinji by treaty with its owner and laid siege to Vellore, whose governor ultimately yielded it for a price after a heroic defence of fourteen months, on 21 August 1678.

The flood of Maratha invasion swept over the Karnatak plains. Only a few fortified places offered resistance, the rich men fleeing to the shelter of the woods or the European forts on the coast at the news of their approach. Sher Khan Lodi was defeated at Tiruvadi (20 km i.e. 13 miles west of Cuddalore) on 26 June and forced to give up all his territories. Then marching to Tirumala-vadi, on the north bank of the Kolerun river, Shivaji invited Vyankaji to meet him and tried to wrest from him three-fourths of what their father had left at his death. But Vyankaji cleverly escaped (23 July) to Tanjore, and Shivaji set out on his return, visiting many holy places on the way. The whole of the Karnatak was 'peeled to the bones' by his system of organized plunder and exaction.

The territory annexed by Shivaji in the Karnatak in the course of 1677 and 1678 was sixty leagues by forty and estimated to yield 20 lakhs of *hun* a year, and it included a hundred forts.

Shivaji left the Madras plains early in November 1677 and entered the Mysore plateau, conquering its eastern and central parts. From Sera in the heart of the Mysore kingdom, he marched home by way of Kopal, Gadag, Bankapur, Belvadi (in the Belgaum district) and Turgal, and returned to his own stronghold of Panhala in the first week of April, 1678.

11.11 The Mughals, Bijapur and Shivaji, 1678–79

In May 1678 the Marathas made a second attempt to get possession of Shivner. They invested the village (of Junnar) at its foot, and at night tried to scale the fort. 'Three hundred Marathas climbed the fort-walls at night by means of nooses and rope-ladders. But Abdul Aziz Khan was an expert *qiladar;* he slew all the infantry of Shivaji who had entered the fort, and sent a message to Shivaji in these words: 'So long as I am *qiladar*, you will never take this fort.'

A rupture now took place between Shivaji and Qutb Shah, and the diplomatic alliance so patiently built up by Madanna Pandit fell to the ground. Qutb Shah's indignation had been rising as he found himself made a mere cat's paw of Shivaji in the Karnatak adventure. He had borne all the expenses of the expedition and supplied artillery and an auxiliary force for it. But not one of the conquered forts was given to him, not one pice of his contribution was repaid out of the fabulous booty carried away by Shivaji from that land of gold. So Abul Hasan arranged for a peace between the new Bijapuri regent, Siddi Masaud, and his rivals (especially Sharza Khan), helped him with money to pacify the unpaid mutinous soldiery, and bound him to wage war against Shivaji and 'confine him to Konkan.' But Dilir Khan spoiled the whole plan by an attack on Bijapur.

Shivaji's eldest son Shambhuji was the curse of his old age. This youth of twenty-one was violent, capricious, unsteady, thoughtless and notoriously depraved in his morals. He had been sent to Parli for being instructed by the saint Ramdas, but escaped with his wife Yesu Bai and a few comrades to join Dilir Khan (13 December 1678). The Khan with his valuable new ally halted at Akluj (80 km i.e. 50 miles south of Bahadurgarh) for some time to prepare for the invasion of Bijapur.

In this danger Siddi Masaud immediately asked for help from Shivaji, as agreed upon. The Rajah sent six to seven thousand well-armed cavalry to guard Bijapur. Masaud could not fully trust his ally. Then Shivaji threw off the mask. He began to plunder and devastate Adil-Shahi territory again. Masaud now made peace with Dilir Khan. A Mughal force was invited to Bijapur and royally welcomed.

Dilir Khan next marched to the fort of Bhupalgarh, (32 km i.e. 20 miles north west of Jath and 78 km i.e. 45 miles south west of Pandharpur), which Shivaji had built as a storehouse of his property and a refuge for the families of his subjects in the neighbourhood during his wars with the Mughals. The assault was launched about 9 a.m., on 2 April, 1679, and the Mughals fought with vigour till noon, when they captured the fort, after heavy slaughter on both sides. Vast quantities of grain and other properties and large number of people were captured by the victors. Seven hundred survivors of the garrison were deprived of one hand and then set free; the other captives were evidently sold into slavery. The fall of Bhupalgarh was followed by a period of puzzling intrigue and counter-intrigue between the Mughal viceroy and the Bijapur nobility, and also quarrels between Masaud and Sharza Khan, Masaud and Dilir, and Masaud and his favourite Venkatadri Murari. About the middle of this year Shivaji sent to Aurangzib a well-reasoned and spirited letter of protest against the *jiziya*, which was drafted by Nila Prabhu in eloquent Persian. (*History of Aurangzib,* Vol. III. Ch. 34 Appendix.)

11.12 Last Campaign of Shivaji

On 18 August, 1679 Dilir crossed the Bhima at Dhulkhed, 64 km (40 miles) due north of Bijapur, and opened a new campaign against Masaud. That helpless regent begged Shivaji, who undertook the defence of Bijapur with great promptitude. Shambhuji fled from Dilir and returned to Panhala about the 4 December.

On 4 November, Shivaji marched out of Selgur (92 km i.e. 55 miles west of Bijapur). His cavalry, 18,000 strong, rapidly moved northwards in two parallel divisions under Shivaji and Anand Rao, and poured like a flood through the districts of Mughal Deccan, plundering and burning all the places in their track and taking an immense booty in cash and kind. In the middle of the month, Jalna, a populous trading town, 64 km (40 miles) east of Aurangabad, was captured and plundered. Here the godly saint, Sayyid Jan Muhammad, had his hermitage in a garden in the suburbs. Most of the wealthy men of Jalna had taken refuge in this hermitage with their money and jewels. The raiders, finding very little booty in the town and learning of the concealment of the wealth in the saint's abode, entered it and robbed the refugees, wounding many of them. The holy man appealed to them to desist, but they only abused and threatened him for his pains. Then the man of God, 'who had marvellous efficacy of prayer,' cursed Shivaji, and popular belief ascribed the Rajah's death five months afterwards to these curses.

After having thoroughly plundered and devastated Jalna for four days, as the Marathas loaded with booty consisting of 'countless gold, silver, jewels, cloths, horses, elephants, and camels,' were retreating, an enterprising Mughal officer Ranmast Khan, attacked their rear-guard. Shidhoji Nimbalkar with 5,000 men held him in check for three days, but was at last slain with many of his men. In the meantime, very large reinforcements were hastenting up to the Mughals from Aurangabad under Kesari Singh and Sardar Khan. When these came to a halt 10 km (six miles) from the fighters, Kesari Singh at night sent a secret message to Shivaji as a brother Hindu, advising him to run away at once before the Mughals could complete their circle and cut him off. Shivaji trusted his chief spy, Bahirji, under whose skilful guidance the Maratha army escaped by an obscure path after three days and nights of anxious and ceaseless marching. But they had to sacrifice much of their booty, besides losing 4,000 horsemen killed and Hambir Rao wounded. From this disastrous expedition, Shivaji returned to Patta-garh (about 22 November) and rested his exhausted and stricken army for some days, and then, at the beginning of December, went to Raigarh. A Maratha division raided Khandesh, in the last week of November, burning and plundering Dharangaon, Chopra, and many other considerable towns adjacent to it.

The character of his eldest son filled Shivaji with the gloomiest anticipations of the future. A profligate, capricious and cruel youth, devoid of every spark of honour, patriotism or religious fervour, could not be left sole master of Maharashtra. Shivaji tried hard to conciliate and reason with Shambhuji. But a born judge of character like Shivaji must have soon perceived that his sermons were falling on deaf ears, and hence his last days were clouded by despair. On 23 March, 1680, the Rajah was seized with fever and blood dysentery. The illness continued for twelve days, and finally the maker of the Maratha nation passed away at noon on Sunday, 4 April, 1680, the full moon of the month of Chaitra. He had not yet completed the 53rd year of his life.

11.13 Shivaji's Kingdom, Army and Revenue

At the time of his death Shivaji's kingdom included all the country (except the Portuguese possessions) stretching from Ramnagar (modern Dharampur State in the Surat Agency) in the north, to Karwar or the Gangavati river in the Bombay district of Kanara, in the south. Its eastern boundary embraced Baglana in the north, then ran southwards along an irregular shifting line through the middle of the Nasik and Puna districts, and encircled the whole of the Satara and much of the Kolhapur districts. A recent but permanent acquisition was the western Karnatak or the Kanarese-speaking country extending from Belgaum to the bank of the Tungabhadra opposite the Bellary district of the Madras Presidency.

Shivaji's latest annexation was the country extending from the Tungabhadra opposite Kopal to Vellore and Jinji, i.e., the northern, central and eastern parts of the present kingdom of Mysore and portions of the Madras districts of Bellary, Chittur and Arcot. This province was really held by an army of occupation and remained unsettled in 1680.

Outside these settled or half-settled parts of his kingdom, there was a wide and very fluctuating belt of land, subject to his power but not owning his sovereignty. In these he levied blackmail (*khandani,* i.e., ransom, in Marathi), as regularly as his army could repeat its annual visit to them. The money paid was popularly called *chauth,* because it amounted to *one-fourth* of the standard assessment of the land revenue of a place. The payment of the *chauth* merely saved a place from the unwelcome presence of the Maratha soldiers and civil underlings, but did not impose on Shivaji any corresponding obligation to guard the district from foreign invasion or internal disorder. His revenue is put by his courtier Sabhasad at the round figure of one *krore* of *hun,* while the *chauth* when collected in full brought in another 80 *lakhs.*

It was Shivaji's settled policy to use his army to draw supplies from foreign dominions every year. 'The troops were to go into cantonments in the home territory during the rainy season (June–September). On the day of *Dasahara* (early in October) the army should set out from the camp for the country selected by the Rajah. The troops were to subsist in foreign parts for eight months and also levy contributions. No woman, female slave or dancing-girl was to be allowed to accompany the army. A soldier keeping any of these was to be beheaded. No woman or child was to be taken captive, but men only. Brahmans were not to be molested, nor taken as hostages for ransom. On return home the booty of every soldier was to be handed over to the State.'

11.14 Shivaji's Central Administration

Shivaji governed by the advice and assistance of a council of eight ministers *(Ashta Pradhan),* composed of (1) the *Peshwa* or *Mukhya Pradhan,* i.e., the prime minister, (2) the *Majmuadar* (Sanskrit title *Amatya*) or accountant-general, (3) the *Waqia-naviis* (Sanskrit *Mantri*) who compiled a daily record of the king's doings and Court incidents, (4) the *Surnis* (Sanskrit *Sachiv*) or superintendent of correspondence, (5) the *Dabir* (Sanskrit *Sumant*) or foreign secretary and head of the intelligence department, (6) the *Sar-i-naubat* (Sanskrit *Senapati*) or commander-in-chief, (7) the *Pandit Rao* (corresponding to the Persian *Sadr* and *Muhtasib* in one), whose duty it was to decide theological questions and caste disputes, to punish heresy and impiety, and to reward learned Brahmans out of the royal alms fund, and (8) the *Nyayadhis* or chief justice. All these ministers with the exception of the Senapati were of the Brahman caste, and all the first six of them had to take command of armies when necessary. The actual work of State correspondence was conducted by members of the Prabhu (Kayastha) caste, most of whom knew Persian well. The pay-accounts of the army were kept by a class of officers called *sabnises* (Persian *Bakhshi*).

But this Council of Eight Ministers was in no sense a cabinet. They merely acted as the king's secretaries; they had no initiative, no power to dictate any policy to him by the threat of resignation. Their function was purely advisory when the king was in a mood to listen to advice, and at other times they merely carried out his general instructions and supervised the details of their respective departments. The Peshwa was more honoured than the other seven *Pradhans,* but they were in no sense subordinate to him. The solidarity of the British Cabinet, as well as its power, was wanting in the Maratha Council of Eight. Shivaji kept all the strings of the administration in his own hands, like Louis XIV or Federick the Great.

11.15 Shivaji's Character and Place in History

But whatever might be the moral quality or the means he employed, his success was a dazzling reality. This jagirdar's son proved himself the irrepressible opponent of the Mughal empire and all its resources. Aurangzib was in despair as to how he could subdue Shivaji, seeing that nearly all his great generals had failed in the Deccan.

To the Hindu world in that age of renewed persecution, Shivaji appeared as the star of a new hope, the protector of their religion.

Shivaji's private life was marked by a high standard of morality. He was a devoted son, a loving father and an attentive husband. Intensely religious from his very boyhood, by instinct and training alike, he remained throughout life abstemious, free from vice, and respectful to holy men. The liberality of his faith is proved by his impartial respect for the holy men of all sects (Muslim as much as Hindu) and toleration of all creeds. His chivalry to women and strict enforcement of morality in his camp was a wonder in that age and has extorted the admiration of hostile critics like Khafi Khan.

He had the born leader's personal magnetism and threw a spell over all who knew him, drawing the best elements of the country to his side and winning the most devoted service from his officers, while his dazzling victories and ever-ready smile made him the idol of his soldiery. His royal gift of judging character was one of the main causes of his success, as his selection of generals and governors, diplomatists and secretaries was never at fault. His army organization was a model of efficiency; everything was provided beforehand and kept in its proper place under a proper caretaker; an excellent spy system supplied him in advance with the most minute information about the theatre of his intended campaign; divisions of his army were combined or dispersed at will over long distances without failure; the enemy's pursuit or obstruction was successful met, and yet the booty was rapidly and safely conveyed home without any loss. His in-born military genius is proved by his instinctively adopting that system of warfare which was most suited to the racial character of his soldiers, the nature of the country, the weapons of the age, and the internal condition of his enemies. His light cavalry, stiffened with swift-footed infantry, was irresistible in the age of Aurangzib.

Shivaji's real greatness lay in his character and practical ability, rather than in originality of conception or length of political vision. Unfailing insight into the character of others, efficiency of arrangements, and instinctive perception of what was practicable and most profitable under the circumstances (*tact des chases possibles*),—*these* were the causes of his success in life. The imperishable achievement of his life was the welding of the scattered Marathas into a nation, and his most precious legacy was the spirit that he breathed into his people. And he achieved this in the teeth of the opposition of four mighty Powers like the Mughal Empire, Bijapur, Portuguese India, and the Abyssinians of Janjira.

No other Hindu has shown such constructive genius in modern times. He has proved by his example that the Hindu race can build a nation, found a State, defeat enemies; they can conduct their own defence; they can protect and promote literature and art, commerce and industry; they can maintain navies and ocean-trading fleets of their own, and conduct naval battles on equal terms with foreigners. He taught the modern Hindus to rise to the full stature of their growth.

12 *Decline and Fall of Bijapur*

12.1 Jai Singh's Invasion of Bijapur, 1665–66

Aurangzib had reason to be displeased with the Sultan of Bijapur. Adil Shah had taken advantage of the war of Mughal succession to evade the fulfilment of the promises made by him in the treaty of August 1657. During Jai Singh's campaign against Shivaji he found out that the Bijapur Government had made a secret alliance with the Maratha chief and helped him with lands, money and other requisites. Above all, the war with Shivaji being over in June 1665, the vast army assembled in the Deccan under Jai Singh's command was standing idly, and profitable employment had to be found for it. An invasion of Bijapur offered the best means of doing it.

In the Treaty of Purandar, Jai Singh's clever diplomacy had detached Shivaji from Bijapur and, indeed, thrown a bone of perpetual contention between the two. The Maratha chief had promised to assist the Mughals in their intended invasion of Bijapur by furnishing 2,000 cavalry of his son Shambhuji's contingent as a mansabdar and 7,000 expert infantry under his own personal command.

Jai Singh also intrigued with many of the feudatories of Bijapur and sent them letters offering them service under the Delhi empire. The old Mughal policy of seducing the ministers and generals of Bijapur was pursued vigorously and with a lavish disregard of expenditure. The most eminent of these deserters was Mulla Ahmad, an Arab of the Navaiyat clan settled in Konkan, who held the second place among the Bijapur nobility. He joined Jai Singh on 29 September, 1665, and was at once created a *6-hazari* in the Mughal peerage; but he fell ill on the way to Delhi and died about 18 December.

Before opening the campaign Jai Singh employed diplomatic trickery, of which he was a past master, to throw Adil Shah into a sense of false security by pretending that he had received no order to invade Bijapur. He also made conciliatory overtures to Qutb Shah to induce him to stand aloof from Bijapur in the coming war.

At last, all his preparations being complete, Jai Singh set out on 19 November 1665 from the foot of fort Purandar, at the head of 40,000 imperial troops, besides 2,000 Maratha cavalry and 7,000 infantry under Netaji Palkar. During the first month of the campaign, Jai Singh's march was an uninterrupted triumph. The Bijapuri forts on the way,—Phaltan, Thathvada, Khatav, and finally Mangalvide (only 84 km i.e. 52 miles north of Bijapur)—were either evacuated or surrendered at call. The first battle with the enemy took place on 25 December. That day a detachment under Dilir Khan and Shivaji marched sixteen kilometres (ten miles) from the imperial camp and fought a Bijapuri army of 12,000 men under the famous generals Sharza Khan and Khawas Khan and their Maratha allies Jadav Rao of Kaliani and Vyankaji, the half-brother of Shivaji. The Deccanis evaded the charges of the heavy cavalry of Delhi, but harassed them by their 'cossack' tactics, forming four divisions and fighting loosely. After a long contest, Dilir Khan's tireless energy and courage broke the enemy by repeated charges, and they retired in the evening. But as soon as the victors began their return march, the elusive enemy reappeared and galled them severely from the two wings and rear. At dawn, 24 December, Sharza Khan with 6,000 cavalry came to the fort of Mangalvide by forced marches. The Mughal faujdar Sarfaraz Khan, disobeyed Jai Singh's instructions, sallied out to fight him and was slain. The remnant of his force fled back to the fort.

After a two day's stay, Jai Singh resumed his march and on 28 December, fought another battle. The Deccani horsemen, as usual, tried to envelop the Mughals, breaking into several loose bodies, each of which attacked its immediate opponent at the first sign of any weakness or disorder in the ranks of the latter. Finally the Mughals charged and the Deccanis gave way, but they kept up a Parthian fight for the ten kilometres (six miles) they were chased. Next day, 29 December, Jai Singh arrived within 20 km (12 miles) of Bijapur. This was destined to be the farthest point of his advance, because by this time Ali Adil Shah II's military preparations had been completed, and his capital and its environs had been rendered impregnable to attack; its regular garrison had been strengthened by 30,000 Karnataki infantry, renowned for their fighting quality. In addition to this, the country round, for a radius of ten kilometres (six miles), had been remorselessly laid waste; the two large tanks of Nauraspur and Shahpur had been drained dry; all the wells in the environs had been filled up with earth; every building had been razed to the ground and every tree cut down, so that 'not a green branch or shade-giving wall was left standing' to afford shelter to the invaders. At the same time a picked force under the noted generals Sharza Khan and Siddi Masaud had been sent off to invade the imperial dominions and create a diversion in Jai Singh's rear, while the main Bijapuri army hovered round that general's camp.

Jai Singh, in his eagerness to grasp the golden chance of attacking Bijapur while undefended and torn by domestic factions, had not summoned big artillery and siege material from Parenda fort but had arrived near Mangalvide by rapid marches. And now his position was critical. A large army was coming from Golkonda to the help of Adil Shah, and the invaders were faced with starvation.

12.2 Jai Singh Forced to Retreat from Bijapur, 1666

So, the Mughal general began his retreat on 5 January, 1666, the Bijapuris hanging on his rear. He reached Sultanpur (on the Sina), 28 km (16 miles) south of Parenda on the 27th and halted there for 24 days.

In this month of January, four great misfortunes befell the Mughals. First, about the 12th, a brave Afghan captain named Sikandar (the brother of Fath Jang Khan), when convoying provisions, material and munitions to the army of Jai Singh, was surprised by a superior Bijapuri force under Sharza Khan 14 km (eight miles) south of Parenda; he was cut down, and all his rich convoy was plundered.

Then, on the 16th, Shiva who had at his own request beea detached to make a diversion in the west by attacking Panhala, met with a dismal failure in assaulting that fort, and lost a thousand men. About the 20th came the bad news that, Shivaji's chief officer Netaji, who was dissatisfied with his master on being reprimanded for his disobedience and slackness during the assault on Panhala, had deserted to Bijapur for a bribe of four *lakhs* of *hun* and led raiding parties into Mughal territory. Jai Singh lured him back (20 March) with many persuasive letters and the acceptance of all his high demands. The fourth misfortune of the Mughals was the sending of 12,000 cavalry and 40,000 infantry by the Sultan of Golkonda to assist Adil Shah.

In his retreat from the environs of Bijapur Jai Singh had to fight two severe battles (on 11 and 22 January), besides almost daily skirmishes by his foraging parties. The raiding parties of Bijapur, under Bahlol Khan and Netaji, in the lately annexed Bidar-Kaliani districts could no longer be ignored. And, therefore, on 20 February Jai Singh issued from his camp at Sultanpur and marched due east into the disturbed area.

The third stage of the war now began, which was to end with his retreat to Bhum, 30 km (18 miles) north east of Parenda, early in June next. During these three months and a half Jai Singh moved about in the small quadrilateral formed by the Bhima on the west and the Manjira on the east, the cities of Dharur in the north and Tuljapur in the south. In the course of this campaign, he fought four more bloody but fruitless battles like those described before; each time the Bijapuris were repulsed in the field and driven some distance off, but they were not crushed, and continued as before to hover round the Mughal camp, cut off stragglers and weak foraging parties, and stop the arrival of supplies.

Mangalvide was too far from the Mughal frontier and too isolated a post to be held easily; Jai Singh, therefore, detached 24 May) Dilir Khan to remove the guns and materials from the fort, distribute the grain and other property, burn whatever could not be carried away, and dismantle the fortifications. This was done. Phaltan had been deemed untenable and its Mughal garrison withdrawn as early as the preceding February, so that not a single place remained to the Mughals out of the gains of the first campaign.

Jai Singh's return march northwards began on 31 May. Reaching Bhum (about 10 June), he halted there for 3 ½ months, and then, on 28 September, started for the environs of Bir (56 km i.e. 37 miles north of Bhum) where he stayed till 17 November, finally reaching Aurangabad on the 26 of that month. Both the combatants were sick of the war, and longed for peace; and negotiations were reopened. The Bijapuris retired within their own frontiers when the Mughals did the same.

12.3 Jai Singh's Failure and Death

Jai Singh's invasion of Bijapur was a military failure. Not an inch of territory, not a stone of a fortress, not a pice of indemnity was gained by it. As a financial speculation it was even more disastrous. In addition to thirty *lakhs* of rupees from the imperial treasury, Jai Singh had spent more than a *krore* out of his own pocket. Profuse as Jai Singh's payments were, they were exceeded by the engagements he made on behalf of his master. Every petty Muslim captain of Maratha chieftain, who offered to desert from Bijapur, was promised a title and a high *mansab* in the Mughal service, besides a large cash bounty for equipping his retainers.

The Emperor was highly displeased with Jai Singh for the military failure and money losses of the invasion of Bijapur. The unhappy general received (October 1666) orders to return to Aurangabad, and on the 23 March following (1667) he was recalled to Court and the viceroyalty of the Deccan was given to Prince Muazzam, assisted by Jaswant Singh. The Rajput veteran of a hundred fights made over charge to his successor at Aurangabad in May 1667, and bent his way towards Northern India in humiliation and disappointment. Not a pice of the *krore* of rupees of his own money that he had spent in the Bijapur war would be repaid by his master. Broken-hearted from disgrace and disappointment and labouring under disease and old age, Jai Singh died from an accidental fall from his elephant on reaching Burhanpur, on 18 August, 1667.

But the Rajah had never a fair chance in this war. His army was hopelessly inadequate for the conquest of so large and rich a kingdom; his war material and food supply were sufficient for a month or two only, and he had no siege-guns. At the same time the power of the Bijapur State was unimpaired in contrast with its exhausted condition when Aurangzib himself captured its capital 20 years later. Small as Jai Singh's army was, relative to the task laid upon it, he was badly served by his subordinates. Many of his officers were unreliable, and refused or delayed in carrying out his orders. And the imperial officers at the base did not keep his army regularly supplied with grain. Success under these conditions was not humanly possible.

12.4 Military Aristocracy Governing Bijapur Provinces Their Character

Military revolt was the curse of the Bijapur sultanate, and the decline of its royal power was attended by the dismemberment of the kingdom into a number of military fiefs. The government was a pure military occupation, and its power was upheld by a number of mercenary generals among whom all offices of power and trust were divided. The chief races who formed the dominant aristocracy were the Afghans (with their fiefs in the western parts, from Kopal to Bankapur), the Abyssinians (ruling over the eastern province, viz., the Karnul district and a part of the Raichur Doab), the Sayyids who headed the Mahdavi sect, and the Arab Mullas of the Navaiyat clan of Konkan. The Hindus, both public servants and vassal Rajahs, were a depressed class. The official body that had made the State its own was alien in origin; tut it had settled in the soil with no idea of returning to its original homes, and it had practically converted itself into a hereditary feudal baronage, each race of which married within its own tribe and thus could not become assimilated to the native population. This alien aristocracy of office naturally formed no integral part of the State. Its aim was purely personal gain, and so long as the pay and estates of its members were secured they did not care who was the sovereign of the country of which they were nominally a part; they had no patriotism because they had no *patria*; they were truly political Bedouins, 'orphans of the heart,' nomads who lived in India but were not of it.

The State founded on the loyalty of such public servants is an edifice built on sand. At each foreign conquest the people merely changed masters. Their life was untouched by the political change, and they, therefore, could not be expected to rally round the crown in its hour of need, as the citizens of a national State are sure to do. The decline of the Adil Shahi monarchy merely illustrates this well-known principle.

12.5 Decline of the Adil Shahi Kings; Struggles for the Regency

Under Muhammad Adil Shah the kingdom of Bijapur reached its greatest expansion, and stretched from the Arabian Sea to the Bay of Bengal, across the entire Indian peninsula. His realm had an annual revenue of 7 *krores* and 84 *lakhs* of rupees, besides 5 ½ *krores* of tribute due from vassal Rajahs and Zamindars. The strength of the army establishment was 80,000 cavalry and 250,000 infantry, besides 530 war elephants.

The storm of Mughal invasion (1657) having blown over, the Bijapur State next showed a revival of power for some time. Ali Adil Shah II developed great capacity and enterprising spirit from 1666. He took the field in person, curbed the growing power of Shivaji, forced the refractory Abyssinian officers of the N.E. province (Karnul) back into submission, humbled the rebel Rajah of Bednur, and finally rolled back the flood of Mughal invasion under Jai Singh. Thereafter the Sultan gave himself up to the pleasures of the harem and the wine-cup, for the rest of his life; but his able *wazir*, Abdul Muhammad, continued to carry on the administration with great success. With the death of Ali Adil Shah II on 24 November 1672, the glory of Bijapur departed. His son Sikandar, a boy of four, was placed on the throne, and the reign of selfish regents commenced which finally ruined the monarchy.

The history of Bijapur from 1672 to the extinction of the dynasty in 1686 is really the history of its *wazirs.* It was a period marked by chronic civil war among the factious nobles, independence of the provincial governors, paralysis of the central administration in the capital itself, occasional but indecisive Mughal invasions and a secret alliance but pretended hostility with the Marathas.

Ali Adil Shah II died on 24 November 1672, and immediately afterwards Khawas Khan, the Abyssinian leader of the Deccani Musalman party, seized the supreme power and crowned the boy Sikandar, the last of the Adil-Shahs. The new prime minister broke his word to the other nobles and refused to yield to them the forts he had promised. At this, the able and experienced *ex-wazir* Adbul Muhammad left the Court in disgust. 'The infancy of the king and the incapacity of the regent threw the monarchy into a decline. Disturbances broke out on all sides.'

'The Emperor began to send Bahadur Khan repeated orders for invading Bijapur.' But the task was obviously impossible for Bahadur Khan with the ordinary contingent of a provincial governor. What the Khan did was to advance from the seat of his government to Pedgaon (afterwards named by him *Bahadur-garh*), a strategic point on the Bhima river 88 km (55 miles) due east of Puna and nearly midway between Aurangabad and Bijapur. His aim was to direct his main forces against Shivaji and win territory from Bijapur by corrupting its nobles and threatening war, rather than by actual invasion.

The Afghans formed 'more than half the Bijapuri army.' Their leader was Abdul Karim, surnamed Bahlol Khan II, whose fief lay at Bankapur. Their harsh demand for arrears of pay and open opposition to his administration had driven the regent to secretly beg the aid of the Mughal viceroy in 'pacifying the Afghans or extirpating them.' So, Bahadur advanced to the bank of the Bhima river, met Khawas Khan (19 October), and arranged terms for suppressing the Afghan faction at Bijapur and making war on Shiva.

12.6 Regency of Bahlol Khan, 1675–77

Sure of Mughal support, the regent formed plans for overthrowing Bahlol Khan, who was commander-in-chief and 'used often to disobey and oppose Khawas Khan.' The Afghan chief, getting scent of the matter, forestalled the blow. Inviting Khawas to a dinner, he plied him with wine, seized him (11 November), and sent him off as a prisoner to Bankapur. He then entered the citadel of Bijapur and made himself *wazir* without a blow. 'Khawas Khan had been prime minister and virtual king for three years, during which, owing to the Khan's indolence and incompetence, affairs went from bad to worse.' But bad as this Abyssinian's regency had been, the rule of Bahlol Khan and his Afghans proved even worse. After seizing the regency he began to place his Afghan followers and relatives in power and removed the Deccanis from office, one by one, and even expelled them from the city. Great disorder broke out throughout the kingdom. The Deccani party was up in arms against Bahlol.

Bahlol Khan's administration rested on the ability and vigour of one man, his chief counsellor Khizr Khan Pani. On 12 January 1676, this man was stabbed to death by a Deccani. Bahlol immediately murdered his helpless captive Khawas Khan (18 January), and then set out from Bijapur to punish Munihaj and other Deccanis. On 21 March a bloody battle was fought between the men of Sharza Khan and the army of the regent near Mokah, in which the Afghans triumphed. Sharza took refuge with Bahadur Khan at Sholapur, who now sided with the Deccani party and denounced Afghan rule at Bijapur. He marched southwards from Sholapur, crossing the Bhima near Halsangi on 31 May; his cavalry began to ravage the environs of Bijapur city. On 13 June, on a plain between Aliabad and Indi (48 km i.e. 30 miles north-east of Bijapur), Bahlol Khan offered him battle. The brunt of the Deccani attack fell on the Mughal right wing under Islam Khan (governor of Malwa) and his Turks, who repelled two onsets. But his elephant stampeded into the enemy's ranks during a gun-powder explosion and Islam Khan and his son were slain. The Mughal base camp on the other side of the Bhima was looted by the Afghans and its guards put to the sword, while the flooded river prevented Bahadur Khan from sending succour to it.

Bahadur Khan's position was further endangered by the arrival of a vast Golkonda army, under the premier Madanna Pandit, to reinforce the Bijapuris. But the newcomers were bribed by the Mughal general, and had also (as I suspect) some difference With Bahlol Khan, and therefore retreated without doing anything. Bahadur Khan marched on the Halsangi, where he assembled a vast force. This huge demonstration of strength cowed Bahlol Khan, who then secured safety for himself by agreeing not to hinder the Mughal conquest of certain Bijapuri districts. Bahadur Khan now took easy possession of Naldurg (14 May 1677) and Kulbarga (7 July) by bribery. But the viceroy's position was rendered untenable by a conflict of policy between him and his second in command, Dilir Khan, (arrived in June 1776), who as an Afghan became the bosom friend of Bahlol Khan and the patron of the Afghan faction at Bijapur. Dilir and Bahlol wrote to the Emperor accusing Bahadur Khan of having formed a secret understanding with the three Deccani Powers and of being really hostile to the success of the imperial enterprises there.

12.7 Dilir Khan and Bahlol Invade Golkonda, 1677

Aurangzib recalled Bahadur, who left the province early in September 1677, and Dilir continued to officiate as viceroy of the Deccan till October 1678. Looking collectively at the Mughal gains in the Deccan during the first twenty years of Aurangzib's reign, we find that he had in 1657 annexed Kaliani and Bidar in the north-eastern corner of the kingdom of Bijapur; the fort and district of Parenda in the extreme north had been gained by bribery in November 1660; Sholapur had been acquired by treaty in July 1668; and now Naldurg and Kulbarga were annexed. Thus, the vast tract of land enclosed by the Bhima and the Manjira eastwards up to an imaginary line joining Kulbarga to Bidar (77° E longitude) passed into Mughal hands, and the imperial boundary on the south reached the north bank of the Bhima, opposite Halsangi, within striking distance of Bijapur city,—while south-eastwards it touched Malkhed, the fortress of the western border of the kingdom of Golkonda.

After the Mughals had effected their conquests in this corner of Bijapur, they turned to settle accounts with Golkonda. They threatened (middle of August) Qutb Shah with invasion unless he seized and delivered up to them Shivaji and Shaikh Minhaj,—the last of whom had taken much money from the Mughal viceroy by promising to join him, but had ended by going over to Golkonda. Dilir and Bahlol invaded Golkonda in September. From Kulbarga, the last Mughal outpost, they advanced to Malkhed, 40km (24miles)eastwards,the first fort on the Golkonda frontier, which they took in one day. But near Malkhed, 128 km (80 miles) from the Qutb-Shahi capital, the tide of invasion was arrested by vast enemy forces. The Qutb Shahis were posted at Mangaligi, 12 km (7 miles north of Malkhed, the Mughal encampment (October). For two months there was constant but indecisive fighting. The Qutb Shahis penetrated far within Bijapuri and Mughal territories and cut off grain convoys coming to the invaders. The Afghans and Rajputs in the allied army suffered terrible hardships from excess of rain and the scarcity of grain caused by the enemy hovering around. Bahlol Khan was struck down by a mortal illness, and his retainers dispersed to save themselves from starvation. Then Dilir made a disastrous retreat to Kulbarga, the enemy hemming him round and making daily attacks. His baggage was looted, and the famished imperialists had to eat the seeds of the toddy-palm and the date-palm.

At Kulbarga Masaud met Dilir Khan and made peace with the Mughals: he was to act as *wazir* at Bijapur, but must obey the orders of Aurangzib, made no alliance with Shivaji, and always help the Mughals in wresting the Maratha chief's usurped territory; Adil Shah's sister, Shahar Banu Begam (popularly called Padishah Bibi) was to be sent to the Mughal Court to marry a son of the Emperor. Dilir then retired northwards.

12.8 Masaud Becomes Regent; Afghan Mutiny; Rebellions in Provinces of Bijapur

Bahlol died on 23 December 1677. Masaud, escorted by a Golkonda army, was installed as regent in February next. But the treasury was empty. He failed to pay up the arrears of the Afghan mercenaries, and then the exasperated Afghans broke out in lawless fury. They seized the house of Bahlol Khan's orphans, widows and other relatives, publicly insulting them to compel payment of their dues. All citizens believed to be rich were caught and tortured by them. 'Chintu Chimna, a Brahman robber, oppressed the people of the city, while the Afghans oppressed those outside the fort-walls.... All the time Masaud sat down in helplessness, shutting the doors of his own house.... Many people emigrated to the Karnatak in fear.'

Nor was the new regent better obeyed in the provinces. To crown his misfortunes, he provoked the wrath of the Mughals by trying to strengthen himself by a secret alliance with Shivaji. This breach of faith on the part of Masaud absolved Dilir Khan from the treaty of Kulbarga, 'respect for which alone had so long kept him back from the invasion of Bijapur.' At the end of the rainy season (October 1678) Dilir Khan moved out of Pedgaon and halted at Akluj.

Meanwhile, Shivaji, according to a treaty, sent six thousand steel-clad troopers to guard Bijapur and reinforce Masaud. But hearty co-operation between the two allies was impossible: Shiva tried to seize Bijapur fort by treachery. The ill-feeling between them daily increased and finally broke out in open quarrel. Then Shivaji resumed plundering the Bijapuri territory. The Maratha troops approached the city, and looted the suburbs of Daulatpur (i.e., Khawaspur), Khusraupur, and Zuhrapur. Masaud, in greater fear of his pretended ally than of his open enemy, sought the protection of Dilir Khan and welcomed a Mughal force at Bijapur.

Dilir Khan made a successful diversion in favour of Bijapur by capturing and destroying Shivaji's stronghold of Bhupal-garh (2 April 1679) and defeating the relieving army of 16,000 Marathas with heavy slaughter. But Masaud's duplicity at last wore out his patience, and he crossed the Bhima at Dhulkhed and marched to Halsangi, only 56 km (35 miles) north of Bijapur. The Adil-Shahi Government had been dissolved and there was utter anarchy in the country and capital in consequence of the feud between Masaud and Sharza Khan. The Mughal viceroy of the Deccan had now become the sole arbiter among the warring factions of Bijapur. 'About 1,000 troopers of Adil Shah, consisting of Deccani Muslims, Afghans and Marathas, entered the Mughal service and gathered round Dilir, while only three or four thousand starving men remained with Masaud in Bijapur, and even these hankered for Mughal pay.'

Aurangzib demanded that the Sultan's sister Shahar Banu, surnamed Padishah Bibi, should be sent to the Mughal harem. This princess was the beloved idol of the royal family and the citizens alike. On 1 July 1679 she left the city of her birth, amidst the tears and wailings of the Court and the populace, to enter a bigoted Sunni's house for the rest of her life, as the wife of Prince Muhammad Azam.

12.9 Dilir Khan Invades Bijapur; Shivaji Assists Adil Shah, 1679

But the sacrifice of the royal maiden was of no avail to the doomed dynasty. Mughal greed was insatiable; Dilir Khan now demanded that Masaud should resign the regency and retire to his own fief, while the Bijapur government would be carried on by a creature of the Mughals. Masaud wisely rejected the proposal. The Mughal general, being thus openly defied at once declared war against Bijapur. But his own position was really weak; his treasure-chest was empty, while his soldiers' pay was in arrears. Secondly, the new viceroy of the Deccan, Prince Shah Alam, was his sworn enemy, and tried his best to foil his undertakings and covered him with discredit. Dilir Khan was thus brought to a halt at the very outset of the campaign, and wrote entreating the prince for money. Masaud utilized the delay in strengthening the defences of Bijapur; he sent an envoy to Shivaji appealing to him to come to the rescue of Adil Shah in his supreme need. Shivaji's response was prompt. He took 10,000 Maratha cavalry to aid Masaud, and despatched 2,000 ox-loads of provisions to Bijapur.

The Mughals took possession of Mangalvide (84 km i.e., 52 miles north of Bijapur) and the country between the Bhima and the former fort, in September 1679. They also raided Salotgi, Kasigaon, and Almala, and besieged Akluj, but without success. Dilir Khan reached Baratgi (10 km i.e. 6 miles north east of the capital) on 7 October. But distracted by the opposition of Shah Alam, the censure of the Emperor for his delay in effecting conquest, and quarrels among his counsellors and allies, he saw failure staring him in the face. Shivaji had arrived at Selgur (midway between Panhala and Bijapur) with a new division 10,000 strong, and had been joined by his advanced division, of the same strength, under Anand Rao, (31 October 1679). On 4 November he divided his army into two bodies; one, 8,500 strong, under his own command, marched northeast by way of Muslah and Almala, while the second, 10,000 men led by Anand Rao, entered Mughal territory by the Sangula route (north-westwards).

With an army swollen to 30,000 horse, he spread a fan of free-booters and raided the imperial dominions in all directions from the Bhima northwards to the Narmada, plundering, burning, and slaying.

12.10 Dilir Ravages the Country Round Bijapur and Attacks the Capital

Stung by the Emperor's reproaches, Dilir Khan resumed the campaign. Despairing of taking Bijapur by siege or *coup de main*, and afraid of being attacked by Shivaji in the rear if he opened siege-trenches, the Mughal general left the environs of the city on 14 November and marched westwards, intending to invade the Miraj-Panhala region. His first work was to ravage the Bijapuri territory with insane cruelty. The villages in his path were utterly sacked; all their men, both Hindus and Muslims, were taken prisoner for being sold into slavery; and the women committed suicide by jumping down into the wells with their children. On 20 November, Shambhuji fled away from Dilir's camp to Bijapur, and thence arrived at Panhala about the 4 December.

From Ainapur Dilir Khan had faced round. Making a wide detour round the south side of Bijapur city, he raided the fertile and flourishing valleys of the Don and the Krishna,—the former of which was known as the granary of Bijapur,—laid waste all the gardens, fields, and villages on the way, took all their inhabitants prisoner, and then reached Aliabad (10 km i.e. 6 miles north-east of the city) on 4 December. From this place he used to march out daily with his guns and men and exhaust his ammunition, soldiers and horses by wildly firing at the impregnable fort-walls from one point or another.

The quarrel between Shah Alam and Dilir Khan daily grew bitterer; the Emperor wrote a strong letter of censure to the general. Dilir's position before Bijapur was no longer tenable. His army refused to obey him. So, on 29 January 1689, he broke up his camp at Begam Hauz and began his retreat, after having wasted 56 days before the fort of Bijapur. He next roamed about like a mad dog, slaying and looting with fiendish cruelty, needlessly inflicting unspeakable misery on the innocent peasants, and turning into a barren wilderness the region from Bijapur city southwards to the Krishna and eastwards to the fork between the Krishna and the Bhima. Practising his usual brigandage all the way, Dilir Khan next invaded the Berad country whose capital was Sagar, then ruled over by Pam Nayak, and reached Gogi (20 February 1680). He met with a crushing defeat when he tried to assault Sagar (13 km, i.e. 8 miles south of Gogi). The Berad infantry, sheltered behind the parapet of the fort, hillocks and even boulders, plied their matchlocks with deadly effect on the Mughal troops densely crowded in the village.

The imperial cavalry galloped away in a panic, assailed at their backs by the fleet-footed Berads and piteously crying for mercy. The Mughal casualties mounted up to 1,700 men on that day. The spirit of his soldiers was utterly broken and they even declined his offer of Rs 5,000 as bounty for facing the enemy again.

12.11 Dilir Khan is Disgraced and Recalled, 1680

At last utterly disgraced he set out on his return journey, on 23 February, moving northwards along the east side of Bijapur, burning the villages on the route and seizing the population for ransom. His officiating viceroyalty of the Deccan had ended in October 1678, when Shah Alam had arrived at Aurangabad to fill that office for the fourth time. The prince continued in the Deccan till May, 1680. His supine administration was rendered more than usually barren of success. The Emperor was displeased and recalled both Shah Alam and Dilir, appointing Khan-i-Jahan (Bahadur Khan) as subahdar of the Deccan for the second time. This general took over charge from Shah Alam at Aurangabad in May, 1680.

12.12 Aurangzib's Policy Towards Bijapur from 1680 to 1684

For four years after Dilir Khan's failure and retreat (February 1680), nothing decisive was done by the Mughals against Bijapur, as they were harried and distracted by the fertile audacity of Shambhuji. Aurangzib wrote a friendly letter to Sharza Khan, the leading general of Bijapur, (13 July, 1681), pressing him to co-operate with the Mughal generals in crushing Shambhuji and recovering the Bijapur territory he had usurped; Shahar Banu, the Bijapuri princess recently married to Azam, also sent a personal appeal to Sharza (18 July) to the same effect. But no response came from any Adil Shahi officer to the Emperor's appeal for co-operation. The Emperor received repeated and clear proofs of the help that the Marathas used to get from the Bijapuri Government. So, Aurangzib decided to increase the pressure on Shambhuji by making a diversion against the Bijapuris and compelling them to concentrate their resources on the defence of their own realm. In April 1682, a large force was sent under Prince Azam to enter Bijapur territory. He ravaged the frontier and took the fort of Dharur (about 224 km i.e. 140 miles, north of Bijapur). The campaign languished for many months, and the prince had not advanced further south than the Nira river when he was recalled to Court (June 1683). A few months later these desultory attacks on Bijapur ceased for a time.

The condition of Bijapur was now hopeless. Five years' wazirship at the decadent Court of Adil Shah had thoroughly disgusted Siddi Masaud. 'With all his efforts he failed to reform the Government or restore order in the administration. No man from peasant to chieftain ate his bread in peace of mind for a single day; none from king to beggar slept in happiness for a single night'. Despairing of improving the administration, he left the Court on 21 November, 1683, and formally resigned his post on reaching his fort of Adoni. Aqa Khusrau was invested with the robe of *wazir* on 19 March 1684, but died in six months (11 October). At this time vigorous steps were taken for the the defence of the realm: Sikandar entrusted this task (3 March 1684) to his bravest general Sayyid Makhdum, surnamed Sharza Khan; his vassal Pam Nayak of Wagingera was invited to come to the capital with his Berad clansmen, who were the best shots in the country.

On 30 March, a letter was received from Aurangzib, calling upon Adil Shah as a vassal, to supply provisions to the imperial army promptly, allow the Mughal troops a free passage through his territory, supply a contingent of 5 or 6 thousand cavalry for the Emperor's war with the Marathas, abstain from helping or harbouring Shambhuji, and expel Sharza Khan from his country! In the meantime the Mughals continued to appropriate bits of the Adil-Shahi kingdom and establish their own outposts in it. At the end of May, Khan-i-Jahan took possession of Mangalvide and Sangola and their environs. So, Sikandar sent a spirited reply to Aurangzib, demanding that the Mughals should return to him the tribute and territory they had exacted in the past, withdraw their outposts from his dominions, march against Shambhuji through their own territory only, and never make peace with the Maratha king till they had recovered from him and restored to Adil Shah every inch of his territory that Shambhuji or Shivaji had usurped.

The Mughal generals were now ordered to plant outposts in Bijapuri territory and they at once came into collision with Sharza Khan, who was guarding the land, but even then war did not formally break out;

for some months after, Sikandar continued to receive letters and robes of honour from the Mughal Court

In January 1685, Sharza Khan returned to the capital, and a. son of Masaud came to deliver his father's counsels to the Sultan. Shortly before this, promise of support had arrived from Golkonda. On 21 February a Maratha contingent under Shambhuji's *diwan* Melgiri Pandit reached Bijapur and was welcomed by the Sultan from the Zuhrapur gate. Diplomatic relations with the Mughals had already ceased, and both sides were preparing for an appeal to the sword. On 1 April 1685, the first trenches were opened and the siege of Bijapur began.

12.13 Siege of Bijapur Begins

The walls of Bijapur city enclose 3½ square kilometres, (i.e, two and a half square miles) of land, forming an ellipse. After crossing the deep moat, 13 to 15 metres (40 to 50 feet) broad, we meet the massive and strong walls, varying in height from 10 to 15 metres (30 to 50 feet), with an average thickness of 6 metres (20 feet) and strengthened with 96 bastions besides ten at the gates. On the top of the walls a battlemented curtain wall 3 metres (ten feet) high runs from bastion to bastion and is loopholed for artillery and small arms. Aurangzib seems to have let the Sharzi Burj (in the west) alone and directed the whole fire of his artillery against the Landa Kasab tower in the south, and breached the curtain wall close by. Between this tower and the Firingi Burj is the Mangali gate, which was renamed *Path Darwaza* after Aurangzib's victorious entrance into the city through it.

In the heart of the city there is an inner fortification, called the *qila ark* or citadel, forming a circle about 1.5 km (a mile) m circumference; all the royal palaces and public offices of the Adil Shahs were situated within this inner enclosure. But the site of the citadel is unfavourable. It is almost the lowest part of the city and is commanded by the rising ground on the north west.'

The Mughals began their siege operations on 1 April, 1685, when Ruhullah Khan and Qasim Khan opened their trenches on the Shahpur or north-west side, 800 km (half a mile) from the fort-wall, with a large tank in their rear, while Khan-i-Jahan ran his approaches near Zuhrapur or Rasulpur suburb in the west. Prince Azam arrived with a large army on 14 June and took over the supreme command, halting at the Begam Hauz, due south of the city.

The Mughals were proverbially slow and clumsy in taking forts by siege. The soil round Bijapur was, in addition, extremely hard; only 30 cm (a foot or two) below the surface one strikes solid rock. The Mughal advance was, therefore, extremely slow and laborious. And the garrison gave them no rest. For more than a year after its commencement, the siege of Bijapur was in no sense an investment. The garrison sallied out whenever they liked, and attacked the siege trenches, while reinforcements and provisions freely entered the fort from outside.

Allies began to flock to Adil Shah in his distress. On 10 June, Siddi Masaud's contingent arrived, next, on 14 August, a Golkonda force, and finally on 10 December a second army from Shambhuji under Hambir Rao.

12.14 Prince Azam in Danger, is Relieved by Firuz Jang

Prince Azam had arrived close to the fort of Bijapur on 19 June, 1685, but in less than a month he had to fight three severe battles with the enemy. On 1 July his trenches were assailed by Abdur Rauf and Sharza Khan, and several Mughal officers were wounded and slain. Next day the Deccanis fell on the supplies coming to the siege-camp and evidently cut them off.

A famine broke out in his camp; the oft-ravaged neighbourhood of Bijapur could yield no food supply, the roads from the north were closed by the activity of the Marathas and the flooded streams, as the rainy season had now set in. 'Grain sold at Rs 15 a *seer*, and that too in small quantities.'

For lack of men the Mughal outpost at India, midway between Sholapur and Bijapur, had been withdrawn, and thus the road from the imperial base to the siege-camp was now closed. Aurangzib saw no means of saving his son other than by ordering him to retire from Bijapur with his army. The prince held a council of war; they all voted for a retreat. But the prince's spirit had been roused; he would not reduce himself to the level of his rival Shah AJam, who had recently come back from Konkan covered with dismal failure. Turning to his officers, Azam exclaimed, 'You have spoken for yourselves. Now listen to me. Muhammad Azam with his two sons and Begam will not retreat from this post of danger so long as he has life. After my death, His Majesty may come and order my *corpse* to be removed for burial. You, my followers, may stay or go away as you like.' Then the council of war cried out with one voice, 'Our opinion is the same as your Highness's !'

When this Spartan resolution of his son was reported to Aurangzib, he at once took steps to send relief. 5,000 pack-oxen were despatched to convey food, with treasure loaded on many hundred spare remounts, and much munition to the prince. A strong escort under Ghazi-ud-din Khan Bahadur Firuz Jang left the imperial camp with the party on 4 October, 1685, and fought its way to the famished army, after repulsing Sharza Khan at Indi. The arrival of Firuz Jang 'turned scarcity into plenty in the Mughal camp, and the famished soldiers revived.' His next success was the cutting off of a force of 6,000 Berad infantry, each man carrying a bag of provisions on his head, which Pam Nayak tried to smuggle into the fort at night. Early in October, Haidarabad, the capital of Qutb Shah was entered by Shah Alam unopposed, its ruler having shut himself up in Golkonda. Many of his officers deserted to Shah Alam. The Mughal control over the Qutb Shaḥi State was confirmed in March, 1686, when the prime minister Madanna Pandit—who had pursued a policy of alliance with Bijapur and the Marathas—was murdered.

12.15 Sufferings and Difficulties of Mughals at Siege of Bijapur

By this time (June 1686) the siege of Bijapur had dragged on for 15 months with no decisive result.

Discord and mutual jealousy had broken out among the Mughal commanders. The Emperor realized that unless he took the command in person, the fort would not fall. On 14 June 1686 he left Sholapur and on 3 July reached the Rasulpur suburb, west of the fort. Orders were at once issued to press the siege vigorously. The city was completely beleaguered. Prince Shah Alam, joining his father, commanded the sector opposite the north-western or Shahpur gate and wanted to steal a march over his brother Azam, the general in charge of the siege. He opened a correspondence with Sikandar Adil Shah and his officers to effect the peaceful surrender of the fort and thus rob Azam of the credit of being called the captor of Bijapur. One of his confidential officers, Shah Quli, even used to enter the fort in secret to negotiate with the garrison. The matter became the talk of the camp and reached the ears of Muhammad Azam Shah and of the Emperor. Shah Alam was censured; some of the officers incriminated were thrown into prison and the others were expelled from the camp. The sufferings of the besiegers were aggravated by a scarcity which was raging in the Deccan on account of the failure of rain that year. But the sufferings of the besieged were ten times worse. 'Countless men and horses died within the fort,' and for lack of horses the Deccanis could not follow their favourite tactics of hovering round their enemy and cutting off stragglers and transport. In the extremity of the siege, a deputation of Muslim theologians issued from the city and waited upon Aurangzib in his camp, pleading, 'You are an orthodox believer, versed in Canon Law, and doing nothing without the warrant of the *Quran* and the decrees of theologians. Tell us, how you justify this unholy war against brother Muslims like us.' Aurangzib was ready with his reply: 'Every word you have spoken is true. I do not covet your territory. But the infidel son of the infernal infidel (meaning Shambhuji) stands at your elbow and has found refuge with you. He is troubling Muslims from here to the gates of Delhi, and their complaints reach me day and night. Surrender him to me and the next moment I shall raise the siege.' The scholars were then reduced to silence.

Shortly after Aurangzib's arrival the sap had been carried to the edge of the moat, but the filling up of the ditch seemed an impossible task. 'From the fort walls the artillery struck down whosoever reached the edge of the ditch. None durst show his head.' For three months the broad and deep moat remained unfilled.

On 4 September Aurangzib advanced his tent from 3 km (two miles) in the rear to a place immediately behind the trenches. Thither he rode fully armed, by a covered lane, and received the salute of the investing officers. Next he rode to the edge of the moat to inspect the battery raised to command the fort bastion and to learn for himself why the conquest was delayed.

12.16 The Fall of the Last King of Bijapur

Bijapur fell a week after this date, but not to assault. The garrison now lost heart. The cause of the Adil Shahi monarchy was hopeless: the king was a plaything in the hands of selfish nobles: all hope of help from outside was gone. The future was absolutely dark. The garrison had by this time shrunk to 2,000 men. In the night of 9 September the secretaries of the two Bijapuri leaders, Nawab Abdur Rauf and Sharza Khan, waited on Firuz Jang and opened negotiations for surrender. Aurangzib received them with favour.

Sunday, 12 September 1686, saw the downfall of the Bijapur monarchy. Amidst the tears and lamentations of his subjects who lined the streets, Sikandar, the last of the Adil Shahi Sultans gave up his ancestors' throne and issued from the capital of his house, at one o'clock in the afternoon, in charge of Rao Dalpat Bundela and went to Aurangzib's camp in Rasulpur.

Meanwhile the large tent which served as the Hall of Public Audience in Aurangzib's camp, had been richly decorated for this historic scene. When Sikandar arrived, a train of high officers welcomed him and ushered him into the Presence. The fallen monarch made his bow at the foot of the conqueror's throne. His extreme beauty and combined grace of youth and royalty excited universal admiration and pity for his fate. Even Aurangzib was touched: he spoke soothingly to Sikandar. The deposed Sultan was enrolled among the Mughal peers with the title of *Khan* (lord), and a pension of one *lakh* of rupees a year was settled on him. All the Bijapuri officers were taken over into Mughal service. On 19 September, the victor, seated on a portable throne, rode into the fort by way of the trenches of Saif Shikan Khan and the southern or Mangali gate, which had once been chosen for the assault. Along the roads of the city he marched, scattering handfuls of gold and silver coins right and left, and viewed the fort walls and bastions and the palaces within the citadel. Then he went to the Jama Masjid and rendered two-fold prayers to God for His favours. In Sikandar's palace: he rested for some hours and received congratulatory offerings from his courtiers. All paintings on the walls drawn in violation of the Quranic law that man should not presumptuously vie with his Creator by depicting living beings, were ordered to be erased, and an inscription recording Aurangzib's victory was placed on the famous cannon *Malik-i-maidan.*

Complete desolation settled on the city of Bijapur after the fall of its independent dynasty. Two years after its conquest, a terrible plague swept away more than half its population. A few years later, Bhimsen noticed how the city and its equally large suburb Nauraspur looked deserted and ruined; the population was scattered, and even the abundant water-supply in the city wells had suddenly grown scanty! Bijapur henceforth continued as a dismal example of departed greatness,—a vast city covered with 'long lines of fallen houses, ruined mansions and lonely patches of jungle.'

The last Adil Shahi Sultan was for some time lodged in the State prison of Daulatabad. Later, he was again carried about with the camp of Aurangzib, as a captive. In this condition he died outside Satara fort on 3 April 1700; he had not yet completed 32 years of age. According to his last wishes, his mortal remains were carried to Bijapur and there buried at the foot of the sepulchre of his spiritual guide Shaikh Fahimullah, in a roofless enclosure.

13 *The Decline and Fall of the Qutb Shahs*

13.1 Accession of Abul Hasan Qutb Shah, 1672

Abdullah Qutb Shah, the sixth king of Golkonda, had succeeded his father in 1626, at the age of twelve, and reigned for 46 years, during the whole of which he was a mere puppet on the throne. The actual administration was conducted for more than 40 years by his mother, Hayat Bakhsh Begam, a lady of strong character, and after her death (1667) by Abdullah's eldest son-in-law Sayyid Ahmad. Abdullah was, throughout his life, indolent and almost imbecile; he never appeared in public to give audience and administer justice according to the custom of the country, nor did he venture outside the walls of the fortress Golkonda. Confusion and misrule were the natural and unavoidable consequences of this state of things.

Abdullah had no son, but three daughters, the second of whom had been married to Aurangzib's son Muhammad Sultan, and the first to Sayyid Ahmad, who claimed descent from one of the noblest families of Mecca and who rose by his ability to the position of prime minister and *de facto* ruler of the State. It was proposed to marry the third princess to Sayyid Sultan; but on the day fixed for the marriage, Sayyid Ahmad told Abdullah that if he gave his daughter to Sayyid Sultan, he would at once leave the kingdom. A hurried search was made for another match for the princess. The choice of the palace agents fell on Abul Hasan, a youth descended on his father's side from the Qutb Shahi family, who had spent the last 16 years in the lazy pampered life of a monk by entering himself as a disciple of the saint Sayyid Raju Qattal. This man was led to the palace and forthwith married to the princess.

On 21 April, 1672, Abdullah died, and at once there arose a dispute for the succession. After some confusion and fighting, Sayyid Muzaffar, a leading general of high Persian origin, supported by Musa Khan *mahaldar* and several other officers of the harem, overpowered Sayyid Ahmad and forced him into prison. Abul Hasan was crowned king, Muzaffar becoming his prime minister. But within a few months, Abul Hasan bought over Madanna, the Brahman *factotum* of Muzaffar, and through him corrupted most of the captains of his personal followers, so that one day Muzaffar was quietly deprived of his wazir-ship, which was conferred on Madanna, with the title of Surya Prakash Rao. This change of ministers took place about 1673 and Madanna's rule continued till his own assassination in 1686, on the eve of the fall of the kingdom. His brother Akkanna became commander-in-chief and his nephew, the gallant and learned Yengana surnamed Rustam Rao, was given a high command. Muhammad Ibrahim, a creature of Madanna, was at first created premier peer.

During the twelve years of Madanna's ministry the internal administration of the country was marked by the same disorder and tyranny as in the reign of Abdullah, and matters naturally declined from bad to worse, 'and nothing was thought of but peeling and squeezing the people.' Madanna continued the same foreign policy as before, but with a necessary variation. There was no estrangement from the Adil Shahi Government; that Court was now the scene of chaos, faction-fights and changes of regency. Madanna, therefore, built his hopes of national defence chiefly on a close alliance with the ever-victorious Maratha king, and promised him a regular subsidy of one *lakh* of *hun* for the defence of Golkonda.

13.2 Mughal Policy Towards the Golkonda King

So long as Bijapur stood, Golkonda was safe. Aurangzib knew it, and therefore did not try to annex the latter kingdom first. Nor was it necessary for him to do so, as he found it more profitable and cheaper to fleece and terrorize the Qutb Shahi Government than to extinguish it. The Mughal 'Resident' at Haidarabad domineered over the king and the people, insulted and taxed them, but without provoking armed protest.

Resigning his royal functions to his wazir Madanna, Sultan Abul Hasan shut himself up in his palace with a host of concubines and dancing-girls. Under his predecessor, Haidarabad had become the Indian Babylon, with its twenty thousand public women (who had to dance before the king in the public square every Friday) and its countless taverns, close to these women's quarters, where 1,200 large leather bottles of fermented palm-juice were consumed daily. But he also promoted several fine arts contributory to luxury; he settled in his capital and supported by his bounty skilled craftsmen of various kinds, whose exquisite manufactures were famous throughout India. The king's own skill in music was of no mean order. He was rightly called Tana Shah or 'the dainty king'.

The enormous wealth of the country was derived from its well-watered fields which at once arrest the eye by their greenness and abundance of tropical fruits as the traveller enters the State from the arid and sterile region round Bijapur, its rich mines of diamond and iron, and its prosperous ports on the east coast from Chicacole southwards to St. Thome. The king had a secure income of 2 ¾ *krores* of rupees. For nearly thirty years after Aurangzib's accession to the throne, the kingdom of Golkonda had enjoyed respite from Mughal attack; the pre-occupation of the Mughals with Shivaji and his patron Adil Shah had prevented them from turning to Golkonda. Qutb Shah had also paid tribute to the imperial Government more regularly than the Sultan of Bijapur.

During the Mughal invasions of Bijapur under Jai Singh in 1665–66, under Dilir Khan in 1679 and under Prince Muhammad Azam in 1685, the Sultan of Golkonda had openly sent his troops to assist his brother in distress. The first two of these acts had been condoned, or atoned for by the payment of tribute. The last brought ruin on him. But, in the eyes of Aurangzib his worst offence was his fraternizing with infidels. He had effectively helped Shivaji with the sinews of war after his flight from Agra in 1666 and thus enabled him to recover his forts from the Mughals. Again Qutb Shah had rapturously welcomed Shivaji on his visit to Haidarabad in 1677 and behaved like a humble vassal of the Maratha king, placing a necklace of gems round his horse's neck and promising him an annual subsidy of one *lakh* of *hun* for the defence of his territory. Above all, he had made the Brahmans, Madanna and Akkanna, his chief ministers, and thus allowed Hindu influence to predominate in his administration.[1]

[1] As the Emperor wrote to his envoy at the Golkonda Court: 'This luckless wretch [meaning Abul Hasan Qutb Shah] has given the supreme power in his State to a *kafir* and made Sayyids, Shaikhs and scholars subject to that man. He has

13.3 War with the Mughals and Capture of Haidarabad, 1685

Aurangzib had begun his attack on Bijapur (in March 1685) by warning Abul Hasan not to assist Sikandar Adil Shah in any way. But at the end of June, a letter from Abul Hasan to his agents was intercepted, in which he had written, 'The Emperor is a great man, and has acted magnanimously up to this time, but now, finding Sikandar, a helpless orphan, he has laid siege to Bijapur and pressed him hard. It is, therefore, necessary that while the Bijapur army and Shambhu, with his countless hordes, are offering resistance from one side, I should, from this side, send 40,000 men under Khalilullah Khan to enter into the war. We shall then see on which front the Emperor can meet and repel his enemies.'

At this Aurangzib at once detached Prince Shah Alam with a vast army to march on Haidarabad. But when the imperial vanguard approached Serum, 13 km (8 miles) east of Malkhed, it found its path barred by a Golkonda army; the Mughal advance was stopped and the troops fell back on Malkhed. Every day there were skirmishes with the enemy. Khan-i-Jahan ran up walls round his camp at Malkhed and practically stood a siege there.

After a time the prince arrived with reinforcements and the Mughals, depositing their baggage at Malkhed, sent their vanguard again under Khan-i-Jahan to hack a way towards Haidarabad. The Deccanis outnumbered this force three to one, and there were frequent fights. Each such encounter was followed by a half of three or four days on the Mughal side. It was already August, and the heavy rain caused great hardship to the Mughal troops and impeded their advance. Their daily losses at last took the heart out of the Mughal soldiery. So, the imperial generals halted and wasted two months in the neighbourhood of Malkhed without fighting. Then a stinging rebuke from the Emperor and an unusually audacious

---

publicly allowed [in his realm] all kinds of sin and vice [viz., taverns, brothels, and gambling houses]. He himself is day and night sunk in the deadly sins, through the intoxication of kingship, and fails to distinguish between Islam and infidelity, injustice and oppression, sin and piety. By refusing to respect God's commands and prohibitions, by sending aid to infidel Powers,... and by recently paying one lakh of *hun* to the *kafir* Shambhu, he has made himself accursed before God and man.' (K. K., ii. 328).

act of sniping on the prince's camp, roused him to seek battle again. After a very bloody contest the Deccanis were pushed back to their camp. Next morning it was learnt that they had fled towards Haidarabad. The cause of this sudden breakdown of the Deccani resistance was dissension between the commander-in-chief Mir Muhammad Ibrahim, and his second in command Shaikh Minhaj, and the seduction of the former by the Mughals. The prince, being now unopposed, rapidly marched towards Haidarabad.

The fight of the commander-in-chief paralysed the defence of Haidarabad. Qutb Khan did not know whom to trust; he fled to Golkonda fort. The king's flight to Golkonda was so precipitate that all his property was left behind. When the people of Haidarabad learnt that the city had been abondoned by the Government and that the enemy were at hand, there was a mad scramble to flee to the fort. The confusion was aggravated by the indiscriminate looting which began immediately. The city presented the spectacle of a sack after assault by an enemy. In every ward, street, and market-place, there were *lakhs* of rupees worth in cash, property, chinaware of the nobles and tradesmen, and carpets of the king and the aristocracy, besides horses and elephants. These were looted in the midst of a terrible uproar. Many Hindu and Muslim wives and children were kidnapped and some of them outraged.

Next day Shah Alam sent a party of his soldiers to protect the citizens, but these men themselves joined in the plunder! After two days the prince appointed Khan-i-Jahan to police the city, and he succeeded in restoring order to some extent. The Mughal army made this its second entry into Haidarabad about 8 October 1685. Qutb Shah continued to send agents to the prince, helplessly appealing to him to make peace. At the prince's recommendation, which reached the Court on 18 October, the Emperor consented to pardon Abul Hasan on the following conditions: (1) He must pay one *krore* and 20 *lakhs* of rupees in settlement of all past dues, and in addition, a tribute of 2 *lakhs* of *hun* every year. (2) He must dismiss Madanna and Akkanna. (3) He must give up all claim to Malkhed and Serum, which the imperialists had already occupied.

13.4 Murder of Madanna, 1686

Shah Alam stayed for some months, first close to Golkonda, and afterwards at Qutb Shah's request he withdrew to Kuhir, (78 km i.e., 48 miles north-west of it), waiting for the collection of the war-indemnity. Abul Hasan put off the dismissal of Madanna as long as he could. At this his discontented nobles lost all patience. They regarded Madanna as the cause of all their sufferings at the hands of the Mughals. A plot was formed against Madanna by the discontented Muslim nobles, whose leader was Shaikh Minhaj, and by Saruma and Jani Sahiba, the widows of Abdullah Qutb Shah, who now ruled over the king's harem with despotic powers. One night, early in March 1686, just after Madanna had left his master's presence, he was set upon and murdered in the streets of Golkonda by Jamshid and other slaves. Akkanna shared his brother's fate on the spot. Then brave and accomplished nephew, Rustam Rao, was pursued to his house and there stabbed to death. The ministers' family residences were plundered. Next, a general attack was made by the mob on the Hindu quarter of the fort and 'many other Brahmans lost their lives and property in the night.' The Dowager Sultan now sent the heads of the obnoxious ministers to Aurangzib as the best of peace-offerings. The Emperor recalled Shah Alam to his side at Sholapur, where the prince arrived on 7 June 1686. Golkonda territory was now completely evacuated by the Mughals. Bijapur fell on 12 September of that year, and its fall set the Mughal forces free to deal finally with the Qutb Shahi Government.

13.5 Aurangzib Besieges Golkonda, 1687

On 28 January 1687 the Emperor arrived within 3 km (two miles) of Golkonda. Meanwhile, Abul Hasan had again fled from his capital to this fort, and the city of Haidarabad was occupied for the third and last tune by the Mughals.

Three kilometres (two miles) due west of the stone bridge over the Musi river which connects the two parts of the city of Haidarabad, stands the fort of Golkonda. It is an irregular rhombus, with a rough pentagon (the *Naya Qila*) annexed to its north-eastern face. A strong crenellated wall of granite, over 6 km (four miles) in length and of great thickness, surrounds the fort, which is further defended by 87 semi-circular bastions, each from 16 to 20 metres (50 to 60 feet) high and built of solid blocks of granite cemented together, some of them weighing more than a ton. The eight massive gates could have safely defied any artillery known to the seventeenth century. Outside is a deep ditch, 16 metres (50 feet) broad, with stone retaining walls. But Golkonda really consists of four distinct forts joined to each other and included within the same lines of circumvallation. The lowest of these is the outermost enclosure into which we enter by the Fath Darwaza, near the south-eastern corner; it is a vast tract covered with mansions of the nobles, bazaars, temples, mosques, soldiers' barracks, powder magazines, stables and even cultivated fields. Here the whole population of Haidarabad used to live in times of danger. Proceeding inside along the grand main road for some 1200 metres (1,250 yards) from the Fath Darwaza, and leaving a set of rather later palaces, harems and offices on a low site on the right, we arrive at the Bala Hisar gate, which leads us, over a flight of steps, to a higher area with exceedingly lofty and strong walls and containing a capacious three-storied armoury, magazines, stables, mosques, audience chambers, harems, gardens, large wells with steps, and even two *serais* and a temple of the monkey-god! Further west, some 200 steps cut in the solid rock lead the traveller up to the very apex of the fortress, the *Bala Hisar* (or Upper Fort), standing on a bed of solid granite, its walls being formed by huge boulders with here and there connecting curtains and parapets that tower far overhead. This is the citadel of the citadel, the kernel of the whole fort. At the north-eastern corner of the fort stands a mound commanding parts of Golkonda; but it was enclosed by a wall and added to the fort, under the name of the *Naya Qila* or New Fort, by king Abdullah as a defensive precaution after Aurangzib's first siege in 1656. North, south and even west of this last area are large tanks, and the water-supply of the fort was unfailing. North of the fort at a distance of 2000 metres (a mile and a quarter), runs a low range of bare fantastically piled up hills skirted by the great old road from Sholapur and the west. Here Aurangzib is said to have established his own quarters at the last siege.

The Mughal attack was directed on the south-eastern and southern faces of the fort, their soldiers moving along both the north and south banks of the Musi, while the northwest gate was bombarded only as a feint.

Arriving within view of Golkonda, Aurangzib at once ordered his generals to assail and drive away the enemy's troops who had assembled in the dry ditch under shelter of the fort walls. One charge of the imperialists swept them away, or as the Mughal official history puts it, 'the wind came and the gnats fled away;' and their property, wives and children were captured. Qalich Khan (the grandfather of the first Nizam) tried to enter the fort pell-mell with the fugitives and capture it by one stroke. But he was hit on the shoulder-blade by a *zamburak* bullet from the fort walls, and in spite of all the remedies tried by the doctors, he died after three days. Regular siege operations were therefore begun, on 7 February.

13.6 Shah Alam Imprisoned

But at the very outset the Emperor's arms were paralysed by bitter personal jealousies in his camp. Prince Shah Alam was of a soft pleasure-loving nature, and constitutionally averse to strenuous exertion and heroic enterprise. He did not wish to see a brother sovereign like Abul Hasan utterly ruined. This generous impulse was mingled with a more sordid feeling: if he could induce Abul Hasan to sue for peace through his mediation, then he himself would be proclaimed in the official reports as the captor of Golkonda. Abul Hasan's agents secretly visited Shah Alam with costly presents, begging him to use his influence with the Emperor to save Abul Hasan's throne and dynasty. The prince gave encouraging replies. In thus negotiating behind the Emperor's back and with an enemy beyond hope of the Emperor's pardon, Shah Alam was playing a dangerous game. And he had enemies in the camp ever on the look-out for a chance to ruin him. His rival Azam's partisans revealed to the Emperor the secret of the communications passing between Shah Alam and Abul Hasan. An order of Shah Alam to bring his women's tents closer to his headquarters, really as a precaution against surprise by the enemy, strengthened Aurangzib's suspicion that the prince was meditating flight to the enemy's fort with his family. All doubts were set at rest when Firuz Jang intercepted and showed to the Emperor one night some letters which the prince had been trying to send to the fort.

Aurangzib acted promptly: imperial troops were at once posted as guards round the prince's camp. Next morning (21 February), Shah Alam with his four sons was invited to the Emperor's tent for consultation. After a few minutes' talk with him, they were asked by the *wazir* to step into a side-room (the chapel) with him to hear some secret instructions of the Emperor. There they were politely asked to consider themselves as prisoners and surrender their swords. The prince's entire family was imprisoned, his property attached, his troops distributed among other commands, and his trusted eunuchs tortured to make them divulge their master's treasonable plots. The more the prince protested his innocence, the more did the Emperor's anger flare up; he increased the rigours of Shah Alam's captivity and ordered that he should not be allowed to cut his hair or pare his nails, nor be supplied with delicate food, cooling drinks or his customary dress. It was seven years before Shah Alam recovered his liberty. After the arrest of the prince, the Emperor hurriedly broke up his Court, ran to his wife Aurangabadi Mahal, and kept slapping his knees and moaning, 'Alas! Alas! I have razed to the ground what I had been rearing up for the last forty years.'

13.7 Aurangzib's Difficulties at Golkonda Siege

But Shah Alam was not the only discordant element in the siege-camp. The many Shias in the imperial service heartily disliked the prospect of the extinction of the last Shia kingdom in India. Apart from the Shias, this war of extermination against Abul Hasan was condemned by many orthodox Sunnis even, as an unprovoked 'war between Muslims' and therefore sinful. The upright and saintly Chief Justice, Shaikh-ul-Islam, had counselled the Emperor not to invade the two Deccani sultanates, and on his advice being rejected he had resigned his high post and retired to Mecca. His successor in office, Qazi Abdullah, tendered the same unpalatable advice and was packed off to the base camp!

This natural distrust of Shias hindered the Emperor's business. At first the only high and distinguished officer at the siege was Firuz Jang. Saif Shikan Khan, the Chief of Artillery, was a Persian and jealous of the superior position and favour enjoyed by Firuz Jang, a Turk. After working strenuously for some time, he resigned 'in order to spite Firuz Jang.' Salabat Khan succeeded him, but failed to do his work well, and resigned in a short time. The next Chief of Artillery was Ghairat Khan, who was surprised by the enemy in a state of gross carelessness and carried off as a prisoner. Then the post went abegging for some time to the ruin of the siege operations. Then at last, Saif Shikan Khan was taken out of prison and restored to this office (22 June 1687). But by that time the field-works constructed after five months of toil, had been demolished by the enemy, and the investment had to be begun anew. The siege had been started on 7 February. But the fort had an inexhaustible supply of munitions and its walls bristled with guns of large calibre. Day and night the garrison kept up an incessant fire on the approaching Mughals. Every day some men were slain or wounded on the Mughal side. But the dauntless courage and tireless perseverance of the troops under Saif Shikan carried the sap to the edge of the ditch in about six weeks. The next step was to fill the ditch and make a path for the assaulting column.

While these slow operations for breaching and assault were going on, the commander-in-chief, Firuz Jang, made an attempt to take the fort by an escalade, on 16 May. He stole out of his camp at 9 p.m., and on reaching a bastion where the enemy's sentries were asleep, he planted a ladder against the wall and sent two men up to the rampart. The two other ladders he had taken with him proved too short, and so a rope-ladder was fastened to the top of the gate. By chance a pariah dog was standing on the wall, seeking a path for descending to the moat and feeding on the corpses lying there. Alarmed by the appearance of strangers, it set up a loud bark, which roused the garrison, and they drove away the Mughals. To the Muslims the dog is an unclean animal. But this dog had saved the capital. Abul Hasan rewarded his canine deliverer by giving it a gold chain, a collar set with jewels, and a gold embroidered coat, and styling it *Sehtabqa* or 'Peer of three degrees,'—in mockery of Firuz Jang's three titles of *Khan*, *Bahadur*, and *Jang*,—and remarking wittily 'This creature has done no less a deed (than Firuz Jang)!'

The garrison promptly retaliated for the surprise that had failed, by making a sortie on the raised battery and slaying the artillerymen. The siege operations had ceased to make any progress for some time past, on account of the confusion in the artillery branch. The enemy's fire was still unsubdued, and the ditch far from filled up. The Mughals now fell into the grip of famine. The Deccanis and their Maratha allies infested the roads and prevented the transport of grain to the Mughal camp. Then, in June, the rain descended in torrents, the swollen water-courses and rivers became impassable, the roads were turned into quagmires. No provisions could reach the besiegers. The incessant rain of the middle of June completely spoiled the siege-works. The raised gun-platforms collapsed into mud-heaps; the walls of the trenches fell down and blocked the passages; the camp became a sheet of water out of which the white tents stood up like bubbles of foam.

13.8 Sorties of the Garrison: Heavy Mughal Losses

The enemy seized the opportunity. In the night of 15 June, amidst a deluge of rain, they raided the Mughal advanced batteries and trenches, slew the careless artillerymen, drove nails into the port-holes of the guns, destroyed the stores of sapping and gun material, then fell on the officers, and carried off into captivity Ghairat Khan (the Chief of Artillery), Sarbarah Khan (a trusty old servant of the Emperor) and twelve other high officers. It was only after three days of struggle and with assistance of a fresh division that the enemy could be expelled and the ruined battery re-occupied by the Mughals. Abul Hasan treated the captive Mughal officers very kindly, gave them rich presents and sent them back to the Emperor. Vigorous measures were taken to retrieve the late disaster and press the attack home. Three mines had been carried from the siege-trenches to under the bastions, and they were ready by 19 June, each chamber stored with 500 *mounds* of gunpowder and the fuses laid.

The next day was fixed for the explosion of the mines and the delivery of the assault, which the Emperor went to supervise in person from Firuz Jang's trenches. The Mughal troops, as ordered, rushed out of their trenches and made a noisy feint against the undermined bastion in order to induce the enemy to crowd at this point and then to kill vast numbers of them by the explosion! Early at dawn the first mine was fired, but the force of the explosion was directed outwards; a vast mass of rock and earth from the glacis was hurled upon the Mughal ranks crowded below: 'In a twinkle of the eye the flying splinters killed 1,100 imperialists, while the fort walls remained intact.'

The enemy seized the opportunity by making a sally and attacking the confounded Mughals, and then seized the trenches and outposts which it had taken the Mughals four months to make and occupy. A force sent by the Emperor drove them out and recovered the position after a long contest and heavy loss. This had been hardly effected when the second mine was fired with the same disastrous consequences. Again the splinters of the blown-up tower fell on the Mughals, and killed more than a thousand of them. The enemy then made a second sortie and took possession of the Mughal field-works and shelters. A severe struggle for them now took place; Firuz Jang was wounded with two other generals,

Rustam Khan and Dalpat Rao Bundela, while vast numbers of his men were slain.

At the news of this serious check, Aurangzib himself, girt round by his staff, advanced from his station in Firuz Jang's tent to aid his hard-pressed troops. Cannon-balls began to fall near his portable throne (*takhi-i-rawan*), and one of them carried away an arm of his body-servant (*khawas*). But he coolly kept his position and cheered his soldiers by his example.

While the battle was raging, a tropical storm burst on the plain with all the violence of wind, rain and thunder. The rain continued to descend in torrents; the dry *nalas* and even low paths became rushing streams. The Mughals, assailed by men and the gods, gave way; and then the Deccanis made their third sortie of the day. They seized the trenches further off and the elevated gun-platforms, carried off as many guns as they could and destroyed the others. The big planks, beams and thousands of bags filled with earth which the Mughals had thrown into the ditch were quickly removed into the fort and used in repairing the breach caused by the explosion! By this time the plain of battle had been turned into a lake of mud. At sunset the defeated Mughals retired to their quarters; the Emperor spent the night in Firuz Jang's camp.

13.9 Mughal Failure; Famine and Pestilence

Next morning (21 June) the Emperor issued forth again to fire the third mine and try his fortune by another assault under his own eyes. The mine did not explode at all. It was then learnt that the enemy had discovered it and flooded the chamber with water. The baffled Emperor stole back to his own tent 'without ceremony.' 'Various other plans were tried, immense wealth was spent, but the siege dragged on.' The *morale* of the imperial army was utterly gone. The famine grew worse than before, and pestilence appeared as its inseparable companion. The city of Haidarabad was utterly depopulated; houses, rivers and plains were all filled with corpses. The same condition prevailed in the Mughal camp. At night piles of the dead used to accumulate. After some months, when the rains ceased, the white heaps of skeletons looked from a distance like hillocks of snow.

Aurangzib with grim tenacity sat sown to starve the fort into surrender. 'The Emperor decided to build a wall of wood and earth round the fort of Golkonda. In a short time it was completed and guards were placed at its doors, ingress and egress being forbidden except on the production of passports.' At the same time, to prevent the garrison from getting fresh supplies, Aurangzib issued a proclamation annexing the kingdom of Haidarabad. He appointed his own magistrates and revenue-collectors for all places in it. The *khutba* was read in the Emperor's name and a Censor of Public Morals (*muhtasib*) was posted by him at Haidarabad.

13.10 Golkonda Surrendered by Treachery

On 21 September, after the siege had lasted nearly eight months Golkonda was captured by bribery. An Afghan soldier of fortune, named Abdullah Pani, surnamed Sardar Khan, who had deserted Bijapur service for the Mughal and then left the Mughals to join Abul Hasan, now sold his master to the enemy. He left the *khirki* or postern gate of the fort open, and at his invitation a party of Mughal soldiers under Ruhullah Khan entered the fort unchallenged, at about 3 o'clock in the morning of 21 September, 1687. They posted some men within to hold the ground and then opened the main gate through which the flood of Mughal invasion now poured into the fort. Prince Azam with the supports advanced from the river to the foot of the wall.

One last feat of the purest heroism cast its radiance on the fall of Golkonda and redeemed its infamy. When the exultant Mughals were swarming into the fort and making their way to the palace, a single rider who had no time to gird his belt on or put saddle on his horse's back, fell like a lunatic on that myriad of enemies. It was Abdur Razzaq Lari, surnamed Mustafa Khan, the one faithful man among that faithless crew of Golkonda. Throughout the siege he had rejected with scorn all the bribes of Aurangzib, including a command of Six Thousand Cavalry in the Mughal army, saying that 'he would rather be ranked among the 72 faithful companions who perished with the Imam Husain at Karbala than with the 22,000 traitors who overcame him.' Alone he rushed against the flood of invaders, shouting, 'While I live, there will be at least one life sacrificed in defence of Abul Hasan.' But covered with 70 distinct wounds, one eye badly damaged, and his horse reeling from wounds and loss of blood,—Abdur Razzaq no longer saw the path before him, but did his best merely to keep his seat and gave his horse loose rein. The animal escaped from the press and dropped him near an old coconut tree in the Nagian Bagh garden near the citadel. Thence he was removed to the Mughal camp and nursed back to life by order of the Emperor.

13.11 Abul Hasan Made Captive

In the meantime, when the roar of the advancing Mughals reached the ears of Abul Hasan, he came out to the audience chamber and sat down on the throne calmly waiting for his unbidden guests. When at last Ruhullah Khan and his party entered, Abul Hasan greeted them kindly, and behaved with royal dignity throughout the painful scene. Then, after bidding his captors to breakfast with him, he finished his meal and left the palace. In the evening he was presented by Azam to the Emperor. After a time he was sent to Daulatabad, and there sighed out his captive life on a pension of Rs 50,000 a year. At the moment of leaving his throne and passing into the rigours of captivity under a sworn enemy, Abul Hasan showed a self-control and a dignity which surprised his captors. To their cries of admiring surprise he replied that though born of royalty he had been trained in youth in the school of poverty, and knew how to take pleasure and pain with equal indifference as gifts of God, 'who had made me a beggar, and then a king, and now a beggar again, and who never withdraws His gracious care from His slaves, but sends to each man his allotted share of food.'[2]

---

[2] K.K. ii. 368–364. But Dr. Careri (in Churchill's *Voyages*, iv. 249) and Manucci (ii. 306–'8) speak of his being insulted and beaten when taken to Aurangzib. Ishwardas tells the characteristic story that at the time of his capture Abul Hasan was merrymaking with his dancing-girls and musicians and, when the girls stopped their dance in alarm at the entrance of the enemy, he cried out to them, 'Go on dancing as before. Every minute that I can spend in pleasure is a great gain.' Firuz Jang raised him from his throne and led him, mounted on a horse, to the Emperor's presence. Abul Hasan, without making *khurnish* or *salam* walked in erect. The Emperor asked, 'How are you?' He replied, 'I neither rejoice ... nor grieve. But I am delighted to gaze at what has made itself visible from behind the screen of the inscrutable.' (93 *a* and *b*.)

The report entered in the Fort St. George Diary on 12th Nov. 1687 is more reliable than Manucci's account. It runs thus: '... News from the French, Dutch and other nations that the Mughal had taken Golkonda fort by treachery on the 2nd of last month [New Style] about midnight ... Upon the king of Golkonda's prostration the Mughal had made a large discourse to him for his corrupt government, wherein he had been very unfaithful, in the charge he had committed

The spoils taken at Golkonda amounted to nearly seven *krores* of rupees in cash, besides gold and silver plate, jewels and jewelled ware. The revenue of the conquered kingdom was 2 *krores* and 87 *lakhs* of rupees.

to him, in encouraging the Brahmans and discouraging the Moors, to the dishonour of their religion and country, whereby he had justly brought these troubles upon himself; and ordered him to be put in chains, of which it is reported he was next day released.'

14 *Reign of Shambhuji, 1680–89*

14.1 The Disputed Succession: Shambhuji Makes Himself King

The death of Shivaji left the newly created Maratha kingdom utterly divided and distracted, while the future looked very uncertain. His eldest son Shambhuji's licentious character promised an unhappy reign to his subjects, while his recent desertion to the mortal enemy of his faith and fatherland had discredited him in the eyes of all right-thinking men. Indeed, his wise father in his last days, after vainly trying to reform Shambhuji, had been constrained to keep him under surveillance in the fort of Panhala. Therefore, after Shivaji's funeral, Rajaram (his younger son, a boy of ten) was proclaimed king by the ministers present in Raigarh, on the lead of Annaji Datto.

This change in the natural order of succession was effected by a party only at the capial. The people in general and the troops outside had not been consulted, and they naturally murmured.

The crowning of Rajaram gave the signal for a division among the Marathas. A faction for Shambhuji was soon formed. The army, gorged with plunder in Shivaji's time, seems to have received no bounty at this change of masters and was eager to transfer its venal sword to Shambhuji, whose helpless condition made him reckless in his promises for gaining adherents. The council of regency as constituted at Raigarh meant Brahman rule, and the commander-in-chief (a Maratha by caste) was not prepared to take his orders from a priestly Mayor of the Palace.

The result was that within a week of Shivaji's death, parties of soldiers began to flock daily to Shambhuji at Panhala, and he openly assumed royal powers, ignoring the Government at Raigarh.

Shambhuji's first measures displayed a degree of sagacity and timely energy which was quite unexpected from a man of his character. He first made himself master of Panhala and then consolidated his possession of the South Maratha country and South Konkan before venturing on a contest with the forces of his rival at the capital in the north.

In the meantime, Annaji Datto had placed Rajaram on the throne at Raigarh, on 21 April, and shortly afterwards started for Panhala with the Peshwa, ostensibly for the purpose of recovering that fort and imprisoning Shambhuji. But the news of the successful *coups* of Shambhuji disheartened them and they hesitated to attack him. Soon, the hands of the selfish double-dealing ministers were forced by the army. At the end of May the commander-in-chief, Hambir Rao Mohite, arrested Annaji and Moro Pant and took them as captives to Shambhuji at Panhala. There all the army chiefs assembled and recognized Shambhuji as their king.

Annaji was cast into prison, loaded with chains; the Peshwa made a timely recantation and thus gained Shambhuji's favour without his trust. The new king then set out for Raigarh, his army swelling to 20,000 men during the march. The capital opened its gates to him (18 June). Rajaram made no opposition, because he was incapable of making any.

Though deposed, he was treated 'with all kindness,' because he had been a mere tool in the hands of designing men.

Shambhuji first sat on the throne on 20 July. The formal coronation was performed with full ceremony and splendour on 16 January 1681. A son and heir was born to him on 18 May 1682, who was destined to revive the Maratha kingship about 30 years later. It was Shivaji II, popularly known as Raja Shahu.

14.2 Shambhuji Renews War with the Mughals

The new monarch gained a long respite from foreign attacks. All the military resources of the Mughal Empire were then concentrated for the war with the Rajputs under the Emperor's own eyes. At the end of October the Maratha armies were out, as usual, after *Dashahara*. One division, both horse and foot, was designed to march towards Surat and another towards Burhanpur, while a third kept Bahadur Khan (recently created Khan-i-Jahan) in check by forming a screen before his encampment near Aurangabad. The news of the raids, however, quickly drew the Mughal general into Khandesh (about 25 November) and the Marathas retreated from the province, but it was for a time only.

At the end of January next (1681) the raiders were back again, evidently emboldened by the news of Prince Akbar's rebellion, which rumour had exaggerated into the downfall of Aurangzib. One band under Hambir Rao sacked Dharangaon and other towns in North Khandesh, and, passing further east, fell on the Bahadurpura suburb of Burhanpur, (30 January) before the approach was even known, and there gathered an immense quantity of booty from the numerous shops and houses in it. Seventeen other wards (*puras*) outside the city-walls were similarly plundered. The surprise was so complete that none could conceal or remove a penny worth of property, or save his wife and children. The smoke of the burning houses first informed the governor of the enemy's presence, but he was powerless to do anything and merely shut himself up in the fort. Lakhs of rupees worth of booty was taken in every *pura*. Many respectable men slew their wives and daughters and then fell desperately fighting the brigands, rather than see their family honour outraged.

For three days the Marathas looted the suburbs to their hearts' content, without the least interruption, and dug up the floor of every house, thus discovering the buried treasure of many generations past. Khan-i-Jahan was too slow in coming up and misjudged the route of the raiders, so that they escaped with all their prisoners and booty. Popular voice in the Deccan charged the Mughal viceroy with having been bribed by Shambhu to follow this wrong strategy. The citizens of Burhanpur complained to the Emperor to this effect and the Muslims threatened to stop their Friday prayers unless they were assured of the safety of their life and honour in future.

At Babulgaon, some 42 km (26 miles) west of the city, Khan-i-Jahan learnt that another Maratha band was coming up from the south by way of Ahmadnagar and Mungi-Paithan to loot Aurangabad. He took horse immediately and set off with his cavalry at 3 o'clock in the morning, arriving near the city at noon, just in time to save it. The city was in the wildest terror. All houses were closed, the men sitting armed and trembling and the women weeping within doors. As soon as the Khan arrived, the enemy fled without fighting.

As usual, after the *Dashahara* day, in October 1681, the Maratha light horse set out to rove in different directions. An attack on Ahmadnagar was actually attempted, as two Maratha princesses (a wife and a sister of Shambhuji) captured by Dilir Khan were lodged in that fort and the Marathas wished to rescue them. Some Maratha soldiers who had secretly entered the fort in disguise were detected and killed by the qiladar and the rest driven away after a fight (end of October).

14.3 Prince Akbar Seeks Refuge with Shambhuji, 1681

Prince Muhammad Akbar, the rebel son of Aurangzib, crossed the Narmada near Akbarpur (9 May) under the guidance of the faithful Durgadas Rathor and made his way to Maharashtra. On crossing the Mughal frontier he was welcomed by several high officers of Shambhuji and conducted with honour to Pali (1 June).

The prince was accompanied by 400 cavalry, a small body of infantry (mostly Rajputs with a few Muhammadans) and 50 camels for transport.

Three hundred Maratha foot soldiers were told to form his bodyguard, and Shambhuji's *subahdars* (collectors) nearabout waited on him to pay their respects. Netaji Palkar was left, in attendance upon him as Shambhuji's representative.

14.4 Conspiracy Against Shambhuji; Kavi-kalash Becomes his Favourite

After gaining Raigarh (18 June 1680), Shambhuji imprisoned Ijis chief enemies, including their leaders, Annaji Datto and Nilkanth Moreshwar Pingle (the son the Peshwa Moreshwar Trimbak). Early in October Moreshwar died, and Shambhuji set his son Nilkanth free and bestowed the vacant prime ministership on him. He also released the arch-traitor Annaji Datto 'from prison and appointed him to the post of Accountant-General (*Majmuadar*).

But in August 1681, Annaji Datto formed a conspiracy with Soyra Bai, Hiraji Farzand, and some other leading men to murder Shambhuji and give the throne to Rajaram, under the protection of Prince Akbar. They intended to kill Shambhuji by putting poison in his food.

But the plot was revealed, and Shambhuji immediately seized the traitors, flung them into prison, and put them to torture. Annaji Datto, his brother Somaji, Hiraji Farzand, Balaji Avji Prabhu, and Mahadev Anant, with three others were killed by being flung in chains under the feet of elephants. Twenty more culprits were sentenced to death later. Rajaram's mother, Soyra Bai, was charged with having poisoned her husband (a year and a half earlier), and was put by Shambhuji to a painful death, through poison or by starvation. All this happened in October 1681. Her father's family, the Shirkes, fell under Shambhuji's persecution; many of their members were killed, and the rest fled to the Mughals.

Shambhuji's character and conduct made it impossible for any of the old servants of the State to regard him with that love and devotion which Shivaji had inspired. On his part, he could never forget that practically all the notable ministers and generals had at first given their assent to removing him from the line of succession. He; therefore, felt that he stood absolutely alone and friendless in his native country; and his whole reign was in fact disturbed by frequent conspiracies and desertion among his officers and rebellions among his vassals.

In this forlorn situation he seemed to have gained a truly devoted servant. A Kanauji Brahman, who had been the hereditary priest of the Bhonsle family at Allahabad, arrived at Raigarh shortly before Shambhuji's grand coronation. By introducing a Tantrik high priest into the Rajah's Court and performing grand sacrifices to the goddess Kali through him, Kavi-kalash accomplished the birth of an heir of Shambhu (May 1682). He thus won the Rajah's heart, and monopolized his trust and the supreme control of the administration, with the title of *Kavi-kalash* or Pinnacle of Poets, while Shambhuji rapidly became a *faineant* king, blindly following the minister's advice, and devoting all his time to wine and women, with fitful outbursts of martial vigour.

In his obscure village refuge Prince Akbar kept up the pageant of an Emperor as far as his reduced means allowed.. Mercenary horse men were constantly joining him, and by the month of August he had collected about 2,000 cavalry in his pay. On 13 November 1681, Shambhuji interviewed Prince Akbar at Padishahpur (= Pali), taking his entire army and retinue with him. Durgadas was with Akbar, But Akbar's sole chance of success of invading the Mughal Empire was now gone. The crisis of the Rajput war had ended in June, when the Maharana made a definite peace with the Emperor. The Mughal forces were now free to hunt Akbar down, and the Emperor himself arrived at Burhanpur on 13 November. Thus, by the middle of November, all the military resources of the empire were concentrated in the Deccan under the Emperor himself, three of his sons and all his best generals. At first he contented himself with following a watch-and-wait policy.

14.5 Aurangzib's Strategic Dispositions, 1682

Shambhuji was busy during the whole month of January 1682 in making a furious attack on Janjira under his own eyes. This was Aurangzib's opportunity. Sayyid Hasan Ali Khan descended from Junnar into North Konkan at the head of 14,000 horse and took possession of Kalian (about 30 January 1682) burning all the Maratha villages on the way. In May next he withdrew from the province, in order to save his horses from the effect of the heavy rainfall of the west coast.

Aurangzib arrived at Aurangabad on 22 March 1682 and sent off Azam Shah and Dilir Khan to Ahmadnagar in the south, while Shihab-ud-din Khan with Dalpat Rao was sent to Nasik on the western frontier. The latter general took some small forts in this region and then (in April) laid siege to Ramsej, 11 km (7 miles) north of Nasik. But it was defended by a gallant Maratha garrison under an expert *qiladar,* and the Mughals could make no impression on it. The Emperor sent Khan-i-Jahan to reinforce the siege. But even this great general could achieve no better success; two assaults failed with heavy losses.

Aurangzib's spirit was now up. He decided on extensive operations against Shambhuji. As the English at Karwar write, 'He is so inveterate against the Rajah that he hath thrown off his *pagri* and sworn never to put it on again, till he hath either killed, taken, or routed him out of his country' (30 July 1682). He sent Ruhullah Khan (23 May) and later Muizz-ud-din (28 September) to defend the Ahmadnagar district, while Prince Azam was sent towards Bijapur (14 June) to overawe that State and prevent it from aiding or sheltering Maratha bands. From Nasik Shihab-ud-din Khan was transferred to Junnar (June), while Ranmast Khan, the able lieutenant of Khan-i-Jahan, was promoted to the command of an independent army corps (September) and ordered to invade Konkan.

Khan-i-Jahan continued the siege of Ramsej for some months more, delivered another assault which failed, and then gave up the siege (October 1682).

Ranmast Khan entered Konkan and occupied Kalian, late in November 1682. Rupaji Bhonsle and the Peshwa opposed him to no effect, though they fought many battles with heavy slaughter.

Khan-i-Jahan united with the prince's force at Ramdoo, on the Godavari, 40 km (25 miles) south of Aurangabad, and pushed on eastwards to Nander. Thence his division went to Bidar, 137 km (86 miles) due south. Next he pursued the raiders in a long running fight which carried him to the frontiers of Chanda and Golkonda. It was a highly creditable feat. During this campaign his troops had to bear great hardship.

In June 1682 Prince Azam marched out of Ahmadnagar to invade Adil Shahi territory. In the course of this campaign he took Dharur. Then he entered Shambhuji's territory and leaving his wife Jahanzeb Banu (popularly called Jani Begam) behind in his camp, with Rao Anurudh Singh Hada and his Rajputs to guard her, he advanced with his army further into the enemy's country. The Marathas, sending off one division to keep Azam engaged, suddenly threatened the Begam's camp in overwhelming force. The heroic daughter of Dara Shukoh mounted her covered litter on an elephant, and advanced 3 km (two miles) from her camp to oppose the enemy.

Calling Anurudh Singh near her elephant she spoke to him *from her own mouth,* 'The honour of the Chaghtais is to the Rajputs the same as their own honour.[1] I call you my son. If God gives us victory with this small force, well. Otherwise, you may rest assured about me; I shall sit down after doing my work [i.e., committing suicide, in order to avoid capture].' Then a great battle was fought. Nine hundred Rajputs fell on Anurudh's side, and many of the Marathas too. At last Anurudh gained the victory, though he was wounded. After some time spent on the bank of the Nira, Azam was recalled to Court in June 1683.

14.6 Failure of Mughal Efforts; Emperor's Distraction and Suspicions

In March 1683, all the Mughal divisions operating against Akbar were recalled to the Emperor's side. Ruhullah and Ranmast Khan evacuated Kalian on 23 March, after burning and razing to the ground the

---

[1] *Sharm-i-Chaghtaia ba Rajputia ek-ast.* (*Akhbarat.*)

fortifications they had built round the city. The retreat was opposed by a Maratha army under Rupaji Bhonsle, who attacked the Mughal rear at Titvala (11 km, i.e. seven miles north-east) of Kalian, killing many men and carrying off a large number of horses.

Thus we see that for more than a year after his arrival in the Deccan, from November 1681 to April 1683, the Emperor accomplished nothing notable, in spite of his immense resources. In truth, he was at this time passing through a domestic and mental crisis; his faith in his family had been totally shaken and he did not know whom to trust or where he would be safe. Hence his policy for some time after was hesitating, suspicious, watchful and seemingly capricious or self-contradictory. On 2 October 1683, the Surat factors write, 'How the king's mind may alter we cannot tell. It is continually wavering and he is extraordinarily peevish and uneasy because of Sultan Akbar. Sultan Azam, Begam [i.e., Jahanzeb Banu] and Dilir Khan degraded for even nothing but only suspected, without any grounds, of being kind to Akbar, that all persons of quality stand on ticklish terms, are mighty careful.'

14.7 The Maratha Navy and Wars with the Siddis, 1680–82

There could be no amity between the English and Shambhuji,. because the Siddi fleet, as well as occasional Mughal squadrons from Surat, used to pass the stormy monsoon months (May to October) in the safe shelter of Bombay harbour every year, and the Siddis settled in the Mazagaon quarter of the island, from which they frequently ravaged the *Kurlas* or rich low-lying tracts of Maratha, territory on the mainland, east of Bombay. Shambhuji by turns threatened the English and offered them his alliance if they would only exclude the Siddis from their harbour; but the President and Council of Surat instructed Bombay, 'You must use all contrivances to keep fair with them; as we would by no means quarrel with Shambhuji Rajah, so upon no account can we with prudence fall out with the Siddi at present, it being a very unfit time.'

The Maratha vessels, being smaller in size and armament than the Siddi's, lay sheltered up the Nagothna creek and in Khanderi harbour during the monsoons, without venturing on pitched battles. But occasional skirmishes took place between the rival gallivats (*jalbas*) in which the Siddis had the advantage, and these seas were often closed to the Maratha trading vessels.

On 7 December 1681 the Siddis burnt the town of Apta, on the Patalganga, 16 km (ten miles) south of Panvel. (They had first sacked it in 1673.) 'On this provocation Shambhuji, accompanied by Sultan Akbar, came down from Raigarh, with 20,000 men and a vast train of cannon, to Danda [18 December] ... and from the hill opposite to Janjira' bombarded that island incessantly for 30 days. But the Mughal invasion of North Konkan and capture of Kalian (*c.* 30 January) forced him to hasten back to Raigarh.

In July 1682, the Marathas getting some boats together delivered an assault on Janjira, but they could gain no footing on the storm-beaten rocky coast and had to retire with heavy loss. On 4 October, Siddi Misri (in Maratha service) with 30 gallivats gave battle to Siddi Qasim's squadron, 12 km (8 miles) south of Kolaba Point. But he was defeated after a brief fight, his other vessels fled away, and he was carried a prisoner, mortally wounded, with seven of his vessels to Bombay.

14.8 Shambhuji's War with the Portuguese, 1683

Shambhu's wrath fell on the Portuguese. They had given him provocation by seizing and fortifying Anjidiv, an island just south of Karwar, which the Maratha king had intended to make his naval base, to counteract the Siddi stronghold of Janjira (April 1682). In December 1682, the viceroy of Goa had allowed the Mughal ships to pass under the Portuguese fort of Thana up the creek to Kalian, with provisions for the Mughal army under Ranmast Khan, then ravaging that district. He had also allowed the Mughal army a free passage through the Portuguese province of Daman ('the North') to the Maratha district of North Konkan. For these breaches of neutrality Shambhuji vowed vengeance on the Portuguese. On 5 April 1683, he launched his attack on them. With 1,000 horse and 2,000 foot he raided the open town of Tarapur and burnt it and all other towns from Daman to Bassein. On 31 July, his Peshwa, with 6,000 infantry and 2,000 cavalry, laid siege to Chaul. Early in the morning of 8 August the Marathas made an assault on the city, but were repulsed with heavy loss. At midnight following 29 August, the Portuguese Viceroy sent a large body of the Indians of Goa across the river to the mainland of Savant-vadi, with a general licence to plunder and burn the villages of Shambhuji. This attempt to imitate the Maratha policy of *mulkgiri* was a failure. But Chaul remained unconquered by the Marathas after a siege of many months.

The Viceroy of Goa planned to make a diversion by laying siege to Phonda; with 800 white troops and 8,000 Kanarese, and five pieces of heavy artillery, he arrived (on 22 October) in the vicinity of Phonda and opened fire on that fort immediately.

The thirtieth of October had been fixed for scaling the breach in the inner wall. But that very day a relieving force under Shambhuji was sighted, the Portuguese army was completely outflanked and lost heart, and decided to raise the siege. Next day they began to retreat, and on 1 November reached Durbata, where they were to embark for return to Goa.

The retreat from Durbata was disastrous for the Portuguese. The Maratha cavalry attacked the Goa infantry with great determination. 'The Kanarese [i.e., the native troops of Goa] ... threw down their muskets and fled. Finally, nearly all the Portuguese did the same, but in vain, for the blacks rode over them, trampling most of our men. All our men fled in utter disorder, each one trying to save himself.... Of the Portuguese infantry nearly a whole company of seamen were killed, the dead and wounded amounting to two hundred.'

14.9 Shambhuji Invades Goa, 1683

From the walls of Phonda Shambhuji marched wih 7,000 cavalry and 15,000 infantry against Goa city. At 10 o'clock in the night of 14 November, forty Marathas entered the island of Santo Estevao, 3 km (two miles) north-east of Goa, by crossing a channel which is fordable at low tide. Then they scaled the fort on the top of the hill, and were soon reinforced by four thousand men from their main army from the other side of the river.

Next morning at 7 o'clock, the Viceroy with 400 men disembarked at the island of Santo Estevao, and vigorously attacked the Maratha infantry. But three hundred cavalry reinforcing them, 'they fell upon our men with great fury.... Our men began a headlong flight down the hill.... Besides the dead, who were said to be more than 150,—there was not one who was not wounded by a ball, sword or stone. The Viceroy had his arm pierced by a ball.... At two o'clock in the afternoon he embarked.... The rest of the men,—about 120,—fled into the river.... Some stuck in the mud, and some swam off. All those who were in the mud died. But next day (16 November) the Maratha left the island in great haste.'

On 1 December one thousand Maratha horse and 3,000 foot entered the districts of Salsette and Bardes lying immediately south and north respectively of the island of Goa and separated from the latter by a creek only. They plundered everything that they could find, took the men prisoners, ravished the women and roamed over the country for a month. Shortly afterwards a deliverer came to terror-stricken Goa in the person of Shah Alam, who occupied Bicholim (an important town belonging to Shambhuji) on 5 January 1684, and three days later a very powerful Mughal fleet reached the harbour of Goa. At the news of the prince's approach Shambhuji fled (23 December) to Raigarh, leaving Kavi-kalash with Akbar to negotiate with the Portuguese for peace.

In the northern theatre of this war, i.e. Daman district, the Portuguese were severely beaten. Many of their towns were taken and burnt by the Marathas; on 22 December Shambhu occupied the island of Karinja, only 16 km (10 miles) south-east of Bombay. After Shambhuji had hurriedly fled northwards to his capital, leaving Kavi-kalash as his plenipotentiary for concluding a peace with the Portuguese through the mediation of Akbar, these two at first took refuge from the Mughals in the forest of Bhimgarh (43 km, i.e. 27 miles east of Goa) and then at Phonda, and made peace with the Portuguese envoy, Manuel S. de Albuquerque (about 20 January) on the basis of the mutual restitution of conquests and prizes and neutrality in future.

But this treaty was a hollow truce. The Maratha king soon prepared for a second encounter with the Portuguese. On 19 September the Portuguese attacked and recovered Karinja island. Languid hostilities with the Portuguese continued till the end of Shambhuji's reign.

14.10 Prince Akbar's Designs and Disappointments at the Maratha Court

Shambhuji was frittering away his strength in small predatory incursions here and there, or engaging in fruitless wars with the Siddis and the Portuguese, having 'too many irons in the fire' to do anything effective, as the Surat factors rightly remarked in December 1683.

Akbar's one thought was, how to gain the throne of Delhi. He valued Shambhuji only as an instrument of this design. Every day that he spent in Maharashtra was a day more of hope deferred. It was also a day more of unwonted suffering to him. Only by leaving Maharashtra could he get back to civilization.

But Shambhuji's interests did not exactly coincide with Akbar's. Why should he go out of the safety of the Deccan hills and jungles into the broad plains of North India where his troops would lose their natural advantage? Why should he denude his country of its defenders by accompanying Akbar in the wild project of invading Hindustan, and thus give Aurangzib an opportunity of conquering Maharashtra in his absence?

At last after 18 months of heart-sick waiting, hope deferred and evasion of promises, Akbar saw through Shambhuji's character and policy and despaired of ever being effectually helped by him. He, therefore, decided to leave Maharashtra. He issued from his asylum at Pali (December 1682) with his Rathor contingent, and took up his residence at Banda in Savant-vadi, which though lying within the Maratha kingdom, is only 38 km (twenty-five miles) north of Goa. From this place Akbar (January 1683) sent an agent to the Viceroy of Goa, presenting him with his own jewelled dagger and begging for his permission to sell some jewels in Goa and his influence with the Portuguese factor at Mangalore (in the kingdom of Kanara) to assist Akbar in chartering a ship there to carry him to Arabia. But by order of the Emperor, during March and April the Siddl lay with his fleet in the Rajapur Creek, on the watch to intercept Akbar, if he took ship at Goa.

In September, Akbar removed from Banda to Bicholim, a town in Shambhuji's territory, less than 16 km (ten miles) north of Goa. Utterly disgusted with Shambhuji, the poor deluded Mughal prince, at last (about 8 November) bought a ship and embarked at Vingurla, wishing to go to Persia. But Kavi-kalash hurriedly arrived from Rajapur and with Durgadas visited Akbar on board, and persuaded him to come back to land with fresh promises of Shambhuji's armed support in India. Then the Luso-Maratha war broke out, in which Akbar acted as the mediator of the Marathas.

Akbar spent a whole year from February 1684 in the Ratnagiri district (at Sakharpen and Malkapur), inviting Kavi-kalash repeatedly to meet him and decide on future plans of action.

14.11 Rebellions Against Shambhuji; Mughal Operations from July 1683

From July 1683 the prospects of the imperialists in the Deccan began to brighten. Akbar was estranged from Shambhuji and meditating flight from India and the Marathas became plunged into a long war with the Portuguese. The Mughals profited by these circumstances. The Emperor's indecision and cautious inactivity ended, and a vigorous offensive was opened in many directions.

Shambhuji's profligacy, capriciousness and violence created a general discontent among his officers and vassals. Aurangzib's bribes aggravated the evil, and there were frequent desertions from the Maratha service. On 26 July 1683, Qazi Haidar, Shivaji's *munshi*, came over to Aurangzib and was created a 2-hazari and a Khan, and later on (1706) rose to be the Chief Qazi of the Empire.

Khem Savant (ruler of Kudal and a vassal of Shambhuji) rebelled against him and, reinforced by the Portuguese, roamed over Savant-vadi, burning and robbing many places in the Maratha kingdom north of Goa (February 1685). He, with two other rebels, named Dulva Nayak (of Phonda) and Ram Dalvi, took refuge in Portuguese territory, made it a safe base for their operations, and kept South Konkan and Kanara in turmoil. The contagion spread. The whole coastal region was soon up in arms against Shambhuji.

The Mughal offensive was opened at the end of the rainy season, about the middle of September, 1683. A few days after 15 September, Shah Alam marched out of Aurangabad with a grand army to penetrate into Savant-vadi and South Konkan by the Ramghat pass, while Shihab-ud-din was sent to Puna (October), from which he made a raid on Nizampur in the Kolaba district across the Ghats (27 December). Prince Azam, who had been sent against Bijapuri territory (on 20 August), returned to Court in October and was transferred to Nasik (November), to guard the northward road to Baglana and Khandesh; the Siddi cruised off Vingurla watching Akbar's movements (October); the Emperor himself marched further south to Ahmadnagar (November); and another army corps (under Khan-i-Jahan) was advanced from Bidar to Akalkot to watch the Golkonda and Bijapur frontiers and prevent those Powers from making any diversion in aid of the Marathas.

14.12 Shah Alam Invades South Konkan

From Aurangabad Shah Alam marched (September 1683) due south through Bijapuri territory, entered the Belgaum district, and captured the fort of Shahpur, Sampgaon (28 km, i.e. 18 miles south-east of Belgaum) and some other large cities and a few forts of that region and much booty. Then he turned sharply to the west, crossed the Ramghat pass 42 km (26 miles) due west of Belgaum and 48 km i.e., (30 miles) north-east of Goa as the crow flies and descended into the plains of Savant-vadi.

Shah Alam reached Bicholim on 5 January, 1684, and there demolished the spacious mansions and pleasure-gardens of Shambhuji and Akbar. Three days afterwards a large Mughal fleet rode into Goa harbour with provisions for the prince's army.

On arriving near Goa, he demanded a huge fee from the Portuguese for having saved them from being plundered by Shambhu! He also plotted to seize Goa by treachery. This rupture with the Portuguese was the worst mistake that the prince could have committed, because it ultimately caused the annihilation of his army through famine.

From the neighbourhood of Goa Shah Alam marched northwards to Malvan and there blew up with gunpowder the famous white temple and other edifices belonging to the Maratha king. Kudal and Banda (in Savant-vadi) were burnt and Vingurla sacked by him during this expedition. Turning south again, he returned to the bank of the Chapora river (north of Goa), either to establish touch with his provision vessels or to make a second attempt on the Portuguese capital.

In February the further progress of the Mughal army was stopped by famine. Portuguese suspicion prevented the Mughal provision fleet from sailing up the creek of Goa to the prince's camp; no corn could be secured locally, as famine was raging in Goa. The prince's only work in Konkan had been, as the English merchants remark, 'to range to and fro, as he pleases, with little resistance. He hath taken no stronghold but ruins the country, lays all waste, and burns all towns he comes near.' The scarcity in his camp reached an extreme point. The soldiers, through fasting, retained only the last breath of their lives. So the baffled prince returned to the *ghat* on 20 February.

His difficulties only thickened. In the narrow Ramghat pass, the air bred a pestilence of such virulence that in a week one-third of his men died, none escaping who was attacked. The horses, elephants and camels perished in an even larger proportion and their carcasses poisoned the air. This failure of transport led to a second famine. Many of his men also died from the great heat and thirst that they underwent.

Shah Alam crossed the pass and descended into the Kanara plains. The enemy hovered round, cut off stragglers and plundered the baggage and convoys 'in all dierctions.' The miserable remnant of his army reached Ahmadnagar on 18 May, without having done anything except burning a few villages and robbing a few towns.

14.13 Shambhuji's Doings After 1683

The minor operations of the years 1683–85 need not be described here. The Mughal campaign in the first half of 1684 was highly successful; many Maratha forts were taken, their field armies repeatedly defeated, and much territory annexed. The crowning feat was the capture of two wives, one daughter and three slave-girls of Shambhuji, who were confined in the fort of Bahadurgarh in July. One wife and one sister of the Maratha king had been captured before by Dilir Khan and lodged in Ahmadnagar fort.

Where was Shambhuji all this time? After the failure of his attack on Goa at the end of 1683, he gave himself entirely up to pleasure, spending his time with women, amusement, and wine, instead of taking the field and emulating the example of valour and untiring exertion bequeathed to him by his father.

About the middle of January 1685, Shihab-ub-din Khan made a fresh dash into Konkan by Borghat and set fire to the village (Pachad) at the foot of Raigarh fort, 'slew many of the infidel chiefs, plundered their wealth and property, made many captives and gained a great victory.' For this brilliant success he was created Khan Bahadur Firuz Jang.

Many Maratha captains were induced by Firuz Jang to desert to the imperial side. Early in December, Kondana was captured by Abdul Qadir. While every Maratha soldier was sorely needed for home defence, they made the mistake of blindly following their policy of *mulk-giri* and raiding Khandesh. But at the end of March 1685 the siege of Bijapur began, the Mughal forces were concentrated there, and the pressure upon the Marathas ceased for a time.

Captain Richard Keigwin, who had seized the fort of Bombay for the East India Company's governor, adopted a vigorous policy and, in April

1684, forced Siddi Qasim, the Mughal admiral, to respect the neutrality of Bombay by ceasing to make the island the base of his operations against the Maratha villages. At the end of April he sent two ambassadors (Captain Henry Gray and Lt. Thomas Wilkins) with Ram Shenvi as interpreter, to Shambhuji, to settle the long-standing differences about the indemnity claimed by the English for Shivaji's sack of their Rajapur factory in March 1661 and other matters and to make a friendly alliance with the Maratha Rajah. The mission was a complete success. Shambhuji granted all the demands of the English and signed two agreements with them containing 30 and 11 articles.

14.14 Mughal Conquest of the Province of Bijapur

After the surrender of Bijapur (12 September 1686), Aurangzib sent his generals to the different parts of the newly-annexed country to make a revenue settlement, maintain peace, and take charge of the forts. But from next February to September the Mughal forces were concentrated at the siege of Golkonda, and it was only after the fall of that fort (21 September 1687) that the imperialists could renew their activity in the provinces of the old Adil Shahi kingdom.

Their first campaign was directed against the Berad clan, who ruled over the land situated in the fork between the Krishna and Bhima, with their capital at Sagar. The terror of Mughal arms inspired by the fall of Bijapur and Golkonda within one year, did the work. Pam Nayak, the Berad chieftain submitted, gave up his fort (28 November), and paid a visit to the Emperor on 27 December 1687, but suddenly died after five days. His country was annexed.

Mughal enterprise was next directed towards the east and the south of the two newly conquered Deccani Sultanates. Firuz Jang invaded the district of Karnul and the fort of Adoni, south of the Tungabhadra, where Siddi Masaud was now reigning in independence. On 6 August 1688, Siddi Masaud was induced to capitulate; his fort was occupied and renamed Imtiaz-garh, and he was enrolled in the Mughal peerage as a *7-hazari*.

Prince Azam captured the strong fort of Belgaon after a siege (about March). In other directions, too, innumerable forts were captured by the imperialists.

The Emperor left Haidarabad on 25 January 1688, and arrived at Bijapur on 15 March. Here his attention was taken up by the necessity of giving relief to the people who had fallen into want through the ruin of the city and its environs. The chief want of the citizens was the lack of drinking water, because the aqueducts were damaged during the siege and the water suddenly dried up (probably from this cause). Mukhlis Khạn, the Mir Atish, was ordered to cut a canal for conveying the water of the Krishna to the city.

A terrible epidemic broke out in the city of Bijapur and the imperial camp, at the beginning of November 1688. 'First a bubo appeared in the arm-pit and the corner of the thigh, then high fever and unconsciousness supervened; medical treatment produced no effect; few men lived beyond two days, but most died in less. Among the victims were the Emperor's old wife Aurangabadi Mahal, Maharajah Jaswant's alleged son Muhammadi-Raj aged 13, Fazil Khan the *Sadar*, and many other grandees. The middle-class and poor people, both Hindus and Muhammadans, who died, cannot be counted, but are conjectured to have been not less than a lakh. Firuz Jang's eyes were lost.'

The Emperor firmly set out on his campaign on 14 December 1688, and a week afterwards the fury of the epidemic abated. He marched on to Akluj, 136 km (85 miles) north of Bijapur and halted.

14.15 Last Efforts of Prince Akbar in India

Akbar made a dash into Mughal territory in June 1686, after the Emperor had left Sholapur to join the siege of Bijapur and Mughal Deccan was denuded of his forces. The attempt, however, failed, because the Emperor with his usual foresight had left Marhamat Khan with a division to guard Ahmadnagar, who fought a severe battle with Akbar near Chakan, and defeated and repulsed him. The prince went back to Shambhuji's dominions and made some futile attempts to break northwards to Surat through Mahuli and Jawhar.

At last, with Zia-ud-din Muhammad (a former follower of Shuja) and 45 retainers, Akbar embarked on a ship hired at Rajapur (commanded by Bendal, an Englishman), and sailed for Persia (in February 1687), but was driven by stress of weather to the port of Masqat. After some months' detention here he reached the Persian Court at Isfahan on 24

January 1688. After thus sending him safely out of India, Durgadas returned to his home in Marwar.

14.16 Internal Condition of the Maratha Kingdom and Shambhuji's Doings, 1685–87

While Aurangzib was directing the full strength of his empire against Bijapur and Golkonda, Shambhuji made no adequate effort to meet the danger that threatened all the Deccani Powers alike. His soldiers plundered places in the Mughal territory as a matter of routine, but these raids did not influence the-military situation. Aurangzib disregarded such pin-pricks. The Maratha king was not wise enough to follow any large and well-thought-out plan for diverting the Mughals from the sieges of Bijapur and Golkonda and averting their fall; his Government was also hopelessly weakened by rebellions among his vassals and plots among his courtiers. Within a few years of the accession of Shambhuji, nearly all the ministers and generals who had contributed to the glory of his father's reign disappeared. His affairs in the outlying parts of his dominions suffered from the lack of competent agents on the spot. The evil was aggravated by fresh conspiracies against the king, which were inevitably followed by the execution or at least imprisonment of more Maratha generals and ministers of leading positions. The Madras Karnatak, a kingdom in itself, had practically passed out of Shambhuji's control and was ruled by his brother-in-law Harji Mahadik with the title of Maharajah in semi-independence.

The economic decay of the Maratha kingdom through Shambhuji's supine rule, the corruption of his officers, and the disorder caused by the rebels, is graphically described in the English factory records. 'In former years there was a quantity of pepper, about 1,500 *khandi* [20 maunds each], it grew in and near about Rajapur; but now grows not the tenth part since that place hath been in Shivaji's hands; it is a miserable poor town [now].'

The cause of this ruin of trade and industry were misrule and the universal hunger for bribes and presents among the Maratha State officials. 'With the Rajah down to the plowman the infection of *peshkasing* is so prevalent that nothing can be well done without it, or withstand it.' The weavers that used to come from Thanah and Chaul to Bombay were about

600 families. But within a year of the Maratha siege of Chaul (1683), 400 of these families for want of encouragement forsook Bombay, 150 of the remainder were dead; so that only 50 families were left in 1685.

Near Karwar the ways were molested by Shambhuji's revolted vassals. 'In his dominions there is little or no safety, and at best a great deal of hazard: trade in general obstructed.'

14.17 Capture and Execution of Shambhuji

After the conspiracies against Shambhuji in June 1680 and October 1681 had been crushed, there was a fresh plot in October 1684, in consequence of which he threw several leading men into prison, where they remained confined till his death. Things then continued quiet at his Court for four years. But in October 1688, the Shirke family again rose against him; they attacked Kavi-kalash and drove him into Khelna for refuge. Shambhuji marched from Raigarh to the rescue of his favourite, defeated and routed the rebels at Sangameshwar, and then went to Khelna. He arrested Prahlad Niraji and many other ministers and leading people on suspicion of complicity in the late rising, and after provisioning Khelna fort, started with Kavi-kalash for returning to his capital. On the way he arrived at Sangameshwar, 35 km (22 miles) north-east of Ratnagir city, and the sacred junction of the Alak-nanda and Varuna rivers, where Kavi-kalash had laid out fine gardens and built nicely-decorated mansions for his master. Here, after sending his army and family back to Raigarh, Shambhuji plunged into drinking and merry-making, with a small escort and in utter carelessness. All vigilance was abandoned, as he believed the place to be impenetrable to Mughal arms.

Shaikh Nizam, 'chief among the servants of Qutb Shah,' had been induced to desert to the Mughals during the siege of Golkonda (28 May, 1687) and created a 6-*hazari* with the title of Muqarrab Khan. This able and active general had been detached to lay siege to Panhala (1688).

On hearing from his spies of Shambhuji's unguarded life of debauchery at Sangameshwar, he lost no time, Taking with himself only 2,000 picked troopers and 1,000 infantry, he made a forced march from his camp at Kolhapur. Very great hardship was undergone in crossing the jungles, broken ground and lofty passes of the Western Ghats, at such a rapid pace. With only 300 troopers he arrived at Sangameshwar 'with the speed of lightning and wind', covering the intervening 144 km (90 miles) in two or three days.

When the invaders entered the town, Kavi-kalash offered them battle. He was wounded by an arrow in his right hand, and being unable to fight, dismounted. The Maratha force had hurriedly assembled, and being now without a leader, it broke and fled away. Shambhuji and his minister then hid themselves in a hole in the floor of the latter's house, but were dragged out by their long hair, and taken to the general on his elephant outside. Twenty-five of Shambhuji's chief followers with their wives and daughters were captured at this place (1 February 1689).

The news of the capture soon reached the imperial camp at Akluj and caused a wild outburst of rejoicing in all parts of the imperial dominions.

On 15 February the imperial camp reached Bahadurgarh, and the captives were brought there. By the Emperor's order, the oppressor of the Deccan was made a mark of public ridicule. Six kilometres (four miles) outside the encampment, Shambhuji and Kavi-kalash were dressed as buffoons with long fool's caps and bells placed on their heads, mounted on camels, and brought to Bahadurgarh with drums beating and trumpets pealing. Hundreds of thousands of spectators lined the roads, to gaze at Shambhuji as at a new kind of wild beast or demon. Thus degraded, the captives were slowly paraded through the entire camp and finally brought to the Emperor who was sitting in full *darbar* for the occasion. At the sight of the prisoner, Aurangzib descended from his throne and kneeling down to the carpet bowed his head to the ground in double thankfulness to the Giver of this crowning victory.[2] The Emperor's counsellors wanted to spare Shambhuji's life and thus induce him to order his officers to surrender all his forts peacefully. Ruhullah Khan was sent by Aurangzib to learn from Shambhuji where he kept his treasures hidden and which of the imperial officers used to correspond with him. Fretting with bitterness of souls at being publicly insulted and now driven to despair, Shambhuji spurned the offer of life, loosened his tongue in abuse of the

---

[2] K.K. (388) narrates a tradition that when Aurangzib was thus praying, Kavi-kalash addressed *impromptu* Hindi verses to Shambhuji saying, 'O Rajah even Aurangzib dare not sit on the throne in thy presence, but must kneel to do thee homage!' Ishwardas (155*b*) says that Shambhuji refused to bow to the Emperor, though urged to do so.

Emperor and his Prophet, and scurrilously asked for one of Aurangzib's daughters to be given to him as the price of his friendship.

The Maratha Rajah had sinned beyond hope of pardon. That very night his eyes were blinded and next day the tongue of Kavi-kalash was cut out. The Muhammadan theologians, pronounced a decree that Shambhuji should be put to death on account of his having 'slain, captured and dishonoured Muslims and plundered the cities of Islam.' The Emperor consented to his death. After undergoing a fortnight of torture and insult, the captives were removed with the imperial camp to Koregaon, on the bank of the Bhima, 19 km (12 miles) north-east of Puna (3 March), and there they were put to a cruel and painful death on 11 March, their limbs being hacked off one by one, and their flesh thrown to the dogs. Their severed heads were stuffed with straw and exhibited in all the chief cities of the Deccan to the accompaniment of drums and trumpets.

14.18 Capture of Raigarh and Shambhuji's Family, 1689

After t he downfall of Shambhuji his younger brother Rajaram was taken out of prison and crowned (8 February) by the Maratha ministers in Raigarh, as Shambhuji's son Shahu was too young to be the head of a State engaged in a life and death struggle with an enemy like Aurangzib. Soon afterwards an imperial army under Itiqad Khan laid siege to the Maratha capital, but Rajaram escaped from it (5 April) in the guise of a *yogi.* Sayyid Abdullah Khan (of Barha), the new subahdar of Bijapur, tried to intercept the fugitives, and came up with them in three days 'near the forts of Subhangarh and Jara on the bank of the Tungabhadra.' The Marathas, who had taken refuge in an island, were attacked at night and a hundred of their chiefs were made prisoners. But Rajaram contrived to escape with his bare life while his comrades were carrying on the fight.

For some time he hid himself in the territory of the Rani of Bednur (now the Shimoga district of Mysore). But at last she let him escape to Jinji (where he arrived on 1 November), and then made her peace with the Emperor by paying a small fine. The Maratha captives taken on the island were confined in the citadel of Bijapur, but in a short time Hindu Rao, Baharji, and some twenty other chiefs escaped from the stronghold—a feat 'which was impossible except with the connivance of their guards.' At this the Emperor put the remaining 80 prisoners to death.

Itiqad Khan (later entitled Zulfiqar Khan) after a long struggle captured the fort of Raigarh on 19 October 1689, and seized in it Shivaji's surviving widows, and Shambhuji's and Rajaram's wives, daughters and sons, including Shahu, a boy of seven. The ladies were lodged in separate tents with every respect and privacy. Shahu was given the rank of a 7-*hazari* and the title of Rajah, but kept a prisoner near the imperial tent.

Thus, by the end of the year 1689, Aurangzib was the unrivalled lord paramount of northern India and the Deccan alike. Adil Shah, Qutb Shah, and Rajah Shambhuji had all fallen and their dominions had been annexed to his empire.

'All seemed to have been gained by Aurangzib now; but in reality all was lost. It was the beginning of his end. The Mughal Empire had become too large to be ruled by one man or from one centre.... His enemies rose on all sides; he could defeat but not crush them for ever. Lawlessness reigned in many parts of Northern and Central India. The administration grew slack and corrupt. The endless war in the Deccan exhausted his treasury. Napoleon I used to say, "It was the Spanish ulcer which ruined me." The Deccan ulcer ruined Aurangzib.' (My *Studies in Aurangzib's Reign,* 17.)

15 *Struggle with the Marathas up to 1700*

15.1 Aurangzib's Movements during the Second Half of his Reign

Leaving Rajputana on 8 September 1681, Aurangzib reached Aurangabad on 22 March following and occupied this, strategic centre, directing the operations of his columns in all directions till 13 November 1683, when he proceeded further south to Ahmadnagar. From this place he arrived at Sholapur on 24 May 1685 so as to be still closer to Bijapur, which his troops had besieged. He went to the Rasulpur suburb of Bijapur on 3 July 1686 in order to press the siege to a conclusion. When the Adil Shahi capital was conquered, he left the place on 30 October, visited Kulbarga and Bidar, and then sat down before Golkonda on 28 January 1687. Here he lay encamped for a year, and then arrived at Bijapur (on his second visit) on 15 March 1688. In this city he lived for the next nine months, till driven out (on 14 December) by a terrible outbreak of the plague. By way of Akluj and Bahadurgarh (on the Bhima) he reached Koregaon in the Puna district, where he encamped from 3 March to 18 December 1689, and then returned to Bijapur (on 11 January 1690). But he soon left it, and after spending February, March and April at different places south of that city, near the bank of the Krishna, he finally encamped at Galgala, on the southern side of that river and 54 km (34 miles) south-west of Bijapur, about 21 May 1690. The rest of this year and the first two months of the next year were passed by him here; and then he went back to the environs of Bijapur for fourteen months (March 1691–May 1692). Thereafter, Galgala was again his, residence, for nearly three years (May 1692–March 1695).

Finally, after a fifth and last visit to Bijapur for five weeks (April–May 1695) he settled at Brahmapuri on the southern bank of the Bhima, which he renamed *Islampuri.* Here he lived for four years and a half (21 May 1695–19 October 1699). At Islampuri his encampment was walled round, and here he left his family in charge of his wazir when he set out on 19 October, 1699, on that endless campaign against the Maratha forts which was to wear out the last years of his life, and from which he returned to Ahmadnagar (20 January 1706), only to die a year later (20 February 1707).

15.2 THE MARATHA RECOVERY, 1690–95

The years 1688 and 1689 were a period of unbroken triumph for the Emperor. His armies took possession of the forts and provinces of the annexed kingdoms of Bijapur and Golkonda, e.g. Sagar (the Berad capital), Raichur and Adoni (in the east), Sera and Bangalore (in Mysore), Wandiwash and Conjeveram (in the Madras Karnatak), Bankapur and Belgaon (in the extreme south-west), besides Raigarh (the capital) and many other Maratha forts. In northern India, too, signal success attended his arms: the Jat rising under Rajaram was put down and that leader was slain (on 4 July, 1688).

But at the end of 1689 the new Maratha king Rajaram was known to have reached the fort of Jinji, which henceforth became a centre of Maratha enterprise in the East Coast, while their ministers left at home organized resistance to the Mughals in the west. The difficulties of Aurangzib were only multiplied by the disappearance of a common head and a central Government among the Marathas, as every Maratha captain with his own retainers fought and raided in a different quarter and on his own account. It now became a people's war, and Aurangzib could not end it, because there was no Maratha Government or State-army for him to attack and destroy. The imperial forces could not be present everywhere in full strength; hence, they suffered reverses here and there. The enemy forts which the Mughals had captured or bought during the first panic following Shambhuji's downfall, now began to be recovered by the Marathas. The tide first turned against Aurangzib in May 1690, when his general Rustam Khan was captured and his whole camp looted by the Marathas.

Throughout 1690 and 1691 the Emperor's chief concern still was to take possession of the almost boundless expanse of fertile territory in the south and the east, which had legally fallen to him as the heir-at-law of Adil Shah and Qutb Shah, At this stage, he evidently underrated the Maratha danger, as he felt that the *State* of the Marathas had been practically annihilated. He had yet to take a proper measure of the Maratha *people.*

In the autumn of 1691 the Mughal position before Jinji became so dangerous that the Emperor had to divert large forces to that quarter. In 1692 nothing was achieved by the imperialists in the western theatre, while in the east coast the year ended with crushing disasters to their arms,—the capture of two high Mughal generals, the abandonment of the siege lines before Jinji, and the arrest of Prince Kam Bakhsh by his colleagues (December 1692–January 1693). So, the first thing to be done in 1693 was to save the situation by pouring reinforcements and supplies into the Eastern Karnatak. In the western theatre, Prince Muizz-ud-din, who laid siege to Panhala in October 1692, toiled unsuccessfully throughout the next year, and was finally expelled by the Marathas in March 1694. In addition to this, there were the incessant raids of the Maratha partisan leaders,—Santa Ghorpare, Dhana Jadav, Nima Sindhia, Hanumant Rao and others.

Meanwhile, over the broad and strategically important tract from Bidar to Bijapur and from Raichur to Malkhed, the activities of the hardy aboriginal tribe of Berads lead by their enterprising chief Pidia Nayak, had become so serious that a large army under a first-rate general had to be posted at Sagar from June 1691 to December 1692. Then the Berad chieftain made his submission, but he renewed his hostility three years later, when another large army had to be sent against him (1696). During 1694 the war in Western Deccan continued to be of the same indecisive and straggling character. Only in the Madras Karnatak the reinforced Mughal general made many conquests and levied contribution from Tanjore, but Jinji remained uncaptured.

At last, by April 1695 Aurangzib came to realize that he had really gained nothing by the conquest of the Adil Shahi and Qutb Shahi capitals and the extinction of their royal lines. He now perceived that the Maratha problem was no longer what it had been in Shivaji's time, or even in Shambhuji's. They were no longer a tribe of banditti or local rebels, but the one dominating factor of Deccan politics, the only enemy left to the Empire, and yet an enemy all-pervasive from Bombay to Madras across the Indian Peninsula, elusive as the wind, without any headman or stronghold whose capture would naturally result in the extinction of their power. They had now assumed the alarming character of being the ally and rallying point of all the enemies of the Empire and all disturbers of public peace and regular administration throughout the Deccan and even in Malwa, the Central Provinces and Bundelkhand.

For Aurangzib, then there was no going back to Delhi; his work in the Deccan was still unfinished; indeed, it was only just beginning.

15.3 The Emperor's Stay at Islampuri 1695–99

Therefore, in May 1695 he sent his eldest surviving son Shah Alam to govern the north-western portion of the Empire (the Panjab, Sindh and afterwards Afghanistan) and to guard the western gateway of India, while he himself settled at Islampuri for the next 4½ years, and thereafter made it the base (*bungah*) at the back of his campaigns. During the Islampuri period (1695–99), the Maratha danger came nearer home and drove the Mughals into the defensive in the Marathi and Kanarese districts of the present Bombay Presidency. The movements of their roving bands were bewilderingly rapid and unexpected. The Mughals could not defend every place; their pursuing columns panted helplessly behind the 'robbers' and wore themselves out in vain. Local representatives of the Emperor were driven to make unauthorized terms with the Marathas by promising them an annual blackmail of one-fourth of the revenue (*chauth*). Worse than these, many imperialists made a concert with the enemy and enriched themselves by robbing the Emperor's own subjects and innocent traders, as these officers had been starving by getting no rent from their devastated fiefs. The Mughal administration had really dissolved, and only the presence of the Emperor with all his troops in the country held it together, but it was now a delusive phantom.

The chief incidents of this Islampuri period where Santa's destruction of two great Mughal generals, Qasim Khan (November 1695) and Himmat Khan (January 1696), the murder of Santa in a domestic feud (June 1697), the Mughal capture of Jinji (7 January 1698), and the consequent return of Rajaram to Maharashtra.

15.4 Aurangzib's Last Campaigns, 1699–1705

This last event forced a change on Aurangzib's policy. Safe in the undisputed possession of the east coast, he could now concentrate all his resources in the western theatre of war. Now, therefore, began the last stage of Aurangzib's career,—the sieges of successive Maratha forts by the Emperor in person. The rest of his life (1699–1707) is a repetition of the same sickening tale: a hill-fort captured by him after a vast expenditure of time men and money, the fort recovered by the Marathas from the weak Mughal garrison after a few months, and its siege began again by the Mughals a year or two later! His soldiers and camp-followers suffered unspeakable hardships in marching over-flooded rivers, muddy roads, and broken hilly tracks; porters disappeared; transport beasts died of hunger and overwork; scarcity of grain was ever present in his camp. His officers, wearied of this labour of Sisyphus; but Aurangzib would burst into wrath at any suggestion of return to northern India and taunt the unlucky counsellor with cowardice and love of ease. The mutual jealousies of his generals ruined his affairs as completely as the French cause in the Peninsular War was ruined by the jealousies of Napoleon's marshals. Therefore, the Emperor must conduct every operation in person, or nothing would be done. The siege of eight forts—Satara, Parli, Panhala, Khelna, Kondana, Rajgarh, Torna and Wagingera,—occupied him for five years and a half (1699–1705).

The siege of Wagingera (8 February–27 April 1705) was the last campaign of the old campaigner of eighty-eight. At Devapur, where he halted (May–October 1705) after the capture of this fort, a severe illness seized him. The whole camp was thrown into despair and confusion. At length Aurangzib yielded to their entreaty and the warning of approaching death, and retreated to Ahmadnagar (20 January 1706), to die there a year afterwards.

15.5 The Sorrow and Misery of Aurangzib's Last Years

The last few years of his life were inexpressibly sad. On its public side there was the consciousness that his long reign of half a century had been a colossal failure. The endless war in the Deccan exhausted his treasury; the Government turned bankrupt; the soldiers starving from arrears of pay (usually three years overdue) mutinied; and during the closing years of his reign the revenue of Bengal, regularly sent by the honest and able *diwan* Murshid Quli Khan, was the sole support of the Emperor's household and army, and its arrival was eagerly looked forward to. While in the Deccan the Marathas remained supreme to the end, lawlessness reigned in many places of northern and central India also. The old Emperor in the far South lost control over his officers in Hindustan, and the administration grew slack and corrupt; chiefs and zamindars defied the local authorities and asserted themselves, filling the country with tumult, and the great anarchy in the empire of Delhi began even before Aurangzib had closed his eyes.

In the Deccan, the Maratha captains, each acting on his own account, incessantly raided Mughal territory and did the greatest possible injury to the imperialists by their guerilla warfare. They seemed to be ubiquitous and elusive like the wind. The movable columns frequently sent out from the imperial headquarters to 'chastise the robbers,' only marched and countermarched, without being able to crush the enemy. When the Mughal forces had gone back, the scattered Marathas, like water parted by the oar, closed again and resumed their attack as before. There was an exultant and menacing Maratha army always hanging five on six kilometres (three or four miles) behind the Emperor's camp wherever it marched or halted.

The wastage of the Deccan war, which raged intensely for nearly 20 years, was one hundred thousand soldiers and followers and three times that number of horses, elephants, camels and oxen on the Mughal side every year. In the imperial camp pestilence was always present and the daily mortality was heavy. The economic exhaustion of the Deccan was complete: 'the fields were left devoid of trees and bare of crops, their places being taken by the bones of men and beasts. The country was so entirely desolated and depopulated that neither fire nor light could be found in the course of a three or four days' journey.' (Manucci)

15.6 Leading Maratha Ministers and Generals at the Accession of Rajaram

In the terrible national crisis when Shambhuji's sons were captured and his successor Rajaram was driven into hopeless flight by the Mughals, the genius of the Maratha *people* saved them and secured their liberty. It is, therefore, necessary to study the leaders of this almost kingless State during the period. At this time (end of 1689), the leading persons in the Maratha State were four: Nilkantha Moreshwar Pingle the *Peshwa*, Ramchandra Nilkantha Bavdekar the *Amatya*, Shankaraji Malhar the *Sachiv*, and Prahlad, the son of the late Chief Justice Niraji Ravji. This Prahlad had been the Maratha ambassador at Golkonda. Three other men, who had hitherto filled only subordinate posts, now forced their way by their genius and enterprise to the first rank of State servants and popular leaders in this crisis of Maratha history. They were Dhana Singh Jadav and Santaji Ghorpare (the two rivals for the office of Senapati) and Parashuram Trimbak, who finally rose to the post of *Pratinidhi* or Agent in 1701.

The able general Zulfiqar Khan invested the Maratha capital of Raigarh in February 1689. But before its fall (on 19 October) Rajaram, the newly enthroned successor of the murdered Shambhuji, slipped out of the fort in the disguise of a Hindu religious beggar *(yogi)* on 5 April and went to Panhala. Ramchandra advised him that it would be a wise strategy to divide the enemy's forces by transferring a part of the Maratha activities to the far off Eastern Karnatak, while the Mughals were kept in play on the western side of the peninsula by his other officers.

The plan of operations for the future was thus arranged: Rajaram was to be escorted to Jinji to make a stand in his eastern province. The supreme control of affairs in the homeland was vested in Ramchandra Nilkantha Bavdekar, the *Amatya*, who was given the new title of *Hakumat-panah* or Dictator, with his headquarters first in Vishalgarh and latterly in Parli, assisted by Shankaraji Malhar (the *Sachiv*) and certain other officers. All officials and captains in the homeland were to take their orders from Ramchandra and obey him like the king himself. Ramchandra had an inborn genius for command and organization. He gathered round himself the ablest lieutenants, and managed to make the mutually jealous and contentious Maratha guerilla leaders act in concert.

Arriving at Jinji on 1 November 1689, Rajaram took over the government from the unwilling hands of Harji Mahadik's widow and son, formed a full Court and began to reign like a king, though in extreme poverty. The Peshwa Nilkantha Moreshwar Pingle accompanied his master to Jinji, but there fell completely into the second place; the king's leading counsellor and the supreme authority in the administration was Prahlad Niraji, on whom the high title of Regent (*Pratinidhi*) was conferred and who thus stood outside and above the cabinet of eight ministers (*Ashta-Pradhan*).

15.7 Aurangzib's Successes and Policy during 1689

When Rajaram fled from Maharashtra, Aurangzib had already won many of the Maratha forts and was rapidly winning others by money or force. In the extreme north, Salhir (21 February 1689) and Trimbak (8 January 1689) had been captured, and in the centre Singhgarh (November 1684) and Rajgarh (May 1689); Raigarh and Panhala were to fall before the year was over, while in North Konkan his able agent Matabar Khan gained many places. The inland parts of Central and Southern Konkan remained in Maratha possession, but the coast was mostly subject to Mughal sway, as the Marathas were forced to lose the port of Chaul, evacuate the island-depot of Khanderi, and transfer their naval headquarters further south to Gheria or Vijaydurg.

In the year 1689 many Maratha forts fell easily into Aurangzib's hands. His one aim now was to occupy the rich and boundless dominions of the fallen Adil Shahi and Qutb Shahi kingdoms. Therefore, during 1689, 1690 and 1691 Aurangzib was too busy in the plains of the south and the east to divert his resources to the barren hill-forts of the west.

15.8 Maratha Recovery: Capture of Rustam Khan, May 1690; Siege of Panhala

But, in 1690, the Marathas began to show signs of recovery from the effects of the disastrous fall of their late king. On 25 May 1690 they gained their first signal victory. The Mughal general Rustam Khan was roving in the neighbourhood of Satara with his family and troops, planning how to capture that fort for the Emperor. The Maratha leaders,—Ramchandra, Shankaraji, Santa and Dhana,—fell upon him in concert. Rustam himself, after receiving many wounds, fell down from his elephant and was carried off into captivity. Fifteen hundred of the Mughals fell on the field. The Maratha general in Satara fort now sallied out and carried off the family of Rustam Khan into the fort. In addition, the Marathas made prize of 4,000 horses, eight elephants and the entire camp and baggage of Rustam's army. After sixteen days, Rustam Khan ransomed himself by promising to pay one lakh of rupees.

Next Ramchanḍra and Shankaraji recovered the great forts of Pratapgarh, Rohira, Rajgarh and Torna, in the course of the same year (1690). After the fall of Raigarh, the Maratha garrison of Panhala lost heart and sold the fort to the imperialists (about December). But the Mughal garrison held it so negligently that the Marathas under Parashuram afterwards easily recovered it by surprise (about the middle of 1692).

Prince Muizz-ud-din laid siege to Panhala in October 1692 and sat down before it till 1694 without success. In October 1693, Dhana Jadav arrived there and effectively spoiled the work done by Muizz-ud-din in a year outside Panhala, reprovisioned the fort, and destroyed the siege-works. Thereafter the siege was practically abandoned; the prince carried on his operations languidly, merely to deceive the Emperor.

In March 1694 the prince, availing himself of the Emperor's permission, began to march away from Panhala, while Lutfullah Khan and many other officers, who had positive orders to stay below the fort, joined him in the retreat. Then Bidar Bakht (the eldest son of Prince Md. Azam) was given this task and he set out from the Court at Galgala on 5 April.

A desultory siege was continued by him till the end of January 1696, when the disasters to Qasim Khan and Himmat Khan further south induced the Emperor to send the prince to Basavapatan, and to entrust the siege of Panhala to Firuz Jang, who, too, could effect nothing. In fact, the capture of Panhala was quite beyond the power of any divisional army.

After the disaster to Rustam Khan (May 1690), the Emperor found it necessary to occupy the North Satara district in force. Lutfullah Khan was detached from Court as thanadar of Khatau (40 km i.e. 25 miles east of Satara). On 6 July, towards the end of the night, Santa Ghorpara at the head of ten thousand horse and numberless infantry surprised him; the camp was saved from plunder by firing from a distance. But the Marathas were only baffled and not crushed. They rallied their forces and reappeared in the East Satara region in superior force. Lutfullah was attacked, but beat the enemy back, though with loss.

There was nothing further of note till the end of 1690, when some Maratha auxiliaries of the Mughals,—namely Nima Sindhia, Mankohi Pandhre and Nagoji Mane,—went over to Rajaram at Jinji with their contingents.

The year 1692 witnessed a renewal of Maratha activity and their conspicuous success in many quarters, one of these being their recovery of Panhala from Mughal hands. Santaji Ghorpare's base was the Mahadev hill to the north-east of Satara, and from this refuge he used to make rapid raids far to the east, over the rolling plains of Bijapur. At the same time the Marathas were dsiturbing the Belgaon and Dharwar districts of Western Kanara. On 8 October, Dhana and Santa with 7,000 men were reported to have seized some forts near Belgaon and invested the latter town itself, and to be feeding their horses in the growing crops. The Emperor stiffened the defence of Kanara, by sending Hamid-ud-din Khan to Belgaon and Matlab Khan to Dharwar, while Qasim Khan the faujdar of Bijapuri Karnatak or north-west Mysore, was reinforced and ordered to guard Bankapur and other places near it. In December both Santa and Dhana went to Madras with large armies to relieve Jinji, and therefore, Maharashtra was for a time denuded of the best national leaders and troops, and the Mughals in the western theatre enjoyed peace for a time.

15.9 Struggle with Santaji Ghorpare and Dhana Jadav, 1694–95

Late in 1693 Maratha activities revived in the west. Amrit Rao Nimbalkar crossed the Bhima to raid Mughal territory. Himmat Khan set out in pursuit of him, but could not catch the elusive Maratha horsemen. At the same time Dhana, Shakaraji and other leaders were attacking the Mughal force before Panhala. Santa Ghorpare had come back from Jinji, and in October 1693 he resumed his raids in the homeland. Himmat Khan went out in pursuit and gained a signal victory over Santa and his Berad allies (about 14 November) at the village of Vikramhalli. Then the Mughal generals quarrelled; Hamid-ud-din and Khwaja Khan gave up the pursuit and returned towards Kulbarga, leaving Himmat alone to follow the enemy. Santa now safely divided his force, detaching 4,000 troopers under Amirit Rao to raid Berar, while he himself marched with 6,000 horsemen towards Malkhed, collecting *chauth*. Desultory fighting with many fruitless marches followed for many months and the Mughals could achieve nothing substantial.

Throughout 1694 and 1695, though the Maratha bands were active and the Berads troublesome all over the Western Deccan, nothing decisive or noteworthy was done on either side till the end of 1695, when Santa defeated and killed two first-rate Mughal generals, Qasim Khan and Himmat Khan.

Such was the chequered history of the contest with the Marathas in Western India till near the end of the year 1695. It was no longer a simple military problem, but had become a trial of endurance and resources between the Mughal Empire and the indigenous people of the Deccan.

15.10 The Eastern Karnatak, its Divisions and History

The Eastern or Madras Karnatak, which must be distinguished from the Western Karnatak or the Kanarese-speaking division of the Bombay Presidency (called Kanara in this book),—extends from near the 15th degree of north latitude to the Kaveri river in the south. In the late 17th century it was divided into two halves by the Palar river, or an imaginary line from Vellore to Sadras. These two parts were called Haidarabadi Karnatak and Bijapuri Karnatak respectively, and each of them was further sub-divided into uplands *(balaghat,* in Persian) and plains (*payinghat*). The upland of Haidarabadi Karnatak included Sidhout, Gandikota, Guti, Garamkonda and Kadapa; Bijapuri Balaghat included the Sera and Bangalore districts of Mysore and their dependent zamindaris. In the lowlands, Haidarabadi Karnatak embraced the sea-coast from Guntur to Sadras; Bijapuri Payinghat extended south from Sadras (12.30 degree of north latitude) to Tanjore. But the conquests had not been consolidated; much of the country was still in the hands of unsubdued *poligars* or petty local chieftains, and Adil Shah held only certain forts and their environs; but even in these his authority was exercised by his nobles, who were independent in all but the name. This situation was further complicated by Shivaji's invasion and conquest of the country (1677–78), as the result of which a new Maratha Government was created in the South Arcot district (capital, Jinji). Shivaji had placed Raghunath Narayan Hanumante as viceroy over this new conquest. Shambhuji, soon after his accession, dismissed and imprisoned Raghunath (early in January 1681), and sent his own sister's husband Harji Mahadik to govern Jinji. But the Maratha, king's absorption in vice, and the increasing Mughal pressure on Maharashtra under the personal direction of Aurangzib, tended to extinguish Shambhuji's authority in the far off province of Jinji and to make the local viceroy his own master. Harji assumed the title of Maharajah, and neglected to send the surplus, revenue to his sovereign at Raigarh.

In October 1686 Shambhuji sent Kesho Trimbak Pingle with 12,000 horse, outwardly to strengthen his garrisons in the Karnatak, but with secret instructions to seize and depose the refractory Harji Rajah and assume the government of Jinji in the king's name. Kesho Trimbak arrived near Jinji on 11 February 1687. But his hopes were doomed to disappointment. Harji had effectually secured Jinji fort in his own hands and made the local army absolutely devoted to himself. Kesho, finding the game lost, marched into Mysore at the head of 18,000 horse. But here he could effect nothing, and soon returned to the neighbourhood of Jinji.

15.11 Mughal Penetration into the Eastern Karnatak, 1687

After the conquest of Golkonda Aurangzib wisely retained the former Qutb Shahi officers at their respective posts for sometime. Muhammad Ibrahim (created by him Mahabat Khan), the highest Golkonda noble to desert to him, was appointed subahdar of Haidarabad, and the Khan's confidant Muhammad Ali Beg (now entitled Ali Askar Khan) was nominated faujdar of the Qutb Shahi Karnatak, with subordinate qiladars and magistrates at Chinglepat, Conjeveram and Punamali. These officers submissively proclaimed Aurangzib as their sovereign (October 1687).[1] But the Emperor changed his mind soon afterwards; Mahab Khan was replaced by Ruhullah Khan in the subahdari of Haidarabad: Qasim Khan supplanted Ali Askar and was directed to march to the Karnatak and conduct a vigorous war against the Maratha forces there (January, 1688).

Harji sent out a detachment of his army to plunder and conquer on his own account the late territory of Golkonda, north of the Palar river, which had recently submitted to Mughal ownership without having as yet received adequate Mughal garrisons. Marching with 2,000 horse, 5,000 foot, and great numbers of pioneers and scaling ladders, he took easy possession of several forts and a hundred towns in this region. On

[1] The governor of Punamali said that as the world turned round like a wheel, he had beaten his drums, and fired his guns, for the victory which the mighty Alamgir had gained over his old master.' (Orme's *Frag.* 157.)

24 December Arcot was captured by assault. The Marathas spread over the country plundering and torturing without regard for sex or creed. Several great Brahmans of Conjeveram with their wives and children took refuge in Madras (27 December 1687–10 January 1688), to save their persons and property from Maratha outrage. On 11 January the Marathas burst into Conjeveram, plundering the city, killing about 500 men, destroying the houses, and putting the terror-stricken inhabitants to flight. Kesho Trimbak took to the same profitable business with his own contingent; after capturing Chitpat and Kaveripak, he established his camp at Conjeveram (January 1688).

But the Maratha occupation was short-lived. Aurangzib had ordered four high generals of the late Golkonda Government—Ismail Khan Maka, Yachapa Nayak, Rustam Khan, and Muhammad Sadiq,—to hasten to the Karnatak plains and succour the Emperor's partisans there. These officers arrived at Conjeveram on 25 February 1688. The Marathas evacuated that town; the Mughal vanguard pursued and fought them, seized Wandiwash and made it their camp, while the Marathas encamped at Chitpat, a day's march southwards. The main armies on the two sides remained in this position for a year, merely watching each other, but they daily sent out detachments and foraging parties who plundered the country indiscriminately. The hapless people, who had not yet recovered from the effects of desolating famine of 1686, had now to endure two sets of robbers instead of one. The trade of the district was ruined, industry ceased, grain and oil seeds became very scarce, and multitudes flocked to the fortified European settlements of the coast as their only refuge.

The year 1689 continued to be as bad for the Karnatak as the year before. The roads were unsafe; Mughal and Maratha armies daily plundered the country. Country-made cotton and other goods could not be brought to the English factory at Kunimedu for export, by reason of the constant warfare and robbery in the region. Harji died about 19 September. His wife Ambika Bai (Shivaji's daughter) continued to govern the fort and province on behalf of her minor sons.

15.12 Rajaram at Jinji

But the arrival of Rajaram at Jinji (1 November 1689) was followed by a peaceful revolution. Harji's widow and her Brahman advisers were reluctant to part with the usurped authority and local independence they had enjoyed for over eight years [*Memoires* of F. Martin]. But Rajaram's right could not be disputed: the government of Jinji passed into his hands. Harji's son was placed under confinement, and money was squeezed out of the late viceroy's widow by calling upon her to render accounts for her husband's long years of administration of the province. She had to make her peace by paying three lakhs of *him*, and Santaji Bhonsle one lakh. For Prahlad Niraja, the king's supreme agent, a new post, that of *Pratinidhi* or Regent, was created, while Nilo Moreshwar Pingle continued to hold the title of *Peshwa* or nominal prime minister. The Regent, Prahlad Niraji, 'threw Rajaram into a life of debauchery' and kept 'the young king constantly intoxicated by the habitual use of *ganja* and opium.' Then 'seizing the reality of power, he caused the Brahmans who had enriched themselves under Harji to disgorge their money and goods by the stroke of confiscation.'

But this squeezing of its former officials could not fill the gaping void of the Maratha Government's financial distress. The ministers at Jinji looked round to raise money from the European settlements on the East Coast; the richer merchants were urged to lend 5,000 or even 1,000 *hun* each. After Rajaram's coming, the French and Dutch agents continued to intrigue against each other among the Maratha ministers,—the Dutch offering a large bribe for a proclamation expelling the newly founded French factory at Pondicherry. The Jinji ministers encouraged the game, 'thinking only how to get the maximum amount of money out of the one or the other.' In January 1690, the Mughal cause suffered a temporary eclipse from the rebellion of the old Haidrabadi local officers lately taken over into the Emperor's service, viz. Muhammad Sadiq, Yachapa Nayak and Ismail Maka. Finding themselves likely to be replaced by old servants of the Emperor and doomed to unemployment or humble offices, they deserted their new master, made an alliance with Rajaram, and began to usurp the country and collect the revenue. The imperial representatives, from Madras to Kunimedu, were hopelessly outnumbered and defeated and forced to flee to the European settlements on the coast (April). The rebellion was extinguished only at the approach of Zulfiqar Khan as the supreme Mughal commander, who reached Conjeveram in August and the environs of Jinji at the beginning of September.

The military situation was now reversed; the Maratha raiding bands were driven back by the Mughals and 'invasion threatened the dominions of Rajaram.' In consternation, that king left Jinji and went to some safer refuge further south in the Karnatak, nearer his ally the Rajah of Tanjore. The miserable country from Jinji to the sea-coast continued to be pillaged by the camp-followers and 'couriers' of both sides. The local people fled with their families for safety far to the south in Tanjore territory, or to the European factories on the coast.

15.13 Siege of Jinji Begins

The rock-fortress of Jinji consists not of one fort, but of three fortified hillocks, Rajgiri, Krishnagiri, and Chandrayandurg,—connected together by strong lines of circumvallation, and forming a rough triangle nearly 5 km (three miles) in circumference. 'These hills are steep, rocky and covered with such enormous boulders that they are almost unclimbable. Each of the three is fortified on all sides with line above line of stone walls, flanked with bastions, filled with embrasures for guns, loopholed for musketry and pierced only by narrow and strong gateways; and from each to the next, connected with these defences, runs a great stone-faced rampart nearly 20 metres (60 feet) thick with a ditch over 26 metres (80 feet) wide outside it. On the three hills are the citadels.'

The gates are three: one in the northern wall, now called the Vellore or Arcot gate but known in the seventeenth century as the 'gate towards Trinomali'; a second in the eastern face, now called the Pondicherry gate, which was the principal entrance into the fort in the seventeenth century; and due west to this second gate, stands a small postern gate (in the wall connecting Chandrayan with Rajgiri), called by the Indians *Shaitan-dari* (or *Port du Diable* in French).

Zulfiqar Khan had reached Jinji early in September 1690, but he merely sat down before it. The investment of such a vast group of forts with the forces under him was out of the question, and he had no heavy guns nor enough munitions for a bombardment. He could not prevent the victualling of the place, as a complete blockade was beyond his power; and 'the Marathas recovering from their first consternation began to harass him incessantly.' In the February following, Rajaram returned to Jinji.

The military superiority of the Mughals was rapidly lost after April 1691, while the activity of the Maratha bands roving around stopped the supply of grain to Zulfiqar's camp. He therefore begged urgently for reinforcements. This general's father Asad Khan, the *wazir,* and Prince Kam Bakhsh, from Wagingera, were sent with a large force and they reached Jinji on 16 December, 1691.

In the meantime, Zulfiqar had abandoned his futile attacks on Jinji and turned to the more profitable work of levying contributions from the zamindars of South Karnatak, Tanjore and Trichinopoly. Thus the year 1691 passed without any decisive success for the imperialists.

The next year was equally barren of results for them, in spite of the great accession to their armed strength brought by the prince and the wazir. Ismail Khan Maka was induced to re-enter the Emperor's service and he joined Zulfiqar's camp with his contingent. With these additions to his forces, Zulfiqar renewed the siege of Jinji in 1692. After some changes he selected Chandrayandurg as his objective and ran trenches towards it. Then he began a bombardment of this hill as well as of the Pondicherry gate. But all his exertions were a mere show, as the country around knew well.

The condition of the Mughal camp in the rainy season of 1692 is thus described by an eye-witness: 'The rain fell with excessive severity. Grain was dear. The soldiers, having to spend days and nights together in the trenches, suffered great hardship; the entire tract looked like one lake.'

15.14 Santa Ghorpare and Dhana Jadav Capture Ali Mardan and Ismail Khan, 1692

The Mughal position became absolutely untenable in winter. Early in December, a vast Maratha force of more than 30,000 horse, raised in western India by Ramchandra (the chief agent of Rajaram) arrived in Eastern Karnatak under the famous generals Dhana Singh Jadav and Santa Ghorpare.

The deluge of the newly arrived Maratha cavalry first burst on the Conjeveram district. The terror inspired by these brigands caused a panic flight of the inhabitants far and near into Madras for refuge. When the division under Santa arrived near Kaveripak, Ali Mardan Khan, the Mughal faujdar of Conjeveram, went out to encounter it, without knowing its vast numbers. But his small force was hemmed round and he was captured with 1,500 horses and six elephants. All the property and materials of his army were looted (13 December). The Khan was taken to Jinji and secured his release by paying the huge ransom of one lakh *hun*.

The other division of the Maratha reinforcements, led by Dhana Jadav, attacked the siege-camps round Jinji. Zulfiqar saw himself hopelessly outnumbered, and wisely ordered his outposts to fall in on his main army. But Ismail Khan, posted west of the fort, had a longer distance to cross: the Marathas helped by their brethren within the fort intercepted him. The Khan offered a brave opposition to ten-fold odds, but was wounded and captured with 500 horses and two elephants, and carried off as prisoner to Jinji. The victorious Marathas immediately proclaimed their authority over the Haidarabad Karnatak.

15.15 Prince Khan Bakhsh Intrigues with Marathas; is Arrested

The revival of Maratha activity and predominance in the surrounding country put a stop to the free and plentiful supply of grain in the Mughal camp. It also stopped the coming of letters from the Emperor's Court. The Mughal army outside Jinji was now besieged in its turn, and its condition became extremely dangerous by reason of internal disputes. Prince Khan Bakhsh was a foolish young man, the spoilt child of his father's old age, untaught to bridle his passions, and ever swayed by his caprices and the counsels of young and worthless favourites. He contrived to offend his guardian, the aged and influential wazir Asad Khan. Through the medium of 'some reckless and mad men' he opened a secret correspondence with Rajaram. The Marathas flattered the prince's humour and mischievously instigated him in new evil projects. Zulfiqar Khan soon learnt the prince's secret, and secured the Emperor's permission to keep him under careful surveillance. As the result of the arrival of Santa and Dhana in December 1692, for some weeks communication with the Emperor's Court and the Mughal base ceased altogether. Alarming rumours arose immediately. It was said that Aurangzib was dead and that Shah Alam had succeeded to the throne. Kam Bakhsh considered himself in a most perilous position. Asad and Zulfiqar were his enemies; they would naturally try to win the favour of the new Emperor by sending Kam Bakhsh in chains to him. His only hope of safety, so his servants assured him, lay in his making terms with Rajaram, escaping to the fort with his family on a dark night, and then trying with Maratha aid to win the throne of Delhi.

This project also was reported to Asad Khan by his spies. The wazir and his son consulted the leading officers of the imperial army; they urged with one voice that the prince should be strictly guarded, the trenches abandoned, and the entire army concentrated in the rear lines.

The withdrawal from the siege lines was effected only after severe fighting. Zulfiqar burst his big guns by firing excessive charges of powder and abandoned them where they stood. The base-camp was four miles in his rear; the garrison made a sortie, joined their brethren outside under Dhana Jadav, and hemmed the Mughal army on all sides. The imperialists lost 400 troopers, 400 horses and 8 elephants, and at the close of the day they reached Asad Khan's camp.

Here the prince had plotted with his silly courtiers to arrest these two generals at their next visit to him and then grasp the supreme power. But this plot, like all others, had leaked out. Zulfiqar Khan, worn out with his day-long fighting and anxieties, reached his father's side at night, learnt of the new plot, and then the two leaders quickly decided that the safety of the entire army and the preservation of the Emperor's prestige alike demanded that the prince should be deprived of the power of creating mischief. They immediately rode to Kam Bakhsh's quarters for arresting him.

The wazir was in a towering rage. He severely rebuked the prince, calling him a dancing-girl's son unworthy to rule over men or to command in war. Then he continued, 'What is this that you have done? You have disgraced yourself, and covered my grey hairs with disgrace.' The prisoner was taken to Asad Khan's own tent and treated with every courtesy. Thus the Mughal army was saved by establishing unity of control.

Santaji Ghorpare, flushed with his signal victory over Ali Mardhan Khan and the unresisted plunder of the Conjeveram district, now arrived at Jinji and turned his great talents and energy against Zulfiqar. Fighting took place daily; 'The enemy exceeded 20,000 men, while the imperialists were small force and many of them were engaged in guarding the prince and the camp. Kam Bakhsh's contingnt was unfriendly and never left their tents to co-operate in the defence. The whole brunt of the fighting fell on Zulfiqar Khan and a few other *mansabdars* with only 2,000 horsemen.'

15.16 Famine in Zulfiqar's Army, His Retreat from Jinji to Wandiwash

But the Mughal army was now in a state of siege and famine was its worst enemy. In a few days scarcity deepened into an absolute want of food. Zulfiqar then marched out with his own division to bring in grain from Wandiwash, 40 km (24 miles) north-east of Jinji. When he set out on his return (5 January 1693), Santa with 20,000 men barred his path at Desur, 16 km (10 miles) southwards, and then enveloped his army. The Mughals, after a hard fight, reached the shelter of the fort of Desur at night. When they resumed their march next morning, the Marathas brought a large force into the field and made a most determined attack. But Dalpat, fighting with desperate bravery, forced the Marathas to withdraw. The Bundelas thus saved Zulfiqar's division and thereby saved also the camp before Jinji.

But the food brought by Zulfiqar at such a heavy cost was all too little for that huge multitude of soldiers and camp followers. The condition of the starving imperialists became worse. 'Every day from dawn to sunset the Marathas assembled round our camp and made demonstrations. All the army, high and low alike, were distracted and depressed.'

Asad Khan now made secret overtures of peace to Rajaram, offering a heavy bribe if he was allowed to retreat to Wandiwash unmolested. Rajaram agreed. On the other side, Dalpat Rao urged Zulfiqar not to withdraw, as it would only bring disgrace on him in the end. But while Zulfiqar was hesitating, his hands were forced by his artillerymen who loaded their effects, left the camp and sent word to their general that, as they were dying from hunger there, they were going away to Wandiwash. Zulfiqar had no help but to start with the prince at noon. Owing to long continued starvation, most of the horses, camels and other transport animals of the army had perished. Most men set fire to their belongings. Many stores of the Emperor and nobles were left behind there. When the Mughal army marched out of the camp, about a thousand Maratha horse came after them, like a rear-guard, and plundered the men of the army of their property. The imperialists reached Wandiwash in three days, on 22 or 23 January 1693. Ten days later, Qasim Khan, the newly appointed faujdar of Conjeveram (*vice* Ali Mardan Khan), was reported to be coming from Kadapa with abundant supplies and a strong force.

Santa Ghorpare tried to intercept him; he attacked Qasim and pressed him so hard that he had to shut himself up in the great temple enclosure of Conjeveram. Next day Zulfiqar arrived to his aid, drove away the Marathas and escorted Qasim Khan to Wandiwash (7 February). Food again became abundant in the Mughal camp, and the troops were further reassured by getting the latest news and letters from the Imperial Court telling them that the Emperor was alive and well. Zulfiqar lay in his camp at Wandiwash for four months (February–May, 1693), abandoning the attack on Jinji for the present. He had to wait for the Emperor's orders about Kam Bakhsh. Escorted by Asan Khan, that prince arrived at the imperial camp at Galgala on 11 June, and was presented to his father in the harem through the intercession of his sister Zinat-un-nisa.

15.17 Operations in Karnatak during 1693–94

The Eastern Karnatak from the latitude of Madras to that of Porto Novo, was at this time occupied by three sets of authorities, often in conflict with one another,—namely, the representatives of the old Hindu local chieftains and Vijaynagar viceroys, whom the conquering armies of the Bijapur and Golkonda Sultans had imperfectly subdued; the officers of the lately subverted Bijapur and Golkonda Governments, who were loath to recognize their new Mughal master; and the Maratha intruders representing the house of Shivaji and Vyankaji. To the first of these classes belonged Yachapa Nayak, whose ancestors had obtained the fort of Satgarh (43 km, i.e. 26 miles west of Vellore) from the ministers of Rajah Pratap Rudra of Warangal, and who once commanded the local levies (*sehbandi*) of Golkonda. When Rajaram reached Jinji, Yachapa joined him, In March 1693 he left Rajaram, recovered Satgarh, and began to extend his territory eastwards. At the close of the year Zulfiqar Khan won him over, by securing for him a *mansab* of 6-hazari.

Ismail Khan Maka, an ex-general of Golkonda and a local zamindar, joined the Mughals wholeheartedly. Santaji Ghorpare besieged Trichinopoly in March; Rajaram himself arrived there soon afterwards, and then went to visit his first cousin and friend Shahji II at Tanjore (May 1693). But a quarrel now broke out in the Maratha ranks; Santaji's temper was found intolerable and he left for Maharashtra in anger, Dhanaji being appointed Senapati in his place.

Zulfiqar set out in February 1694 to conquer the South Arcot district. The fort of Peru-mukkal, 30 km (18 miles) north of Pondicherry, was stormed for him by Dalpat Rao's Bundelas. Then he marched down the East Coast, towards Tanjore, by way of Pondicherry and other European factories, capturing many forts in the South Arcot district, and skirting Cuddalore at the end of February. When (in March 1694) the Mughal general with his army arrived near Tanjore, Maharajah Shahji II found resistance vain, especially as his ever hostile neighbour, the Nayak of Trichinopoly, joined the Mughals. So, Shahji had to yield; on 22 May he signed a letter of submission, promising to obey the Emperor's orders like a faithful vassal in future, to ease from assisting Rajaram in any way, to pay the Mughal Government a tribute of 30 lakhs of Rupees annually, and to cede the forts of Palamkota, Sittanur and Tunganur with their dependent districts as well as several other places.

But Rajaram, who had mortgaged Palamkota to Vyankaji, seized that fort for himself, so that Zulfiqar had to lay siege to it. After six days the garrison capitulated. Then the Mughal army returned to its base at Wandiwash and made another attack on Jinji in September. In this month Zulfiqar suddenly arrested Yachapa at a darbar and had him beheaded on the charge of treason.[2]

15.18 Zulfiqar's Movements and Difficulties, 1695

Zulfiqar Khan renewed the siege of Jinji towards the close of the year 1694, but it was a mere show intended to deceive the Emperor. The fact of his treasonable collusion with the Marathas was notorious in the country. He had, during the course and particularly at the end, of the siege of Jinji, an understanding with Rajaram, in expectation of the death of the very old Aurangzib and the civil wars that would surely follow among his sons. 'It is the practice of generals to prolong operations for their own profit and ease.'

[2] Manucci (iii. 271–272) gives horrible details of the suicide of his wives and children and also asserts that Zulfiqar falsely accused Yachapa of treason and killed him, because the Nayak had written a letter to the Emperor exposing Zulfiqar's treasonable collusion with the Marathas and deliberate prolongation of the siege of Jinji, and offering to capture the fort in eight days by his own troops alone, but the letter had been intercepted by Asad Khan.

Nothing was achieved by the Mughals during 1695, while the scarcity of grain which raged there for the entire year intensified their sufferings. Siege was laid to Vellore in October, but it held out for many years (falling on 14 August 1702).

15.19 Operations of Zulfiqar during 1696

Dhana Jadav arrived near Vellore at the end of December. Zulfiqar immediately raised the siege, sent off his camp baggage and family to Arcot, and prepared for action. In March 1696, Santa Ghorpare too arrived on the scene. The Maratha bands spread to several parts of the country, the imperialists with their depleted numbers could not defend so many places. Zulfiqar wisely concentrated his forces; but throughout this year 1696 he was hampered by his extreme want of money. He therefore confined himself solely to the defensive in the fort of Arcot, as his strength was still weak. The Marathas, as usual, hovered round him, there being a secret understanding between the two sides to spare each other. In November and December Santa entered Central Mysore, and Zulfiqar, under orders of the Emperor, pursued him there and co-operated with Prince Bidar Bakht, who had reached that province from the north-west for expelling the Marathas from beyond the Tungabhadra. These two Mughal forces united near Penu-konda (125 km, i.e. 75 miles north of Bangalore). The elusive Marathas disappeared without offering battle, and Zulfiqar returned to Arcot in February 1697.

15.20 Siege of Jinji Renewed: Fall of the Fort

He again left Arcot to collect tribute from Tanjore and other places in the south. Then he returned to Wandiwash from canton for the rainy season of 1697. Happily for him, the Marathas were now very much weakened by a bitter and final rupture between Dhana and Santaji. Rajaram had sided with Dhana, an internecine war raged among the Marathas, and finally Dhaaa had been defeated by his rival and driven back to Maharashtra (May 1696). Early in November 1697 Zulfiqar renewed the siege of Jinji in right earnest.

He himself took post opposite the northern gate, Ram Singh Hada against the Shaitandari, and Daud Khan Pani before Chikkali-durg, one kilometre (half-a-mile) south of Jinji. Daud Khan captured Chikkali-durg in one day by a reckless assault at close quarters, and then, coming to Jinji itself, entrenched opposite Chandrayangarh, the southern fort. If Zulfiqar had wished it, he could have taken the entire fort the next day. But his secret policy was to prolong the siege in order to keep his army together, enjoy his emoluments, and escape the hardships of active duty on some new expedition.[3] He let the Marathas know that his attacks were for show only, and thus the siege dragged on for two months more.

At last it became necessary for Zulfiqar to capture the fort if he wished to avoid disgrace and punishment by his master. Rajaram received timely warning, and escaped to Vellore with his chief officers, but leaving his family behind. Then Zulfiqar gave the order for the assault. Dalpat Rao scaled the northern walls of Krishna-giri and captured the outer fort after a severe struggle. The garrison retreated to an inner fort called *Kalakot,* which Dalpat's Bundelas entered pell-mell with them and occupied. The surviving Marathas took refuge in Rajgiri or the highest fort. Meantime Daud Khan had made his way into Chandrayangarh and advanced through the city or the low inner plain of Jinji towards Krishna-giri. The inhabitants fled to the top of Krishna-giri, but finding no safety there, capitulated. A vast amount of booty in horses, camels and things fell into the hands of the imperialists (8 January, 1698). Rajaram's family was naw invested in Rajgiri, but their situation was hopeless. Ram Singh Hada made his way to the summit of Rajgiri by crossing the chasm at its foot by means of a wooden gangway. The Maratha royal family was promised safety; four wives, three sons and two daughters of Rajaram now came out of the citadel and were kept in honourable captivity. Another wife of the Rajah avoided surrender by death; she flung herself down from the summit of the fort into the sheer depths below. Nearly 4,000 men, women and children were found in the fort, but very few combatants.

From Jinji Zulfiqar (now honoured with the title of Nasrat Jang) returned to his base at Wandiwash, and then pursued Rajaram from Vellore to Garamkonda. But the Maratha king had a good start of him

[3] Wilkes (i. 133). 'To preserve appearances it was necessary to report (to the Emperor) frequent attacks and repulses. On the other side, Daud Khan, second in command of the Mughal army, drank largely of the best European liquors, and when full of the god would perpetually volunteer the extirpation of the infidels. Zulfiqar necessarily assented to these enterprises, but always gave secret intelligence to the enemy of the time and place of attack; and the troops of Daud Khan were as often repulsed with slaughter.'

and escaped to Vishalgarh in safety (February). Thus the entire work of the Emperor's long siege of Jinji was undone. The bird had flown away.

15.21 Qasim Khan Defeated by Santa Ghorpare, Dies at Dodderi, 1695

The Maratha captains infested various parts of Mughal Deccan in the usual manner throughout October and November 1695. Early in November, Santa, who had been looting the Bijapur district, vainly pursued by an imperial detachment under Himmat Khan south of the Krishna, now turned southwards to convey his rich store of plunder to his own estate in N. W. Mysore.

Aurangzib, then encamped at Islampuri, ordered Qasim Khan to intercept the raiders. To reinforce Qasim Khan, he sent a detachment from his own camp under some of his highest younger officers, including Khanazad Khan (afterwards Lord High Steward). Though 4,800 troopers in actual muster, it was a very choice corps, being composed of men from the Emperor's guards and personal retinue and the contingents of the nobles who had to patrol round his tent on different days of the week. They joined Qasim Khan about 33 km (12 miles) from the Marathas' expected track. Santa, who had been roving at a distance, heard of his enemy's position and movements, came up with them by swift marches, and skilfully matured a plan for their destruction, which the luxury and thoughtlessness of the Mughal generals crowned with the most complete success imaginable. Qasim Khan rose to the height of hospitality and ostentation in order to receive worthily the noble guests coming to him from Court, and discarded the simple and light kit of a general who would wage war with the Marathas wisely. Santa Ghorpare showed the highest tactical power in making his dispositions and moving his three distinct and scattered divisions so as to ensure the perfect timing of their movements and exact co-operation among them. He divided his army into three bodies, of which one was sent to plunder the Mughal camp, another to fight the soldiers, and the third was held in reserve ready for action wherever required. Barmappa Nayak, the zamindar of the Chittaldurg district, now sided with the Marathas in the hope of a share of the spoils, and thus the Mughals were ringed round by enemies and cut off from all information.

An hour and a half after sunrise (about 20 November) the first Maratha division fell upon Qasim Khan's advanced tents (ten kilometres i.e. six miles to the front), slew and wounded the guards and servants, carried off everything they could, and set fire to the heavy tents. On the news of it reaching Qasim Khan he hurried towards the point of attack. Before he had gone 3 km (2 miles), the second body of the enemy appeared in front and the battle began. The enemy's numbers were overwhelming, and they had a very large body of *Kala-piada* musketeers,—the best marksmen and bravest infantry of the Deccan,—in addition to their numberless mobile light cavalry. A great battle was fought and many were slain on both sides. Then the reserve division of Santa fell upon the camp and baggage left behind by the Mughals and looted everything. This news reached Qasim and Khanazad in the heat of the battle and shook their firmness. They took counsel together and fell back on Dodderi.[4] The fort of Dodderi was small and the food-store in it limited. So its imperial garrison shut its gates upon their newly arrived comrades. The two Khans had to encamp outside. As the night closed, the enemy completely encircled them; for three days the Marathas only appeared in sight without fighting, till some thousands of infantry sent by Barmappa Nayak, joined them. Then they seized the opportunity and made an attack on the fourth day. The imperial artillery munitions had been plundered in their camp and what little was carried with the soldiers was now exhausted; so, after vain exertions for some hours, they sat down in despair, a helpless target for the Kanarese musketeers. Fully one-third of the Mughal army had been slain at the two camps, during the retreat, and on the banks of the tank of Dodderi.

Then the chiefs saved their own lives by sneaking into the fort, abandoning their soldiers. The Muslim soldiery now faced utter starvation. Qasim Khan was a great eater of opium, and the lack of the drug caused his death on the third day. [But many people suspected that he committed suicide to escape disgrace at the hands of the enemy and censure by the Emperor.]

When the food supply was absolutely exhausted and the water in the fort became scanty and unwholesome, Khanazad Khan, in despair

[4] *Dodderi,* 14° 20′ N., 75° 46′ E., in the Chittaldurg division of Mysore, 35 km (22 miles) east of Chittaldurg, and 154 km (96 miles) in a straight line south of Adoni. South of it stands a large reservoir of water.

of relief, sent his diwan and a Deccani captain of the imperial army to Santa to beg for terms of capitulation; the ransom was fixed at 20 lakhs of Rupees; and all the cash, articles, jewels, horses and elephants of the doomed army were to be given up. The lean woebegone and bedraggled remnant of the imperial army filed out of the fort 13 days after entering it. The enemy gave them bread from one side and water from the other. After resting for two days, Khanazad started for the Court with a Maratha escort. He had lost everything.

15.22 Santa Slays Himmat Khan at Basavapatan

In less than a month from this stroke, Santa achieved another and equally famous victory by killing Himmat Khan Bahadur, who had been deputed to co-operate with Qasim Khan and had taken refuge in Basavapatan (67 km, i.e. 40 miles west of Dodderi) on account of the smallness of his force. On 20 January 1696, Santa appeared before Himmat Khan's position at the head of ten thousand cavalry and nearly the same number of infantry. His Karnataki foot-musketeers—the best marksmen in the Deccan—took post on a hill. Himmat Khan, with a very small force, advanced to the attack and dislodged them from it, but as he was driving his elephant towards the place where Santa was standing, he was suddenly shot by a bullet in the forehead. After some days the Marathas withdrew with the captured baggage of the Khan.

On 28 January the Emperor learnt of Himmat Khan's death and the blockade of his troops in the fort of Basavapatan by Santa; and a great effort was made to gather troops and retrieve the position of N. W. Mysore. Hamid-ud-din Khan started on 1 February for the relief of Basavapatan. Some 32 km (20 miles) before his destination he was attacked by Santa (26 February). But the Marathas were defeated and driven out of that region, and Basavapatan was relieved.

15.23 Military Arrangements of the Imperialists During 1696

Prince Bidar Bakht had been ordered (end of January) to march from Panhala to Basavapatan. Arriving at this place in a few weeks, he stayed there for some time, sending out detachments to punish the rebel zamindars of the district. Barmappa Nayak of Chittaldurg made a humble submission and promise of loyalty, on 16 May. Prince Muhammad Azam had been sent from the Emperor's camp at Islampuri to Pedgaon (Bahadurgarh), 145 km (90 miles) north of it in February 1696, and this place remained his headquarters till he was recalled to the Emperor's side at Miraj three years later.

In March 1697, Santa Ghorpare returned from the East Coast to the Satara district, and Firuz Jang was despatched against him. But a civil war among the Maratha generals weakened their power during the first half of the year 1697.

15.24 Civil War Between Santa Ghorpare and Dhana Jadav; Death of Santa

Flushed with his far-resounding victories over these two first-rate Mughal generals in the west, Santa went to Jinji to wait on Rajaram (March 1696). He seems to have claimed the office of Senapati, contrasting his own brilliant performances with Dhana's poor record of victories. But his vanity, imperious temper and spirit of insubordination gave great offence to the Court at Jinji and the result was an open rupture near Conjeveram (May 1696). Rajaram sided with Dhana and placing Amrit Rao Nimbalkar in the van of his army, attacked his refractory general. But Santa's genious again triumphed; Dhana was defeated and driven precipitately to his home in western India; Amrit Rao fell on the field.

After ranging through the eastern Karnatak for many months, Santa finally returned to his homeland in March 1697. Here an internecine war now raged between him and Dhana, all the other captains being ranged on the two sides. They fought together in the Satara district in March 1697. But fortune now deserted Santaji; his severity and insolence had disgusted his officers, and most of them deserted to Dhana, while the rest were killed or wounded. Santa, despoiled of all and deserted by his army, fled from the field with only a few followers to Mahaswad, the home of Nagoji Mane whose wife's brother Amrit Rao he had killed. Nagoji gave shelter and food for some days, and then dismissed him in safety. But his wife Radha Bai, with a woman's unquenchable vindictiveness, sent her surviving brother after him. The pursuer came upon Santaji when, exhausted by fast travel, he was bathing in a *nala* near the Shambhu Mahadev hill, in the Satara district. The party from Mahaswad surprised him in this helpless situation and cut off his head (June 1697).

Santaji had an inborn genius for handling large bodies of troops spread over a wide area, changing his tactics so as to take prompt advantage of every change in the enemy's plans and condition, and organizing combined movements. The success of his tactics depended on the rapid movement of his troops and on his subordinates carrying out his orders punctually to the minute. He, therefore, insisted on implicit obedience from his officers and enforced the strictest discipline in his army by draconic punishments; and hence naturally 'most of the Maratha nobles, became his enemies.'

The two lifelong rivals, Santa and Dhana, were both army leaders and organizers of the highest ability, courage and activity, but with contrasting characters. Dhana made war like a gentleman. He was moderate in victory, generous to the vanquished, polite in his address, practised in self-control, and capable of taking long views and making statesmanly arrangements. His inborn courtesy to the Mughal generals who had the misfortune to encounter him, is noticed with praise by the Muslim historians. Moreover, he served his country's Government unselfishly for many years.

Santaji Ghorpare, on the other hand, was, in comparison with Dhana, a barbarian devoid of culture or generosity, unable to restrain his passions or to take thought of the distant future. He loved to hustle all whom he met with, not excepting his king. He showed no mercy and expected none. By his temperament, Santa was incapable of co-operating with others, and he had not the patriotism to subordinate his own will to the needs of his nation. He exercised no influence on the political history of the Marathas or even on the general effect of Aurangzib's campaigns. He merely flashed through the Deccan sky like a lonely meteor.

15.25 Rajaram's Return Home and Activities in 1698–99

Nothing remarkable seems to have happened in the second half of 1697, except a heavy flood of the Bhima river which washed away the Mughal camps at Pedgaon and Islampuri (19 July) and spread universal misery and ruin. But in January next, Jinji fell to the Mughals. Rajaram fled from it and reached Vishalgarh in Maharashtra in the following month. It is not probable that any unusual activity was shown by the Marathas immediately after Rajaram's return home. He seems to have taken time to recover from the effects of the loss of Jinji. Some of his followers at this time deserted his service in despair and joined the Mughals.

Early in 1699 Rajaram set out on a tour of inspection in Konkan, visiting all his forts, and returned to Satara at the end of June. Forming plans for an extensive raid through Khandesh and Berar, he sallied out of Satara, about 26 October.

Evidently Aurangzib's intention to besiege this fort first had leaked out, for, immediately after the Emperor's starting from Islampuri (19 October), Rajaram removed his family from Satara to Khelna and himself left it on 26 October in order to escape falling into the Emperor's hands. Dhana Jadav, Ramchandra, Dado Malhar and other generals, with 7,000 cavalry, escorted him to Chandan-Wandan, whence, after a three days' halt, he took the route to Surat.

The Emperor immediately sent urgent orders to Bidar Bakht to pursue and defeat this hostile force. 7 km (4 miles) beyond the fort of Parenda, Bidar Bakht came upon the Marathas. After a bloody fight, they were broken and driven towards Ahmadnagar (13 or 14 November). On 26 December, Rajaram was reported as having dismounted some 50 km (30 miles) from the imperial camp below Satara fort and intending to go to Vishalgarh. The Maratha king's raid into Berar had been nipped in the bud. But one division under Krishna Savant plandered some places near Dhamuni and returned. This was the first tie that a Maratha force crossed the Narmada.

Meantime, battles had been fought with the other Maratha bands too. On 9 January 1700 Nasrat Jang (Zulfiqar) fought Dhana, Ranuji Ghorpare, and Hanumant Rao beyond Masur, and defeated them, killing 500 of their men. A few days later, Dhana attacked the outpost of Khanapur and carried off its Mughal officer, Avji Adhal.

In the meantime the Emperor's siege of Satara continued and battles took place in its environs between the Mughal invaders and the Maratha field armies.

15.26 Death of Rajaram; Tara Bai's Policy

On 2 March 1700, Rajaram died at Singhagarh, of a fever which was most probably caused by the hardships of his raid and the vehement pursuit by the Mughals. His family was then in the fort of Vishalgarh. His favourite natural son Kama was immediately afterwards crowned as king by his ministers, with the help of Dhana Jadav, but died of small-pox in three weeks. Then his legitimate son by his wife Tara Bai was placed on the throne as Shivaji III, with the support of Ramchandra, 'the Regent of the West.' An internecine quarrel now broke out in the Maratha Court between Rajaram's surviving widows, Tara Bai and Rajas Bai (the mothers of Shivaji III and Shambhuji II respectively), each standing up for her own son and supported by a faction among the officers and generals. But the ability and energy of Tara Bai, the elder wife, gave her the supreme power in the State.

Immediately after learning of her husband's death, Tara Bai offered submission to the Emperor, asking for a 7-hazari *mansab* and the deshmukhi rights over the Deccan for Rajaram's legitimate son, and proposing to supply a contingent of 5,000 men for service under the imperial victory of the Deccan, and to cede seven forts. Aurangzib refused this offer. Towards the end of May, Ramchandra's agent Ramaji Pandit and Parashuram's agent Ambaji visited Prince Azam and begged him to intercede with the Emperor for sparing Rajaram's young son in return for the surrender of the Maratha forts. These overtures seem to have been insincere and came to nothing.

15.27 The War in Konkan, 1689–1704

Going southwards from Surat, the traveller meets successively with the following divisions of the long coast-strip between the Western Ghat range and the Arabian Sea—first, *Kolvan* or the broken country inhavited by the wild Koli tribe (forming the Jawhar and Dharampur States), then *North Konkan* (or the modern Thana and Kolaba districts, parallel to the Nasik and Puna districts which lie east of the Ghats), and lastly *South Konkan* (or the modern Ratnagiri district, which runs parallel to the Satara and Kolhapur ditsricts of the Deccan plateau across the mountain range). At the southernmost point of Ratnagiri, the coast is broken, near Vingurla, by the territory of the ancient Maratha family of *Savants of Vadi* (popularly known as the 'Desais of Kudal' in the Seventeenth century), and immediately south of it, by the Portuguese province of *Goa.* Still further south begins *Kanara,* with the Karwar district along the coast, and the States of Sunda and Bednur in the interior, far to the east, leading into the Mysore plateau.

Through a gap in the Western Ghats near the city of Nandurbar, some distance north of Dharampur, an invading force from the coastal region could easily enter the rich provinces of Khandesh and Berar,—while

Kolvan afforded a convenient base for the plundering either of Surat in the north or of Baglana in the east, and from Baglana, southwards across the Chandor range, for incursions into the Nasik district.

Shivaji had conquered Konkan between 1657 and 1662 and the Koli country in 1670–73. After his death the Mughals had made descents into N. Konkan in 1682 and 1683 and temporarily occupied its capital Kalian, but more to ravage and bum the places than to hold them. In December 1683 the Marathas reoccupied Kalian and remained in undisturbed possession of Konkan for the next five years, though their coast-villages lay subject to depredation by the Siddis. Mughal progress in this region began only in 1689 and under a very able local officer.

Matabar Khan, a Sayyid of the Navaiyat clan of Arabs long settled in Kalian, when employed as thanadar of the Nasik district, first distinguished himself (1688) by his enterprising spirit and farsightedness. He enlisted a strong infantry force of the local hill-men, won over many of the zamindars in the neighbourhood and captured many Maratha forts by force or bribery, e.g., Patta (Vishramgarh), Kulang, Trimbak (on 8 January 1689), and several smaller ones after the fall of Shambhuji. The triumphant Mughal general crossed the Ghats and descended into Konkan. In this province he took Kalian (27 March), Prabal, Karnala, Dugad, Manikgarh, and finally Mahuli (in August). Thus all North Konkan from the Koli country southwards to the latitude of Bombay passed into imperial possession. Most parts of the district had been ruined by twenty years of Maratha predominance and frequent warfare. He established imperial rule over them, restored order, and planted colonies of peasants so as to revive their cultivation and prosperity.

After these successful campaigns Matabar Khan returned to Kalian (1690) and lived there in comparative peace for some years, beautifying that city with a governor's mansion, a hall of public audience, a mosque, a Turkish bath, a portico, a garden and a terrace with a tank and fountains, and other structures. The magnificent tomb of his wife in Kalian was built at the cost of one lakh of Rupees.

But early in 1693, the Marathas recovered their power and the Mughals lost their dominant position and were driven to assume the defensive. Roving Maratha bands began to raid Mughal territory and recover the forts recently acquired by the imperialists. Konkan served the Marathas as an excellent base for organizing these operations, as the Western Ghats formed a screen in their front, while the possessions of the friendly Portuguese along the western coast afforded a safe refuge to the wives and children of their fighters even when the enemy descended into the eastern belt of Konkan. The local Portuguese governor was bribed by them to give them shelter and to supply provisions to their forts and villages in North Konkan.

Matabar Khan, therefore, invaded the Portuguese territory of 'the North' (i.e., Bassein and Daman), making prisoners of the enemy's subjects and defeating their armies. The viceroy of Goa at last made peace by humble submission to the Emperor and the offer of presents.

The news-letters of Aurangzib's Court contain many examples of Matabar's vigilant care for his charge, his strict maintenance of efficiency in the administration, and his assistance to the Siddi chief of Janjira in the military operations further south for upholding the imperial power. Death overtook this able and faithful servant at the end of February 1704.

16 The Last Phase of Aurangzib's Career

16.1 Policy of the Maratha Government, 1689–99

When Rajaram, the newly crowned king of the Marathas, fled away to the Madras coast (July, 1689), affairs in the Maharashtra country were left to his ministers. Ramchandra Nilkanth was created Regent of the West, with the title of *Hakumat-Panah*, and he guided the fortunes of this virtually kingless State with remarkable wisdom and tact. He checked the progress of the Mughals, organized raids into imperial territory, sent succour repeatedly to his master in Jinji, and kept peace among the intractable and mutually jealous Maratha generals.

Rajaram, in addition to being plunged into debauchery in the Karnatak, was naturally weak-minded. His position made him powerless. He was a king without an army or treasury of his own, or subjects under his undisputed rule. Any Maratha captain who could get togther a thousand or even five hundred men of his own, could dictate the terms of his obedience to his nominal king. Rajaram was, therefore, profuse in his gifts of titles and unconquered lands: All the Maratha *sardars* went to the king at Jinji, and he gave them titles, army commands, and grants for the different districts where they were to go, loot the country, and impose the *chauth*. Rajaram's political impotence is best illustrated by his duplication of offices and titles at a time when his kingdom was shrinking to nothing. He could not afford to disoblige any of his proud and selfish chiefs. The office of *Senapati* (commander-in-chief) was changed five times in Rajaram's short reign of eleven years; and, in addition, five officers at one time enjoyed titles varying in terminology but all meaning 'leader of the army' and all being entitled to the rank banner and other paraphernalia of the *Senapati*!

But this decentralization of authority was exactly suited to the situation in Maharashtra. The Maratha captains, each acting on his own account, carried on a guerilla warfare and caused the greatest loss and disturbance to the Mughal territories. The imperialists did not know what point to defend, nor where to find a vital enemy position for their attack. The extremely mobile Maratha bands covered long distances and delivered attacks at the most unexpected quarters; and such roving bands were countless. The result was universal unrest throughout the Deccan. At this stage the Marathas avoided pitched battles. Their encampments during the rainy months were in obscure and inaccessible places. Their bands did not hold together all the year round but dispersed to their several homes after the campaigning season of six months (October to April) was over.

There was mutual jealousy among the ministers left in Maharashtra as well as at the Court of Jinji. Parashuram Trimbak formed a faction of his own and drew Santaji Ghorpare into it. The natural consequence was that Dhana Singh Jadav was backed by Ramchandra. Santa's insubordination proved unbearable; he would not obey the Regent of the West, nor co-operate in any national enterprise (like the relief of Panhala in 1693) planned by him, preferring to conquer an independent estate for himself. Ramchandra had, therefore, to secure the king's consent to Santa's dismissal. Then another minister Shankaraji Malhar took Santa under his wing. Another refractory and selfish general of great power was Nima Sindhia. Ramchandra struggled against these difficulties as best he could, and on the whole he succeeded fairly well. The rivalry between Santa Ghorpare and Dhana Jadav precipitated a civil war in 1696, and three battles were fought between them. The murder of Santa (June 1697) created a blood-feud between his son Ranuji and his brother Baharji (surnamed *Hindu Rao*) on the one hand and Dhana's party on the other, which took long to heal. But this internal discord among the Marathas gave the Mughals only a brief respite.

Ramchandra cleverly provided shelters for the families of the Maratha combatants in South Konkan and the Portuguese territory of Daman, which had not yet been penetrated by Mughal armies, and also in the Berad country and the north-western corner of Mysore, which the Emperor was not yet free to invade.

16.2 Tara Bai Rules as Queen-mother; Internal Dissensions in the Maratha State

When Rajaram died, on 2 March 1700, and then his natural son Karna after a three weeks' reign, Tara Bai crowned her own: (legitimate) son Shivaji, a boy under ten years, and ruled with the help of Parashuram Trimbak. Thus a second regency ensued in the Maratha kingdom. The supreme guiding force in Maharashtra now was not any minister but the dowager queen Tara Bai Mohite. Her administrative genius and strength of character saved the nation in the awful crisis that threatened it in consequence of Rajaram's death, the disputed succession to his throne, and Aurangzib's repeated victories from 1699 to 1701. The hostile Muslim historian Khafi Khan is constrained to call her wise, enterprising, expert in administration and popular with the army. 'Under Tara Bai's guidance, Maratha activity began to increase daily. She took into her own hands the control of all affairs,—such as the appointment and change of generals, the cultivation of the country and the planning of raids into Mughal territory. She made such arrangements for sending troops to ravage the six subahs of the Deccan, nay even up to Sironj and Mandesor in Malwa,—and winning the hearts of her officers, that all the efforts of Aurangzib against the Marathas down to the end of his reign failed.'

Immediately after the death of Rajaram, Parashuram Trimbak, out of jealousy for the other ministers then in Satara, came out of his own fort of Parli and offered to join the Mughals. But Tara Bai won this supremely able officer over to her interests by creating him *Pratinidhi* and giving him her full trust. But it was only after a hard struggle that Tara Bai's supremacy was established. Some of the generals obeyed her, some did not. Rajas Bai, the junior wife of Rajaram and the mother of Shambhuji II, whom she set up as a rival king, began to quarrel with Tara Bai and form her own faction. There was a third party among the Maratha leaders, who wanted to secure national unity by placing Shahu on the throne, as he represented the elder branch of Shivaji's descendants. These dynastic quarrels were complicated by the cross-currents of personal rivalry among the Maratha generals, especially Dhana Jadav and Santa Ghorpare and their partisans.

16.3 Shaba's Captive Life, 1689–1707; Maratha Partisans of the Mughals

Shahu, the eldest son of Shambhuji, had become a prisoner of the Mughals at the age of seven, when Raigarh surrendered in October 1689, and he was kept under strict watch, though kindly treated, close to the Emperor's tent and within the circle of the red canvas screen (*gulal-bar*) of the imperial quarters. With him were his mother Yesu Bai and his half-brothers Madan Singh and Madhu Singh.

In 1700 Shahu had a severe attack of illness, which seems to have left his body and mind shattered for the rest of his life. The Court news-letter gives the following account of it—Rajah Shahu came to the audience on 26 August and made his bow. The Emperor after looking at him remarked that his colour had turned entirely yellow, and asked the reason for it. Hafiz Ambar (eunuch) replied that the rajah did not eat any cooked *dal,* bread or rice, but only sweets (*pakwan*), on the ground that Hindus must not eat cooked food in prison, and he regarded himself as a prisoner.

As difficulties thickened round Aurangzib and the Deccan tangle seemed insoluble, he began to form plans for settling the contest with the Maratha generals through Shahu. First, on 9 May 1703, he sent Hamid-ud-din Khan to urge Shahu to become a Muslim, as the heirs to some other Hindu thrones had already been tempted to do in this reign. But Shahu refused to apostatize. Next the Emperor tried to create a division among the Marathas by releasing Shahu. The terms of his release were to be settled by treaty with the leading Maratha generals, through the mediation of Prince Kam Bakhsh. For approaching the national leaders and winning them over, Raibhan, the son of Vyankaji Bhonsle of Tanjore, was taken into the Emperor's service, created a *6-hazari,* and sent to visit Shahu (10 July 1703). But the move failed. As Bhimsen bluntly puts it—'The prince repeatedly sent his men to Dhana. But as the Marathas had not been vanquished and the entire Decean had come into their possession like a deliriously cooked pudding, why should they make peace?... The envoys of the prince returned in disappointment, and Rajah Shahu was again placed under surveillance in the *gulal-bar*.'

Aurangzib felt himself utterly helpless. In the last year of his life (1707) he decided to make another attempt at peace with the Marathas. Shahu was transferred from his own camp to that of Nasrat Jang (25 January). Raibhan, too, was posted under him in the hope of his being able to persuade the Maratha generals to make terms with the Emperor as the price of the release of Shahu. Nasrat Jang wrote conciliatory letters to the Maratha generals and invited them to come and join Rajah Shahu. But it was to no effect. A civil war had indeed broken out among the Marathas, Rajas Bai trying to seize Tara Bai and thwarting all her plans; but the Emperor's hope of taking advantage of it and creating a further division by bringing Shahu into it, failed. It was only after Aurangzib's death that Prince Azam, then marching towards Agra, connived at the escape of Shahu to the Deccan.

It is not true that all the leading Maratha families were on the national side during the struggle with Aurangzib. Many of them served the Mughal Government, and for various reasons. The noble house of Jadav Rao of Sindhkhed, in which the great Shivaji's mother had been born, entered the Mughal army early in Shah Jahan's reign (1630), after the murder of Lakhi Jadav Rao, and they remained on the imperial side for several generations. Kanhoji Shirke and his sons, from whose family Rajaram's mother came, had been persecuted by Shambhuji and had fled for refuge to the Mughal Emperor, who gave them high posts. The Shirkes as well as Nagoji Mane (the thanadar of Mhasvad and a Mughal partisan from 1694) remained consistently loyal and rendered long and meritorious service to the Mughals. Three other devoted Maratha servants of the Emperor were Avji Adhal (thanadar of Khanapur) who was made captive by the Marathas on 23 January 1700, Ramchandra (thanadar of Khatau) who died fighting at his post on 18 August 1700, and Baharji Pandhre, sometimes thanadar of Kashigaon.

Another Maratha chief in Mughal pay was Satvaji Dafle, who had a more chequered career. This family had been barons under the Adil Shahi kings. On the fall of that monarchy they took service with the Mughal conqueror. Satva's son, Baji Chavan Dafle, gave up his life most heroically in leading the storming party at the siege of Satara (13 April 1700). Satva himself had deserted the Mughals before 1695 and continued to raid the imperial territory, but came over to the Emperor in August 1701, when he was created a *5-hazari,* and given the Jagir of Jath in reward of his late son's gallantry.

Several thousands of Mavles, or Maratha hill infantry, served under Aurangzib. But on the whole the presence of hired Maratha auxiliaries on the Mughal side had merely the effect of keeping them out of mischief, and did not add much to the strength of the imperial army. For one thing, their equipment and armament were far inferior to those of the regular Mughal troops. Then, they fought half-heartedly for their paymaster, and their captains frequently changed sides.

16.4 Aurangzib's Siege of Satara

On 19 October 1699, Aurangzib started from Islampuri on that campaign against the great Maratha strongholds which was to occupy the next six years of his life, One by one the famous hill-forts of Satara, Parli, Panahla, Vishalgarh (Khelna), Kondana (Singhgarh), Rajgarh, and Torna were captured by him, besides five places of lesser note. But it should be remembered that with the sole exception of Torna, none of these were taken by assault; all capitulated after a time and for a price; their garrisons were permitted to march out with their personal effects, and their commands were given costly rewards for ceasing resistance.

At Islampuri Aurangzib left his wife Udaipuri and her son Kam Baksh, and his daughter Zinat-un-nisa, with all the surplus baggage and unnecessary officials, and the families of his soldiers and camp-followers. The wazir Asad Khan remained in charge of them with a suitable force. Zulfiqar, surnamed Nasrat Jang, was given a roving commission for fighting the Maratha field armies that hovered round the siege camp or threatened the base at Islampuri.

Marching from Islampuri the Emperor reached Masur, (33 km i.e., 21 miles south of Satara) on 21 November. Basantgarh, a fort 10 km (6 miles) south west of Masur, was evacuated by its garrison in terror, and the imperialists entered it on 25 November and named it the 'Key to Victory' (*Kilid-i-Fath*), as a happy omen of their success in the ensuing campaign.

Marching thence, the imperialists arrived before Satara on 8 December. Aurangzib took up his quarters at the village of Karanja, two and a half km, i.e. a mile and a half to the north of the fort walls. The Mughal army with its followers and transport animals was concentrated in one spot, 9 km (five miles) round, and this encampment was walled round to keep out the Maratha raiders. Siege operations began on 9 December. The rocky soil made digging a very slow and difficult work. The garrison fired upon the Mughals day and night without cessation with every kind of missile. But the lines of investment were not complete. The enemy entered and issued from Satara almost to the end of the siege.

The garrison made frequent sorties, all of which were repulsed with more or less loss. But the greatest danger to the Mughals came from the Maratha field forces, which practically reduced the besiegers to the position of a beleagured city. Foraging parties could leave the Mughal camp only under very strong escorts, led by the foremost nobles. Dhana, Shankara, and other enemy leaders spread through the Mughal possessions, raiding villages, cutting off outposts and closing the roads to the grain-dealers (*banjaras*).

Tarbiyat Khan by hard labour dug a mine 24 yards long and carried it under the fort-wall. But assault by breaching was deemed inadvisable. Then, a surprise escalade was attempted by 2,000 Mavles in Mughal pay, on 23 January, but the attempt failed. On 13 April two mines were fired. The first killed many of the garrison and buried the havladar Pragji Prabhu under the debris of the wall, but he was dug out alive. The second exploded outwards; a tower was blown up and fell upon the Mughal troops densely assembled at the foot of the wall for the assault; nearly two thousand of them perished. This explosion made a breach in the wall, 18 metre (20 yards wide). Some brave imperialists, notably Baji Chavan Dafle, the son of Satva Dafle (the founder of the State of Jath in the Bijapur district), ran up to the top of the wall, shouting to their comrades, 'Come up! there is no enemy here!' But none followed them; the men in the Mughal trenches who survived were too dazed and alarmed by the catastrophe to stir outside. The garrison now recovered from their surprise, and rushing up to the breach, slew the gallant forlorn hope.

Meantime Rajaram had died (March) and his minister Parashuram proposed submission to the Mughals. Tarbiyat Khan had demolished 63 metre (70 yards) of the fort walls, 400 of the garrison had been killed by the mines. Considering all these facts, Subhanji, the qiladar of Satara, lost heart and made terms with the emperor through Prince Azam. On 21 April he hoisted the imperial flag on his fort and vacated it with the garrison the next day. The fort was renamed *Azamtara* in honour of Prince Md. Azam.

16.5 Parli Fort Captured

The Mughals soon afterwards opened siege trenches before Parli, 10 km (6 miles) west of Satara. This fort had been the seat of Shivaji's *guru* Ramdas Swami and it was serving as the headquarters of the Maratha Government while Satara was invested by the enemy. Parashuram, the chief revenue officer of the Maratha Government, being disheartened by the death of Rajaram and the fall of Satara, escaped from Parli, but that fort continued its resistance under his subordinates.

The invaders suffered terribly from excessive rain and the scarcity of grain and fodder. But Aurangzib held grimly on. Terms were at last made with the qiladar of Parli, and he evacuated the fort (on 9 June) for a bribe.

These two sieges had caused an enormous waste of men, horses and transport animals in the imperial army. The treasury was empty, the soldiers were starving at their pay being in arrears for three years. Heavy and unprecedented rain began to fall early in May and continued till the end of July. On 21 June the return march towards Bhushangarh commenced, but the sufferings of the miserable soldiers were only aggravated by the change. Most of the transport animals had perished during the siege. The few cart-oxen and elephants that survived had nothing but their skins and bones left. Only a small part of the property of the Emperor and the nobles could be carried away by these weak animals and porters. Much had to be left in the forts or burnt. Many persons of noble birth had to walk on foot through the mud for mile after mile. One march was followed by two days' halt, in order to allow the stragglers time to come up. Only 5 kilometres (3 miles) were covered by a day's march. The Krishna was in such high flood that the opposite bank could not be seen from this. Great difficulty was felt in crossing such a huge army over the swollen river. Only seven half-broken and clumsily-patched up boats were available for ferrying the men across, and the people often fought to get seats in them. Bhushangarh was reached on 25 July, the army having taken 35 days to cover 72 km (45 miles). Here a month's halt was made. Then the imperial camp was shifted (on 30 August 1700), Khawaspur, on the Man river, 60 km (36 miles) off. The imperialists lay encamped on both its banks and even its dry bed. But on the night of 1 October, while the men were fast asleep, a high flood caused by heavy and untimely rainfall on the hills, came suddenly sweeping through the river bed, overtopped its banks and spread over the plains beyond. Many men and animals perished; many more, including even the nobles, were left absolutely poor and naked; nearly all the tents and property were damaged.

When the flood first struck the camp, a little before midnight, a loud cry arose throughout the army. The Emperor, imaging that the Marathas had burst into the camp, rose in alarm, but stumbled and dislocated his right knee. The doctors failed to set it properly, and he remained a little lame for the rest of his life. The Court flatterers used to console him by saying that it was the heritage of his ancestor, the world-conqueror Timur the Lame!

But vigorous efforts were made to replenish his army. Orders were sent to the governors of Northern India to enlist strong men and buy good horses in every province and send them to the Deccan. Two thousand horses were bought in Kabul, and 2,000 mares locally, besides the remounts purchased in other provinces.

The Marathas put the misfortunes of the imperialists to the best account. In addition to their normal raids, Hanumant Rao plundered the *thana* of Khatau and killed its Mughal officer Ramchandra (a Maratha), 18 August, 1700. The Berad chief, Pidia Nayak, posted his infantry all over the Bijapur district levying *chauth*, while the Marathas plundered up to the very tank of Shahpur, outside Bijapur city, (*c.* 15 November). Ranuji Ghorpare killed the Mughal thanadar of Bagehwari (50 km i.e. 30 miles south-east of Bijapur) and looted that outpost as well as Indi (north-east of Bijapur city).

16.6 Siege of Panhala, 1701

Panhala was the next point of attack. The Emperor arrived there on 9 March 1701 and formed a complete circle of investment, 23 km (14 miles) in length, round Panhala and its sister fort of Pavangarh. A mobile force under Nasrat Jang was sent out to 'chastise the robbers wherever they should raise their heads.' But in that stony region the progress of mining was necessarily very slow, and the dreaded rainy season was approaching. In addition to the notorious rivalry between the Emperor's two highest generals,—Nasrat Jang and Firuz Jang,—which made it impossible to employ both at the same place, there now broke out a bitter jealousy between Tarbiyat Khan and Fathullah Khan and another between the older officers in general and a very able upstart from Gujrat named Muhammad Murad. The mutual jealousies of the generals made true co-operation among them impossible. They secretly thwarted one another, and thus spoiled their master's business and prolonged the siege. When Tarbiyat Khan was urged to deliver an assault, he ironically replied, 'The preparations for an assault are complete. Please order Md. Murad, who has done such heroic deeds, to support us on the day of storming.' With this spirit animating Aurangzib's generals, it was only natural that all his efforts came to nothing, and the siege dragged on for two months, without success seeming to come any nearer. To gain Panhala before the rains began, a large bribe was paid to Trimbak, the qiladar, and he delivered the fort on 28 May, 1701. The efforts of the Marathas to relieve the siege of Panhala were many. Their generals, Dhana Jadav, Ranuji Ghorpare, Ramchandra and Krishna Malhar constantly hovered round the siege camp, cutting off foraging parties and convoys of provisions. Nasrat Jang and Hamid-ud-din with movable columns toiled in vain after the fleet Maratha rovers and fought many a bloody battle without decisive result.

After the fall of Panhala, Aurangzib (on 29 May, 1701) retreated from it to encamp in the safer and more fertile region of Khatau (42 km i.e 25 miles east of Satara and on the left bank of the Yerla river). Quick as his departure was, it had not been made soon enough. A cyclone passed over the camp 'blowing away tents and sheds like paper. Kings and beggars had to sit down in the sun. Veiled ladies became exposed to the public gaze.'

Fathullah Khan, highly promoted and created a Bahadur, was sent ahead to take Wardhangarh (13 km i.e. 8 miles north-west of Khatau) and three other forts in the neighbourhood,—Chandan, Nandgir and Wandan.

16.7 Siege of Khelna

The Emperor next set out for the conquest of Khelna (or Vishalgarh). The fort stands 50 km (30 miles) west of Panhala, on the crest of the Sahyadri hill, 1,035 m (3,350 feet) above the sea and overlooking the

Konkan plain lying on its west. The district is wet and cool, and the hills were thickly covered with trees and dense underwood in the seventeenth century. The easiest means of reaching the fort is by the Amba pass, 8 km (5 miles) north of it, and some 58 km (35 miles) north-west of Kolhapur. The 13 km (8 miles) leading to the defile were very difficult ground. There was in that age no road here for wheeled traffic, and the ups and downs were so sharp and the path so narrow that even horses could not use it with ease or safety.

Leaving Wardhangarh on 7 November 1701, the Emperor arrived near Malkapur in 12 marches. Here he halted for a week, while pioneers were set to make a road ahead. But the Amba pass itself had yet to be made fit for the passage of an army. This formidable task was accomplished by Fathullah Khan after one week's incessant toil with a host of pioneers and stone-cutters. Then Asad Khan was detached on 26 December to begin the siege. On 16 January 1702, the Emperor's tent was pitched 1½ km (1 mile) from Khelna. His followers suffered terrible hardship and loss in crossing the pass and bringing his camp and equipage to the foot of the fort.

The siege dragged on for five months (January—June 1702). During this year Nasrat Jang with his mobile division marched in pursuit of the Maratha field forces nearly 10,000 km (6,000 miles) in Berar and Telingana and fought 19 great battles with them, besides numberless skirmishes. The Mughal artillery beat in vain against the solid rock of the walls of Khelna; only a few stones were loosened from the tower, and success seemed as far off as ever. On the other hand, the catapults of the garrison showered huge stones upon the advancing siegeworks. They also raided the trenches at night. All the valiant exertions of Fathullah Khan Turani on the north side were thrown away against that impregenable rock. No better success was achieved at the Konkani (or western) gate of the fort. Here Muhammad Amin Khan had stormed the fortified hillock opposite this gate and commanding its fausse braye (*rauni*) on 4 March. Bidar Bakht, who replaced the Khan, delivered an assault led by Jai Singh, the young Rajah of Amber, on 27 April, and captured the *rauni*, in spite of heavy losses. The next step was to drag big guns up to the position and batter down the Konkani gate with them.

But the terrible monsoon of the Bombay Coast now burst on the heads of the devoted Mughal army. The qiladar Parashuram accepted a large bribe from Bidar Bakht and on 4 June planted the prince's banner on the ramparts, and in the night of 7 June the garrison evacuated the fort.

The sufferings of the Mughal army during its return from Khelna were terrible. The Emperor beat a hasty retreat from its neighbourhood, on 10 June only three days after the fall of the fort. But the rain had already begun with tropical fury and the Mughal army underwent terrible hardships in crossing the dreadful Amba pass again in this weather. 'The camels refused to set foot on this path. The elephants sank into the mud like donkeys. The only goods carried were on the heads of Porters.' A sudden rise of a *nala* on the way, 'running like a race-horse,' cut the imperial army into two, and many were drowned. *Nalas* in a similar condition intersected the path of retreat at three places. Grain sold at one Rupee a seer. 'Fodder and firewood appeared in the isolated camp only by mistake.' Many men also perished of cold amidst the incessant rain, from having no tent or change of clothing left to them. At some stages only a small canvas cover was all that could be pitched for the Emperor himself. In this condition, after covering 50 km (30 miles) in 38 days, the miserable army arrived near Panhala (17 July 1702).

The Mughals finally reached Bahadurgarh or Pedgaon oa the northern bank of the Bhima, on 13 November, 1702.

16.8 Sieges of Kondana (Singhgarh), Rajgarh and Torna

After a stay of only 18 days, the Emperor set out on 2 December to capture Kondana (Singhgarh), which was reached on the 27 December. The imperial family, ofiices, and heavy baggage were removed from the Base Camp at Islampuri to Bahadurgarh,, and the former post was made Nasrat Jang's cantonment. Bidar Bakht was sent to Aurangabad as viceroy and later (February 1703) given the subahdari of Khandesh in addition. The siege began, but there was no life in the work of the besiegers, and three months were wasted in this way. The rainy season was now approaching. So, the Emperor's servants secured the fort on 8 April 1703, by heavily bribing the qiladar.

From Kondana the army marched back to Puna in a week (1 May), in the neighbourhood of which it spent nearly seven months. The excessive rainfall of 1702 had been followed by a drought in 1703–4, and there was famine throughout Maharashtra, with its natural companion, pestilence. Large numbers of the poorer classes perished,—two millions, according to Manucci.

From the neighbourhood of Puna, the Mughal army reached Rajgarh in 18 days, and began its siege on 2 December, 1703. They bombarded it for two months, and then captured the first j gate by assault on 6 February 1704. The garrison under their chiefs Firangji and Hamanji retired to the inner citadel, and kept up the resistance for ten days more At last the qiladar made terms, hoisted the imperial flag on his tower, and fled away at night (16 February).

Aurangzib next laid siege to Torna, 13 km (8 miles) from Rajgarh, on 23 February. In the night of 10 March Amanullah Khan with only 23 Mavle infantry silently scaled the fort-wall by means of rope-ladders, blew his trumpets, and charged the enemy. Those of the garrison which resisted were put to the sword, the rest fled to the citadel and cried for mercy. This was the only Maratha fort that Aurangzib captured by force without resort to bribery.

From Torna the imperial camp arrived at Khed (11 km i.e. 7 miles north of Chakan) and encamped there for six months, from 17 April to 21 October, 1704. From this place the Emperor started on 22 October for Wagingera, the Berad capital, which was reached after a slow march of three-and-a-half months, on 8 February 1705, and immediately besieged. This was the last campaign of Aurangzib.

16.9 The Berad People and Their Country and Chieftain

The country extending east of Bijapur city, and enclosed by the Bhima and the Krishna rivers, is the home of the Berads, a race of aboriginal Kanarese, also called Dheds, and regarded as one of the lowest in the scale of Hindu castes. They are a virile and hardy people, not much advanced from savagery, but at the same time not toned down like the over-refined upper castes of Hindu society. They eat mutton, beef, pork, domestic fowls, etc., and drink to excess. Dark, muscular, and .of middle height, with round faces, flat cheeks, thin lips and lank or frizzled hair, the Berads can bear fatigue and hardship, but have no taste for settled industry or peaceful arts. Their tribal organization under the heads of families and the judicial authority of their hereditary headmen ensured discipline and solidarity among them, and they supplied the most steady and accurate musketeers of South India in the seventeenth and eighteenth centuries. Their gallantry in war and contempt for wounds and death were as conspicuous as their skill in making night-attacks and surprises,—which we might naturally expect from such expert cattle-stealers. Contemporary Persian historians call them *Be-dar* (fearless), by a play on their name.

The cradle-land of the Bedars was Mysore, from which they advanced into the Raichur doab and then further north into the country beyond the Krishna and even the Bhima. The Berad Nayaks or chieftains of Shorapur, lying in the fork between the Krishna and the Bhima, had their earliest capital at Sagar, some 120 km (72 miles) east of Bijapur city. When this was lost to the Mughals (1687), the Nayak built a new capital at Wagingera, 20 km (12 miles) south-west of Sagar. At the close of Aurangzib's reign even this fort was taken from him, and the Nayak removed his seat to Shorapur, on the eastern face of the same hill-mass as Wagingera and 6 km (4 miles) from it. Having lost their dominion to the Mughals at the surrender of 1687, the Berad chiefs had now no resource left except to rebel, build new strongholds among the hills, and rob the Mughal territory around in imitation of the Marathas and afterwards in concert with them. The Kulbarga district was kept in constant disturbance and the roads were closed to caravans by persistent but elusive bands of Berad horsemen for many years after the fall of Sagar.

Pedda Pidia Nayak, the nephew and adopted heir of Pam Nayak (reign 1678–88), had waited on Aurangzib as early as 1683 and been given a post in the imperial army. After the Mughal conquest of Sagar and the death of his uncle, he busied himself in fortifying Wagingera and raising an army. He collected twelve thousand excellent musketeers of his tribesmen and steadily increased his artillery and munitions of war.

Pidia's robberies in the Kulbarga district became too serious to be overlooked any longer. At last, on 27 May 1691 the Emperor sent his son Kam Bakhsh from Bijapur, in charge of Bahramand Khan, to attack Wagingera. On 20 July the prince was sent off to the Madras Karnatak, and the operations against the Berads were entrusted to Ruhullah Khan. The latter could not achieve the task; the Berads twice fell on his entrenchment and destroyed it; many on the Mughal side were slain, including the celebrated Ranmust Khan. So Ruhullah Khan opened negotiations with the enemy, who bribed and lulled him into inactivity. Azam was sent to relieve Ruhullah (18 December 1691). The prince stayed there for a year, ravaging the country and checking Berad activities. Pidia then submitted, appealed to the prince's mercy, presented him with two lakhs of Rupees and made peace with the Emperor by paying an indemnity of seven lakhs. But in December 1692 the Emperor removed Azam from Sagar, and Pidia soon afterwards resumed his old brigandage and usurpation of land. When Firuz Jang was sent against him (April 1696), he 'played the same jackal's trick on him' and escaped destruction by promising a tribute of nine lakhs.

16.10 Aurangzib Captures Wagingera, 1705

At last, towards the close of the year 1704, after the great Maratha forts had all been captured, the Emperor turned to Wagingera and began its siege on 8 February, 1705.

On the plain in the south, facing the fort gate, there is a village called *Talwargera*, enclosed by a mud wall and containing the market for the supply of the garrison. Close to it was *Dhedpura*, a hamlet of grass huts, where the families of the common Berads lived and from which they tilled the surrounding lands. These three were the only inhabited places there; but close to the fort in the east and north were a number of hillocks which would be of great service to besiegers. One of these, called *Lal Tikri* from its red soil, slightly commanded a portion of Wagingera itself and had a very important bearing on the defence of that fort. The Berads had not thought of protecting any of these outlying eminences by redoubt or outpost.

The strength of Wagingera lay not so much in its natural position or artificial defences, as in the courage and number of its garrison, the deadly accuracy of their musketry fire, and its ample supply of guns, rockets and artillery munitions.

For many weeks after the commencement of the siege, the Mughals could do nothing. Every day the enemy sallied forth and attacked the imperialists. The bombardment from the fort walls continued incessantly and made the advance of the Mughal trenches, or even their maintenance within range of the fort guns, impossible.

One morning while the Mughal generals were out reconnoitring for weak points in the defences, they suddenly charged up Lal Tikri, drove away the Berad musketeers on its top and seized the position. But it was impossible for them to dig themselves in on that rocky height.

The Berads immediately sent three large bodies of their infantry, who swarmed up the hillside 'numberless like ants and locusts,' and plied their muskets and hurled stones with deadly accuracy on the imperialists crowded helplessly on the top. The position had at last to be abandoned after heavy losses.

The Mughal trenches started from a spot between Lal Tikri and the hillock opposite Talwargera, while an outpost was established under Muhammad Amin Khan between Lal Tikri and these trenches, to guard against enemy attacks from that hill. The hillock facing Talwargera was occupied by Kam Bakhsh's troops and another mound near by was held by Baqr Khan.

But on 26 March a Maratha force of five to six thousand horse under Dhana Jadav and Hindu Rao (brother of Santa Ghorpare) arrived near the fort to support their Berad allies, because the families of many Maratha generals had taken refuge there. The first task of the Marathas was to remove their families safely from this fort. While the main body of the new-comers kept the imperialists in play by a noisy feint against the siege lines in front of the fort assisted by a heavy fire from the walls, another body of 2,000 picked troopers brought their women and children out by the back-door of Wagingera, mounted them on swift mares, and escaped, their rear being guarded by a body of infantry that sallied out of the fort.

Pidia had promised the Marathas a daily subsidy of several thousand Rupees as long as they would assist in the defence of his capital. They halted in the neighbourhood and made frequent attacks on the Mughals. The Mughal army itself was now thrown into a state of siege. Its activities ceased and it was confined to its own lines. Grain and fodder became extremely scarce in the camp. The Emperor censured his generals, but it had no effect.

Pidia now made proposals of submission to the Emperor, but his real object was to gain time and call up heavy reinforcements from far and near.

Abdul Ghani, a glib-tongued lying Kashmiri pedlar, one day brought to Hedayat-kesh (the chief of the imperial Intelligence Department) a letter from Pidia proposing peace. Aurangzib gave a favourable reply to the letter. Pidia next sent his brother Som Singh to the Mughal camp, offering to give up the fort and asking that the zamindari, the headship of the clan, and a *mansab* might be granted to his brother. Som Singh stayed in the camp and spread the tale that Pidia had turned mad and fled with the Marathas. The Kashmiri next brought a message from the Berad chief's mother repeating this story and begging that Som Singh might now be allowed to return as the fort would be vacated in seven days. The Emperor agreed and stopped the fighting.

And then the bubble burst. The whole thing was a fraud. Pidia was alive and sane and still within the fort; he refused to surrender it and renewed his attacks. The Emperor almost went mad with rage and shame.

Meanwhile, he had summoned his ablest generals from all sides. Nasrat Jang arrived on 27 March and the next day he galloped up to the hillock of Lal Tikri from which the Mughals had been dislodged in the early days of the siege. He climbed the hill, and drove out the enemy, who ran into the village of Talwargera at its foot, and began to ply their muskets from behind its mud wall. Many Rajputs fell in the attack on Lal Tikri and outside the village. But Nasrat Jang directed Dalpat Bundela to a neighbouring hillock which was still in the enemy's hands. The Berads fled from the second mound too and hid in the village of Dhedpura. On this day twenty-one bullets and one rocket hit Dalpat Rao's elephant. The banners of Nasrat Jang were pitted with shotholes like a crocodile's hide, and two of his elephant drivers were wounded and one killed. Similarly, there were heavy casualties in the centre and rear of the Mughal general's force, but Nasrat Jang kept hold of the position he had gained with so much blood near the wall. A few days later the Khan captured some wells situated on the skirt of the hill whence the enemy used to draw their water. On 27 April he delivered an assault on Talwargera. The imperialists entered the *peth* (walled village), slaying all who resisted, and the rest fled.

The Berads now found that further struggle was hopeless. Pidia fled out of the back-door at night, Nvith the Maratha companions of his day of adversity. When night came and the sound of musketry from within died down, some Mughal soldiers entered the fort and found the place entirely deserted. Then began a wild scene of confusion, rapine and burning. At the news of the fort being vacated, there was a wild rush of camp-followers, common soldiers and all the ruffians of the camp, in the hope of plunder before the Government agents should come and attach the property. The fire from the burning roofs spread to a powder magazine, and there was a terrible explosion,, many people being blown up. After two or three days, a second magazine exploded. Wagingera was captured, but its chieftain had escaped and lived to give trouble to the victors. Thus, all Aurangzib's labours for these three months were lost.

16.11 Desolation of the Country Caused by Aurangzib's Wars; Universal Disorder

At the end of the seventeenth century the great empire founded by Akbar and raised to world-famed prosperity and splendour by Shah Jahan, was in a state of hopeless decay; administration culture, economic life, military strength and social organization—all seemed to be hastening to utter ruin and dissolution. The material waste caused to the empire by this quarter century warfare was frightful. The desolation of the Deccan was complete. As a contemporary European observer, Manucci, notes,—'Aurangzib withdrew to Ahmadnagar leaving behind him the fields of these provinces devoid of trees and bare of crops, their place being taken by the bones of men and beasts. Instead of verdure all is blank and barren. There have died in his armies over a hundred thousand souls yearly, and of animals, pack-oxen, camels, elephants, etc., over three hundred thousand.... In the Deccan provinces from 1702 to 1704 plague [and famine] prevailed. In these two years there expired over two millions of souls.'

As he began his retreat northwards from the environs of Wagingera, the exultant Marathas in a vast horde of 50 to 60 thousand men followed his army a few miles in the rear, cutting off his grain supplies and stragglers and even threatening to break into his camp.

The eye-witness Bhimsen writes,—'The Marathas became completely dominant over the whole kingdom and closed the roads. By means of robbery they escaped from poverty and gained great wealth. I have heard that every week they gave away sweets and money in charity, praying for the long life of the Emperor who had proved [to them] the Feeder of the Universe! The price of grain grew higher and higher; in the imperial camp in particular vast numbers perished (of hunger) and many kinds of illegal exactions and practices appeared, Ever since His Majesty had come to the throne he had not lived in a city but elected all these wars and hard marching, so that the inmates of his camp, sick of long separation, summoned their families to the camp and lived there. A new generation was thus born [under canvas]; they passed from infancy to youth, from youth to old age, and passing beyond old age girt up their loins for the journey to the world of the angels, and yet never once saw the look of a house, but only knew that in this world there is no other shelter than a tent.... When the Marathas invade a province they take from every pargana as much money as they desire and make their horses eat the standing crops or tread them under foot. The imperial army that comes in pursuit can subsist only when the fields are cultivated [anew]. All administration has disappeared.... The realm has been desolated. The ryots have given up cultivation; the jagirdars do not get a penny from their fiefs. The system of the Maratha Government paying salaries to its officials disappeared. So, the Maratha State servants supported themselves by plundering on all sides, and paying a small part of their booty to the king.' The effect of the enemy's robbery and stoppage of rent from the Mughal officers' jagirs was aggravated by a long-continued famine. Hence, the condition of the Mughal army grew worse from the high price of grain and the devastation of jagirs, while the resources of the Marathas increased through robbery. They even attacked walled cities like Haidarabad, Bijapur, Aurangabad, and Burhanpur.'

The break-down of the administration and of public peace created a vicious circle aggravating the evil, as Bhimsen has clearly pointed out: 'The mansabdar, on account of the small forces under them, cannot gain control over the territories granted to them in jagir. The local zamindars, growing stronger, have joined the Marathas, levied troops, and stretched the hand of oppression over the realm.... As the imperial dominions have been given out in *tankha* (fief) to the jagirdars, so too the Marathas have made a distribution of the whole empire among their generals, and thus one kingdom has to maintain two sets of jagirdars!.... The peasants subjected to this double exaction have collected arms and horses and joined the Marathas.' Many of the Mughal mansabdars, goaded by poverty, began to plunder the innocent and loyal peasants to support themselves, and some went into shares with the Maratha raiders.

16.12 Maratha Systems of Spoliation and Warfare

The Marathas had reduced spoliation to a system, 'Wherever these raiders arrived they engaged in a revenue collection of the place and passed months and years there with wives and children in peace of mind. They divided the parganas among themselves and in imitation of the imperial

Government they appointed their own *subahdars, kamavish-dars* (revenue collectors) and *rahdars* (road guards). Their subahdar was a leader of troops: whenever he heard of a large caravan coming, he overtook it at the head of [some] seven thousand cavalry and looted it. Everywhere *kamavish-dars* were posted for collecting the *chauth.* When a kamavish-dar was opposed by a strong zamindar or imperial faujdar and could not levy the blackmail, the Maratha subahdar came to his aid, besieged and desolated the habitations there. The duty of the Maratha *rahdar* was this,—when traders wanted to travel unmolested by these people, the *rahdar* took a sum of money from each cart or bullock (three or fourfold the imperial faujdar's transit duty), and left the road open to them. In each subah the Marathas built one or two small forts *(garhis),* which they made their place of refuge and from which they issued to raid the country around.' (Khafi Khan).

After 1703 the Marathas were masters of the situation all over the Deccan and even in parts of Northern India. The Mughal officers became helpless and reduced to the defensive. A change now came over the Maratha tactics with this growth of their power: they were no longer, as in Shivaji's and Shambhuji's times, light forayers who 'cut and ran' or merely looted defenceless traders and villages and dispersed at the first report of the Mughal army's approach. On the contrary, as Manucci noticed in 1704, 'These [Maratha] leaders and their troops move in these days with much confidence, because they have cowed the Mughal commanders and inspired them with fear. At the present time they possess artillery, musketry, bows and arrows, with elephants and camels for all their baggage and tents. In short, they are equipped and move about just like the armies of the Mughal.'

In the internal administration the break-down of Aurangzib's Government was equally conspicuous. The officials became incorrigibly corrupt and inefficient, all the forbidden exactions (*abwab*) were revived by the local governors in violation of his orders, the Emperor in his old age was disobeyed by his distant officials, and the administration lost its efficiency.

16.13 Aurangzib Retreats to Ahmadnagar, 1705

Immediately after the capture of Wagingera (27 April, 1705), the Emperor removed his camp to Devapur, a quiet green village near the Krishna,

13 km (8 miles) south of the fort. Here he fell very ill on account of his age (ninety lunar years) and incessant labour.

Despair seized all men in his camp. At first he had courageously struggled with disease, and had through sheer strength of mind continued for some days to transact business as usual and even to peep out of his bedroom window to assure the public that he was alive. But the strain of this work only increased his malady, till he was seized with great pain, which at times made him senseless. The wildest rumours spread about his death and wars among his sons.

He lay in this state for ten or twelve days, and then he began to rally, but slowly, and still feeling very weak. At this time, one day in extreme agony he muttered these verses of Shaikh Ganja:

> *'By the time you reach your 80th*
> *or 90th year,*
> *You will have received many a hard blow*
> *from the hand of Time;*
> *And when from that point you reach the*
> *stage of a hundred years,*
> *Death will put on the garb of your life.'*

Amir Khan, who was in attendance by the sick-bed, tried to console the sufferer by saying, 'Peace be on your Majesty! Shaikh Ganja composed those verses merely as introductory to the following couplet:

> *'Then, it is better for you to be cheerful.*
> *Because by being cheerful you can remember God!'*

On 23 October, 1705, Aurangzib broke up the encampment at Devapur and set out northwards in a *palki*. Travelling slowly by easy stages, he reached Ahmadnagar, on 20 January 1706, after an interval of 23 years since the day when he had started from it to begin his Deccan conquests. This place he declared to be his 'Journey's end'.

16.14 Sorrow and Despair of Aurangzib's Last Years

The last years of Aurangzib's life were unspeakably gloomy. In the political sphere he found that his lifelong endeavour to govern India justly and strongly had ended in anarchy and disruption throughout the empire. A sense of unutterable loneliness hunted the heart of Aurangzib in his old age. One by one all the older nobles had died out, and the sole personal friend and survivor of the generation in which his youth had been nurtured that was now left to him was Asad Khan the wazir, and even he was some five years Aurangzib's junior. As the aged monarch looked round his Court circle he only found on all sides younger men, timid sycophants, afraid of responsibility, afraid to tell the truth, and eternally intriguing in a mean spirit of personal greed and mutual jealousy. His Puritan austerity had, at all times, chilled the advances of other men towards mih. Men shrank in almost supernatural dread from one who was above the joys and sorrows, weakness and pity of mortals, one who seemed to have hardly any element of common humanity in him, who lived in the world but did not seem to be of it. His sole companions, when free from the ever-engrossing State affairs, were his daughter Zinat-un-nisa, already an old maid, and his last wife Udipuri, a low animal type of partner, whose son Kam Bakhsh broke his imperial father's heart by his freaks of insane folly and passion.

His domestic life was darkened, as bereavements thickened round his closing eyes. His best-loved daughter-in-law, Jahanzeb Banu, died in Gujrat in March 1705. His rebel son Akbar had died in exile in a foreign soil in 1704. Still earlier, his gifted .daughter, the poetess Zeb-un-nisa, had ended her days in the prison of Delhi (1702). And now Gauhar-ara Begam, the sole survivor among his numerous brothers and sisters, died in 1706 and the news of it dragged out of his heart the pathetic cry, which he repeated again and again, 'She and I alone were left among Shah Jahan's children.' In May 1706, his daughter Mihr-un-nisa and her husband Izid Bakhsh (Murad's son) both died together in Delhi, and next month Buland Akhtar, the son of Akbar. Two of his grand-children died shortly before his own death (1707), but his ministers mercifully withheld the news from the sinking man.

16.15 Imperial Dominions Harassed by Marathas, 1706–7

Aurangzib had left desolation and anarchy behind him when he set out for Ahmadnagar. But his retreat to this city did not bring rest to his army or peace to his empire. In April or May 1706, a vast Maratha army under all their great generals, appeared 6 km (4 miles) from the imperial encampment and threatened it. Aurangzib sent Khan-i-Alam and other officers who succeeded after along and severe contest in repulsing the Marathas from the neighbourhood.

In Gujrat, a terrible disaster befell the imperialists. Inu Mand, a former brewer of Khandesh, who had taken to highway robbery, made a league with the Maratha generals. Inviting Dhana Jadav and his army, he sacked the large and rich trading centre of Baroda (March 1706). Nazar Ali, the faujdar of the place, was defeated by the Marathas and captured with his men.

Similarly, the province of Aurangabad was frequently ravaged by the Maratha bands under Dhana Jadav and other leaders.

In July Maratha activity near Wagingera forced the Emperor to detach Tarbiyat Khan to that region to punish them. Pidia Berad, in alliance with Hindu Rao, gained Penu-konda, 'the key to both the Karnataks,' by bribing its Mughal qiladar, who had been starving from his salary being left in arrears. Flushed with their gain of such a fort, the Marathas turned to Sera, the capital of Bijapuri Karnatak Uplands, the district round which they had plundered before, in June 1704. Daud Khan, the faujdar of Karnatak, afterwards recovered Penu-konda. Siadat Khan, an officer of the Court, was wounded in both eyes by musket-shot, captured, and held to ransom by the enemy. They also recovered Basantgarh from the imperialists about this time.

When the rainy season ended (September 1706), Maratha activity was renewed with tenfold intensity. Dhana Jadav now made a dash for the old dominions, Berar and Khandesh; but Nasrat Jang, leaving his camp near Miraj, headed him off into Bijapur and thence beyond the Krishna. A long train of caravans coming from Aurangabad to the imperial camp was plundered of everything near Chanda, 40 km (24 miles) from Ahmadnagar.

16.16 Last Days of Aurangzib

While dangers were thus thickening round Aurangzib's forces, the internal troubles of his camp became event more ominous. Muhammad Azam's inordinate vanity and ambition urged him to secure the succession for himself, by removing all rivals from his path. So, he poisoned the ears of the Emperor against Azim-ush-shan, the able third son of Shah Alam, and had him recalled from the government of Patna. He also drew over to his side the prime minister Asad Khan and some other nobles. Then he looked out for an opportunity to make a sudden attack on Kam Bakhsh and kill him. Every day Azam's hostile designs against Kam Bakhsh became snore evident, and therefore the Emperor appointed the brave and faithful Sultan Husain (Mir Malang) paymaster of Kam Bakhsh's forces, and charged him with that prince's defence.

Early in February 1707, Aurangzib had one more of the attacks of languor and ill-health which had become rather freequent of late. He recovered for a time and began once more to hold public darbars and do business of the State. But he felt that this time the inevitable could not be far off, and that the peace of his camp and the safety of the vast host assembled there were threatened by Azam's growing impatience and violent ambition which might break bounds any day. So, he appointed Kam Bakhsh subahdar of Bijapur and sent him away with a large force to his charge on 9 February. Four days later (13 February), Md. Azam was despatched to Malwa as its governor; but that cunning prince, knowing his father's death to be very near, marched slowly, halting every other day.

Four days after sending away the last of his sons from his side, the aged and worn-out monarch was seized with a severe fever; but for three days he obstinately insisted on coming to the Courtroom and saying the five daily prayers in full congregation. In these days he often recited the couplet of foreboding—

> *'In a twinkle, a minute, in a breath,*
> *The condition of the world changes'.*

During this last period he dictated two pathetic letters (See next appendix) to his sons Azam and Kam Bakhsh, entreating them to cultivate brotherly love, peace and moderation, and illustrating the vanity of all earthly things.

In the morning of Friday, 20 February 1707 Aurangzib came out of his bedroom, went through his morning prayer,, and began to count his beads and repeat the Islamic confession of faith in the oneness of the Godhead and the prophetship of Muhammad. Gradually unconsciousness crept on, his breathing became harder and harder; but such was the mastery of that indomitable spirit over the natural weakness of the body that his fingers continued to move over his rosary and his lips to gasp out the *Kalimah,* till about eight o'clock when all was over. He had ever wished to die on the Muslim Sabbath Friday, and the prayer had been granted by a gracious Deity to one of His truest servants.

Muhammad Azam arrived in the camp on 22 and after mourning for his father and consoling his sister Zinat-un-nisa Begam, he took part in carrying the corpse a short distance, and then sent it away to Khuldabad near Daulatabad, for burial in the enclosure hallowed by the earthly remains of the saint Shaikh Zain-ud-din.

A low simple tomb, without any marble platform below or dome over it, but having the trough in its covering slab filled with earth for growing green herbs (in imitation of his sister Jahanara's tomb outside Delhi),—now covers all that remains of the greatest of the Great Mughals save one.

APPENDIX

Aurangzib's last letter to Azam

'Peace be on you!

'Old age has arrived and weakness has grown strong; strength has left my limbs. I came alone and am going away alone. I know not who I am and what I have been doing. The days that have been spent except in austerities have left only regret behind them. I have not at all done any (true) government of the realm or cherishing of the peasantry.

'Life, so valuable, has gone away for nothing. The Master has been in my house, but my darkened eyes cannot see His splendour. Life lasts not; no trace is left of the days that are no more; and of the future there is no hope.

'My fever has departed, leaving only the skin and husks behind it. My son Kam Bakhsh, who has gone to Bijapur, is near me. And you are nearer even than he. Dear Shah Alam is farthest of all. Grandson Muhammad Azim has, by order of the Great God, arrived near Hindustan (from Bengal).

'All the soldiers are feeling helpless, bewildered, and perturbed like me, who having chosen to leave my Master, am now in a state of trepidation like quicksilver. They think not that we have, our Lord Father (ever with us). I brought nothing with me (into the world), and am carrying away with me the fruits of my sins. I know not what punishment will fall on me. Though I have strong hopes of His grace and kindness, yet in view of my acts anxiety does not leave me. When I am parting from my own self, who else would remain to me? (Verse)

Whatever the wind may be,
I am launching my boat on the water.

'Though the Lord Cherisher will preserve His slaves, yet from the point of view of the outer world, it is also the duty of my sons to see that God's creatures and Muslims may not be unjustly slain.

'Convey to my grandson Bahadur (i.e., Bidar Bakht) my parting blessing. At the time of going away I do not see him; the desire of meeting remains (unsatisfied). Though the Begam is, as can be seen, afflicted with grief, yet God is the master of hearts. Shortness of sight bears no other fruit than disappointment.

'Farewell! farewell! farewell!'[1]

Aurangzib's last letter to Kam Bakhsh

'My son, [close to my heart like] my liver! Although, in the days of my power, I gave advice for submission to the will of God and exerted myself beyond the limits of possibility,—God having willed it otherwise, none listened to me. Now that I am dying, it will do no good. I shall carry away with myself the fruits of all the punishments and sins that I have done. What a marvel that I came [into the world] alone and am [now] departing with this [large] caravan? Wherever I cast my eyes, no caravan-leader save God comes into my view. Anxiety about the army and camp-followers has been the cause of [my] depression of mind and fear of final torment. Although God will undertake the protection of his people, yet it is also obligatory on Muslims and my sons. When I was full of strength, I could not at all protect them; and now I am unable to take care of myself! My limbs have ceased to move. The breath that subsides, there is no hope of its return. What else can I do in such a condition,, than to pray ? Your mother Udipuri [Begam] has attended me during my illness; she wishes to accompany me [to the next world]. I consign thee and thy children to God. I am in trepidation. I bid you farewell.... Worldly men are deceivers (literally, they show wheat as sample but deliver barley); do not do any work in reliance on their fidelity. Work ought to be done by means of hints and signs. Dara Shukoh made unsound arrangements and hence he failed to reach his point. He

[1] Translated by me from Br. Museum Addl. 26240. The version given in the lithographed edition of the *Ruqat* has been rejected.

increased the salaries of his retainers to more than what they were before, but at the time of need he got less and less work out of them. Hence he was unhappy. Set your feet within the limits of your carpet.

'I have told you what I had to say and now I take my leave. See to it that the peasantry and the people ... are not unjustly ruined, and that Musalmans may not be slain, lest punishment should descend on me.' [India Office MS. 1344, *f.* 26*a*].

Aurangzib's last will

[From India Office Library MS. 1344, *f.* 49*b*. Said to have been written with his own hand and left under the pillow on his death-bed.]

'I was helpless [in life] and I am departing helpless. Whichever of my sons has the good fortune of gaining the kingship, he should not trouble Kam Bakhsh, if the latter remains content with the two provinces of Bijapur and Haidarabad. There is not, nor will there [ever] be any wazir better than Asad Khan. Dianat Khan, the diwan of the Deccan, is better than other imperial servants. With true devotion entreat Muhammad Azam Shah,—if he agrees to the mode of partitioning the empire which was proposed in my lifetime, then there will be no fighting between armies and no slaughter of mankind. Do not dismiss my hereditary servants nor, molest them. The occupant of the throne should have [one of] the two subahs of Agra and Delhi, and whoever agrees to take the former [of these] will get four subahs of the old kingdom—Agra *(sic),* Malwa, Gujrat, and Ajmir and the *chaklas* dependent on them,—and four subahs of the Deccan, namely Khandesh, Berar, Aurangabad and Bidar and their ports. And whosoever agrees to take the latter (i.e., Delhi) will get the eleven subahs of the old kingdom—Delhi, Punjab, Kabul, Multan, Tatta, Kashmir, Bengal, Orissa, Bihar, Allahabad and Oudh.' [Another version is given in Eraser's *Nadir Shah,* 36–37. See Irvine's *Later Mughals,* i. 6.]

Another alleged will of Aurangzib is given in the *Ahkam-i-Alamgiri* ascribed to Hamid-ud-din Khan Bahadur (§ 8 of the text and translation published by me). It runs thus:

'Praise be to God and blessing on those servants of Him who have become sanctified and have given satisfaction to Him.

I have [some instructions to leave as my] last will and testament:

First,—On behalf of this sinner sunk in iniquity [i.e., myself] cover [with an offering of cloth] the holy tomb of Hasan (ON HIM BE PEACE!), because those who are drowned in the ocean of sin have no other protection than seeking refuge with that Portal of Mercy and Forgiveness. The means of performing this great auspicious act are with my noble son, Prince Alijah (Azam); take them.

Second,—Four Rupees and two annas, out of the price of the caps sewn by me, are with Aia Beg, the *mahaldar.* Take the amount and spend it on the shroud of this helpless creature. Three hundred and five Rupees, from the wages of copying the Quran, are in my purse for personal expenses. Distribute them to the faqirs on the day of my death. As the money got by copying the Quran is regarded with respect of the Shia sect.[2] do not spend it on my shroud and other necessaries.

Third,—Take the remaining necessary articles from the agent of Prince Alijah, as he is the nearest heir among my sons, and on him lies the responsibility of the lawful or unlawful [practices at my funeral]; this helpless person (i.e., Aurangzib) is not answerable for them, because the dead are at the mercy of the survivors.

Fourth,—Bury this wanderer in the Valley of Deviation from the Right Path with his head bare, because every ruined sinner who is conducted bareheaded before the Grand Emperor (i.e., God), is sure to be an object of mercy.

Fifth,—Cover the top of the coffin on my bier with the coarse white cloth called *gazi.* Avoid the spreading of a canopy and innovations like [procession of] musicians and the celebration of the Prophet's Nativity *(maulud).*

Sixth,—It is proper for the ruler of the kingdom *(i.e.,* my heir) to treat kindly the helpless servants who in the train of this shameless creature [Aurangzib] have been roving in the deserts and wilderness [of the Deccan]. Even if any manifest fault is committed by them, give them in return for it gracious forgiveness and benignant overlooking [of their faults].

Seventh,—No nation is better than the Persians for acting as clerks *(mutasaddi).* And in war, too, from the age of the Emperor Humayun and the present time, none of this nation has turned his face away from the field, and their firm feet have never been shaken. Moreover, they have not once been guilty of disobedience or treachery to their master.

[2] The reading in MS. N. may be taken to mean, 'As the money got by copying the Quran is suspected by the Shia sect to be unlawful [kind of wealth].'

But as they insist on being treated with great honour, it is very difficult to pull together with them. You have anyhow to conciliate them, and should employ subterfuges.

Eighth,—The Turani people have ever been soldiers. They are very expert in making charges, raids, night-attacks and arrests. They feel no suspicion, despair or shame when commanded to make a retreat in the very midst of a fight, which means, in other words, 'when the arrow is drawn back';—and they are a hundred stages remote from the crass stupidity of the Hindusthanis, who would part with their heads but not leave their positions [in battle]. In every way you should confer favours on this race, because on many occasions these men can do the necessary service, when no other race can.

Ninth,—You should treat the Sayyids of Barha, who are worthy of blessing, according to the Quranic verse, 'GIVE UNTO THE NEAR RELATIONS [OF THE PROPHET] THEIR DUES,' and never grow slack in honouring and favouring them. Inasmuch as, according to the blessed verse, 'I SAY I DO NOT ASK OF YOU ANY RECOMPENSE FOR IT EXCEPT LOVE TO [MY] KINSMEN,' love for this family IS THE WAGES OF [MUHAMMAD'S] PROPHETSHIP, you should never be wanting [in respect for them], and it will bear fruit in this world and the next. But you should be extremely cautious in dealing with the Sayyids of Barha. Be not wanting in love for them at heart, but externally do not increase their rank, because a strong partner in the government soon wants to seize the kingship for himself. If you let them take the reins ever so little, the result will be your own disgrace.

Tenth,—As far as possible the ruler of a kingdom should not spare himself from moving about; he should avoid staying: in one place, which outwardly gives him repose but in effect brings down a thousand calamities and troubles.

Eleventh,—Never trust your sons, nor treat them during your lifetime in an intimate manner, because, if the Emperor Shah Jahan had not treated Dara Shukoh in this manner, his affairs would not have come to such a sorry pass. Ever keep in view the saying, 'THE WORD OF A KING IS BARREN.'

Twelfth,—The main pillar of government is to be well informed in the news of the kingdom. Negligence for a single moment becomes the cause of disgrace for long years. The escape of the wretch Shiva took place through [my] carelessness, and I have to labour hard [against the Marathas] to the end of my life, [as the result of it].

TWELVE IS BLESSED [among numbers]. I have concluded with twelve directions. *(Verse)*

If you learn [the lesson], a kiss on your wisdom.
If you neglect it, then alas! alas!

17 *Affairs of Northern India*

17.1 Thirty Years' Warfare in Marwar

When the Emperor went to the Deccan in person after patching up a peace with the Maharana (June 1681), the Rajput war so far as Mewar was concerned was ended, but not in respect of Marwar. The Emperor's troops continued to hold the chief towns and strategic points of the Rathor country, but the Rathor patriots remained in a state of war. They occupied the hills and deserts and every now and then swooped down upon the plains, cutting off convoys and trade caravans, capturing weakly held Mughal outposts, and rendering the cultivation of the fields and traffic on the roads impossible except under the protection of the imperial garrisons. No wonder that famine was constantly present in Marwar, and that the Rathor bard records that in certain years 'the sword and pestilence united to clear the land'.

A generation of time passed away in Marwar in ceaseless conflict, captures and recaptures. But the resources of the empire were far superior to those of a small desert province ravaged by perpetual warfare. The Rathor national opposition, therefore, would have gradually grown weaker and finally died out through attrition, if only the Emperor had not been plunged into a more serious conflict in the Deccan, which drained all his resources. The military situation in Maharashtra reacted on the situation in Jodhpur, and worked for the ultimate success of the Rathor patriots and the restoration of their chieftain to his ancestral throne immediately after Aurangzib's death.

The history of these 27 years (1681–1707) in Marwar falls into three well-defined periods. From 1681 to 1687 it was a people's war, because their king was a child and their national leader Durgadas was absent in the Deccan. The Rathor people fought under different captains, group by group, with no central authority and no common plan of action except to attack the Mughals wherever they could. This desultory warfare afforded many examples of Rathor bravery and devotion, but its military effect was nothing more than to keep the Mughal garrisons in constant alarm and to make their occupation of Marwar financially ruinous. It was rather an advantage to the Rathors that at this stage they had no common leader, because a pitched battle of all the forces of the tribe with the better armed and better organized imperialists would have led to their decisive defeat and prevented them from raising their heads for a generation to come, whereas by adopting guerilla tactics they wore out the Mughals and minimized the disadvantage of their own inferior numbers and equipment.

The second stage of the war began in 1687, when Durgadas returned from the Deccan and Ajit Singh came out of concealment. The success of the Rathors was at first brilliant. Reinforced by the Hadas of Bundi, they cleared the plains of Marwar and, sweeping onwards beyond the limits of their own country, raided Malpura and Pur-Mandal (1687), and even defeated the subahdar of Ajmir (1690), and carried their ravages into Mewat and the west of Delhi. But they could not recover their own country. In the very year 1687 in which Ajit Singh and Durgadas appeared together at the head of the national forces, an exceptionally able and enterprising officer named Shujaet Khan became governor of Jodhpur on behalf of the Emperor, and held that office for 14 years, during which he succeeded in maintaining the Mughal hold on Marwar.

Shujaet Khan, in addition to the faujdari of Marwar, held the subahdari of Gujrat. He always kept his retainers up to their full number and was prompt and quick in his movements. He used to spend six months (sometimes eight) every year in Marwar and the other six in Gujrat. Thus, he succeeded in checking the Rathors when it came to fighting, while he also made an understanding with them, paying them one-fourth of the imperial custom duties on all merchandise if they spared the traders on the roads (1688). This was another form of the *chauth.*

But on 9 July 1701 Shujaet Khan died, Prince Muhammad Azam succeeded him as governor of Marwar and renewed hostilities with Ajit, and the third stage of the Rajput war of independence began, which after much bloodshed and many reverses on both sides ended in the complete break-down of the imperial policy of greed and the final recovery of Marwar by its national ruling dynasty (1707).

After the Mughal occupation of their capital and other cities, the Rathors took refuge in the hills and out of the way nooks; but the plains lay exposed to the raids of their roving bands; and encounters frequently took place between them and the army of occupation near one or other of these outposts with varying success. The situation of the country is best described in the words of the bard Karani-dan: 'An hour before sunset every gate of Maru was shut. The Muslims held the strongholds, but the plains obeyed Ajit.... The roads were now impassable.'

17.2 Durgadas Again in Marwar, 1687–98

Durgadas's return from Maharashtra in 1687 greatly stimulated Rathor activity, and happily just then they gained a valuable ally. Durjan Sal Hada, the leading vassal of Bundi, on being insulted by his chieftain Anurudh Singh (a loyal feudatory and general of Aurangzib), armed his kinsmen and retainers and seized the fort of Bundi by a sudden attack. He then came over to Marwar, married a sister of Mukund Singh Champawat (a Rathor leader), and strengthened the Rathor national army with his thousand horsemen of the Hada clan.

The united Rathors and Hadas, having slaughtered or driven away most of the Mughal outposts in Marwar, made a daring raid into the imperial dominions in the north and even menaced the capital Delhi. After his return, Durjan Sal was killed in a battle near Mandal.

In 1690 Durgadas gained a conspicuous success; he routed and drove back on Ajmir the new governor of that province, Safi Khan, who had taken post on the Marwar frontier. He kept up plundering and distributing the parts of Marwar in Mughal occupation and rendered the roads unsafe for travellers. This alarming situation recalled Shujaet Khan, who very tactfully won over many of the Rajput headmen (*thakurs* and *pattawats*) and inspired them with ardour of the Emperor's cause.

Aurangzib was anxious to get back Akbar's daughter Safiyat-un-nisa, who had been sheltered by the Rathors ever since her father's flight in 1681. The negotiations for this purpose which had failed in 1692 were renewed in 1694 and entrusted to the able and wise Shujaet Khan, who employed as his intermediary in this affair the historian Ishwardas, a Nagar Brahman of Patna (now in the Gaikwar's territory) formerly employed as a revenue collector (*shiqdar* or *amin*) in Jodhpur.

After Ishwardas had repeatedly approached Durgadas, the latter agreed to make terms for his chieftain and himself, by giving up Akbar's daughter to the Emperor ... Ishwardas escorted the princess to the imperial Court. On their arrival there, Aurangzib immediately spoke of appointing a tutoress to give his grand-daughter that education in the Islamic scriptures which she must have missed so long in that uncivilized and inaccessible Hindu State. But the Begam informed him that Durgadas had been so attentive to her welfare that he had secured for her a Muslim mistress from Ajmir, under whose tuition she had already studied the Quran and committed it to her memory.

This fact convinced the Emperor of Durgadas's devotion and induced him to forget all his past offences.

The next thing was to recover Akbar's son Buland Akhtar from the Rathors. But in effecting this there was nearly two years' delay, mainly because Durgadas demanded the restoration of Jodhpur to Ajit Singh, while Aurangzib wished to satisfy the heir of Jaswant with only a small portion of Marwar.

But Ajit Singh's position was now one of distress and despair. He was weary of roving in the wilderness, hunted by Mughal columns and subjected to every hardship. So, in 1698, Durgadas abated his demands. Ajit was pardoned by the Emperor and given a *mansab* in the imperial army, with the parganas of Jhalor, Shanchod and Siwana as his jagir, of which he was also appointed faujdar.

Durgadas conveyed Buland Akhtar to the imperial Court then at Islampuri on the Bhima (1698). This poor royal lad had been brought up ever since his birth among the rude Rajput peasantry, without seeing any city or Court, or talking with any cultured person. He did not even know the polished Hindustani language. Aurangzib was shocked and his Court was amused to find a grandson of the Emperor who could speak only the Rajput patois (*Rajasthani boli*) Buland Akhtar felt overcome with shyness like a country youth suddenly brought to a large and polished city. Moreover, he had been taught during his life among the Rathor nationalists to regard Aurangzib as a sort of demon and the relentless enemy of his father and family; and now he was being torn away from the protectors of his boyhood and the comrades of his youth and delivered over to that very Aurangzib. He thought it the wisest course under the circumstances not to open his lips at all but to pretend dumbness. He was, however, gradually educated and polished, and lived to be employed in the Court, close to the Emperor's person, in charge of one of the royal seals. Durgadas was rewarded by being created a 3-hazari *mansabdar* and appointed faujdar of Patan.

17.3 AJIT AND DURGADAS, 1701–7

This reconciliation with Durgadas took place in May 1698, but in 1701–2 he was driven into rebellion a second time. In fact, both he and Ajit Singh had continued to distrust the Mughal Government and kept themselves at a suspicious distance from the Court. The new governor of Gujrat, Prince Muhammad Azam Shah, was ordered by the Emperor to send Durgadas to the imperial camp if he could, otherwise to kill him there, so that Durga might no more instigate Ajit Singh and the other Rathors.

Muhammad Azam summoned Durgadas to wait on him at Ahmadabad, the seat of his government. But the arrival of couriers in succession to hasten his visit excited the Rajput's suspicion, which passed into alarm when he heard reports about the prince's troops having been drawn up armed. Therefore, Durgadas set fire to his tents and baggage and immediately rode away towards Marwar with all his followers, by forced inarches.

When Durgadas was back again in Marwar as an enemy of the empire, Ajit Singh joined him in open rebellion (1702) and made some attacks on the Mughals. But the two could effect nothing. The economic exhaustion of Marwar was complete, and war-weariness had seized the Rathor clansmen after a quarter century of continuous guerilla fighting. To aggravate the evil, disagreement now broke out between Ajit and Durgadas, of which the Emperor was not slow to take advantage. Ajit was impatient of advice, imperious in temper, and jealous of Durgadas's well-merited influence in the royal council and popularity among his clansmen. This internal discord among the Rathor leaders helped Aurangzib's designs just when all seemed to be going against him, and it enabled him to keep Ajit Singh out of his kingdom and capital for five years more.

In 1704 Aurangzib, at last admitting his growing helplessness against a sea of enemies, made a sort of peace with Ajit by giving him Mairta as jagir. In November 1705, Durgadas, too, unable to maintain himself in barren independence, made his submission to the Emperor through Prince Azam, and was restored to his old *mansab* and post in Gujrat.

Next year, the last of Aurangzib's reign, a Maratha incursion into Gujrat was followed by a crushing disaster to the Mughal army at Ratanpur. Ajit Singh raised his head in rebellion for the third time. Durgadas again fled the Mughal camp and began to act in concert with him, causing risings in Therad and other places. But Prince Bidar Bakht, then in charge of Gujrat, sent a force against Durgadas, who now fled to the broken Koli country, south of Surat. Ajit Singh had now been in open rebellion for some time. He fought Muhakam Singh of Nagor who was on the Emperor's side, at Drunera, and by defeating him gained an increase of prestige and strength. Just after this, news of Aurangzib's death at Ahmadnagar arrived, and on 7 March 1707 Ajit took horse for Jodhpur, expelled Jafar Quli (the deputy faujdar of the city), and took possession of his father's capital. Mairta was evacuated by Muhakam Singh, who fled wounded to Nagor. Sojat and Pali were regained. The fort of Jodhpur was purified with Ganges water and *tulsi* leaves. Durgadas's life's task was thus crowned with success.

17.4 Jat Disturbances near Agra

The endless wars in whicn Aurangzib became involved in 1679 and which were to continue till his death, began very soon to react on the political condition of Northern India. In unvarying succession Northern India continued to be annually drained of its public money and youthful recruits, in order to fill the ever-gaping void caused by the Deccan wars. Years passed away, and yet the Emperor did not return to his capital, nor did any of the princes. The rich old provinces of the empire, north of the Narmada, were left in charge of second-rate nobles with insufficient troops. At the same time, the long caravans of merchandise, State revenue, army provisions, and the families and property of the nobles, so frequently making their way to the far-off South under slender escort, offered an irresistible temptation to robber tribes. The great royal road leading from Delhi to Agra and Dholpur and thence through Malwa to the Deccan, passed directly through the country of the Jats, a brave, strong and hardy people whose predatory instinct can be kept in check only by the terror of superior force.

In 1685 the opportunity created by the Emperor's Deccan invasion was seized by two new leaders of the Jats, Rajaram and Ramchehra, the petty zamindars of Sinsani and Sogar, who were the first to train their clansmen in group organization and open warfare. Every Jat peasant was practised in wielding the staff and the sword; they had only to be embodied in regiments, taught to obey their captains, and supplied with fire-arms to make them into an army. As bases for their operations, refuges for their chiefs in defeat, and storing places for booty, they built several small forts (*garhi*) amidst their almost trackless jungle, and strengthened them with mud walls that could defy artillery. Then they began to raid the king's highway and carry their depredations up to the suburbs of Agra.

Rajaram's lawless activities could not be checked by Safi Khan, the governor of Agra. The Jat gangs closed the roads to traffic, and plundered many villages of the district. Rajaram soon showed even greater audacity, by attacking and killing (near Dholpur) the renowned Turani warrior Aghar Khan when on his way from Kabul to the Emperor's camp at Bijapur. Prince Bidar Bakht was sent (in December 1687), to assume the supreme command in the Jat war.

But before the prince could arrive, the Jat leader committed more atrocities. Early in 1688, he attacked Mir Ibrahim of Haidarabad (newly entitled Mahabat Khan), then marching to-his viceroyalty of the Panjab. Shortly afterwards he plundered Akbar's tomb at Sikandra, taking away its carpets, gold and silver vessels, lamps, etc., and damaging the building.[1]

Bidar Bakht, on his arrival, infused greater vigour into the Mughal operations. In an internecine war raging between two Rajput clans, Rajaram, who was fighting for one party, was, shot dead (4 July 1688).

Bishun Singh Kachhwa, the new Rajah of Amber (Jaipur), was appointed by the Emperor as faujdar of Mathura with a special charge to root out the Jats and take Sinsani as his own jagir. Bidar Bakht and Bishun Singh laid siege to Sinsani. But the campaign in the jungles of the Jat country severely taxed the invading army, which had to undergo great hardship

---

[1] Ishwardas, 1326. Manucci (ii. 320) adds: 'They began their pillage by breaking in the great gates of bronze which it had, robbing the valuable precious stones and plates of gold and silver, and destroying what they were not able to carry away. Dragging out the bones of Akbar, they threw them angrily into the fire and burnt them.'

from, scarcity of provisions and water. But the besiegers held tenaciously on. A mine was successfully fired (end of January 1690), the wall was breached, and the Mughals stormed the fort after three hours of stubborn opposition, the Jats losing 1,500 men. On the imperial side, 200 Mughals fell and 700 Rajputs were slain or wounded. Next year (21 May 1691) Rajah Bishun Singh surprised the other Jat stronghold of Sogar.

The result of these operations was that the new Jat leader went into hiding in 'nooks and corners' unknown to the imperialists, and the district enjoyed peace for some years, after which a new leader arose among them. This was Churaman, the son of Bhajja, a brother of Rajaram. This Churaman had a genius for organization and using opportunities, and succeeded in founding a dynasty which still rules over Bharatpur. 'He not only increased the number of his soldiers, but also strengthened them by the addition of fusiliers (musketeers) and a troop of cavalry, whom he shortly afterwards set on foot;.. .and having robbed many of the ministers of the Court on the road, he attacked . the royal wardrobe and the revenue sent from the provinces.' But this full development of Churaman's power took place after the death of Aurangzib. About 1704 he recovered Sinsani from Mughal possession. It was, however, wrested from the, Jats a second time on 9 October 1705 by Mukhtar Khan, the governor of Agra.

17.5 Pahar Singh Gaur and His Sons Disturb Malwa, 1685

Pahar Singh Gaur, a Rajput zamindar of *Indrakhi* in western Bundelkhand, was serving the Emperor as faujdar of Shahabad Dhamdhera in Malwa. He was a man of matchless bravery and as chivalrous as he was brave. Taking the side of Lal Singh Khichi (Chauhan) against the latter's oppressive overlord, Anurudh Singh Hada (the Rajah of Bundi), Pahar Singh defeated the Bundi Rajah and plundered all his camp and baggage, worth lakhs of Rupees (early in 1685). He then openly broke with the imperial Government, and took to plundering the village of Malwa. At this time that province was being administered, in the absence of Prince Muhammad Azam, by Rai Muluk Chand, the assistant (*peshdast*) to his diwan. He attacked and slew the rebel (December 1685). But the rising continued under Pahar Singh's son Bhagwant, who collected a large body of fierce peasants and began to plunder the country round Gwalior, entirely closing the roads to traffic. Muluk Chand marched against him with his troops. A pitched battle was fought near Antri, in which the imperialists broke and fled; but the Gaur soldiers plundered all the baggage, horses, etc. of the Mughals, and returned to their base to secure the booty, and Bhagwant Singh, who was thus left almost alone in the field, was killed by some Mughal officers (March 1686).

But the trouble did not end even then. Devi Singh, another son of Pahar Singh, joined Chhatra Sal Bundela, and took to plundering the imperial territory and molesting the people in Bundelkhand. In 1690, Gopal Singh, the grandson of Pahar Singh, assembled a large army and captured the fort of *Indrakhi,* belonging to Bakhtawar of the Bhadauria clan. Safdar Khan, the faujdar of Gwalior, was killed during an attack on these rebels (May 1690).

But two years later the Gaur rebels submitted to the Emperor and we find them serving in his army.

17.6 Gangaram's Rising in Bihar; Copal Singh's in Malwa

Gangaram, a poor Nagar Brahman of Gujrat, was diwan of Khan-i-Jahan Bahadur, and managed his estates (*jagirs*) in Allahabad and Bihar, while the Khan was serving in the Deccan. The sudden rise of this obscure Hindu excited the jealous hate of the other servants of the Khan, who had been displaced from his favour; and they poisoned his ears against his absent diwan, by charging him with a design for independence and self-aggrandizement. The Khan summoned the diwan to his presence. Gangaram, disgusted with such a lightminded master and despairing of his life and honour, flew to arms. Collecting some four thousand soldiers, he plundered the city of Bihar and advancing laid siege to Patna. The rebel set up a bogus Prince Akbar and called upon the people to rally round his standard (March 1681). But he had neither the skill nor the materials necessary for taking a walled city, and turned to the more profitable work of plundering the neighbouring villages, while the governor shut himself up in the fort. At length imperial reinforcements arrived from Dacca and Benares and raised the siege of Patna. After some time Gangaram entered Malwa and in concert with Rajput rebels plundered Sironj (October 1684). He died shortly afterwards at Ujjain.

Rao Gopal Singh Chandrawat, the zamindar of Rampura in Malwa, was serving in the Emperor's army in the Deccan. He had sent his son Ratan Singh home to manage his affairs. This wicked youth became a convert to Islam, and thus secured from the Emperor the grant of his ancestral estate, which was newly named *Islampura!* At the news of it, Gopal Singh left the Mughal army, returned home, and tried to raise a body of men for recovering Rampura (June 1700). But the Malwa governor's forces repulsed him. At last Gopal Singh in despair made his submission to the Emperor, and was appointed faujdar of Kaulas (in Haidarabad). Early in 1706, he again fell into extreme poverty on his being deprived of the faujdari of Kaulas. He then joined the Marathas for a living, and accompanied them in the sack of Baroda in the month of March in that year.

17.7 English Trade with Bengal

The English nation established their first trade factory at Surat in 1612 and exchanged foods with Agra and Delhi by land route. From Agra attempts were made in 1620 and 1632 to open up trade at Patna in Bihar, but the cost of land transport from Surat was prohibitive, especially for bulky goods like saltpetre, and this project was wisely abandoned. There was also an agency at Masulipatam, a port of the Golkonda kingdom.

In 1633 an English factory was opened at Balasore and another at Hariharpur, 40 km (25 miles) south-east of Cuttack. A little later, in 1640, the building of Fort St. George was begun at Madras, on a piece of land bought from a Hindu Rajah of the Vijaynagar dynasty, and thus 'the English established their first independent station in India'. It lay, however, outside the Mughal empire. In 1651 the English opened their first commercial house in Bengal at Hughli on the Ganges, 38 km (24 miles) north of Calcutta. Their chief exports were saltpetre (brought down in boats from Singhia or Lalganj, north of Patna), silk and sugar. Prince Shuja, then governor of Bengal, granted a *nishan* (or prince's order) by which the English were allowed to trade in Bengal on payment of Rs 3,000 a year in lieu of all kinds of customs and dues (1651). Balasore continued for several years as the place for loading and unloading Europe-going ships with Bengal merchandise.

In 1658 the Home authorities reorganized the English establishments in India. All the Company's factories were to be subordinate to the President and Council of Surat, besides which there were to be chief agencies at Madras and Hughli.

The trade with Bengal was very prosperous about 1658. Raw silk was abundant; the taffetas were various and fine; the saltpetre was cheap and of the best quality; the gold and silver sent from England were eagerly taken up by the Indians.

In 1661 further changes were made in the government of the English factories in India; all the Bengal establishments were made subordinate to the Presidency of Madras, which now became of equal rank with Surat. The Bengal trade continued to grow rapidly: in 1668 the Company exported from the province goods worth £34,000, in 1675 the value rose to £85,000, in 1677 to £100,000, and in 1680 to £150,000. Subordinate factories were opened at Dacca in 1668, and at Malda in 1676. In addition to buying local manufactures, the English sent out European dyers to Bengal to improve the colour of the silk cloth bought locally, and they also inaugurated the Bengal Pilot Service for navigating the Ganges from Hughli to the sea (1668). The first British ship sailed up the Ganges from the Bay of Bengal in 1679.

17.8 Friction between the English Traders and the Mughal Officials in Bengal

In the meantime, the differences between the English traders and the local Mughal officers on account of the illegal exactions and obstructions of the latter had come to a head. The local officials at Hughli continued to stop the Company's boats and seize their goods. In vain agent Hedges offered to Shaista Khan large sums of money in order to be excused the payment of customs. At last the English traders lost all patience and decided to protect themselves by force, break with the Indian rulers, and seize and fortify some convenient place on the Indian coast where their trade would be safe from molestation. This war actually broke out in 1686.

The complaints of the English traders against the local agents of the Mughal Government were three:

(*i*) The demand of an *ad valorem* duty on the actual merchandise imported, instead of the lump sum of Rs 3,000 per annum into which it had been commuted during the viceroyalty of Prince Shuja, and also the enhancement of the rate of duty from time to time. The English also claimed that Aurangzib's *farman* of 15 March

1680 entitled them, on the payment of a consolidated duty of 3 ½ per cent at Surat, to import goods and to trade absolutely free of customs and other exactions at all *other* places in the Mughal empire.

(*ii*) Exactions by local officers under the name of *rahdari* (road patrol charge or internal transit duty); presents (*Peshkash*), writer's fee, and *farmaish* (supplying manufactures to order of the governor, for which it was not customary to take the price).

(*iii*) The practice of high officials (such as Shaista Khan and Prince Azim-ush-shan, subahdars of Bengal),—a practice sometimes resorted to by local faujdaı.. also,—to open the packages of goods in transit and take away articles at prices capriciously fixed by them far below the fair market price. Some governors (notably Azim-ush-shan) tried to enrich themselves by seizing goods at low prices and then selling them in the market at normal prices,—a practice called *sauda-i-khas.*

On 10 April 1665 Aurangzib issued an order that in all provinces there would be two uniform rates of custom duty on imports in future, namely 2½ per cent for Muslims and 5 per cent for Hindus. The Mughal Government seems to have found it difficult to assess and levy the *jiziya* per head from the Europeans in the same manner as from the Hindus, and consequently it seems to have offered them (March 1680), a compromise by turning the *jiziya* into an addition to the import duty on their goods, raising the latter to 3½ per cent.

The claims of the English in Bengal (*a*) to escape the duty on the actual value of their imports by a fixed annual payment of Rs 3,000 (as conceded by Shuja in 1651) and (*b*) to trade absolutely free in all other parts of India on payment of customs at Surat (in virtue of Aurangzib's *farman* of 1680), are both false and indefensible on any reasoning.

Shuja was merely a provincial governor. He could, as he pleased, let off some favoured body of merchants on easy terms during his own viceroyalty, but his grant (*nishari*) could not bind his successors in office, unless it was confirmed by the Emperor and turned into an imperial charter (*farman*). The English interpretation of Aurangzib's *farman* of 1680 was equally wrong. Payment of duty on the goods landed at Surat could, by no exercise of ingenuity, exempt from duty a different cargo that had come from Home or China not through Surat but directly to Bengal, and which, therefore, could not have paid any duty at Surat.*

As for the second and third grievances of the English, we must remark that the exactions here complained of had been declared illegal by Aurangzib and were practised only in disregard of his orders. *Rahdari* had been abolished in the second year of his reign, while 'benevolences' and forced presents were condemned in the general order abolishing *abwabs* issued on 29 April 1673. The 'forcing of goods' by his grandson Azim-ush-shan for his private trade, called forth Aurangzib's sternest censures when it was brought to his ears (about 1703). But the traders thus wronged by the local officers could have redress on those rare occasions only when their cries reached the ears of the old Emperor in the far off Deccan, and the redress was merely an order on paper.

Purity of administration was impossible in a society devoid of public spirit and accustomed to submit helplessly to every man in power, in public life as well as private. The Emperor could not look to everything; he could not be present everywhere; he had to act through agents, and these men did not share his integrity and regard for his subjects.

17.9 The English War with Aurangzib in Bengal, 1686–89

The Indian merchants and brokers employed by the East India Company at Qasimbazar (Bengal) made a large claim against Job Charnock, the chief of the factory there, and his colleagues. The Indian judge of the place decreed the sum of Rs 43,000 against the Englishmen (1684–85). As Charnock refused to comply with the order, his factory was invested by Mughal troops (August 1685). But in April next, he escaped to Hughli and took the chief direction of English affairs in Bengal. The war began in six months' time from this.

On 28 October 1686, three English soldiers, in trying to enter the market of the Mughal town of Hughli in defiance of the order of the local faujdar, were wounded and carried prisoner to the faujdar. An advance

* The exact terms of the Emperor's *farmans* (1637 and 1650) and Shuja's *naishans* (1651 and 1656) and also Mir Jumla's *parwanah* (1660) are given in my larger *History of Aurangzib,* Vol. V., 2nd ed., pp. 290–291. Sir W. Doster admits that the English claim was invalid.

made by Captain Leslie from the English factory (near Golghat) to rescue them was beaten back with loss, and the thatched huts surrounding the English factory were set on fire to arrest their progress. But reinforcements soon arrived from the English camp 5 km (3 miles) down the river, and advanced, sacking and burning the faujdar's house and the town lying beyond it. In the evening the English ships came abreast of Hughli, captured a ship of the Mughals, and 'kept firing and battering most part of the night and next day, burning and plundering all they met with'. The faujdar fled away in disguise; on the Indian side sixty soldiers were killed and four or five hundred houses burnt down together with a great number of barges and boats.

Shaista Khan, on hearing of the sack of Hughli by the English, decided to crush these disturbers of public peace. Vast detachments of cavalry were sent to Hughli and the English factory at Patna were ordered to be seized. On 20 December, the English withdrew from Hughli with all their property, and falling 40 km (24 miles) down the river halted at Sutanati (modern Calcutta).

The war was renewed in February 1687. The English burnt down the imperial salt-warehouses near Matiaburuj and then stormed the forts at Thana (modern Garden Reach, south-west of Calcutta). Sailing down the river they seized the island of Hijli, on the east coast of the Medinipur district (Contai subdivision),—a swamp of deadly malaria, but rich in fruits, corn and game, and the seat of salt manufacture by evaporating sea-water. Here all the English land and sea forces in the Bay of Bengal were assembled. Next March a body of 170 English soldiers and sailors landed at Balasore, took the Mughal fort, and burnt the two towns called Old and New Balasore, after looting them for two days. The Indian shipping in the docks were burnt, and two vessels belonging to Prince Azam and Shaista Khan were seized as prizes.

About the middle of May 1687, Abdus Samad, a lieutenant of Shaista Khan, arrived before Hijli with 12,000 men to expel the English. The invaders had been daily losing men from disease, both on land and in the ships, during the trying months of March and April, and their provisions had now run very short. Their losses in the meantime had been terrible: 200 soldiers had perished and only a hunderd, weakened by fever, survived; the forty officers had sunk to five only. On 11 June the English evacuated Hijli fort, carrying off all their ammunition and artillery, their drums beating and their banners flying. On 16 August Shaista Khan issued a letter in which he rebuked the English for their recent acts of violence, but permitted them to build a fort at Uluberia (about 32 km, i.e. 20 miles south of Calcutta) and renew their trade at Hughli. So, Charnock returned with his ships and halted at Sutanati (September 1687).

Next year Captain Heath arrived from England, replacing Charnock as Agent in Bengal. The new chief decided to withdraw from Bengal proper, and on 8 November 1688 sailed away from Sutanati with all the men and property of the Company. Sailing to Balasore with 300 soldiers, Captain Heath, on 29 November, stormed the Mughal fortification (called Point of Sand) at the easternmost point of Old Balasore, capturing its artillery and stores. Next day he seized New Balasore (further inland, to the west) and committed great excesses, ill-treating Christians and non-Christians, men and women alike. Arriving before Chatgaon about 18 January 1689, he planned to wrest that fort from the Mughal officers and make it the safe and independent base desired by the English for their trade in Bengal. A council of war dissuaded him from this mad project, and at last in utter disgust Heath sailed away for Madras (17 February), abandoning all his Bengal projects.

The Emperor, on hearing of these acts of hostility, had immediately ordered the arrest of all the Englishmen, the occupation of their factories all over his dominions, and the prohibition of all trade or other intercourse with them. But the English were supreme at sea, and could stop the journey of pilgrim-ships to Mecca. The loss to his customs revenue through the stoppage of their trade was also serious. Therefore, after a time he was inclined to come to terms with them. Ibrahim Khan, who came to Bengal as subahdar in May 1689, was a mild and just man, friendly to the English. He wrote to Madras inviting the factors to return to Bengal. At last in February 1690, peace was finally concluded between the Mughal Government and the English on the West Coast. As Aurangzib wrote on 22 February 1590, 'The English [of Surat] having made a most humble, submissive petition... and [promised] that they would present the Emperor with a fine of Rs 150,000,... and behave themselves no more in such a shameful manner ... His Majesty hath pardoned their faults and agrees ... that they follow their trade as in former times.' After this settlement, the Emperor also wrote to Ibrahim Khan, on 23 April following, to let the English trade freely in Bengal as formerly, without giving them any further trouble.

From Madras Charnock arrived once more at Sutanati on 24 August as Agent. This was the foundation of Calcutta and of the British Power in Northern India. On 10 February 1691 an imperial order (*hasb-ul-hukm*) was issued by the grand wazir to the diwan of Bengal, allowing the English to carry on their trade in that province without molestation on paying Rs 3,000 a year in lieu of all customs and other dues.

17.10 English War with the Mughals on the West Coast

As in Bengal, so also on the Western Coast of India, the English traders suffered from the vexations and illegal interference and greed of the local officers of the Mughal Government, which the Emperor could not check. In addition, they were in 1680 asked to pay the *jiziya* in the form of one per cent additional import duty, which would have amounted to Rs 20,000 annually. The friction continued; the local agents of the E.I.Co. were powerless to find a remedy.

But Sir Josiah Child, the Chairman of the Company in London, was a man of a fiery disposition and exceptional force of character. He decided on a policy of firmness, independence, and if necessary of reprisal, against the Mughal empire. Such a policy required three things, namely (*a*) the withdrawal of the English factory from Surat, which was really a 'fool's paradise,' (*b*) concentrating the Company's trade and officers in Bombay as 'the Key of India', in order to be free from the intolerable restraints and indignities to which the Company's servent were subjected at Surat, and (*c*) seizing the Indian shipping at sea in retaliation for the oppression done to English trade in the Mughal dominions.

But Sir John Child, the 'General and Director in Chief' of all the Company's factories in India, was weak and incompetent. In obedience to orders from Home, he left Surat for Bombay on 25 April 1687, in order to be beyond the reach of the Mughals. The imperial governor of Surat, taking this to be a preparation for war, put troops round the English factory, with the effect that Benjamin Harris, the chief of the Surat Council, and Samuel Annesley, his second in office, could not go outside.

At last, on 9 October 1688, Sir John Child appeared with a fleet before Swally and sent to the governor of Surat a list of the grievances of the

English, demanding compensation for past injuries and a new charter confirming and extending their privileges. The governor began open hostility by suddenly imprisoning the English factors and their Indian brokers, placing a guard over the English factory, and sending a force to Swally to seize Child. The latter escaped, and retaliated by blockading the mouth of the river below Surat and then sailing down the coast and capturing all sorts of Indian shipping indiscriminately.

The Mughal Government's reply was to put the captive Englishmen at Surat in irons, in which deplorable condition they remained for 16 months (December 1688–April 1690). At the same time, the Siddi of Janjira, as Mughal admiral, delivered an attack on Bombay (May 1689) and landed on the island, occupying its outlying parts. The English garrison was driven within Bombay fort and besieged there by a daily increasing mob of Muslims. Governor Child, therefore, made an abject appeal for pardon, sending a mission to Aurangzib under G. Weldon and Abraham Navarro (10 December 1689). The Emperor pardoned them, by an order dated 25 December 1689. The English were restored to their old position in the Indian trade on condition of paying a fine of one-and-a-half lakhs of Rupees, and restoring the goods taken from Indian ships.

17.11 European Pirates in Indian Seas, Seventeenth Century

European piracy in the Indian Ocean had begun with the coming of Vasco da Gama at the end of the fifteenth century. It excited no moral reprobation in Christendom. Merchants and adventurers of all classes and nationalities flocked from Europe to the Indian seas in the sixteenth and seventeenth centuries and with the growth of Indian trade there was a corresponding growth of piracy by different nations.

In 1635, Cobb, the captain of a ship licensed by Charles I of England, plundered two Mughal vessels at the mouth of the Red Sea, though one of them had a pass from the Surat factory. In 1638, Sir William Courten, under a grant from the same king, sent out four ships which robbed Indian vessels and tortured their crews. For these misdeeds of their fellow-countrymen, the innocent servants of the East India Company at Surat were kept in prison for two months, and released only on the payment of Rs 170,000 as compensation.

In the second half of the seventeenth century an even more lawless face of men than the old Buccaneers appeared and extended their operations to the Indian Ocean, acting generally in single ships and plundering vessels of every nationality. 'Of these men, chiefly English, the most notorious were Teach, Evory, Kidd, Roberts, England and Tew, with many others less known to fame.... Roberts alone was credited with the destruction of 400 trading vessels in three years.... The chief cause of their immunity lay in the fact that it was the business of nobody in particular to act against them.... Their friends on shore supplied their wants and gave them timely information of rich prizes to be looked for, or armed ships to be avoided. Officials high in authority winked at their doings, from which they drew a profit.... Not only were the greater number of pirates of English blood, but pirate captains of other nationalities often sailed under English colours. The native officials, unable to distinguish the rogues from the honest traders, held the E.I.Co.'s servants responsible for their misdeeds.'

In 1681 two ships under English colours seized vessels in the Red Sea worth six lakhs of Rupees. Next year a number of sea-rovers from the West Indies made their appearance and infested the Malabar coast, hoisted the red or black flag, and robbed Indian and European vessels alike. There were besides, other European pirates in the Persian Gulf at the mouth of the Red Sea, in the Mozambique Channel, and some lying off Achen (Sumatra).

The most famous of these pirates was Henry Bridgman, who took the *alias* of Evory. On 30 May 1694, while acting as the mate of an English ship hired by the Spanish Government, he overpowered the officers, renamed his ship *Fancy*, and took to a life of piracy, with 46 guns and 150 fighters on board. After notable captures in the Gulf of Aden, he took off Socotra (September 1695) the *Fath Muhammadi*, a richly laden ship of Abdul Ghafur, the prince of Surat merchants. A few days later he achieved his crowning feat, the capture of the *Ganj-i-sawai*, a ship belonging to the Mughal Emperor and being the largest vessel of the port of Surat. Every year it used to sail to Mokha and Jidda, carrying Indian pilgrims for Mecca and Indian goods for sale in Arabia. It had 80 guns and 400 muskets on board, but its captain, Muhammad Ibrahim, was a coward.

He was returning from Mokha, when between Bombay and Daman he was attacked by the *Fancy*, a second pirate ship and two boats. The artillery fire of the Europeans was most effective; in a short time the Mughal vessel had lost 25 soldiers killed and 20 wounded. A gun on board the *Ganj-i-sawai* burst, setting the ship on fire and killing or burning several of the crew. While the Indians were distracted by the fire and engaged in putting: it out, the pirates boarded the ship from all sides. No resistance was made by the crew. The captain hid himself in a lower cabin, after placing swords in the hands of the Turkish slave-girls whom he had purchased at Mokha and whom he now bade fight like men!

For three days the pirates looted the ship at leisure; the women on board, many of them belonging to the Sayyid and other respectable families, were outraged, and several of these victims committed suicide. Then Evory left the unhappy ship, which was carried by its crew to Surat on 12 September. When its passengers, stripped of everything, unfolded the tale of plunder and rape, the people of Surat were roused to uncontrollable indignation at this outrage on the Muslim faith. The sufferers ascribed the attack to Englishmen closely connected with Bombay.

Itimad Khan, governor of Surat, was a friend of the English and an officer of unrivalled uprightness and purity. Amidst the popular clamour he kept his head, and by his judicious measures saved the local Englishmen from being lynched by the Muslim fanatics. He sent a party of regular troops under his lieutenant Ashur Beg to occupy the factory (14 September), and confine the merchants there pending the receipt of the Emperor's orders. A similar fate overtook the English traders at Swally and Broach. Their trade was totally stopped.

During his captivity, Annesley (President of the English Council at Surat) with tireless activity sent off petitions to the Surat governor, to the agents and friends of the English in Aurangzib's camp, and to the Emperor himself and his ministers,—asserting the innocence of the Company's servants and demanding their release. Sir John Gayer, governor of Bombay, was equally active; he wrote to Itimad Khan and to the Emperor, strongly protesting against the arrest of his countrymen and appealing for justice. 'We are merchants and not pirates,' he repeated.

17.12 Aurangzib's Policy towards European Traders

Aurangzib deeply resented this flagrant offence against his flag and his religion, but he was too wise a man to be swayed by his passions. He desired above all things to secure a regular escort of European war-vessels for the pilgrim-ships to Mecca, and this embargo on European trade was only an instrument for putting pressure on them to gain that end cheaply but effectually.

The Dutch offered to clear the Indian seas of the pirates and to be responsible for the safety of the pilgrims to Arabia if they were given the exclusive right of trading in the Mughal empire free of duty. This was declined by the Emperor. Annesley wrote to the Mughal Government undertaking to supply convoy for the Indian vessels in the Arabian Sea or stand responsible for their safety, on condition of the English being paid four lakhs of Rupees annually. The Emperor higgled hard over the amount to be paid for each escorting ship,—offering only half the actual running cost for the double voyage. At last Annesley signed a bond for supplying escort, and the English prisoners were set at liberty on 27 June, 1696.

In 1696 a syndicate of English noblemen had fitted out the *Adventure,* a very strong 30-gun vessel, to act as a privateer against the French and at the same time destroy the pirates in the Indian Ocean. Its captain was William Kidd, 'destined to blossom into the most redoubtable pirate who ever besmirched the honour of England.' Arriving off Calicut early in 1697, he took to a life of piracy, shamelessly describing his robberies as legitimate acts of privateering authorized by the king of England. Kidd's success drew many restless English seamen into his party. 'Distributing his forces with the skill of a sea-strategist,' Captain Kidd dominated the Indian Ocean, with his munitions and stores drawn from a base in Madagascar. 'All told, the pirate fleet mounted 120 guns, and was manned by not less than 300 Europeans, of whom the great majority were Englishmen.'

Besides taking many of the E.I.Co.'s ships, he captured on 2 February 1698, the *Queda Merchant,* 400 tons, bound from Bengal to Surat with a rich cargo worth 4 lakhs of Rupees belonging to Mukhlis Khan, one of the great nobles of the empire. Late in 1698 Chivers (a Dutch pirate) captured a fine ship with a cargo worth 14 lakhs belonging to Hassan Hamidan, a merchant of Jidda and Surat.

The English merchants of Surat could not escape any longer. The wise and upright collector of the port, Itimad Khan, had died in February 1697 and had been succeeded by Amanat Khan, an unscrupulous and rapacious tyrant. 'It was useless to assert that the English were not to be identified with the pirates, when ... many English seamen of the piratical craft were actually recognized by reliable native sailors as former servants of the E.I. Co.' The Mughal governor, on 23 December 1698, surrounded the Surat factory and gave Annesley an ultimatum either to yield to the Emperor's demand for giving a bond to guard the sea against pirates or to leave the country in ten days. The Dutch and the French were similarly treated. Meantime the factories were segregated, and Indians who tried to communicate with them were bound and flogged by order of the governor. In August 1698 came an imperial order that the English, French and Dutch would be held responsible for all losses at sea and that the three nations should pay total damages amounting to 14 lakhs.

Finally, the English, French and Dutch agreed to act in concert to suppress piracy and signed bonds by which they *jointly* engaged to make good all future losses. On receiving this agreement, Aurangzib reversed his embargo on European trade in the Mughal dominions, and he wrote to the Surat governor to settle the matter in his own way. In terms of this agreement, 'the Dutch convoyed the Mecca pilgrims and patrolled the entrance to the Red Sea, besides paying Rs 70,0000 to the governor of Surat; the English paid Rs 30,000 and patrolled the South Indian seas, while the French made a similar payment and policed the Persian Gulf' (March 1699).

On 8 April 1699 a new English Company was established at Surat, with Sir Nicholas Waite as President. Sir William Norris was sent out from England as the English King's ambassador to the Mughal Court in the interests of the new Company. He visited Aurangzib in the siege camp before Panhala (April 1701); there was an exchange of presents between the two Governments, but nothing was secured by the ambassador in return for his very expensive mission and waste of sixteen months (27 January 1701–18 April 1702). Aurangzib had demanded, as the price of a *farman* for the new Company's factories, that the English should give an undertaking to clear the seas of the pirates, while Norris knew it to be an impossible task.

Meantime, in February 1701, Sir John Gayer had been seized and imprisoned by Amanat Khan at Surat, through the machinations of Waite, who had procured an order from Aurangzib to that effect by bribing the Surat news-writer. Poor Gayer was kept in confinement for six years with only occasional intervals of liberty. A return prepared in January 1702 showed that the captives at Surat numbered 109 persons, including 21

English officials of the Company ... and 15 seamen. Their imprisonment varied in rigour according to the caprice of the governor.

On 28 August 1703 two ships of Surat, one belonging to Abdul Ghafur and another to Qasimbhai, when returning from Mokha were captured by the pirates off Surat. The news of the outrage reached Surat on 31 August and the governor, Itibar Khan, seized all the Indian brokers of the European Companies, and blockaded their factories, cutting off their food supply and every kind of communication with outside. Three lakhs of Rupees were extorted by the governor from Vittal and Keshav Parekh, the brokers of the old English Company, and three lakhs more from the brokers of the Dutch. In this the governor had merely enforced the indemnity bond which his predecessor Amanat Khan had extorted from the Europeans in Februray 1699 to the effect that they would stand security for any losses caused to Indian shipping by the pirates. Aurangzib, on hearing of it, disapproved of Itibar Khan's action and set aside the agreement extorted in February 1699.

But in truth there was no peace for the Europeans. The captivity of Sir John Gayer and his Council continued with the usual relaxations, under fresh orders from the Mughal Court in July 1704. The Dutch made reprisals by capturing a rich vessel bringing Indian pilgrims back from Mecca. Among them were Nur-ul-Haq (a son of the late Chief Qazi Abdul Wahab) and Fakhr-ul-Islam. Both were held in high veneration by Aurangzib for sanctity of character and respectable birth. 'Without ill-treating them, the captors sent a message to the governor of Surat calling on him to repay the money he had taken from them by force. On being paid, they would restore the ships.' Aurangzib at last realized how helpless he was at sea and that he must make an unconditional surrender to the Europeans if his subjects were ever to make pilgrimages to Mecca. He instructed Nejabat Khan to secure the release of these two holy men and the other captives on any terms that he could get, and forbade him to take indemnity bonds from the Europeans in future.

18 *Some Provinces during Aurangzib's Reign*

18.1 Bengal: Its Natural Wealth and Growth under Mughal Peace

Among all the provinces[1] of the Mughal empire, Bengal was most lavishly favoured by Nature. Its copious rainfall, makes the labour of artificial irrigation unnecessary. Its numberless rivers and tanks with their abundance of fish and its fruit-laden orchards richly supplement the corn-fields. The climate alone is vile and justifies Aurangzib's epigram that this province was 'a hell full of bread'. Such a country needed only peace to be full of wealth and population. That peace and good government were supplied to Bengal by the Mughal empire throughout the Seventeenth century.

In the sixteenth century Bengal had been an unhappy scene of anarchy and desolation from the decay and dismemberment of its independent provincial sultanate and the long wars of Mughal conquest. The misery of the people was extreme, from the annihilation of wealth and culture through political turmoil. In the midst of this internal decay and exhaustion of the old order, its conquest by Akbar came as a blessing to the province. But during Akbar's reign Mughal rule in Bengal was more like an armed occupation than a settled administration. His viceroys had to content themselves with the nominal submission of the old independent Afghan princelings and Hindu ruling zamindars. The Emperor's subahdars merely received the tribute, but did not establish direct imperial administration over the poeple, except in the district round the capital and the strategic

[1] It is neither possible nor necessary to give here the history of every *subah* of the Mughal empire during this reign. The historian is concerned with those provinces only whose affairs assumed an imperial importance.

cities held by their assistants, the faujdars. The huge though irregular armed forces under the various zamindars remained quiescent but undestroyed. They only waited for some weakening of the Emperor's power, some catastrophe at Delhi, to assert their independence once again. After the accession of Jahangir his new viceroy, Islam Khan, who governed the province for six years (May 1608–11 August 1613), was a most ambitious, active and high-spirited noble. By a series of campaigns he crushed all the independent zamindars of Bengal, destroyed the last remnant of Afghan power in Mymensingh, Sylhet and Orissa, and imposed full Mughal peace and direct imperial administration upon all the parts of Bengal. Thereafter Bengal enjoyed profound internal peace for nearly a century and a half and recovered wealth and population, trade expanded by rapid strides, industries developed, and a great indigenous literature grew up in the hands of the Vaishnav sect. The Arrakanese, and subsequently their agents, the Portuguese pirates of Chatgaon, were a pest to the riverside districts of East Bengal; but this evil was removed early in Aurangzib's reign (1666) by Shaista Khan; the trade of the English and the Dutch grew by leaps and bounds from the middle of the century onwards, and their factories and purchase-agencies stimulated production and wealth in the country.

18.2 Governors of Bengal in Aurangzib's Reign

Shaista Khan's first viceroyalty of Bengal extended over 14 years (1664–77). During this unusually long period of office in one province, he first ensured the safety of the Bengal rivers and sea-board by destroying the pirates' nest at Chatgaon, won over the Firingi pirates and settled them near Dacca. His internal administration was equally mild and beneficent. He immediately stopped the resumption by the State of the old rent-free lands which the local officers had begun during the interregnum following Mir Jumla's death.

Every day he held open Court for administering justice and redressed wrongs very promptly. This he regarded as his most important duty. Shaista Khan restored absolute freedom of buying and selling, and also abolished two illegal exactions of his predecessors, namely, a tax of one-fortieth (*zakat*) on the income of merchants and travellers, and an excise duty (*hasil*) from every class of artificers and tradesmen, the latter tax yielding 15 lakhs of Rupees a year in his own jagirs alone. The long interval of peace secured by his arms to Bengal was employed by him in adorning his capital Dacca with many fine buildings, and constructing *sarais* all over the country. On the whole, he was a generous nobleman of the grand old style. Shaista Khan was sent back to Bengal in January 1680. His second term covered nine years from 1680 to 1688; the most noticeable event of this period was the war with the English E.I. Co. already described. The popular tradition is that during his governorship rice sold in Bengal at the rate of eight maunds to the Rupee, which was not incredible in the rice-bowl of Dacca and Barisal in that age of no exportation.

Ibrahim Khan arrived in June 1689, as subahdar. He was an old man of mild disposition and sedentary habits and a great lover of books. Without strength of purpose or capacity for action, he let matters drift, till the administration of the province entirely broke down, and every one did what he liked. He personally administered justice, was free from venality and caprice, and promoted agriculture and commerce. His first act after coming to Bengal was to make terms with the English and induce them to settle in Bengal again.

But Bengal in the late Seventeenth century was no place for a bookworm. The lawless elements in the province seized the opportunity presented by Ibrahim Khan's supine administration and slothful unmartial character. Shova Singh, the zamindar of Cheto-Barda in the Medinipur district, rebelled, and in alliance with Rahim Khan, the chief of the Orissa Afghans, began to plunder the lands of his neighbour, Rajah Krishna Ram, the farmer-general of the revenue of the Bardwan district. Krishna Ram advanced against them with a small force, but was defeated and slain, and his wife, daughters and entire property and the town of Bardwan itself were captured by the rebels. Nurullah Khan, faujdar of West Bengal, timidly shut himself up in the fort of Hughli, where the rebels soon blockaded him. He slipped out of it at night with his bare life, but all his wealth and the fort fell into Shova Singh's hands.

On the outbreak of the rebellion, the three European nations in Bengal had enlisted Indian soldiers to guard their property and obtained the subahdar's permission to fortify their settlements of Calcutta, Chandernagar and Chinsura. These places at once became the only havens of refuge amidst the general disturbance in Bengal. The Dutch of Chinsura recovered Hughli fort for the imperial Government in August.

Shova Singh's next step was to detach Rahim Khan with the main part of his army to take the rich cities of Nadia and Murshidabad, while he returned to his headquarters at Bardwan. Here he was stabbed to death by a daughter of Rajah Krishna Ram. The rebel army chose Rahim as their chief, and he now crowned himself with the title of Rahim Shah. By this time all Bengal, west of the Ganges, had passed into the hands of these men, while Ibrahim Khan lay inactive at Dacca. Rahim's army had now increased to 10,000 horse and 60,000 infantry. He plundered the rich cities of Murshidabad, Malda and Rajmahal.

Immediately on hearing details of this rising and Ibrahim Khan's negligence, the Emperor dismissed him from the viceroyalty of Bengal and appointed his grandson, Azim-ush-shan to the post (middle of 1697). The prince was then in the Deccan, and pending his arrival Zabardast Khan (the son of Ibrahim and faujdar of Bardwan) recovered Rajmahal and Malda, and next attacked the rebel camp at Bhagawangola and after a two days' fight captured it (May 1697). Rahim was successively driven out of Murshidabad and Bardwan into the woods.

In November prince Azim arrived at Bardwan, and halted there for many months. Zabardast having left the province, he rebels now reappeared and renewed their activity on all sides. Rahim, after plundering the Nadia and Hughli districts, arrived near Bardwan to confront the imperial army. Here he treacherously slew Khwajah Anwar, the prince's chief minister, at an interview, and then delivered an impetuous attack on the imperial army, but was killed. Their leader being gone, the rebel army melted away.

Muhammad Hadi, a highly competent finance officer, was transferred by the Emperor from the diwani of Haidarabad to that of Bengal with the title of Kar Talb Khan (November 1700) and later created subahdar of Orissa (January 1703) with the title of Murshid Quli Khan. 'The prudent management of the new diwan soon raised Bengal to the highest degree of prosperity. Particularly careful in the choice of his officers, he obtained through their means complete information about the actual capacity of the lands and the amount of customs duties. The diwan took the collection into his own hands, and by preventing the embezzlements of the zamindars and jagirdars, augmented the annual revenue.'

Murshid Quli refused to let Azim-ush-shan interfere with revenue matters in any way. The foolish prince instigated a plot of some troopers to mutiny and murder the diwan. The conspiracy was defeated by Murshid Quli Khan's presence of mind, courage and tact. But, to guard against further attempts on his life, he removed the revenue office (in 1703) from Dacca, where the prince lived as governor, to a more centrally situated village on the bank of the Ganges, whose name of Maqsudabad he changed to Murshidabad in honour of himself. This was destined to be the capital of Bengal for half the eighteenth century. Aurangzib, on hearing of the incident, grew very angry, and ordered the prince to remove to Bihar, which had been added to his,charge in January 1703. For the next three years (1704–7) Azim lived at Patna, which he was permitted by the Emperor to name Azim-abad after his own name.

Murshid Quli Khan repeatedly sent to the Emperor large sums as the surplus revenue of the province. The money came most poportunely to Aurangzib, whose other resources had been exhausted by the endless war with the Marathas. Under Murshid Quli all felt that a strong master had come to the province. He collected the revenue by his own agents directly and thus saved the profits which middiemen or zamindars used to make. The orders of Murshid Quli Khan were so absolute that the most refractory men trembled in his presence, and his commands were implicitly obeyed. Two days in the week he administered justice in person, and was so impartial in his decisions and rigid in their execution that no one dared commit oppression.

A few years after the death of Aurangzib he was appointed subahdar of Bengal and soon became its independent ruler, as the Delhi Government sank into hopeless decline. Under him Bengal entered on a career of peace and marvellous material prosperity, which was interrupted only by the follies and crimes of his unworthy successors.

18.3 Malwa, its Importance in Mughal Times

The Mughal province of Malwa extended north to south between the Jamuna and the Narmada rivers. West of it, across the Chambal, lies Rajputana, and east of it Bundelkhand, from which the river Betwa separates it. The most notable element of its population are the Rajputs, divided into an immense number of petty clans or minor branches of famous clans, and not organized in compact tribal States as in Rajputana proper. But their number and importance were not so preponderant as to throw into insignificance other races of inhabitants, such as the Jats who were spread over the northern side, and the Gonds concentrated in full strength in the south and the south-east,—besides a strong infusion of Muhammadan immigrants (mostly Afghans) settled in definite centres. The undeveloped primitive races, though strong in number, lived in out of the way corners and among the hills and jungles.

Malwa was rich in agricultural wealth,—producing large quantities of the higher crops, such as opium, sugar-cane, grapes, musk-melons and betel-leaf, besides sheltering large herds of elephants in its forest tracts. In industries it occupied the first rank among the Mughal subahs after Gujrat. In Mughal times its importance was enhanced by the fact that all the great military roads from the northern capitals, Agra and Delhi, to the Deccan passed through this province.

A preponderantly Hindu province, with a sturdy Rajput population, was not likely to take Aurangzib's policy of temple destruction and poll-tax on the Hindus with tame submissiveness. They often fought the agents of Islam in defence of the seats of their religion. But, on the whole, the disturbances in Malwa during the first half of this reign were all on a small scale and confined to a few localities. With the exception of the raids of Chhatra Sal Bundela and Bakht Buland Gond, Malwa continued to enjoy peace and uneventful administration till near the end of the seventeenth century. But after Rajaram's return home from Jinji began a movement which was destined in less than fifty years to completely change the political history of the province.

18.4 Maratha Incursions into Malwa, 1699–1706

In November 1699, a Maratha band led by Krishna Savant *cro*-ssed the Narmada for the first time and raided Malwa up to the environs of Dhamuni. The path thus opened was never again closed, till at last in the middle of the eighteenth century Malwa passed into regular Maratha possession. In January 1703, the Marathas crossed the Narmada again, and caused disturbances up to the environs of Ujjain. In October 1703, Nima Sindhi burst into Berar, defeated and captured Rustam Khan, deputy governor of the province (on behalf of Firuz Jang), and then raiding the Hushangabad district and crossing the Narmada he advanced into Malwa at the invitation of Chhatra Sal. After plundering many villages and towns, he laid siege to Sironj, but Firuz Jang who had entered Berar in pursuit of another Maratha force, hastened with light equipment on the track of the raiders, overtook them near Sironj, and immediately delivered his attack (middle of November). Nima fled away on horseback. Many of the Marathas and their local Rajput and Afghan allies were slain or wounded. The followers and cattle of Rustam, whom Nima was dragging along with himself, were released.

In February 1704 Firuz Jang, following up his success, surprised Nima's army, which was off its guard, near the jungle of Dhamuni, slaying many and recovering much booty. There were heavy losses on the Mughal side too.

It was a great deliverance for the Mughals. The Maratha activities in Berar had held up the reports of news-writers and official letters for 5 or 4 months on the bank of the Narmada. The danger from which Malwa had just escaped, through Firuz Jang's courage and activity, brought home to Aurangzib's mind the gravity of the situation. Prince Bidar Bakht, a brave and skilful general, then acting as governor of Aurangabad and Khandesh, was appointed viceroy of Malwa on 3 August, 1704. He continued to govern Malwa till March 1706, when he received urgent orders to go to Gujrat and take charge of its defence.

The prince's favourite lieutenant was the young gallant Jai Singh *(sawai),* the new Rajah of Jaipur, who had gained his good opinion by his conspicuous services.

Among the rebels who troubled Malwa were Nasiri Afghan, Gopal Singh Chandrawat, Gopal Chaudhuri of Sironj, Abbas Afghan, and Umar Pathan. In fact, the local disturbers of peace in Malwa in the closing years of the reign were too many to be counted. 'Marathas, Bundelas, and Afghans out of employment are creating disturbances in the province.' (1704). The result is summed up in Aurangzib's own words: 'The province of Khandesh has been totally desolated ... Malwa too is ruined,—very little habitation is now left.'

18.5 Chhatra Sal Bundela's Early Life

Champat Rao Bundela's fourth son, Chhatra Sal (born in. 1650), lived to defy the imperial Government with success for half a century, keep his own province in constant turmoil, invade Malwa, and finally to carve out an independent principality in Eastern Malwa, with its capital at Panna. His long life of 81 years ended in 1731.

Left helpless by their father's outlawry and death, Chhatra Sal and his elder brother Angad were first employed by Jai Singh in his own contingent, in the war against Shivaji (1665), and afterwards rewarded for their gallant services by being created imperial mansabdars *(3-sadi* and *hazari* respectively) in August following.

Chhatra Sal was next employed in the Mughal attack on Deogarh by Dilir Khan. But the young Bundela prince felt that he was not being rewarded as he deserved, and that a subaltern's career in the Mughal army did not offer full scope to his soaring ambition. He dreamt of taking to a life of adventure and independence in imitation of Shivaji, whom he visited.

But the Maratha king advised him to return to his own country and use his local influence to promote risings against Aurangzib, so as to distract the Mughal forces. Chhatra Sal, on his return home, began to attack the mighty Mughal empire.

The policy of temple destruction on which Aurangzib launched in 1670, created an opening which Chhatra Sal at once seized. The Hindu population of Bundelkhand and the adjoining province of Malwa took up arms in defence of the altars of their gods. They sighed for a bold leader who would repeat Champafs spirited defiance of the Mughal Emperor and protect their religion. Chhatra Sal was, therefore, hailed as the champion of the Hindu faith and Kshatriya honour. Even Sujan Singh, the loyal Bundela Rajah of Urchha, sent him a secret message of praise and good wishes.

18.6 Chhatra Sal's War with Mughal Government

"The news of Chhatra Sal's advance (1617) was grateful to Bundela ears.' The rebels elected Chhatra Sal as their leader and the king of all the Bundelas, his army numbering 335 men. But he soon received large reinforcements. The hope of plunder drew to his side vast numbers of recruits from this martial tribe, especially Champat's old followers in brigandage. In the earlier part of his career, Chhatra Sal's raiding activities were mostly directed against the Dhamuni district and the rich city of Sironj which lay 108km (65 miles) west of it. He looted the villages of these two regions year after year. Successive Mughal faujdars of Dhamuni resisted him with indifferent results.

In a short time Chhatra Sal's repeated successes decided the waverers. Many other petty chiefs joined him, and even Durjan Sal, the Hada usurper of Bundi, allied himself with the rebels of Bundelkhand. Chhatra Sal followed the Maratha system of sparing the places that paid him a blackmail of one-fourth of their standard revenue *(chauth)*. As Aurangzib became more and more deeply entangled in the Deccan, Chhatra Sal achieved more brilliant triumphs, including the capture of Kalinjar and Dhamuni and the loot of Bhilsa. The range of his raids was greatly extended; the whole of Malwa from the Jamuna to the Rajput border and the Narmada was his happy hunting ground, and he became a nucleus round which all lawless men of this region assembled.

In March 1699, Sher Afkan Khan, the faujdar of Ranod 116 km (70 miles) north of Sironj, marched against him, and attacked him near Suraj-Mau. After a severe battle, Chhatra Sal fled into the fort, which the Khan besieged, but the Bundela chief escaped from it. But Chhatra Sal had his revenge next year. On 24 April 1700 Sher Afkan Khan attacked him near Jhuna and Baraa, slew about 700 of his men, and dispersed the rest after wounding

Chhatra Sal himself. But the Khan was mortally wounded by a musket-shot.

In 1705 Firuz Jang induced the Emperor to make terms with the irrepressible Bundela. Chhatra Sal was created a *4-hazari* in the Mughal peerage and induced to visit the Emperor in the Deccan. Here he lived in peace for a year and a half, and then, on Aurangzib's death, returned home to renew his career of independence.[2]

18.7 The Gond Kingdom and Their Relations With the Mughals

Gondwana covers much of the modern Central Provinces, and stretches on both sides of the Vindhya range. In the northern half of this region a great kingdom had been established in the sixteenth century by the Gond Rajah of Garha. But Akbar's generals dismembered the kingdom and sacked its capitals Garha and Chauragarh. The later Rajahs reigned

[2] The full history of Chhatra Sal's later career, based upon original Persian and Marathi sources, is given in my edition of Irvine's *Later Mughals*, ii 227–241, and Dr. Raghuvir Singh's *Malwa in Transition*.

at Chauragarh, with diminished power and territory, and rapidly sank into obscurity in the middle of the seventeenth century.

The predominance among the Gonds now passed to the chiefs of Deogarh, in the centre of Gondwana and south of the Narmada river. Some 40 km (25 miles) south of Deogarh lay Chanda, the seat of another Gond Rajah, who was the constant enemy and rival of the house of Deogarh. These were the only Gond States that counted for anything in the reign of Aurangzib, and their accumulated treasure, herds of elephants, and collections of gems locally quarried, made them objects of cupidity to the Mughal Government. In 1637 a Mughal army, released from operations in the Deccan, entered Gondwana, levying contributions from the local chiefs. It stormed Nagpur, the seat of the Deogarh Rajah Kukia. The fort was restored to him on his promising an annual tribute.

But the tribute fell into arrears, and in 1655 a Mughal army marched into Deogarh territory and forced the Rajah (Kesari Singh) to make an abject submission. The arrears grew to 15 lakhs at the end of 1666.

An imperial army under Dilir Khan marched into Gondwana in January 1667. Manji Malar, the Rajah of Chanda, had been refractory and done some acts of lawlessness. But on the arrival of the Mughal army at Mandura on his frontier (February 1667), he offered submission, and promised a war contribution of one krore of Rupees and an annual tribute of two lakhs. Dilir Khan stayed there for two months, during which he realized 77 lakhs of Rupees out of the promised contribution.

Kuk Singh, Rajah of Deogarh, was frightened by the fate of the Chanda chieftain. He humbly waited on Dilir Khan, agreeing to pay three lakhs as fine, and deliver 18 lakhs within a fixed period. He, however, did not keep his promise, and in August 1669 Dilir Khan had to repeat his invasion. The Mughals overran Deogarh. The Rajah with his entire family (two brothers and one sister) embraced Islam, as the price of restoration to his kingdom, and on 29 March Dilir Khan left Nagpur for the south.

But the attitude of the Gond Rajah was not changed with his change of religion under temptation. He continued refractory. In March 1686, one claimant to this State was converted to Islam with the title of Rajah Bakht Buland and given the throne. He lived to extend the area, power and prosperity of his kingdom very largely, and to give the greatest trouble to Aurangzib in the last years of his reign.

Ram Singh, Rajah of Chanda, was deposed in October 1683 and the throne given to Kishan Singh. But the old Rajah refused to yield possession to his rival. So, a Mughal force under Itiqad Khan entered his capital on 2 November 1684 and installed Kishan Singh. This Rajah was succeeded by his eldest son, Bir Singh, in July 1696. In August 1700 he was summoned to the Emperor's camp as his tribute had fallen into arrears. He reached the Emperor's army on 27 April 1701 and paid one lakh into the Berar treasury.

18.8 Bakht Buland, Gond Rajah of Deogarh, Asserts His Independence

In June 1691, Bakht Buland was deposed by the Emperor, and the throne of Deogarh was given to another Muslim Gond named Dindar. Bakht Buland, after being kept under surveillance for some years, recovered his freedom (August 1695) by giving security for his future conduct, though the Emperor remarked, 'He will run away; keep a watch on him.' Soon after this, trouble began again in Deogarh. Dindar proved defiant, and a Mughal force with the help of the Chanda Rajah Kishan Singh, captured Deogarh and drove Dindar into flight (March 1696). Kan Singh, the second son of Kishan Singh, secured the throne of Deogarh by turning Muslim (under the name of Rajah Neknam). Bakht Buland now lost all hope of his restoration. The time was opportune for a bold stroke, to test fortune by a throw of the dice, as Deogarh and Chanda had both changed their rulers in the same year (1696), and their new Rajahs were mere lads. He, therefore, slipped away from the imperial army, returned to Deogarh, and raised the standard of rebellion with remarkable pertinacity, resourcefulness and success. The Emperor, in impotent anger, ordered his name to be changed from *Bakht Buland* ('Fortunate') to *Nagun Bakht* ('Luckless'). The rebel's activity spread over a wide area. Berar was his nearest hunting ground. A detachment from Firuz Jang's army defeated Bakht Buland and captured Deogarh (June, 1699). The rebel escaped from his doomed capital and entered Malwa with a vast force; he next occupied the kingdom of Garha and restored Narendra Shah to his ancestral throne (July).

Bakht Buland in July sent Rs 30,000 to Chhatra Sal with a request to recruit a body of the famous Bundela musketeers for him. In October, he sent two envoys to Rajaram in Satara fort, to invite him to Deogarh, in order to create a diversion in Aurangzib's rear; but the Maratha king declined under the advice of his generals. Early in March 1701, Bakht Buland and his uncle Nawal Shah, the zamindar of Jamgarh, in concert with the Marathas assembled a force of 4,000 troopers and 12,000 infantry, and attacked Ali Mardan Khan, governor of Berar, but they were defeated with great slaughter, Nawal Shah being killed and Bakht Buland wounded. Risings by Bakht Buland's Muslim allies are reported in February 1703 (near Ujjain under Abbas) and January 1704 (under Sayyid Abdul Qadir).

'During Bakht Buland's reign the rich lands to the south of Deogarh, between the Wainganga and Kanhan rivers, were steadily developed. Hindu and Muhammadan cultivators were encouraged to settle in them on equal terms with Gonds, until this region became most prosperous.' Industrious settlers from all quarters were attracted to Gondwana, many towns and villages were founded, and agriculture, manufactures, and even commerce made considerable advances. On the death of Aurangzib, this Deogarh chief extended his kingdom; the Seoni district was ceded to him by Narendra Shah and he also annexed the ancient historical Gond principality of Kherla. But the glory of Deogarh departed on the death of his successor Chand Sultan (1739), and the Maratha house of Nagpur secured his kingdom.

18.9 Condition of Kashmir under the Mughals

The Mughal Emperors treated Kashmir merely as a pleasure resort. They did not try to improve the face of the land or the condition of the people.

The common people of Kashmir were sunk in the deepest ignorance and poverty; many of the villagers lived in primitive simplicity and went about almost naked for want of clothing; they merely wrapped a blanket round their bodies for warmth. Long distances and lack of roads made it impossible to import grain from outside, and every valley had to be self-contained in the matter of its food supply; and when a natural calamity like flood or heavy snowfall cut the communications, the inhabitants perished helplessly of famine in thousands. The province was off the routes of the civilized world; difficulty of transport raised the cost of marketing its produce. The province had no local industry. Even shawl-weaving was mostly a Government monopoly, and the people earned from it only the wages of daily labour at the State factories. The fine Kashmiri paper was consumed only by the Court, and made to order.

So backward were the people in civilization that even the upper classes of Kashmiris were deemed unfit to be employed in the imperial service as mansabdars till near the end of Aurangzib's reign. We learn that it was only in 1699 that the Emperor was first induced by the then *subahdar* to appoint people of Kashmir as mansabdars. No Kashmiri Hindu gained any office under the Mughal empire, and as for the common Muslims of the province, if they were villagers they were despised as ignorant savages, and if townsmen as lying flatterers and cowardly cheats, so that in Mughal India a Kashmiri came to be a by-word for a smooth-spoken rogue. Ignorance, poverty, and the feudal organization of society,—which kept the masses in a servile condition, also accounted for their sale of the chastity of their wives and daughters.

The ignorance of the people was only equalled by their superstitiousness. A huge parasite class of Muslim saints and their disciples flourished in this charming climate and exploited the credulity of the people. In the cities of Kashmir, the sectarian bitterness between the Shias and the Sunnis often led to fierce rioting and even civil war, and the strong arm of the governor (when he did not happen to be the partisan of either sect) could only maintain an armed truce among the local population. Quarrels between individual members of the rival sects quickly passed into mass conflicts; the Sunni mob of the capital, roused by the qazi's harangues, plundered and burnt the Shia quarter, and massacred every Shia whom they could catch. Sometimes there were pitched battles in the streets between the armed rioters and the governor's troops. Even the viceroy's residence was not safe from the Sunni mob and soldiery, if he was suspected of harbouring any Shia whom they wanted to lynch.

The villagers were half-naked boors, living in abject poverty, ignorance, and filth. The townsmen, too, had not a much happier lot. The sudden and dangerous floods to which the lake is subject, forced them to build their homes in the cramped high ground above the edge of the river or the lake. The frequency of earthquakes made it necessary for their house to be light wooden structures. The intense cold of the country made fires necessary in every household day and night. The natural consequence of this chain of causes was that conflagrations were frequent, and when they broke out they spread from one end of the city to another, making a clean sweep of these crowded human warrem of timber and grass.

18.10 Aurangzib's Viceroys and their Doings in Kashmir

In Aurangzib's reign, there were twelve subahdars in Kashmir during 48 years. The life of the province varied as the characters of its successive governors varied. Some of them, like Itimad Khan and Fazil Khan, administered justice with great diligence and honoured learning. Others, like Saif Khan, introduced innovations in the form of illegal exactions to enrich themselves.

The long roll of natural calamities during the half century of Aurangzib's reign includes two earthquakes (June 1669 and 1681), two conflagrations of the capital (1673 and 1678), one flood (1681), and a famine (1688). The most notable events of this period in the history of Kashmir were Aurangzib's royal progress through it (1663), of which Bernier has left a graphic account (with a wrong date) and the conquest of Greater Tibet (1666) whose ruler, styled Daldal Namjal in the Persian chronicles, bowed to Islam.

In 1684 took place what was probably the worst fight between the Shias and the Sunnis. The Hasanabad quarter of Srinagar was a Shia stronghold. A resident of it named Abdus Shakur and his sons had done some injury to a Sunni named Sadiq.

Their enmity grew into a long-standing quarrel. In the course of it these Shias publicly did some acts and made some remarks designed to insult the memory of the first three Khalifs (who were usurpers, according to Shia theology). The offenders took refuge with the governor Ibrahim Khan. The qazi Muhammad Yusuf, in pious frenzy, roused the mob of the city and they set fire to the Hasanabad quarters. During the riot, the governor's son Fidai Khan came out to support the men of Hasanabad, while the mob, strengthened by the Kabul officers just returned from Tibet and some local mansabdars, opposed him. Many were slain and wounded on both sides and the mob rioted with terrible fury.

Ibrahim Khan, finding himself worsted in the contest, at last handed Abdus Shakur and other accused Shias over to the qazi, by whom Shakur and his two sons and one son-in-law were put to death under canonical sentence. The Sunni rioters were masters of the city and sacked the mufti's house, though he was a Sunni. Baba Qasim, the preceptor of the Shias, was seized on the road and put to death with disgrace. Fidai Khan rode out and slew a local leader of the Sunnis with many of the mob. But in the meantime, Shaikh Baqa Baba had assembled another crowd, and set fire to Ibrahim Khan's mansion! That governor then arrested and imprisoned Baqa Baba, the qazi, news-writer, and bakhshi of the province, and the leading men of the capital. This strong action cowed the people into submission. Aurangzib, on hearing of these occurrences, removed Ibrahim Khan from the viceroyalty and ordered the Sunni captives to be released.

About 1698–99 an event happened which roused the religious fervour of the Muslims to the point of overflowing. This was the bringing into the country of the reputed hair of the Prophet Muhammad which Khwajah Nuruddin had secured in Bijapur, and which was sent after the Khwajah's death to Kashmir along with his corpse. The entire Muslim population poured out into the streets and open spaces, to behold and to touch the blessed relic.

Another incident, illustrating the gross credulity of the people of Kashmir, took place in May 1692, which in that year was the Muslim month of fasting (Ramzan). A stranger of some position named Mir Husain had come to Kashmir and taken up his residence near the Takht-i-Sulaiman hill, where he set up his hermitage. In the month of Ramzan he prepared a grand illumination in honour of the season. Most of the people of Srinagar went there for excursion and sight-seeing. In the third quarter of the day such a violent storm of wind, rain, thunder and lightning burst upon the place that the whole city was darkened as in the darkest night. It continued so for some time, and then the people, believing that the Sun had set, broke their day's fast. But after 2 or 3 hours the tempest ceased, the Sun reappeared, and all felt themselves befooled and disgraced, for a Muslim can hardly commit a greater sin than eat anything in the day-time of the month of Ramzan. It is characteristic of the intelligence and education of the people of the capital city of Kashmir that all of them, high and low alike, ascribed this abnormal phenomenon to the magic art of that heretic hermit. The 'faith-defending, truth-knowing' Emperor believed in the charge and ordered the magician to be expelled.

18.11 Gujrat, its Advantageous Position and Diversified Population

The wealth of Gujrat was mainly due to its handicrafts and commerce. The former could flourish only in walled cities and in the villages nestling in their shelter. In commerce, not only did its people, both Hindus and Muhammadans, possess a natural capacity surpassing that of other natives of India, but Gujrat enjoyed a position of exceptional advantage. All the merchandise of the rich inland districts of Khandesh, Berar, Malwa and even Upper India had to cross Gujrat for shipment abroad. On the coast of this province stand the greatest ports of India,—Broach in Hindu times and Surat in Muslim. Gujrat was, therefore, pre-eminently the gate of India in Mughal times, in respect of the outer Muslim world. Through Surat passed the enormous volume of Muslim pilgrims to the holy cities of Arabia and of Shia votaries to the shrines of Najaf and Karbala. Travellers, merchants, scholars, fortune hunters, and political refugees from Persia, Arabia, Turkey, Egypt, Zanzibar and even Khurasan and Barbary used to enter India through the Gujrat ports by the short, comfortable, cheap and usually safe ocean highway, while the land route across the Sulaiman and Hindu Kush ranges fell into growing neglect.

This geographical advantage has given Gujrat a very composite population and a large foreign strain from very early times, especially the fire-worshipping Persians and that branch of the Ismailia heretics of Islam who are popularly known as Bohras as well as the unorthodox sect of Mahdavis. These and other emigrant clans or families along with the remnants of the Muslim tribes that had held sway over the land before the coming of the Mughals, have given an unparallelled diversity to the racial complexion of the province. On the Hindu side the population is even less homogeneous; there were in the fringe areas of Gujrat in the seventeenth century many primitive races not yet broken to civilization and orderly political life, such as the Kolis (in the south), the Bhils in Baglana (south-east), the wild Rajputs and pseudo-Rajputs in the eastern frontier, and the predatory Grasias scattered throughout the province, besides the Kathis of the west. These were an ever present menace to the peace of the country. To them were added in Aurangzib's reign another race of disturbers, the Marathas, who at last swept Mughal rule out of the province.

18.12 Governors of Gujrat under Aurangzib

During Aurangzib's reign of 50 years Gujrat was governed for him by twelve viceroys, of whom Mahabat Khan (6 years, 1662–68), Md. Amin Khan (10 years, 1672–82), Shujaet Khan (17 years, 1684–1701), and Prince Md. Azam (4 years, 1701–5) ruled the province longest. In the remaining 13 years there were as many as eight subahdars.

Gujrat had an evil reputation for famines in the middle ages, and the reign of Aurangzib was no happier in this respect. We read of famines in 1681, 1684, 1690–91, 1695–96 and 1698. In 1681 there were bread-riots in the capital. The drought of 1696 was so terrible that 'from Patan to Jodhpur no water nor blade of grass could be seen.' In addition to these natural calamities, pestilence desolated many of the cities, lingering for years together in them. Among the noteworthy public disturbances was the overflow of the Rajput war across the north-eastern frontier of Gujrat (1680) when Bhim Singh, then son of Maharana Raj Singh, raided Vadnagar, Vishalnagar and some other rich cities.

18.13 Maratha Invasion of Gujrat, 1706

The greatest disaster that the Marathas inflicted on the Emperor's troops occurred early in 1706, during the interval between the departure of Prince Azam from Ahmadabad (25 November 1705) and the arrival of Bidar Bakht there (30 July 1706). The Marathas under Dhana Jadav took prompt advantage of this defenceless condition of the province for the time being. At Ratanpur (in Rajpipla), the two divisions of the imperial troops were signally defeated one after the other by Dhana. Two of their chiefs, Safdar Khan Babi and Nazar Ali Khan, were captured and held to ransom; their camps were looted, and large numbers of Musalmans perished or were taken captive (15 March 1706).

When Abdul Hamid Khan (deputy governor) himself arrived with another army, his small force was surrounded by the exultant victors near the Baba Piara ford, all the chiefs including the deputy governor himself were taken prisoner, and their entire camp and baggage plundered. Then the Marathas levied *chauth* not the surrounding country and retired after plundering the towns and villages that failed to pay it. The Kolis had taken advantage of these disorders to rise and sack the rich trading centre of Baroda for two days.

18.14 Religious Persecution of the Bohra and Khoja Sects

A spiritual guide of the Ismailia sect named Qutb had been put to death by order of Aurangzib early in his reign. In 1705 the Emperor, learning that Khanji, the head of the Ismailia sect and successor to Qutb, had sent twelve emissaries *(dais)* who were secretly perverting Muslims to this heresy, ordered the twelve men and certain other members of this community to be arrested and sent to him under careful guard, with the money collected by them and the sixty and odd holy books of their faith. This was done. At the same time orthodox teachers were appointed by the State to educate the children and illiterate people of the Bohras in every village and city in Sunni doctrines and practices. Their mosques had been converted to Sunni usage earlier in the reign.

Another branch of these sectaries, called *Khojas* in Kathiawad and *Mumins* (or Mehtas) in Gujrat, consisted mostly of Hindus converted to Islam by a saint named Sayyid Imam-ud-din, whose tomb at Karmatah (15 km i.e., 9 miles outside Ahmadabad) was their chief shrine. They paid idolatrous adoration to their spiritual guide, kissing his toes and heaping up gold and silver on his feet, while he sat in royal splendour behind a screen and they supported him by a regular volunary tax of one-tenth of their annual income. Aurangzib ordered the arrest of their spiritual head, Sayyid Shahji. The man killed himself by poison on the way, but his son, a boy of twelve, was sent to Aurangzib. At this all his followers in Gujrat rose to wreak vengeance on the governor, saying that he had murdered their religious head. They fought and killed the faujdar of Broach, captured that city, and held it in a body 4,000 strong (October 1685). The subahdar after a long siege recovered the fort and butchered the fanatics within it.

19 *Aurangzib's Character and the Effect of his Reign*

19.1 PEACE THE ROOT-CAUSE OF INDIA'S PROSPERITY

To all outer observers the Mughal empire seemed to have attained to its highest splendour and power when Aurangzib ascended the throne of Delhi. 'The wealth of Ind' had become poverbial in far off countries, and the magnificence of the Court of the Great Mughal had 'dazzled even eyes which were accustomed to the pomp of Versailles.' And when a trained administrator and experienced general like him, who was also a puritan in the simplicity and purity of his private life, succeeded to the guidance of this rich heritage in the fulness of his physical and mental powers, all people hoped that he would carry the empire to unimaginable heights of glory. And yet the result of Aurangzib's long and strenuous reign was utter dissolution and misery. The causes of this strange phenomenon—it is the duty of the historian to investigate.

In a warm, moist and fertile country like India,—where the lavish bounty of Nature speedily repairs the ravages of hostile man and beast, of inclement sun and rain,—order is the root of national life, in an even greater degree than in other lands. Given peace without and the spirit of progress within, the Indian people can advance in wealth, strength and civilization with a rapidity rivalled only by the marvellous growth of their vegetation after the first monsoon showers. A century of strong and wise government under Akbar and his son and grandson had given to the richer and more populous half of India such peace and impulse to improvement. A hundred victories since the second Panipat had taught the Indian world to believe that Mughal arms were invincible and Mughal territory inviolable. Shivaji broke this spell. Mughal peace—the sole justification of the Mughal empire—no longer existed in India at Aurangzib's death.

In a predominantly agricultural country like India, the tillers of the soil are the only source of national wealth. Directly or indirectly, the land alone adds to the 'annual national stock.' Even the craftsmen depend on the peasants and on the men enriched with the land revenue, for the sale of their goods, and if the latter have not enough foodstuff to spare, they cannot buy any handicraft. Hence, the ruin of the peasants means in India the ruin of the non-agricultural classes too. *Pauvres paysans pauvre royaume,* is even truer of India than of France. Public peace and security of property are necessary not only for the peasant and the artisan, but also for the trader, who has to carry his goods over wide distances and give long credits before he can find a profitable market. Wealth, in the last resort, can accumulate only from savings out of the peasant's production. Whatever lowers the peasant's productive power or destroys his spirit of thrift by creating insecurity about his property, thereby prevents the growth of national capital and impairs the economic staying power of the country. Such are the universal and lasting effects of disorder and public insecurity in India. And the reign of Aurangzib affords the most striking illustration of this truth.

19.2 Economic Drain of Aurangzib's Ceaseless Warfare

The economic drain caused by Aurangzib's quarter century of warfare in the Deccan was appalling in its character and most far-reaching and durable in its effect. The operations of the imperial armies, especially their numerous sieges, led to a total destruction of forests and grass. The huge Mughal forces, totalling 1,70,000 troops according to the official records with perhaps ten times that number of non-combatants, soon ate up everything green wherever they moved. In addition, the Maratha raiders destroyed whatever they could not carry off,—feeding their horses on the standing crops, and burning the houses and property too heavy to be removed. Hence, it is no wonder that when at last in 1705 Aurangzib retired after his last campaign, the country presented a scene of utter desolation. 'He left behind him the fields of these provinces devoid of trees and bare of corps, their places being taken by the bones of men and beasts.' (Manucci). This total and extensive deforestation had a most injurious effect on agriculture. The financial exhaustion of the empire in these endless wars left Government and private owners alike too poor to repair the buildings and roads worn out by the lapse of time.

The labouring population suffered not only from violent capture, forced labour, and starvation, but also from epidemics which were very frequent during these campaigns. Even in the imperial camp, where greater comfort, security and civilization might have been expected, the annual wastage of the Deccan wars was one lakh of men, and three lakhs of horses, oxen, camels and elephants. At the siege of Golkonda (1687) a famine broke out. 'In Haidarabad city the houses, river and plain were filled with the dead. The same was the condition of the imperial camp .... Kos after kos the eye fell only on mounds of corpses. The incessant rain melted away the flesh and skin.... After some months when the rains ceased, the white ridges of bones looked from a distance like hills of snow.' The same desolation overtook tracts which had hitherto enjoyed peace and prosperity. The acute observer Bhimsen writes about the Eastern Karnatak, 'During the rule of the Bijapur Golkonda and Telinga (dynasties) this country was extensively cultivated. But now many places have been turned into wilderness on account of the passage of the imperial armies, which have inflicted hardship and oppression on the people.' And he noticed the same thing in Berar also.

In 1688, Bijapur was visited by a desolating epidemic of bubonic plague, which is estimated to have carried off a hundred thousand lives in three months. So, too, we read of a plague in Prince Azam's camp in August 1694. The English factors at Surat report similar devastating epidemics throughout Western India in 1694 and 1696 (when 95,000 men perished). To take one example only, the drought and plague of 1702–4 killed two millions of men. In addition to disease, great natural calamities like flood, drought and excessive and unseasonable rainfall were frequent in the Deccan at the beginning of the eighteenth century, which aggravated the sufferings of invaders and natives alike and still further reduced the population. The state of war, spread over nearly a generation of time, had left no savings, no power of resistance in the common people; everything they produced or had stored up was swept away by the hordes on both sides, so that when famine or drought came, the peasants and landless labourers perished helplessly like flies. Scarcity was chronic in the imperial camp and often deepened into famine. The former remarkable cheapness of grain now became a forgotten myth in many parts of India.

19.3 Injury to Trade and Industry by War, Disorder, and Official Exactions

There being in many places no peace or safety for tillage, the starving and exasperated peasantry took to highway robbery as the only means of living. In the Deccan they gathered arms and used to join the Marathas in their raids. Raiding bands were, also, locally formed, which gave employment to many and chances of glory and wealth to the more spirited among the villagers. Trade almost ceased in the Deccan during this unhappy quarter century. Caravans could travel south of the Narmada only under strong escort; hence, they had to wait in the fortified towns for months before they could get an opportunity of advancing further towards their destination in safety. We even read of the royal mail and baskets of fruits for the Emperor's table being held up for five months at the Narmada by Maratha disturbances in the roads beyond it.

Even where war was not raging (as in Bengal), the weakening of the central Government emboldened provincial governors to disregard imperial prohibitions, and to make money by forcing goods from traders at absurdly low prices and then selling them in the public marts, and also by exacting forbidden *abwabs* from craftsmen and merchants. (See my *Mughal Administration,* Ch. 3.) In the absence of security at home and the impossibility of making purchases at distances, arts and crafts ceased to be practised except in the walled cities. Village industries and industrial classes almost died out. The Madras coast, for instance, with its teeming weaving population, was so unsettled by the Mughal-Maratha struggle for the Karnatak (1690–98) that the english and the French factors found it difficult to get enough clothes for loading their Europe-going ships. Thus ensued a great economic impoverishment of India—not only a decrease of the 'national stock', but also a rapid lowering of mechanical skill and standard of civilization, a disappearance of art and culture over wide tracts of the country.

The Mughal soldiers on their march often trod down the crops, and though the Emperor had a special body of officers for compensating the peasants for this loss (*Paimali-i-zarait*), his financial difficulties led to the neglect of this humane rule. The worst oppressors of the peasants, however, were the tail of the army—the vast nondescript horde of servants, day labourers, *darvishes* and other vagrants who followed Aurangzib's 'moving city of tents' in the hope of picking up crumbs where such a crowd had gathered together. Particularly the Beluchi camel-owners who hired out their animals to the army, and the unattached Afghans searching for employment, plundered and beat the country people most mercilessly. The *banjaras* or wandering grain-dealer tribe, who moved in bodies, sometimes of 5,000 men, each with his couple of bullocks loaded with grain, were so strong in their strength of numbers and contempt for the petty officers of Government, that they sometimes looted the people on the wayside and fed their cattle on the crops in the fields, with impunity. Even the royal messengers (called *mewrahs* in Gujrat) who carried Government letters, reports of spies, and baskets of fruits for presentation to the Emperor, used to rob the people of the villages they passed by. In the trail of the Maratha soldiers appeared the Berads and even the Pindaris—who were brigands pure and simple.

Then, there were the land-stewards of rival jagirdars,—the incoming and the outgoing—of the same village. Under the plea of the never-to-be satisfied arrears of revenue, the late jagirdar's collector tried to squeeze everything out of the peasantry before he left, and even continued to stay in the village for some months after the arrival of his successor. And the new-comer, in order not to starve himself, passed the half-dead peasants through his fiscal grinding-mill.

19.4 Bankruptcy of Mughal Government

The English conquest of India was of a pulsatory character; it was achieved not by an uninterrupted succession of advances, but each aggressive governor-general was followed by a pacific economical non-interventionist. A Western Hastings filled the financial void created by the wars of Clive and Vansittart, and laid the basis for the military expansion of a Wellesley, while the bankruptcy caused by Wellesley's frenzy of conquest was repaired by the recuperation of a sober plodding Barlow or Minto. The pacific Bentinck undid the ravages in the Treasury made by the bellicose Marquis of Hastings and Earl of Amherst. Not so Aurangzib. Ever since 1679, when he embarked on the spoliation of the kingdom of Marwar, his reign was one long warfare. He did not realize the necessity of intervals of peace and retrenchment, which would give breathing time to his subjects, recoup the losses of war, and lay by a reserve for future wars. He soon ran through his current revenue, the yield of the new tax (*jiziya*) imposed on the Hindus in 1679, and even the accumulated treasures of his ancestors in the vaults of Agra and Delhi forts.

Thus, the last reserve of the empire was exhausted, and public bankruptcy became inevitable. The salaries of the soldiers and civil officers alike fell into arrears for three years. The men, starving from lack of pay and the exhaustion of their credit with the local grocers, sometimes created scenes in the Emperor's Court, sometimes abused and beat their general's business manager. The imperial Government made reckless promises of money grant and high command to every enemy captain who was induced to desert and every enemy *qiladar* who was persuaded to surrender his fort. It was not humanly possible to keep all of these promises. The result was that the entire land in the empire proved insufficient for the total amount of *jagir* needed to satisfy the dues of all the officers included in the swollen army-list. Even when the grants of land in lieu of salary were drawn up by the Pay Office, they remained for years as mere orders on paper, the actual delivery of the villages to the grantees being impossible. The interval between the order and the actual possession of the jagir, it was sarcastically said, was long enough to turn a boy into a grey-beard. Even a minor Maratha hill-fort cost on an average Rs 45,000 in cash to take it by bribing its qiladar, and the Emperor might well despair of taking all of them at this rate. And yet he obstinately went on capturing fort after fort by heavy bribery or by regular sieges which were ten times more costly.

The spirit of the Mughal army in the Deccan was at last utterly broken. The soldiers grew sick of the endless and futile war,[1] but Aurangzib would listen to no protest or friendly advice. Even his grand wazir Asad Khan, who had ventured to suggest that now that Bijapur and Golkonda had been conquered he had no more work to do and might as well return to Delhi, received a sharp reprimand, 'I wonder that a wise old servant like you has made such a request.... So long as a single breath remains in this mortal body, there is no release from labour.' A generation of imperial followers grew up in the Deccan who had never entered a city or house of brick or stone, but passed all their lives in tents, marching from one encampment to another. The Rajput soldiers complained that

[1] 'Owing to my marching through deserts and forests, my officers long for my death.' Aurangzib to Muazzam in *Anecdotes,* §11.

their race would not be able to serve the empire in the next generation, as they had to pass their life-time in the Deccan campaigns, without getting any respite for going home and rearing up children. One home-sick noble in the Deccan camp offered the Emperor a bribe of one lakh of Rupees for transferring him to Delhi!

19.5 Administrative Decline and Public Disturbances

The inflated expenditure and incessant warfare in the Deccan adversely reacted on the situation in Northern India. The older, and more settled peaceful and prosperous provinces of the empire were drained of their manhood, wealth, and talent. Their best soldiers, highest officers, and all their collected revenue were sent to the Deccan, while the subahs of Hindustan were henceforth left to be governed by minor officers with small contingents and incomes quite inadequate for maintaining viceregal authority. All classes of lawless men began to raise their hands in the north as well as in the south, though later and more fitfully in Hindustan than in the Deccan. The proud zamindars, whose grand-fathers had been ruling princes before the coming of the Mughals, the Afghan families settled in various districts (especially Bengal, Jaunpur, Malwa, Allahabad and North Orissa) and sitll dreaming of their lost empire in India, claimants to principalities dispossessed by order of Aurangzib, predatory tribes like the Jat peasantry west of Agra and the Mewatis south-west of Delhi, and turbulent Rajput villagers like the Bais of Oudh and Ujjainias of South Bihar,—all rose in defiance of the Government and began to lay hands on their weaker neighbours. The local viceroys could not cope with them, for, their income, inadequate even on paper for their heavy duties, was actually dwindling very fast. The general unrest naturally caused a falling off in the rent collection from the peasants. It is difficult to imagine a system more ruinous to the peasants and therefore in the long run more harmful to the State also, than the actual administration of Mughal *jagirs.* It ended in a mad looting of the peasants by rival jagirdars' agents or successive agents of the same jagirdar. 'There is no hope of a jagir being left with the same officer next year. When a jagirdar sends a collector to his jagir, he first takes an advance from the latter by way of loan. This collector, on arriving in the village, fearing lest a second man who had given a larger loan to the jagirdar was following (to supplant him), does not hesitate to collect the rent with every oppression. The ryots have given up cultivation; the jagirdars do not get a penny.' (Bhimsen). The same ruinous policy was followed in revenue collection in the Crownlands. (See my *Studies in Mughal India*, 223.)

Thus, a vicious circle was formed: political disorder (to which we must add a wrong system of land administration) led to less and less money coming from the jagirs; this diminished income forced the governors to keep fewer and fewer troops in their pay; the decrease in their armed strength encouraged greater lawlessness among the people, from which followed a further impoverishment of the peasants and falling off in the land revenue.

War was the only occupation of the Rajputs and indeed of all the Hindus who claimed to belong to the Kshatriya caste. The Mughal peace established in northern India had left to them chances of employment only in the transfrontier regions on the west or in the still unsubdued parts of the Deccan. Rajputs had fought under the imperial banner in Central Asia and Qandahar. But in Aurangzib's reign Mughal military activity was contracted within the frontiers, though Kabul was still a part of his empire. His annexation of the remaining Deccan principalities caused unemployment among the Rajputs in two ways,—first, because he was under the necessity of giving employment to the masterless local troops of the subverted monarchies, and secondly, because fewer territories were now left for him to conquer. In these circumstances aspiring scions of Rajput houses could only fight with their kinsfolk for their ancestral 'homes', take to robbery, or apostatize in order to get grants of estates from Aurangzib.

19.6 Decay of Indian Civilization under Aurangzib, Its Causes and Signs

The retrogression of mediaeval Indian civilization under Aurangzib is noticeable not only in the decline of the fine arts, but still more in the low intellectual type of the new generation. As the seventeenth century wore on, the older nobility nourished on the manly traditions of Akbar and Shah Jahan, gifted with greater independence of spirit, and trained with greater resources and responsibility,—gradually died out, and their places in camp and Court were taken by smaller men, supplied with poorer resources by the suspicious Aurangzib, afraid to exercise responsibility and initiative, and seeking to advance themselves by sycophancy. The exceptionally prolonged life of Aurangzib with its ever increasing store of experience and information, made him intellectually dwarf the younger generation. His self-sufficiency and obstinacy increased with age; till at last none dared contradict him, none could give him honest advice or impart unpleasant truth. With the lack of leisure amidst the incessant warfare and rough camp-life in the far off South, the culture of the aristocracy decayed, and, as the nobles set the tone to society, the whole of the intellectual classes of India steadily fell back to a lower level. A coarse Jafar Jatali took the place of a chaste Faizi for their delectation.

The growing pessimism of the older men, which we find reflected in the letters and anecdotes of the time and even in the works of thoughtful historians, bears witness to the moral decay of the governing classes. It was too deep and too sincere to be set aside as an example of the familiar oriental habit of imagining a golden age in the past and looking down upon the present generation as the degenerate successors of their glorious ancestors. The historians Bhimsen and Khafi Khan were struck by the hopeless change for the worse that had seized the Indian world and looked wistfully back at the virtues and glories of the men of the times of Akbar and Shah Jahan. We find the aged Aurangzib himself dolefully shaking his head over the prospect of the future and predicting a deluge after his death. It is true, as Sadullah remarked in reply to a pessimist, 'No age is without men of ability. What is needed is a wise master to find them out, cherish them, get his work done by them, and never lend his ears to the whispers of selfish men against such officers.' But this wise principle was not followed in Aurangzib's latter years, and it was altogether discarded by his successors. Career was not freely opened to talent. The public service was not looked upon as a sacred trust, but as a means of gratifying the apostate, the sycophant, the wellgroomed dandy, the great man's kinsmen, and sons of old official families. Bigotry and narrowness of outlook under Aurangzib and vice and sloth under the later Mughals, ruined the administration of the empire and dragged down the Indian people along with the falling empire.

19.7 Moral Degeneration of the Mughal Aristocracy

This moral decay was most noticeable among the nobility and it produced the greatest mischief. The character of the older nobility in the late seventeenth century was deplorable. In a mean spirit of jealousy they insulted and thwarted 'new men' drawn from the ranks and ennobled for the most brilliant public services, and yet they themselves had grown utterly worthless. We have a significant example of the moral degeneration of the Mughal peerage. The prime minister's grandson, Mirza Tafakhkhur used to sally forth from his mansion in Delhi with his ruffians, plunder the shops in the bazar, kidnap Hindu women passing through the public streets in litters or going to the river, and dishonour them; and yet there was no judge strong enough to punish him, no police to prevent such crimes. 'Every time such an occurrence was brought to the Emperor's notice by the new-settlers or official reports, he referred it to the prime minister and did nothing more.'

All the surplus produce of a fertile land under a most bounteous Providence was swept into the coffers of the Mughal nobility and pampered them in a degree of luxury not dreamt of even by kings in Persia or Central Asia. Hence, in the houses of the Delhi nobility luxury was carried to an excess. The harems of many of them were filled with immense numbers of women, of an infinite variety of races, intellect and character. Under Muslim law the sons of concubines are entitled to their patrimony equally with sons born in wedlock, and they occupy no inferior position in society. Even the sons of lawfully married wives became, at a precocious age, familiar with vice from what they saw and heard in the harem, while their mothers were insulted by the higher splendour and influence enjoyed in the same household by younger and fairer rivals of servile origin or easier virtue. The proud spirit and majestic dignity of a Cornelia are impossible in the crowded harem of a ploygamist; and without Cornelias among the mothers there cannot be Gracchi among the sons.

There was no good education, no practical training, of the sons of the Mughal nobility. They were too much petted by eunuchs and maid-servants and passed through a sheltered life from birth to manhood, every thorn being removed from their path by attendants. Early familiarized with vice, softened in their fibres by pleasure, they were yet taught to have an inordinately high opinion of their own wealth and importance in the scale of creation. Their domestic tutors were an unhappy class, powerless to do any good except by leave of their pupils, brow-beaten by the eunuchs (with the support of the ladies of the harem), disobeyed by the lads themselves, and forced to cultivate the arts of the courtier and the sneak, or to throw up their thankless office. The free give and take life in a public school (which hardens character and at the same time removes its angularities), the salutary discipline of training as subalterns in an orderly army, were unknown to the sons of the Mughal aristocracy. Hence, their moral decline was startingly rapid and unchecked. Most of them, and even sons of Aurangzib like Shah Alam and Kam Bakhs, were beyond correction. As Aurangzib, worn out with giving them unheeded counsels, cries out in despair, 'I have become a babbler by talking and talking; but none of you have taken heed from my words.'

In addition to unbridled sexual licence and secret drinking and gambling, many members of the nobility and the middle class were tainted by pederasty, a vice from which many of the so-called saints were not free. All Aurangzib's prohibitions and all the activity of his Censors of Public Morals failed to hold the Mughal aristocracy back from drink. The freak pleasures and queer fancies of some of the nobles are noticed in the contemporary accounts. (Manucci, iv. 254–6, 262.)

19.8 Popular Superstitions

All classes alike were sunk in the densest superstition. Astrology governed every act of life among rich and poor alike. Relic worship was universal among Hindus and Muhammadans alike. Even the orthodox Aurangzib adored and walked devoutly round the pretended footprints and hair of the Prophet Muhammad (*asar-i-sharif*), as if these were representations of the Deity. It is difficult to distinguish between his attitude towards them and a Hindu's worship of Vishnu's footmarks on stone. Man-worship of the grossest form degraded the character of the masses. Besides the adoration of *gurus* and *mohants* by Hindus and Sikhs, the Muslims, equally with the members of those two creeds, venerated saints and religious mendicants, and besought them to work miracles, and give them amulets, spells or marvellous medicines. Pretended magicians did a roaring trade in these things, as well as in the philosopher's stone,—being patronized by the nobles as well as the common people. Alchemy was believed to be an exact science, and men of the highest status and education supported and encouraged the professors of this art, even undertaking to introduce them to the Emperor.

The darker aspect of the subject was not wanting, and we read of human sacrifice being performed to aid the quest for gold and the *elixir vitoe*, though it was criminal in law and punished whenever detected. Some Muhammadan doctors used human fat to cure their patients. Hindu superstition is further illustrated by the worship of long-armed men as incarnations of the monkey-god Hanuman.

As a natural consequence of their ignorance and pride, all classes felt contempt for foreigners. It is true that European gun-founders, artillerymen and doctors (a few) were patronized by the wealthy, because their superior efficiency had been demonstrated before their eyes; and European objects of luxury were eagerly bought. But no attempt was made by any Indian noble or scholar to learn European language,[2] arts or military system. A modern Indian nationalist will best realize how blindly selfish the autocratic the Mughal Emperors and the Indian aristocracy of the sixteenth and seventeenth centuries were, if he considers that while they spent lakhs of Rupees every years in buying European objects of luxury or art, not a single printing-press, not even a lithographic stone, was imported either for popular education or public business.

The moral and intellectual tone of Indian society was greatly lowered by the abundance of slaves. In addition to captives of war and vanquished families reduced to bondage, men and women were sold by their parents for money in famine times, or in discharge of debts. A defaulting debtor could himself be sold with his family at the demand of his creditor. This was an ancient legal practice of the Hindus and Muhammadans alike. One way of punishing criminals of certain cases was to turn them into slaves and sell them to the public; the sale of female slaves of this class is noticed in the 'Peshwas' Diaries.' Slavery lingered down to the first quarter of the nineteenth century even in the British district of Purnia. (Martin's *Eastern India*.) People often made eunuchs of their children and sold them; Orissa and Sylhet were notorious for this offence, which was strongly condemned by Aurangzib.

---

[2] At the Mughal Court interpretation was done for European visitors by Armenians or by Europeans who knew Persian. Only one Muhammadan (Mutamad Khan, *c.* ESZA) is spoken of in Aurangzib's letters as knowing the English language. A few Shenvi Brahmans of Goa territory, who knew Portuguese, translated Marathi documents into the former language for the benefit of the English at Bombay. In Madras the English and French factories employed Brahman interpreters who knew their masters' languages besides 'Moor' (*i.e.,* Persian).

19.9 Official Bribery; Life and Character of the Official World

The educated middle class was composed entirely of officials, if we except the handful of physicians and superior priestly families. Among the traders and lesser landowners there were many who ranked with the middle class in wealth, but not in education, nor did they ever cultivate literature. The Mughal administration, both civil and military, could be carried on only with help of a vast army of clerks and accountants. Their official pay was very low (like that of the East India Company's factory 'writers' in the seventeenth century).

But the exaction of official perquisites or gratuities from men who had to get business pushed through the public offices, was the universal and admitted practice, as in Tudor and Stuart England. In addition, many officials from the highest to the lowest took bribes for doing undeserved favours or deflecting the course of justice. Official corruption was, however, admitted in society to be immoral, and was practised only in secrecy. There were many officers above corruption even in Aurangzib's reign. But the receiving and even demanding of presents by men in power was the universal rule and publicly acknowledged.[3] Even the Emperor was not exempt from it. Aurangzib asked an aspirant to a title, 'Your father gave to Shah Jahan one lakh of Rupees for adding *alif* to his title and making him *Amir* Khan. How much will you pay me for the title I am giving you?'

The ministers and influential courtiers round the Emperor's had the opportunity of reaping a golden harvest, by selling to suitors their good offices in speaking for them to the sovereign when in private attendance on his (*taqarrub*). Thus, Qabil Khan in 2 ½ years of personal attendance on Aurangzib amassed 12 lakhs of Rupees in cash, besides articles of value and a new house. They were besought and bribed with presents and money to yield their protection to officers, to conceal the shortcomings

[3] Nur Jahan's father, when prime minister under Jahangir, was shameless in demanding presents. So also was Jafar Khan, one of the earlier wazirs of Aurangzib. Jai Singh offered a purse of Rs 30,000 to the wazir for inducing the Emperor to retain him in the Deccan command. Bhimsen expresses his disgust at having to pay everybody at Court in order to get or retain a petty Civil office. The qazis grew enomously rich by taking bribes, the most notorious of them being Abdul Wahab. So also did many sadars.

(*ghaibpushi*) of the latter, to intercede for them with the Emperor (*wasila*), and in general to watch over their interests at Court during their absence. This pressure was passed from the Emperor downwards to the peasant, each social grade trying to squeeze out of the class below itself what it had to pay as present to the rank above it, the cultivator of the soil and the trader being the victims in the last resort.

The drink habit was widely prevalent among the clerks, both of the Kayastha and Khatri castes,—as well as among the Rajput soldiers. In spite of the prohibition of the *Quran,* the Muslim nobles and officers, both military and civil, were in many cases addicted to it. The Turks were specially notorious for it. The lower official class, on account of their having to do their works far away from their homes, kept small harems of local concubines. It was only the annihilation of distance by railways and the moral reform effected by English education and theistic religious movements in the late nineteenth century, that put an end to this general immorality.

The clerks, both Hindus and Muhammadans, formed a brotherhood bound together by community of duties and interests, education and ideals, social life and even vices. The official world was inspired by intense hatred and contempt for intruders into its preserve. Officers were expected to be reserved for old families of clerks and accountants. Any official who was not a 'hereditary servant' (*khanahzad*) of State but had sprung from the ranks, was despised as a *novum homo* used to be in the official world of the dying republic of Rome. This attitude was universal, from the higher nobility to the petty clerks.

19.10 The Purity and Simple Delights of the Life of the Masses

The above picture of social life in Mughal India appears very dark, and must be declared incomplete and therefore untrue, if we do not consider certain other aspects of it. We are bound to admit that among the teeming millions of the Indian people domestic life was pure and not without its simple colour and joys. This virtue alone saved the people from the doom of extinction which overtook the degenerate Romans of the later empire. We had many popular songs, ballads and stories, which assuaged the stricken human soul, taught heroic patience, and infused tenderness into the most unlettered hearts. The epic of Tulsidas, which is even now acted annually in every centre of population and recited in every Hindu home in the Hindi-speaking provinces, filled millions of our people with love of duty, manliness, and the spirit of self-sacrifice, and taught them wisdom in public and private life.

In Bengal, Tirhut, Orissa and Assam and certain other parts, the Vaishnavism taught by Shankardev and Chaitanya introduced an unwonted gentleness and fervour, and tamed the rude, if manly, savagery of the Tantric worship and animism that used to prevail there before. The seventeenth century was the great period of the expansion of this new Vaishnavism,—which was marked by enthusiastic personal devotion (as in the Christian revival movement), tenderness to children and the weak, the cultivation of literature (both Sanskrit and the current speech of the people), and the infusion of song and dance and a delicate romantic sentiment into the everyday life even of the poorest. It also bridged social gulfs and established a democracy of the spirit. Apart from this new popular religious literature, the masses[4] in different parts had their folk-songs, like the ballad of Ranjha and Hir (in the Panjjab), which went to their very hearts and relieved for a time the dead-weight of labour and political tyranny which pressed them down. The *Kirtan* or chorus-singing of religious narratives in verse (interspersed with songs) was the universal popular substitute for the sermon, the lecture, and literature throughout India—in the south as much as in the north.

The Muhammadans of that age (except the Hindi-speaking portion) had no vernacular religious poetry for the masses. But they had the annual celebrations (*urs*) of different saints at their tombs, which were attended by tens of thousands of pilgrims from distances, and where fairs were held which attracted men and women of all creeds. In addition, both sexes dwelling in cities, had their usual weekly outing to the garden-tombs of saints in the suburbs. The opportunity was utilized for pleasure rather than piety, and the spread of immorality that it caused led Aurangzib (like Firuz Shah Tughlaq before him) to issue an order for stopping the practice. But it was too popular to be put down. Visits to these periodical

[4] I have spoken of popular romance and religious poetry in the vernacular. But a vernacular literature for the *upper* classes was just missed by Aurangzib. It came into being under Wali of Aurangabad only ten years after his death.

fairs and seats of pilgrimage were the sole joy of the Indian village population, and men aad women were passionately eager to undertake them. Pilgrim-centres like Ajmir, Kulbarga, Nizam-ud-din Auliya, and Burhanpur for the Muslims, and Mathura, Allahabad, Benares, Nasik, Madura and Tanjore for the Hindus, served also to diffuse culture and to break down provincial isolation and narrowness of mental horizon.

19.11 Character of Aurangzib

In the mediaeval world, and nowhere more so than in India, the king was held responsible for the happiness of his people, and with good reason. He was God's representative on earth, invested with unlimited, unquestioned authority and the entire property in the land. Therefore, when towards the close of Aurangzib's reign all things began to go wrong, the contemporary historians turned to examine the Emperor's character, in order to account for the destruction of the empire and of public peace.

Aurangzib was brave in an unusual degree. All the Timurids, till the days of his unworthy great-grandsons, had personal courage; but in him this virtue was combined with a coldness of temperament and a calculating spirit which we have been taught to believe as the special heritage of the races of Northern Europe. Of his personal fearlessness he had given ample evidence from the age of fifteen, when he faced a furious elephant unattended, to his 87th year, when he stood in the siege trenches before Wagingera. His calm self-possession, his cheering words amidst the thickest danger, and his open defiance of death at Dharmat and Khajwa have passed into the famous things of Indian history.

In addition to possessing constitutional courage and coolness, he had early in life chosen the perils and labour of kingship as his vocation and prepared himself for this sovereign office by self-reverence, self-knowledge, and self-control. Unlike other sons of monarchs, Aurangzib was a widely read and accurate scholar, and he kept up his love of books to his dying day. Even if we pass over the many copies of the *Quran* which he wrote with his own hand, as the mechanical industry of a zealot, we cannot forget that he loved to devote the scanty leisure of a very busy ruler to reading Arabic works on jurisprudence and theology, and hunted for rare old MSS. of books like the *Nehayya*, the *Ahiya-ul-ulum*, and the *Diwan-i-Saib* with the passion of an idle bibliophile. His extensive correspondence proves his mastery of Persian poetry and Arabic sacred literature, as he was ever ready with apt quotations for embellishing almost every one of his letters. In addition to Arabic and Persian, he could speakTurki and Hindi; freely. To his initiative and patronage we owe the greatest digest of Muslim law made in India, which rightly bears his name,—the *Fatawa-i-Alamgiri* and which simplified and defined Islamic justice in India ever after.

Besides book-learning, Aurangzib had from his boyhood cultivated control of speech and action, and tact in dealing with others. As a prince, his tact, sagacity and humility made the highest nobles of his father's Court his friends; and as Emperor he displayed the same qualities in a degree which would have been remarkable even in a subject. No wonder that his contemporaries called him 'a *darvish* clad in the imperial purple.'

His private life,—dress, food and recreations,—were all extremely simple, but well-ordered. He was absolutely free from vice and even from the more innocent pleasures of the idle rich. The number of his wives fell short even of the Quaranic allowance of four,[5] and he was scrupulously faithful to wedded love. The only delicacies he relished,—the reader will smile to learn,—were the acid fruit *corinda* (*Carissa carandas*) and a sort of chewing gum called *khardali.* His industry in administration was marvellous. In addition to regularly holding daily Courts (sometimes twice a day) and Wednesday trials, he wrote orders on letters and petitions with his own hand and dictated the very language of official replies. The Italian physician Gemeli Careri thus describes the Emperor giving public audience (21 March 1695): 'He was of a low stature, with a large nose, slender and stooping with age. The whiteness of his round beard was more visible on his olive-coloured skin.... I admired to see him endorse the petitions (of those who had business) with his own hand, without spectacles, and by his cheerful smiling countenance seem to be pleased with the employment.'

Muslim historians have observed that though he died in his 90th year, he retained to the last almost all his faculties unimpaired. His memory was wonderful: 'he never forgot a face he had once seen or a word that he had once hard.' All his physical powers retained their vigour to the

[5] Dilras Banu died in 1657; Nawab Bai was relegated to a retired life at Delhi after 1660; Aurangabadi seems to have stayed with him till her death in 1685, so that Udaipuri (married about 1660) was his only companion (after Aurangabad) for the last half of his reign.

end, if we except a slight deafness of the ear, which afflicted him in old age, and a lameness of the right leg, which was due to his doctor's unskilful treatment of an accidental dislocation.

19.12 His Besetting Sin of Over-centralization: Its Disastrous Effect on the Administration

But all this long self-preparation and splendid vitality, in one sense proved his undoing, as they naturally begot in him a self-confidence and distrust of others, a passion for seeing everything carried to the highest perfection according to his own idea of it,—which urged him to order and supervise every minute detail of administration and warfare personally. This excessive interference of the head of the State kept his viceroys and commanders and even 'the men on the spot' in far off districts in perpetual tutelage; their sense of responsibility was destroyed, initiative and rapid adaptability to a changing environment could not be developed in them, and they tended to sink into lifeless puppets moved to action by the master pulling their strings from the capital. No surer means than this could have been devised for causing administrative degeneration in an extensive and diversified empire like India. High-spirited, talented and energetic officers found themselves checked, discouraged and driven to sullen inactivity. With the death of the older nobility, outspoken responsible advisers from his council, and Aurangzib in his latter years, like Napoleon I after the climax of Tilsit, could bear no contradiction, could hear no unpalatable truth, but surrounded himself with smooth-tongued sycophants and pompous echoes of his own voice. His ministers became no better than clerks passively registering his edicts.

Such a king cannot be called a political or even an administrative genius. He had merely honesty and plodding industry. He was fit to be an excellent departmental head, not a statesman initiating a new policy and legislating with prophetic foresight for moulding the life and thought of unborn generations in advance. That genius, though unlettered and often hot blooded, was Akbar alone among the Mughals of India.

Obsessed by his narrow ideal of duty and supremely ignorant of the real limitations of his character,—and not out of political cunning, as Manucci suggests,—Aurangzib practised saintly austerities and self-abasement and went regularly and even ostentatiously through all the observances of his religion. He thus became an ideal character to the

Muslim portion of his subjects. They believed him to be a saint who wrought miracles (*Alamgir, zinda pir!*) and he himself favoured this idea by his acts. Politically, therefore, Aurangzib with all his virtues was a complete failure. But the cause of the failure of his reign lay deeper than his personal character. Though it is not true that he alone caused the fall of the Mughal empire, yet he did nothing to avert it, but deliberately quickened the destructive forces always present in a rigid theocratic form of government, because he was a reactionary by instinct and no reforming statesman. And these forces I shall examine now.

19.13 True Character and Aim of the Mughal Government

The Mughal did much for India in many ways. But it failed to weld the people into a nation, or to creat a strong and enduring State.

The glitter of gems and gold in the Taj Mahal or the Peacock Throne, ought not to blind us to the fact that in Mughal India man was considered vile;—the mass of the people had no economic liberty, no indefeasible right to justice or personal freedom, when their oppressor was a noble or high official or landowner; political rights were not dreamt of. While the nation at large was no better than human sheep, the status of the nobles was hardly any higher under a strong and clever king; they had no assured constitutional position, because a constitution did not exist in the scheme of government, nor even had they full right to their material acquisitions. All depended upon the will of the autocrat on the throne. The Government was in effect despotism tempered by revolution or the fear of revolution. The whole power and all the resources of a country produce a Court,—the centre of the Court is the prince; finally, then, the ultimate product of all this gathered life is the self-sufficiency of the sovereign.

In Mughal India, as in all other absolute monarchies, popular happiness even under the best of sovereigns was unstable, because it depended upon the character of one man. 'The Mughal system of education and training entirely failed to maintain a line of promising heirs-apparent.... As the princes grew up, the jealousy of rival queens forbade their taking a leading part in the politics of the capital.... A prince who took his proper part in the council of the State was suspected of intriguing against the monarch.... Hereditary succession is only tolerable under a system where the responsibility falls on a ministry, which screens the viciousness or incompetence of the occupant of the throne.' 'Such a ministry the Mughals were never able to organize. The monarch was obliged to fall back on the mob of adventurers who crowded round his *darbar*,... whose function was more to amuse their master than to act as a modern Cabinet.... It was never the Mughal policy to foster the growth of a hereditary aristocracy.' (Crooke).

By its theory, Islamic Government is military rule—the people are the faithful soldiers of Islam, the Emperor (*Khalifa*) is their commander. In an army it is not for the officers, any more than for the privates, to reason why or to seek reply from the supreme leader. The Khalifa-Emperor is the silhouette of God (*zill-subhani*), and is God's Court there is no 'why or how.' No more could there be in the Padishah's administration, which was a sample of God's Court (*namuna-i-darbar-i-ilahi*). By the basic principle of Islamic Government, the Hindus and other unbelievers were admittedly outside the pale of the nation. But even the dominant sect, the Muslims, did not form a nation; they constituted a military brotherhood, a perpetual camp of soldiers.

19.14 Difference in Life and Ideal Makes Fusion of Hindus and Muhammadans Impossible

According to the root principles of Muslim polity, there can be no political rights for minorities, the nation must be merged in the dominant sect, and a community homogeneous in creed and social life must be created by crushing out all divergent forms of faith, opinion and life. The nation as a purely political creation was inconceivable and impossible in such a state of things. The evil was aggravated by the fact that in India the politically depressed class or 'official minority' was a numerical majority, outnumbering the dominant sect as three to one, and at the same time economically better qualified, stronger in capital and wealth-producing power, and not inferior in intellect or physical vigour.

No fusion between the two classes was possible even with the passage of centuries, as they differed like opposite poles in ideal and life. The Hindu is solitary, passive, other-worldly; his highest aim is self-realization, the attainment of personal salvation by individual effort, private devotions, and lonely austerities. To him birth is a misfortune and his fellow-beings so many sources of distraction from his one true goal. Not by enjoyment of God's gifts but by renunciation, not by joyous expansion but by repression of emotion, is he to attain to true bliss. The Muslim, on the other hand, is taught to feel that he is nothing if not a soldier of the militant force of Islam; he must pray in congregation; he must give proof of the sincerity of his faith by undertaking *jihad* or active exertion for the spread of his religion and the destruction of unbelief among other men. He is a missionary, and cannot be indifferent to the welfare of his promoting the salvation of others by all means at his command, physical as much as spiritual. Then, again, Islam boldly avows that it is good for us to be here, that God has given the world to the faithful as an inheritance for their enjoyment.

The practical outlook and social solidarity of the Muslims have made them develop the arts and civilization (excepting literature) in a much higher degree than the Hindus; their pleasures are of a more varied and elegant kind, and the Hindu aristocracy in Mughal times were only clumsy imitators of the Muslim peers. The general type of Muhammadans (excepting beggars and menial labourers) are more refined and accustomed to a costlier mode of life, while Hindus of the corresponding classes, even when rich, are grosser and less cultured. The lower classes of the Hindus, however, are distinctly cleaner and more intellectual than Muslims of the same grades of life.

19.15 Hindus Politically Depressed and Degraded under Aurangzib

Apart from the restrictions about food, difference of religious doctrine and ritual, rules forbidding intermarriage, etc., this polar difference in their outlook upon life made a fusion between Hindus and Muslims impossible. In addition to these, the Quranic polity made life intolerable for the Hindus under orthodox Muhammadan rule. Aurangzib furnishes the best example of the effects of that polity when carried to its logical conclusions by a king of exemplary morality and religious zeal, without fear or favour in discharging what he held to be his duty as the first servant of God. Schools of Hindu learning were broken up by him, Hindu places of worship were demolished, Hindu fairs were forbidden, the Hindu population was subjected to special fiscal burdens in addition to being made to bear a public badge of inferiority; and the service of the State was closed to them, as we have seen in Ch. VIII.

Thus, the only life that the Hindu could lead under Aurangzib was a life deprived of the light of knowledge, deprived of the consolations of religion, deprived of social union and public rejoicing, of wealth and the self-confidence that is begotten by the free exercise of natural activities and use of opportunities,—in short, a life exposed to contsant public humiliation and political disabilities. Heaven and earth alike were closed to him as long as he remained a Hindu. Hence, the effect of Aurangzib's reign was not only to goad the Hindus into constant revolt and disturbances but also to make them deteriorate in intellect, organization, and economic resources, and thereby weaken the State of which they formed more than two-thirds of the manpower.

19.16 Decline of the Muslims in India: Its Causes

The Muslim portion of the population, too, did not prosper under such a polity, though for a different reason. The Turks are soldiers and nothing else; their manhood is a naturally embodied army, and war is their only profession. A standing army as necessarily prevented from cultivating continuous domestic life. The ruling race among the so-called Mughals were really Turks. Hence, Muslim society in the Mughal period, in many of its civilian ranks also, frequently displayed garrison manners, as the organisation of their Government was of a military type and the soldiers set the tone to society.

The intellectual decline of the Muslims was hastened by the peculiar position of the faithful in India. They had made India their permanent home; many of them were Indians by race; and all had become so in their personal appearance, thoughts, manners and customs. And yet their religious teachers urged them to look back to ancient Arabia and drew their mental sustenance from the far off age of the Prophet. The language of their religion must be Arabic, which not one on a hundred among the Muslims of India fully understood; their cultural language was Persian, which a few more learnt with difficult and used with an impurity that excited the laughter and scorn of the Persian-born. The Indian Muslim considered it beneath his dignity (till well into the eighteenth century) to use the vernacular for literary purposes. Hence, the immense majority of this sect were without any literature of their own; their education was hampered and their private life (except in the case of the few who could use Persian freely) was deprived of intellectual joys. They could not have even a *living* growing religious literature. Hindustani amatory or devotional songs and Sufi verses in Persian were not adequate instruments for the diffusion of culture or the removal of general ignorance among a whole community.

Thus, the orthodox Muslim ever felt that he was in India, but not of it. He durst not, for peril to his soul,—so he was taught,—strike his roots deep into his native soil. He must not take to his heart its traditions, language and cultural products; he must import these from Persia and Arabia. Even his civil and criminal law must be derived from the writings of jurists and the decisions of judges in Baghdad or Cairo. The Muslim in India was an intellectual exotic; he could not adapt himself to his environment. The Quranic precepts for the guidance of civil society and the regulation of human conduct and relations, were framed in a far off age for a nomadic people. It was absurd, so a rationalist like Akbar argued, that they should be considered binding on men of the sixteenth or seventeenth century living in a country that had nothing in common with Arabia.

The intellectual vacuity caused by this unnatural straining after a foreign and impracticable ideal, not only arrested the mental and social progress of the Indian Muslims, but also made their hearts a fertile soil for noxious weeds. The eternal human craving for a personal religion, for a living faith, could not be satisfied by repeating an Arabic book by rote (*hifz-i-kalamullah*), or by going through one monotonous physical drill five times a day in a public gathering (*jamait*). The thirsty soul turned to every fabled living saint in its neighbourhood and to the greedy successors in attendance at the tombs of famous saints of the past,—both of whom were believed to be capital of working miracles.

The racial character of the Semitic people who created the Quran and Sunni Canon Law was essentially different from that of the Indians, and the mere fact of a body of the latter race having accepted the religion of the Arabs could not counteract this ethnic difference. These were insurmountable handicaps, to Indian Islam.

19.17 Deterioration and Inherent Weakness of Hindu Society

The Hindus of mediaeval India presented an equally unhappy spectacle. They could not possibly form a nation, or even one compact sect.

A social solidarity like that of the Muhammadans was inconceivable among a people divided into countless mutually exclusive castes, with their rancorous disputes about rights to the sacred thread and the Vedic chant, access to public water-supplies and temples, besides *touchability*, and in Southern India also *approachability*. And time and prosperity seemed only to aggravate these differences. 'Caste grows by fission', and the multiplication of new sub-castes was in active progress through the operation of internal forces during Muhammadan rule, dividing and weakening Hindu society still further.

No enlightened or patriotic priesthood arose to save the Hindu peoples. The separatist tendency is as strong in their religion as in their society; and, indeed, an organized priesthood or State Church is opposed to the root principles of the Hindu scheme of salvation. Stray sheep running after stray shepherds fall easy victims to the quack and the voluptuary. Even if we pass over the degrading forms of man-worship that marked the religious practices of the Vallabhacharya, Kartabhaja and other sects of *guru*-adorers, or the licentiousness promoted by temple dancers (*devadasis* or *muralis*) and small prurient esoteric sects, and turn our eyes to the ordinary idol-worship of the millions, we find the priesthood bringing their worshippers down to the lowest intellectual level by holding up to their adoration a god who eats, sleeps, falls ill of fever (as Jagannath does for a week every year), or pursues amorous dalliances which a Nawab of Oudh might envy or a Qutb Shah imitate in his own harem. Reform was possible only outside the regular Hindu Church followed by the masses,—i.e., among the small non-conforming sects, where men were prepared to leave all things and follow truth; but, even there, only during the first generation or two after their foundation, before they too sank into gross *guru*-worship.

19.18 How Hindus and Muslims Lived Together in India: Occasional Union, Latent Danger or Fight

In spite of what has been said before, Hindu and Muhammadan societies often touched each other at certain points. The true ideals of both creeds were the same, namely, the worship of one Supreme Being, abstinence from earthly joys, tenderness to all creatures. But bigots and the mass of ordinary people could not rise to such a high plane of thought. Muslim saints, famous for striking acts of self-mortification or miracle-working power, were often adored by Hindu princes and people. Similarly, the cult of Sufism brought members of the two sects together in friendly communion. Sufism, however, was not so much a living creed as an emotional-intellectual enjoyment, which affected the select few, being confined to the educated and official classes.

The masses could not appreciate such lofty ideas as mystic pantheism and the universal brotherhood of man. Fanatics had greater sway over their hearts than philosophers. The lower classes, after some fighting between Hindus and Muslims or Shias and Sunnis (the forces of Government being always on the side of the orthodox creed),—at last came to a settlement in every locality, recognizing the boundaries rights and limitations of each creed on a basis which acquired the sacredness of custom with the passage of time. Thus, they lived amicably within their own narrow limits. But this religious truce held good only so long as the local society was static. With the least change in the relative strength of the two sects or in their temper, with the visit of an active orthodox preacher from outside or the accession of a bigot to the throne, the sleeping volcano of mob passions would again wake to fury. Examples of it are furnished by the massacre of the Shias at Srinagar in 1685, the destruction and pollution of Hindu temples by Aurangzib, the plucking out of the *jiziya*-collector's beard by Rajputs in Malwa, and retaliation on mosques by some Rathor and Maratha princes of high spirit. Indian society was, therefore, in a state of unstable equilibrium in every centre of mixed population in Aurangzib'g reign.

19.19 Indian Peoples Lack the Spirit of Progress; Hence Their Decline

Finally, the Indian people of the Mughal age, both Hindus and Muslims, were stationary, prone to venerate the wisdom of their ancestors and to look down upon the latest age as the worst. Experiment and free thought were hence apt to be condemned as an impious questioning of sacred authority and an insolent up of our own puny intellect against that of the sages of yore. The progressive spirit died out of India at the death of Akbar. Then followed a stationary civilization, and such a civilization is bound to decay as it finds improvement impossible.

'The rigidity of Islam has enabled its followers in all lands to succeed up to a certain point. But there they have stopped, while progress is the law of life in the living world. While Europe has been steadily advancing, the stationary East has been relatively falling back, and every year that passes increases the distance between Europe and Asia in knowledge, organization, accumulated resources, and acquired capacity, and makes it increasingly difficult for the Asiatics to compete with the Europeans. The English conquest of the Mughal empire is only a part of the inevitable domination of all Africa and Asia by the European nations,—which is only another way of saying that the progressive races are supplanting the conservatives ones, just as enterprising families are constantly replacing sleepy self-satisfier ones in the leadership of our own society.' [My *Mughal Administration,* Ch. 15 § 11.]

19.20 The Significance of Aurangzib's Reign: How an Indian Nationality can be Formed

The detailed study of this long and strenuous reign of fifty years drives one truth home into our minds. If India is ever to be the home of a nation able to keep peace within and guard the frontiers, develop the economic resources of the country and promote art and science, then both Hinduism and Islam must die and be born again. Each of these creeds must pass through a rigorous vigil and penance, each must be purified and rejuvenated under the sway of reason and science. That such a rebirth of Islam is not impossible, has been demonstrated in our own days by the conqueror of Smyrna. Ghazi Mustafa Kamal Pasha has proved that the greatest Muslim State of the age can secularize its constitution, abolish polygamy and the servile seclusion of women, grant political equality to all creeds, and yet not cease to be a land of Islam.

But Aurangzib did not attempt such an ideal, even though his subjects formed a very composite population, even though the entire Indian world lay at his feet and he had no European rivals hungrily watching to seize his kingdom. On the contrary, he deliberately undid the beginnings of such a national and rational policy which Akbar had set on foot.

History when rightly read is a justification of Providence, a revelation of a great purpose fulfilled in time. The failure of an ideal Muslim king like Aurangzib, with all the advantages he possessed at his accession and his high moral character and training,—is, therefore, the clearest proof the world can afford of the eternal truth that there cannot be a great or lasting empire without a great *people,* that no people can be great unless it learns to form a compact *nation* with equal rights and opportunities for all,—a nation the component parts of which are homogeneous, agreeing in all essential points of life and thought, but freely tolerating individual differences in minor points and private life, recognizing individual liberty as the basis of communal liberty,—a nation whose administration is solely bent upon promoting national, as opposed to parochial or sectarian interests,—and a society which pursues knowledge without fear, without cessation, without bounds. It is only in that pure light of goodness and truth that an Indian nationality can grow to the full stature of its being.

20 The Empire of Aurangzib: Its Resources, Trade and Administrative System

20.1 The Empire: Its Extent and Revenue

At the death of Aurangzib (1707), his empire consisted of 21 *subahs* or separate provinces, of which 14 were situated in Hindustan or Northern India, six in the Deccan, and one (namely, Kabul) in what now forms Afghanistan. Their names are:

(*i*) *Subahs of Hindustan*—Agra, Ajmir, Allahabad, Bengal, Bihar, Delhi, Gujrat, Kashmir, Lahore, Malwa, Multan, Orissa, Oudh, and Tatta (or Sindh).

(*ii*) *Subahs of the Deccan*—Khandesh, Berar, Aurangabad (old Ahmadnagar), Bidar (old Telingana), Bijapur, and Haidarabad. A century earlier, *i.e.,* at the end of Akbar's reign (1605), the Mughal empire had embraced all the fourteen subahs of Hindustan and only the first two of the above provinces of the Deccan,—the annexation of Ahmadnagar by Akbar being nominal. Qandahar or South Afghanistan was long entered in the official records as a subah of the Mughal empire, but it was in name only, as it frequently changed hands between the kings of Persia and Delhi and was finally lost by the Mughals in 1649; it was even at the best of times a barren possession and a very losing concern. Kabul or North Afghanistan, though held by the Mughal Emperors till its annexation by Nadir Shah (1739), had a revenue of only 20 lakhs of Rupees in Akbar's time and 40 lakhs in Aurangzib's reign, much of which was often unrealized. So, we shall leave these two provinces of Afghanistan out of our consideration in this chapter.

The Mughal empire under Aurangzib included in the north Kashmir and all Afghanistan south of the Hindukush; on the south-west a line 60 km (36 miles) south of Ghazni separated it from the Persian kingdom. On the west-coast it stretched in theory up to the northern frontier of Goa and inland to Belgaon (in the Bombay Karnatak or Kanara) and the Tungabhadra river. Thereafter the boundary passed west to east in a disputed and ever shifting line through the centre of Mysore, dipping south-eastwards to the Kolerun river (north of Tanjore). In the extreme north-east, the river Monas (west of Gauhati) divided the empire from the independent kingdom of Assam. But it should be always borne in mind that in the south-west, south and south-east, *i.e.*, throughout Maharashtra, Kanara, Mysore and the Eastern Karnatak, the Emperor's rule was disputed and most places had to obey a double set of masters or spoliators (*do-amli*),—as the English and French factory records painfully illustrate.

Excluding Afghanistan, the Mughal empire had a revenue of Rupees of 13 *krores* and 21 *lakhs* under Akbar, and 33 *krores* and 25 *lakhs* under Aurangzib. This was the standard or maximum State demand from land, but this amount was never fully realized and the actual collection often fell very short of it. This figure stood for the land revenue alone and did not include the proceeds of taxes like the *zakat* (one-fortieth of the annual income of Muslims, to be spent solely in religious charity) and *jiziya.* A rough idea of the proportion of the different sources of State-income can be formed from the figures for Gujrat in Aurangzib's reign:—land revenue Rs 113 lakhs, *jiziya* 5 lakhs, custom-duties of Surat port alone 12 lakhs per annum. (The other ports did negligible trade, except Masulipatam and Hughli towards the end of the reign.) The amounts of land held as military fief (*Jagir*) and Crownland (*khalsa sharifa*) can be judged from the following figures (*circa* 1690): land revenue assessed on *jagirs* 27.64 krores and on *khalsa* 5.81 krores of Rupees (for the whole empire).

20.2 The Official Peerage

The government both civil and military was conducted by means of officials entered in the army-list and graded in successive ranks (*mansab*) from commanders of (nominal) twenty thousand horse down to commanders of twenty (in Akbar's reign ten) men only.

Of these, all who held any grade from 3 *hazari* upwards were called grandees *(umara-i-azam)* or grand commanders (popularly styled *'umdat-ul-mulk* or *'umda'*), those between 500 and 2,500 *zat* as simply *umara,* and those below the command of 500 horse (nominal) were styled *mansabdars* or officers.

Number of	*c.* 1596	*c.* 1620	1647	*c.* 1690
Grandees *(i.e., 3-hazari* and upwards including the princes)	63	112	99	–
Total, including both *umara & mansabdars*	1,803	2,945	8,000	14,449

From the above we can see the enormous inflation of the army-list under Aurangzib and the heavy financial burden that it produced.

Out of the 14,449 mansabdars under Aurangzib, about 7,000 were *jagirdars* and 7,450 were *naqdi* (or paid in cash), *i.e.,* nearly half and half. The annual salary and allowances of the mansabdars, including the pay of their troops (who under Shah Jahan's rule, had to be actually at least one-fourth of the nominal number of their grade) were as follows, for the first class in each grade:

7-hazari............3.5 lakhs of Rs
5-hazari............2.5 „
Hazari ....half a lakh „
Commander of twenty.........Rs 1.000.

The actual armed strength of the empire in 1647 was 2 lakhs of troopers brought to the muster and branding.

8 thousand *mansabdars,*
7 thousand *ahadis* and *barqandazes,*
1,85,000 *tabinan* or additional troopers of the princes, *umara* and *mansabdars,—and*
40,000 foot-musketeers, gunners, and rocket-men.

These numbers underwent a still further increase with Aurangzib's fresh warfare and annexations in the Deccan, till at last his finances hopelessly broke down under the weight of his army bill.

In the Mughal empire there prevailed what Bernier calls 'the barbarous and ancient custom' of the sovereign confiscating the property of every one who died in his service. In other words, there was no hereditary property among the nobility, but the Emperor always took possession of the treasures and houses of his noblemen on their death and made a gift to their children of only what he pleased; the heirs had no legal right to their fathers' legacy. The result was very harmful to the State and to Indian civilization. The nobles lived extravagantly and squandered their all on luxury, as they knew that they could leave nothing to their family and that the Emperor alone would profit by their frugality. Again, the insecurity of the nobles' fortunes prevented the accumulation of private capital and the economic growth of the country which depends on capital. The general level of civilization and culture, too, was lowered, because each generation had to work from the bottom upwards, instead of benefiting by the acquisitions and progress achieved by its predecessor.

The political effect of this escheat system was most disastrous; it prevented India from having one of the strongest checks on royal autocracy, namely, an independent hereditary peerage, whose position and wealth did not depend on the king's favour in every generation and who could therefore afford to be bold in their opposition to royal tyranny. It also made the Mughal nobility a selfish band, prompt in deserting to the winning side in every war of succession or foreign invasion, because they knew that their lands and even personal property were not legally assured to them, but depended solely on the pleasure of the *de facto* king. Mediaeval India had no independent nobility or powerful trading class to act as a barrier between the omnipotent Emperor at the top and the countless poor peasants and labourers at the bottom. Such a Government is most unstable and unsound.

20.3 Manufactures and Trade

The Mughal Government was its own manufacturer, in State factories called *kar-khanahs,* for large quantities and an immense variety of articles. These have been described in detail in my book *Mughal Administration,* Ch. X ('State Industries'). The private industries of the various provinces are enumerated separately in my *India of Aurangzib.* Foreign trade, however, occupied a negligible position on the economics of the Mughal empire, on account of its small volume,—the total yield of the import duty being probably less than 30 lakhs of Rupees a year, while the land revenue brought to the State one hundred and eleven times that amount. As Bernier acutely observes: 'Nor can the commerce of a country so governed be conducted with the activity and success that we witness in Europe.... In case, indeed, where the merchant is protected by a military man of rank, he may be induced to embark in commercial enterprises; but still he must be the slave of his patron, who will exact whatever terms he pleases as the price of his protection.'

The value of the Indian products exported by the English E.I. Company during the first sixty years of its trade (1612–72), did not average more than a hundred thousand pounds (or eight lakhs of Rupees) per annum. (In 1681 it rose to £230,000 for Bengal alone). While the trade of the Dutch Company with India was at this time probably at least as large as that of the English Company, the trade of the Portuguese was certainly smaller. There is no evidence to show that any very considerable volume of trade by sea was in the hands of native merchants, but a small amount of traffic continued to be carried on by the overland route to Persia and Turkey (and also Tibet). The fact is that the people of India at that time obtained little by international exchange except precious metals together with a few articles of luxury enjoyed by the rich. These imports were in the main paid for by her export of cotton goods, supplemented by a small variety of raw produce such as pepper, indigo, and saltpetre. India was thus economically almost self-supporting. (G.J. Hamilton, 32–33).

The low range of import duties (namely, 3½ per cent *ad valorem,* of which 1 per cent was for the *jiziya*) imposed by the Mughal Emperors proves that there was a general desire to encourage trade. There was no question of an attempt to protect native manufactures (by prohibitive import duties). The export trade seems to have been approved (by the Delhi Government) as the recognized means for obtaining a supply of the precious metals and of articles of luxury consumed at the Court. (G. J. Hamilton, 20).

The English E.I. Co.'s trade with the East during the first half of the seventeenth century was to a large extent confined to dealings in five classes of goods. In the English market the products most sought for were the *spices* from the Archipelago and the Spice Islands, the raw *silk* of Persia, and the *saltpetre* and *indigo* of India. No doubt a fair quantity of the finer *cotton* cloths, as also a small quantity of manufactured silk goods were imported into England. But for the most part of the Company's purchases of cotton goods were made not for import into England, but for the markets of the Further East and of Persia. India, indeed, possessed almost a monopoly in the manufacture of cotton goods, in foreign markets,... but she had not even a considerable export trade in silk goods. Raw silk came (to England) chiefly from Persia and from China, while even in the first half of the seventeenth century, China supplied the greater part of the manufactured silk articles imported into England. (G. J. Hamilton, 31–32).

The chief imports into India in the Mughal times were *silver* and *gold* (in specie), and to a lesser extent *copper* and *lead.* 'We were practically dependent upon foreign countries for these metals, though not for iron and steel,—which last were, however, imported as cheaper. For high class woolen clothing Europe (notably France) was our sole supplier, and large quantities of imported broadcloths and other woolen fabrics (Arabic *saqarlat,* scarlet) were consumed in India by the Court and the rich. Next in value were horse, of which large numbers came by ship from the Persian Gulf and by the land-route from Khurasan Central Asia and Kabul through the north-western passes. Hill ponies (called *tangan* or *gunt*) were imported from the Eastern Himalayan States, Tibet and Bhutan, through Bengal, Kuch Bihar, Morang and Oudh. Large quantities of fruits—fresh in winter and dry all the year round, were consumed in Upper India, and came from Central Asia, Afghanistan and Persia. Spices (such as cloves, nutmegs, cinnamon and cardamom) were supplied by the Dutch from the Spice Islands, which had a monopoly of these commodities. Articles of luxury like musk and porcelain came from China, pearls from Bahrain (Persian Gulf) and Ceylon, elephants from Pegu and Ceylon, superior brands of tobacco from America, glass-ware, wine and curiosities from Europe, and slaves from Abyssinia; but the quantity of these was very small, as befitted their high price and limited consumption. The European Companies very occasionally sold artillery and munitions (in small quantities) to our local rulers, in their sudden need, but there was no regular trade in these things and, indeed, the transactions were mostly done in secret as unlawful. A thin stream of traffic entered India from the Himalayan regions by way of Oudh (and later through Patna); they brought to us, loaded on ponies and sheep(!), small quantities of gold, copper, musk and the tail of the yak cow (for use as fans or fly-whiskers), and also spare hill-ponies; and after selling them took back salt, cotton, glass-ware, etc. European paper, imported by the Portuguese and later by the Dutch (but still popularly called 'Portugal paper'), was largely consumed by the independent Sultans of the Deccan. But the Mughal Emperors had their own factories for very fine paper (now known in Europe as 'India paper') in Kashmir and a few other places, while the needs of ordinary office work and private persons were supplied by a class of Muslim manufacturers (called *kaghazis*) who plied their industry in every town, with a special suburb (*pura*) of their own near the capitals.

Our most important exports in those days were common cotton cloth (called *calicoes*), either plain or printed (*chintz*), which were largely consumed in the Indian Archipelago, and towards the close of the seventeenth century in England also,—muslin or very fine cotton fabrics,—and raw products like saltpetre, indigo, silk and pepper (besides certain other cooking spices). Small quantities of white sugar were exported from Hughli, diamonds and rubies *via* Masulipatam, slaves from Bengal and Madras, and also cotton yarn for making candle-wicks in England. Towards the end of the century silk taffetas and brocades began to be exported in larger quantities, and a distinct improvement in the dyeing and weaving of silk was effected in Bengal by the English Company. The whole Madras coast from Masulipatam to Pondicherry, (and next, but far behind it, Kanara or the country from Hubli to Karwar) were the seats of the most productive cotton industry in India; but the wars following the overthrow of the Golkonda sultanate and the rise of the Marathas, completely ruined these regions and the primacy in cotton manufacture passed on to Bengal at the beginning of the eighteenth century.

20.4 The Administrative System

The Muslim State was essentially a military Government and depended for its very existence on the absolute authority of the monarch, who was also the supreme Commander of the Faithful in war. He had no regular council of ministers. The *wazir* or *dewan* was the highest officer below the Emperor, and the other ministers were in no sense his colleagues but admittedly inferior to him. Many important questions were decided by the Emperor and the wazir alone without the knowledge of the other ministers. But none of the ministers, not even the wazir himself, could serve as a check on the royal will; their office depended entirely on his caprice. They, therefore, could not form a Cabinet in the modern sense of the term. Every Muslim sovereign is, in strict theory, the head of the Church and the State alike; he is the *khalifa of the age to his subjects.*

The chief departments of the Mughal administration were:

1. The Exchequer and Revenue (under the *Diwan* or Chancellor).
2. The Imperial Household (under the *Khan-i-saman* or High Steward).
3. The Pay and Accounts office (under the *Bakhshi* or Paymaster).
4. Canon Law (under the *Qazi of Qazis*).
5. Religious endowments and charity (under the *Sadr of Sadrs*).
6. Censorship of Public Morals (under the *Muhtasib*).

   Inferior to these, but ranking almost like departments, were—
7. The Artillery (under the *Mir Atish*), and
8. Intelligence and Posts (under the *Darogha of Dakchauki*).

The Imperial Diwan received all revenue papers and despatches from the provinces and field armies, and decided all questions connected with the collection or assessment of the revenue. He also appointed and controlled the diwans of all the provinces. All orders of payment had to be signed by him. He wrote letters 'by order' (*hasb-ul-hukm*) in his own person to communicate the Emperor's wishes, and often drafted royal letters to important persons and foreign rulers.

The salary bills of all officers—both civil and military (because both were alike *mansabdars*)—had to be calculated and passed by the Bakhshi, and in the case of a field army the payment also was made through his department. At the end of Aurangzib's reign, owing to the great expansion of the empire, there were one Chief Bakhshi (called the First Bakhshi) and three assistants, called the 2nd, 3rd and 4th Bakhshis. Each field army was placed under a general appointed for the occasion. Though at several periods we find officers invested with the title of *sipah salar* or 'chief of the army,' it was only a title of honour and these officers, did not really command the entire Mughal army. The Emperor alone was the commander-in-chief.

The Khan-i-saman or High Steward was the head of the Emperor's household department; he controlled all the personal servants of the Emperor, supervised his daily expenditure, meals, stores, etc., and accompanied him during his journeys. The State factories or *karkhanahs* were managed and paid by him.

The Emperor was theoretically the highest judge in the realm, and used to try cases personally every Wednesday. But the court held by him was a tribunal of the highest appeal rather than a court of first instance. The Qazi was the chief judge in all criminal suits of the Muslims and most civil cases, and tried them according to Muslim law, assisted by a *mufti*, who stated the abstract law bearing on the case after consulting Arabic books on jurisprudence, while the Qazi pronounced the sentence.

The imperial Qazi, called the *Qazi-ul-quzat*, always accompanied the Emperor, and appointed and dismissed the local qazis of the cities and large villages in every province.

The Chief Sadr (called the *Sadr-us-sadur*) was judge and supervisor of the endowments of land made by the Emperor and the princes for the support of pious men, scholars and monks. It was his duty to see that such grants were applied to their proper purpose and also to scrutinize fresh applications for grants. He was also the Emperor's almoner and had the distribution of the charity fund of the State. The provincial sadrs were appointed and supervised by him.

It was the duty of the *Muhtasib* to regulate the lives of the people in strict accordance with the Quranic rules, and to enforce the Prophet's commands by putting down the drinking of distilled spirits, *bhang* and other liquid intoxicants, gambling and the practice of immorality as a profession or in public. The punishment of heretical opinions, blasphemy against the Prophet, and neglect of the five daily prayers or of the fast during the month of Ramzan, also lay within his province. The demolition of newly built temples was entrusted to him.

The administrative agency in the provinces of the Mughal empire was an exact miniature of the Central Government. There were the governor (officially styled *nazim* and popularly *subahdar*), the *diwan, bakhshi, qazi, sadr, buyutat* (keeper of Government property and official trustee), and the *muhtasib*, but no *Khan-i-saman*. Each *subahdar* tried to play the Emperor within his own jurisdiction.

The provinical administration was concentrated in its chief town. At important centres or sub-divisions there were *faujdars* to maintain order, punish rebels and wrongdoers, and assist in the collection of revenue when opposed. The villages were neglected and, either contemptuously or through insufficiency of official staff, left to live their own lives, often as small self-governing units or 'village communities.'

In the big cities the *kotwal* or prefect of police not only enforced law and order, but had also to discharge many functions of a modern municipality, control the markets (weights and prices), and maintain the Quranic rules of morality.

The Central Government kept itself informed of the occurrences in all parts of the country by means of spies and news-reporters, both public and secret. These agents formed four classes: *waqai-navis, swanih-nigar, khufia-navis* (secret letter-writer), and *harkarah* (spy and courier). They had to send reports at regular intervals. Every public office had an open reporter or diarist attached to it. All the reports reached the Emperor through the Postmaster-General (*Darogha-i-Dakchauki*).

In spite of the repeated prohibitions of the Emperors, many local officers (and even subahdars) used to exact illegal cesses (called *abwabs*) under an immense variety of heads and from all classes of artisans, traders, labourers, and people in general.

A list of 67 such *abwabs* is given with explanatory notes in my *Mughal Administration,* ch. 5. A further source of oppression was the practice of some subahdars to seize the goods of merchants in transit, pay an inadequate price or no price at all for them, and then sell these goods in the open market for their own profit (what the English traders called 'the forcing of goods') or appropriate the choice articles to their own use. Only a strong and vigilant Emperor could stop it.

Chronology

[All the dates in this book are in the Old Style or unreformed calendar. To convert them to the New Style, add ten (sometimes eleven) days.]

1618 Oct. 24, Birth of Aurangzib.
1627 Apr. 10 Birth of Shivaji.
1628 Feb. 4, Shah Jahan crowns himself. [Jahangir died on 29 Oct. 1627].
1633 May 28, Aurangzib fights an elephant.
1635 Sept.–Dec., Aurangzib commands in Bundela war.
1636 May, partition treaty between Shah Jahan and Adil Shah.
1636 July–1644 May, Aurangzib's first viceroyalty of the Deccan.
1636 Oct., Shahji Bhonsle submits to Mughals and enters Bijapur service.
1637 May 8, Aurangzib marries Dilras Banu (who d. 8 Oct. 1657).
1638 Feb. 15, Zeb-un-nisa, Aurangzib's eldest child, born, (d. 26 May 1702).
June, Aurangzib annexes Baglana.
1639 Dec. 19, Md. Sultan born, (d. 3 Dec. 1976).
1643 Oct. 4, Muazzam (Shah Alam I) born.
1644 May, Aurangzib dismissed and degraded. Is reinstated in November.
1645 Feb.–1647 Jan., Aurangzib governor of Gujrat.
1647 March 7, Dadaji Kond-dev dies; Shivaji becomes independent, gains Adil-Shahi forts.
May 25, Aurangzib reaches Balkh city; retreats in October.
1648 March–1652 July, Aurangzib governor of Multan and Sindh.
1649 May 14–Sep. 5, Aurangzib's first siege of Qandahar.
1652 May 2–July 9, Aurangzib's second siege of Qandahar.

1652–58, Aurangzib's second viceroyalty of the Deccan.

1655 Nov. 21, Qutb Shah imprisons Mir Jumla's son.

1656 Jan. 15, Shivaji annexes Javli, gains Raigarh 6 Apr-Jan., Aurangzib invades Golkonda; Mughals occupy Haidarabad 23 Jan., Aurangzib's siege *of* Golkonda Feb. 7–March 30. Peace in April.

July, Mir Jumla goes to Delhi, is appointed wazir.

Nov. 4, Md. Adil Shah dies, Ali II. succeeds.

1657 War with Bijapur: Aurangzib takes Bidar by siege 2–29 March, Kaliani 4 May–1 Aug., retreats. Oct. 4.

Sep. 6, Shah Jahan falls ill at Delhi, reaches Agra Oct. 26.

Nov. Shuja crowns himself in Bengal.

Dec. 5, Murad crowns himself, captures and robs Surat Dec. 20.

1658 Feb. 5, Aurangzib starts from Aurangabad to contest the throne.

Feb. 14, Shuja defeated at Bahadurpur by Sulaiman Shukoh.

April 15, Aurangzib and Murad defeat Jaswant at Dharmat.

May 23, *Official beginning of first year of Aur.'s reigm.*

„ 29, Dara defeated at Samugarh.

June 8 Shah Jahan made prisoner in Agra fort.

„ 25, Aurangzib imprisons Murad, (who is killed Dec. 4, 1661). July 21, Aur.'s first coronation.

1659 Jan. 5, Shuja defeated at Khajwa.

March 13, Dara defeated at Deorai.

June 5, Grand coronation of Aurangzib

„ 9, Dara and Sipihr Shukoh captured.

Aug. 30, Dara executed.

Nov. 10, Shivaji kills Afzal Khan.

1660 May 9, Shaista Khan occupies Puna, storms Chakan Aug. 15.

„ 6, Shuja flees from Dacca, which Mir Jumla occupies. (Shuja perishes in Arracan, Feb. 1661).

Dec. 27, Sulaiman Shukoh brought to Delhi as prisoner (killed May 1662).

1661 Feb. 3, Shivaji defeats Kar Talb Kh. at Umbarkhind. May, Mughals take Kalian from Shivaji.

„ 22, Persian envoy Budaq Beg interviews Aurangzib

Dec. 19, Mir Jumla captures Kuch Bihar city.

1662 March 17, Mir Jumla captures Garhgaon, capital of Assam.
May 12, Aurangzib falls ill, complete recovery on June 24.
1663 Jan. 1, Assam king makes treaty with Mir Jumla, who begins retreat on Jan. 10 but dies on Mar. 31.
April 5, Shivaji's night attack on Shaista Khan.
May 14—Aurangzib 16, Aurangzib visits Kashmir.
1664 Jan. 6–10, Shivaji loots Surat (first time)
„ 23, Shahji Bhonsle dies.
1665 March 30, Jai Singh begins siege of Purandar; Shiva interviews Jai Singh 11 June, Treaty of Purandar 13 June.
April 10, Aurangzib doubles custom duty on Hindus.
Nov. 20, Jai Singh starts on invasion of Bijapuf, begins retreat 5 Jan. 1666; dies 28 Aug. 1667.
1666 Jan. 22, Shah Jahan dies.
„ 26 Shaista Kh. conquers Chatgaon
May 12, Shivaji is presented to Aurangzib, escapes 19 Aug., returns to Rajgarh 12 Sep. 1666., submits to Mughals c. Sep. 1667.
1667 Feb. 24, Kam Bakhsh born.
March, Yusufzai rebellion in Peshawar.
1668 Feb. Aurangzib forbids music at Court.
„ Aurangzib recognizes Shivaji as a *Rajah.*
1669 April 9, Aurangzib orders temple destruction throughout his realm; Vishwanath temple of Benares destroyed in Aug., Keshav temple of Mathura in Jan, next.
1670 c. Jan. 1, Shivaji renews war with Mughals, recovers his forts, raids extensively.
Oct. 3–5, Shivaji loots Surat (second time).
Oct. 17, Shiva defeats Daud Khan at Dindori.
Dec. Shiva robs Khandesh and Berar.
1671 Jan., Aurangzib dismisses all Hindu officers from revenue department. Chhatra Sal begins war against Aurangzib in Bundelkhand, (d. as king in 1731).
1672 ?.... Afridi rising under Acmal.
March, Satnami rebellion.
Apr. 21, Abdullah Qutb Sh. dies, Abdul Hasan succeeds.
Nov. 24, Ali Adil Shah II. dies, Sikandar succeeds, Khawas Khan becomes wazir (deposed 11 Nov. 1675).

1673 Shivaji gains Panhala 6 Mar., Parli 1 Apr., Satara 27 July.

1674 Feb. 24, Pratap Rao killed at Nesari, Hambir Rao succeeds as Senapati.

April 7, Aurangzib leaves Delhi for Hasan Abdal, where he stays till Dec. 1675.

June 6, Shivaji's coronation; death of Jija Bai 18 June.

1675 April–May, Shivaji captures Phonda fort and Karwar district.

Nov. 11, Bahlol Khan becomes wazir of Bijapur, (d. 23 Dec. 1677).

Dec. Guru Tegh Bahadur beheaded.

Vyankaji conquers and annexes Tanjore.

1676 June 1, Bahlol defeats Bahadur Khan at Halsangi, Islam Khan slain.

Oct. 8, Asad Khan created wazir of Aurangzib.

1677 *c.* Jan. 1, Shivaji starts on Karnatak expedition, halts at Haidarabad during Feb., at Shri Shaila 24 Mar.–1 Apr., gets Jinji fort 13 May, besieges Vellore 23 May (it falls on 21 July 1678), routs Sher Khan at Tiruvadi 26 June, meets Vyankaji at Tirumalavadi *c.* 18-23 July, ascends Mysore plateau on return home *c.* 5 Nov., Vyankaji attacks Shantaji 16 Nov., Shiva reaches home (Panhala) c. 4 Apr. 1678.

March 19 Amir Khan appointed governor of Afghanistan, (arrives 8 June 1678, d. 28 Apr. 1698).

July 7, Bahadur Khan captures Kulbarga, is replaced by Dilir in Aug., Dilir invades Golkonda, is repulsed at Malkhed in Sep.

Nov. 18 Aurangzib introduces puritanical simplicity at his Court.

1678 Feb. 21, Siddi Masaud becomes wazir of Bijapur, resigns Dec. 1683, is succeeded by Aqa Khusrau, who dies 11 Oct. 1684.

Dec. 10, Jaswant Singh dies at Jamrud.

„ 13, Shambhuji escapes to Dilir Khan,—returns to Panhala *c.* 4 Dec. 1679.

1679 Feb. 19, Aurangzib reaches Ajmir, invades Marwar, which he gives to Indra S. May 26.

April 2, Aurangzib reimposes *jiziya* on non-Muslims.

July 15, Ajit S. conveyed out of Delhi by Durgadas.
Sep. 25, Aurangzib reaches Ajmir again, annexes Marwar to empire in Oct.
Oct. 7–Nov. 14, Dilir. Khan threatens Bijapur fort, thereafter plunders the country around.
Nov. 4, Shivaji starts to raid Mughal districts, sacks Jalna 15–18 Nov., is defeated by Ranmast Kh., retreats to Patta *c.* 21 Nov.

1680 Jan. 23, Aurangzib enters Udaipur, visits Chitor 22 Feb., returns to Ajmir 22 Mar. April 4, Shivaji dies.
June 18, Shambhuji enters Raigarh as king.
Oct. 22, Maharana Raj S. dies, Jai S. succeeds. Shaista Khan's second governorship of Bengal 1680–88.

1681 Jan. 1, Prince Akbar crowns himself Emperor.
„ 16, Prince Akbar fleets away on failure of his rebellion, reaches Pali in Maharashtra 1 June.
Jan. 30–Feb. 1, Marathas loot all suburbs of Burhanpur.
March, Gangaram Nagar (rebel in Bihar) besieges Patna fort, (d. 1684).
June 14, Maharana Jai S. makes treaty of Rajsamudra with Aurangzib.
Sep. 6 Jahanara dies.
„ 8, Aurangzib starts from Ajmir for the Dèccan, reaches Burhanpur 13 Nov., and Aurangabad on 22 Mar., 1682.
Oct., Shambhuji puts Annaji, Soyra Bai and other conspirators to death.
Nov. 13, Shambhuji interviews Akbar at Pali.

1682 January, Shambhuji bombards Janjira.
Apr., Mughals besiege Ramsej, retire unsuccessful in October.
May 18, Shahu (or Shivaji II) born.
Nov., Mughals occupy Kalian, evacuate it on 23 March next.
Dec., Akbar removes from Pali to Banda.

1683 Apr. 5, Shambhuji begins war with Portuguese.
Sep., Akbar removes to Bicholim and tries to hire a ship for Persia.
„ 20 Shah Alam leaves Aurangabad on Ramghat expedition.
Oct. 22, Viceroy of Goa lays siege to Phonda, makes disastrous retreat 31 Oct.

Nov. 14, Marathas occupy S. Estevao and threaten Goa.
Dec. 1, Marathas invades Bardes and Salsette districts (ravage for one month).

1684 Jan. 5, Shah Alam reaches Bicholim proceeds to Goa; ravages Savantvadi and S. Ratnagiri, returns to Ramghat 20 Feb. and to Ahmadnagar 18 May.
Jan. 20. Akbar arranges peace between Shambhuji and Portuguese at Bhimgarh.
May, Shambhuji makes friendly treaty with English of Bombay.
Shia-Sunni fight in Srinagar.

1685 Jan. Vyankaji dies, Shahji II succeeds at Tanjore.
Feb., Khem Savant rebels against Shambhuji.
Apr. 1, Mughals begin siege of Bijapur.
Jat rising under Rajaram begins.
c. Oct. 8, Mughals Occupy Haidarabad (2nd time).
Oct., Khoja fanatics seize Broach fort.
Dec., Muluk Chand slays Pahar S. Gaur in Malwa, but Gaur rebellion continues till 1692.

1686 *c.* Mar. 7, Madanna murdered at Golkonda.
July 3, Aurangzib arrives at Bijapur siege.
Sep. 12, Fall of Bijapur, Sikandar Adil Sh. deposed, (d. 3 Apr. 1700).
Oct. 28, English in Bengal sack Hughli and begin war.

1687 Jan. 28, Mughals occupy Haidarabad (finally).
Feb. 7, Siege of Golkonda begins, it falls on Sep. 21.
Feb. 21, Shah Alam imprisoned.
Feb. Akbar sails for Persia, reaches Isfahan on 24 Jan., 1688, (d. 1704).
March, Durgadas returns to Marwar, Rathors press Mughals hard, Durjan Sal Hada seizes Bundi.
June 11, English rebels evacuate Hijli.
Nov. 28, Pam Nayak surrenders Berad capital Sagar, (d. 1 Jan. 1688).

1688 Jan. 11, Marathas plunder Conjeveram.
c. Feb. Rajaram Jat plunders Akbar's tomb at Sikandra, (is killed 4 July).
March, Azam captures Belgaon.

Aug. 6, Siddi Masaud yields Adoni fort.
Oct. English traders make war on Aurangzib on West Coast.
Nov. Bubonic plague in Bijapur (lasts two months).

1689 Feb. 1, Shambhuji and Kavi-kalash captured, reach imperial camp on 15 Feb., beheaded 3 March.
Feb. 8, Rajaram crowned at Raigarh, escapes from it 5 Apr., and reaches Jinji 1 Nov.
March 27, Matabar Khan recovers Kalian.
Oct. 19, Zulfiqar captures Raigarh with Shahu.
Dec. 25, Aurangzib pardons English traders, peace made.

1690 *c.* Jan. 28, Mughals storm Sinsani.
May 21, Aurangzib encamps at Galgala till Mar. 1695 (except Mar. 1691–May 1692).
„ 25, Marathas capture Rustam Khan near Satara.
Aug. 24, English found Calcutta.
Aug. Zulfiqar reaches Conjeveram.
c. Sep. 2 Zulfiqar arrives before Jinji begins siege.

1691 Dec. 16, Asad Khan and Kam Bakhsh reach Jinji.

1692 Dec. 13, Santa Ghorpare captures Ali Mardan Khan (faujdar of Conjeveram).
„ 16 Dhana Jadav captures Ismail Khan Maka outside Jinji.
c. „ 20, Kam Bakhsh arrested by Asad Khan.

1693 Jan 23, Zulfiqar abandons siege of Jinji and retires to Wandiwash.
? Matabar Khan makes war on Portuguese of North Konkan.

1694 Feb.–May, Zulfiqar levies tribute from Tanjore and conquers S. Arcot district.
Sep., Zulfiqar renews siege of Jinji, raises it in Dec.

1695, and encamps at Arcot (Jan. 1696–Mar. 1697).
Akbar's daughter restored to Aurangzib by Durgadas.

1695 May 21–1699 Oct. 19, Aurangzib encamps at Islampuri.
May, Shah Alam released and sent to the Panjab as governor.
Sept. 8, Piracy on the *Ganj-i-sawai.*
Oct., Mughals lay siege to Vellore, (it falls on 14 Aug., 1702).
Nov. Santa Ghorpare besieges Qasim Khan in Dodderi, Khan dies.

1696 Jan. 20 Santa kills Himmat Kh. at Basavapatan.

March, Santa reaches E. Karnatak; then invades Central Mysore in Nov.–Dec.

c. May, Rebellion of Shoya S. and Rahim Kh.; Bakht Buland Gond begins war in Deograh.

1697 Mar., Dhana defeats Santa in Satara district.

June, Santa murdered.

May–June, Zabardast Khan expels rebel Rahim Khan (who is slain Aug. 1698).

Nov., Prince Azim-ush-shan, new subahdar of Bengal, arrives at Bardwan.

„ Zulfiqar renews siege of Jinji.

1698 Jan. 8, Zulfiqar captures Jinji.

May, Akbar's son Buland Akhtar restored to Aurangzib by Durgadas. Emperor favours Durgadas and Ajit with jagirs and *mansab.*

1699 Feb., Rajaram reaches Vishalgarh.

Mar., Agreement between Emperor and European traders for guarding the Indian seas.

Oct. 19, Aurangzib leaves Islampuri to besiege forts.

„ 26, Rajaram issues from Satara.

Nov., First Maratha raid into Malwa (under Krishna Savant).

Dec. 9, Aurangzib begins siege of Satara, (it falls on 21 April 1700).

1700 March 2, Rajaram dies at Singhgarh; his son Karna crowned, but dies 23 March, when Shivaji III (son of Tara Bai) succeeds.

June 9, Aurangzib captures Parli.

Oct. 1, Imperial camp at Khawaspur washed away, Emperor's knee dislocated.

1701 March 9, Aurangzib besieges Panhala, (it falls on May 28).

Apr., Sir W. Norris visits Aurangzib as ambassador. Murshid Quli Khan appointed diwan of Bengal.

1702 Jan. 16, Aurangzib arrives before Khelna, siege begins, it falls on 7 June.

Durgadas and Ajit again rise against Aurangzib.

Dec. 27, Aurangzib begins siege of Kondana (Singhgarh), it falls on 8 Apr., 1703.

1703 Oct., Nima Sindhia raids Berar and Malwa, is expelled by Firuz Jang in Feb. next.

Dec. 2, Aurangzib lays siege to Rajgarh, it falls on 16 Feb., 1704.

1704 23 Feb., Aurangzib besieges Torna, it falls on 10 March.

1705 Feb. 8, Aurangzib besieges Wagingera, it falls on 27 April.

May–Oct., Aurangzib halts at Devapur, falls ill.

Nov., Durgadas again submits to Aurangzib, but rebels in April next.

1706 Jan. 20, Aurangzib reaches Ahmadnagar.

March, Marathas invade Gujrat, crushing defeat of Mughals at Ratanpur (15 March) and Baba Piara ford; Baroda sacked.

1707 Feb., Aurangzib sends away Kam Bakhsh to Bijapur (9th) and Azam to Malwa (13th), falls ill 17th, dies 20th.

March 8, Ajit S. recovers Jodhpur.

Index

A

Abbas Afghan, 339
Abdul Aziz Khan, 16–17, 180, 184
Abdul Ghafur, 328, 332
Abdul Ghani, 296
Abdul Hamid Khan, 349
Abdul Karim. *See* Bahlol Khan II
Abdul Muhammad, 197
Abdul Qadir, 241, 344
Abdul Wahab, 332
Abdullah, 29, 31, 114
Abdullah Khan, 91, 175, 247
Abdullah Pani, *See* Sardar Khan
Abdullah, Qazi, 220
Abdun Nabi Khan, 127
Abdur Rauf, Nawab, 207, 210
Abdur Razzaq Lari, *See* Mustafa Khan
Abdus Samad, 324
Abdus Shakur, 346
Abhay Chand, 88
Abul Fazl, 8
Abul Hasan, 106
Abul Path, 161
Abyssina, 91
Acmal Khan, 111–12, 115
Adab-i-Alamgiri, 43
Adil Shahi dynasty/Sultans of Bijapur, 148, 156–57, 185, 196–97, 200–1, 204–6, 209–10, 213, 233, 242, 249, 251, 256, 285
  Ali Adil Shah II (1657–72), 33, 35, 44, 148, 156–58, 164, 180, 191–94, 196–97
  Muhammad Adil Shah (1626–56), 10, 32–33, 146–48, 154, 196
  Sikandar Adil Shah (1672–86), 183, 197, 201, 202, 205–8, 210–11, 214–15, 248, 259
  decline and struggles for the regency, 196–98, 248, 256
administrative system in Aurangzib's reign, 384–87
  decline and public disturbances, 357–58
Afghanistan, 41, 135, 252, 378–79, 383
  war, 96*ff*
Afghans, 145, 164, 181, 196–97, 334, 355
  relations with Mughal empire, 108–10, 112
Afridi(s), 108, 116
  risings, 80, 111–14
Afridi, Dariya Khan, 113
Afzal Khan of Bijapur, 34, 156–58, 168
Aghar Khan, 113–14, 317
Agra, 57–58, 70, 71, 80, 85, 127, 168–72, 320, 357, 378
  advances of Aurangzib, 51–52
  fort, 91–94
Ahmad Khan, 154

Ahmad, Sayyid, 212–13
Ahmad Shah, 1
Ahmadabad, 42, 60, 62, 64, 89, 123, 134, 315, 349–50
Ahmadnagar, 4, 10, 146, 155, 174, 177, 180, 229, 232–33, 240–41, 249–50, 277, 298, 302–3, 316
  Aurangzib's retreat, 300–1
Ahoms, 96–97, 99–104
  conquest of Kamrup (1658), 97–98
Ajit Singh, 135–37, 144, 312, 314, 315–16
Ajmir, 62–65, 80, 134–36, 138, 140–41, 307, 312–14, 366, 378
Akbar, 9, 18, 25, 37, 147, 317, 333, 351, 358–59, 368, 376, 378–79
Akbar, Muhammad (son), 3, 11, 14, 83, 93, 229, 231, 233–34, 237, 240, 302, 319, 341–42
  campaign in Marwar, 139–40
  designs and disappointments at Maratha court, 237–39
  last efforts in India, 243–44
  proclaims himself emperor, 140–42
  failure and murder of Tahawwur Khan, 142–43 rebellion of, 134*ff*, 149–50
Akkanna, 213, 214, 216–17
Alam, Sayyid, 72, 73, 77
Alamgirnamah, 4
Alawardi Khan, 74
Ali Mardan Khan, 16, 18, 22, 115, 264–65, 266–67, 344
Ali Naqi, 40, 60
Ali Quli Khan, 75
Amanat Khan, 331–32
Amanullah Khan, 293
Ambaji, 278
Ambika Bai, 261
Amin Khan, Muhammad, 28–29, 66, 110, 111–12, 291, 296, 349
Amir Khan, 66, 82
  governs Afghanistan, 114–16
Amirit Rao, 258
Anand Rao, 176, 178, 186, 202
Annaji Datto, 227–28, 230
Annesley, Samuel, 326, 329–30
Aqa Khusrau, 205
Arab conquerors, 119
Arab Mullas, 196
Arabian Sea, 32, 196, 278, 330
Arcot, 153, 187, 259, 261, 263, 269–70
Arif, 15
Arjun Dev, fifth Sikh guru, 130
Arrakanese, 106–7, 334
Asad Khan, 264, 265, 266, 267, 268n^2, 286, 291, 302, 303, 307, 356
Asaf Khan, 6
Asan Khan, 268
Ashraf, 115
Askaran, 135
Asoka, 1
Assam, 5, 82, 102, 379
  treaty of peace, 101–2
  war, 96*ff*
Asurar Ali, 97
Attock, 110, 112
Aurangabad, 21, 29, 45, 173, 229, 299, 307, 378
Aurangabadi Mahal, 12, 220, 243
Aurangzib retreats to Ahmadnagar, 1705, 300–1
Aurangzib
  advances to Agra, 51–52
  anxieties and policy on the eve of the war of succession, 42–44
  campaigns in Balkh (1647), 15–17
  bigotry and temple destruction, 120, 123–24, 375
  Bijapur, invasion (1657), 32–35, 42; policy from 1680 to 1684, 204–6

character and effect of his reign, 351*ff*
childhood and education, 6–7
and Dara Shukoh, relation, 36–37
won the battle of Dharmat, 48–51, 67
in disgrace, 14–15
early life (1618–52), 1*ff*
empire, its resources, trade and administrative system, 378*ff*
European traders, policy towards, 330–32
family, 11–14
first half of reign, 79*ff*
first viceroyalty of the Deccan (1634–44), 9–11
Golkonda kingdom, invasion (1656), 29–31; besieges, 217–19; difficulties, 220–21
illness (1662), 81–82
Islamic ordinances, 85–88
last campaigns (1699–1705), 253
last days, 303–5
last phase of Career, 281*ff*
last will, 307–10
minor expeditions, 25–26
preparation for contesting the throne, 44–46 conquest of Palamau, 83–84
relations with the outer Muslim world, 89–91
besieges Qandahar, 18–20
reign, significance, 376–77
religious policy, 117*ff*
Samugarh battle (1658), 53–55
Satara, siege of, 286–87
second viceroyalty (1652–58), 21*ff* movements during second half of reign, 249–50 sorrow and misery of last years, 253–54, 301–2 strategic dispositions (1682), 232–33
success and policy during (1689), 256
Viceroys and their doings in Kashmir, 346–47
Wagingera captured, 1705, 295–98
war, desolation of the country caused by, 298; in Rajputana, rebellion of Akbar, 134*ff*
wrangles with Shah Jahan about Golkonda booty, 31–32
Ausa, 11
Avji Adhal, 277, 285
Azam Shah, Prince Muhammad, 11, 139, 201, 204, 206, 207–8, 209, 214, 224, 232–34, 243, 257, 274, 285, 287, 294–95, 304–6, 307–8, 312, 315, 318, 349, 353
Azim-ush-shan, Prince, 303, 322–23, 336–37

B

Babar, 16, 18
Badakhshan, 15–16
Badakhshi, Shah Muhammad, 88
Badr-un-nisa, 14
Baglana, 11, 26, 143, 176–78, 181, 187, 239, 279, 348
Bahadur Chand, Rajah, 84
Bahadur Khan (Khan-i-Jahan), 54, 61, 64, 66, 149, 175, 178–82, 197–99, 204, 205–6, 215, 228–29, 232–33, 240, 319
Bahadur Shah I, 132
Bahadur Shah Zafar, 5, 12
Bahadurgarh, 180, 249, 246, 292
Bahadurpur battle, 69–70
Bahirji, 187
Bahlol Khan, 34, 180–82, 194
Bahlol Khan II (Abdul Karim), 197
invades Golconda (1677), 199–200

regency (1675–77), 198–99
Bahmani kingdom, 16, 146
Bahramand Khan, 294
Baji Prabhu, 159, 167
Bakhtawar, 319
Bakhtiyar Khan, 67
Bakshis, 385
Balaji Ayji Prabhu, 230
Balkh, 40, 91, 164
campaigns of Aurangzib (1647), 15–17
Baluches, 108
Banda, Sayyid, 158
Bangashes, 115
Baqa Baba, 347
Basant, 62
Baud Khan, 76
Bavdekar, Ramchandra Nilkantha, 255–57, 264, 278, 281–82, 285, 289–90, 317
Bay of Bengal, 26, 27, 32, 196, 321, 324
Beg, Ashur, 329
Beg, Budaq, 89
Beg, Haji Said, 163
Beg, Isa, 45
Beg, Mirza Jan, 77
Beg, Muhammad Ali, 260
Beg, Muhammad Murad, 30, 75
Beg, Nazar, 66–67
Bengal, 378
English war with Aurangzib (1686–89), 323–26
governors in Aurangzib's reign, 334–37
its natural wealth and growth under Mughal peace, 333–34
pirates of Chatgaon and their ravages, 104–6 War, 76–78
Berads, 295, 297
Berar, 177, 179, 279, 291, 348, 378
raid by Shivaji, 176–77
Bernier, 6, 64, 66, 73*n*, 346, 381, 382
Bhabanath, 97
Bhagu, 109–10
Bhairav Khind, 165
Bhajja, 317
Bhakkar, 62, 65
Bhaskar, Krishnaji, 157
Bhim Singh, 138
Bhimsen, 210, 353, 359
Bhonsle, Minaji, 155
Bhonsle, Rupaji, 233, 234
Bhonsle, Santaji, 262
Bhonsle, Shahji, 11, 151–52, 153–54, 156, 176, 183
Bhonsle, Vyankoji Datto, 152, 176, 183, 184, 192, 268–69, 284
Bidar Bakht, 257, 270, 274, 277, 291–92, 306, 316–17, 349
Bihar, 67, 70, 76, 82–84, 114, 307, 337, 357, 378
rising of Gangaram, 319–20
war, pursuit of Shah Shuja, 73–76
Bihroz, Rajah of Kharagpur, 74
Bijapur, 3, 5, 10–12, 25, 27, 34, 42–44, 79, 116, 146–49, 152–56, 158–69, 164, 166, 168, 172, 213, 224, 232, 239–40, 242, 244, 247–48, 249–51, 258–59, 268, 272, 287, 289, 293–94, 299, 303–4, 307, 317, 347, 353, 356, 378
Aurangzib invaded (1657), 21, 32–35, 215 decline and fall, 191*ff*, 217; fall of the last king, 209–11
invasion of Jai Singh (1665–66), 191–93, 195; forced to retreat (1666), 193–94, 214
military aristocracy governing, 195–96
Mughal conquest, 242–43
Shivaji, relations, 173, 179–86, 190

Bir Singh, 343
Birbal, Rajah, 109
Birbhan, 128
Bolan Pass, 65
Borah, Baharji, 163
Bukhara, 16–17, 36, 91
Buland Akhtar, Prince, 72, 77, 82, 302, 314
Bundela(s), 170, 267
  War (1635), 8–9
Bundela, Bir Singh, Rajah of Urchha, 8–9, 83
Bundela, Champat Rai, 83, 339
Bundela, Chhatra Sal, 319, 343–44; early life, 339–40
  war with Mughal government, 340–41
Bundela, Rajah Devi Singh, 50, 83
Bundela, Rao Dalpat, 5, 210, 223, 232, 267, 269, 271, 297
Bundela, Subhkaran, 45, 83,166
Bundela, Sujan Singh, 50
Bundelkhand, 9, 171, 252, 337
Burhanpur, 46, 85, 195, 299
Burhanpuri, Bhimsen, 5

C

Canon Law, 209
Chaghtais, 233
Chaitanya, 365
Chakan, 152, 172, 243
  occupied by Shaista Khan, 159–60
Chakradhwaj, 103–4
Chand Sultan, 344
Chanda, 9, 179
Chandra Rao, 154
Chandrawat, Rao Amar Singh, 50, 178
Chandrawat, Gopal Singh, 319–20, 339
Chandrayandurg, 263, 264
Chandrayangarh, 270–71
Charles I, 327
Chatgaon
  conquest by Mughals, 5, 106–8
  pirates and their ravages in Bengal, 104–6
Chaudhuri, Gopal, 339
Chauragarh, 341–42
chauth, 144, 188, 252, 258, 281, 289, 300, 312, 341, 349
Child, Josiah, 326–27
Chimanji Bapuji, 161
Chintaman temple, Ahmadabad, 123
Christian revival movement, 365
Churaman, 317
civil war, 172, 181
  between Santa Ghorpare and Dhana Jadav, 275–76
commutation-money (*jiziya*), 118–19
Constantinople, 89, 91
conversions to Islam, forcible, 127, 131, 134
Courten, William, 327

D

da Gama, Vasco, 327
Dafle, Baji Chavan, 285
Dafle, Satvaji, 285, 287
Dalvi, Ram, 239
Danishmand Khan, 66, 80*n*
Dara Shukoh, 6, 12, 14, 15*n*, 19, 30–31, 35, 36–38, 39, 40–43, 44, 51–52, 55, 57–60, 70, 74, 78, 82, 85, 91–92, 94, 123, 127, 233, 306, 309
  movements after Dharmat, 52–53
  humiliation and murder, 66–67
  persecution of theologians and heretics, 88–89 in Rajputana, battle of Deorai, 62–64
  Samugarh battle (1658), 53–57; after, 61–62

Datta Trimbak, 171
Daud Khan, 62, 77, 84, 166, 174, 176, 178, 270–71, 303
  defeated by Shivaji, 176–77
Daulatabad, 13, 32, 44, 45, 211, 225, 305
  captured by Malik Amber, 10
Dayaldas, 144
Deccan, 44, 79,112, 116, 239, 252, 253, 300, 311, 323, 380
  causes of Mughal weakness, 149–50
  history in seventeenth century, 146–49
  improvements made in administration, 24
  Mughal Deccan decay and misery, 21–22
Deccani Sultantes, 242
Delhi, 61, 85, 89, 101, 378
Delhi Sultanate, 146
Deogarh, 9, 11, 25, 340
Deorai battle, 62–64
Devi Singh, 9
Dhamuni, 9, 277, 338–41
Dharmat, 47–48, 69
  battle of, 48–51, 57, 67
Dheds, 293
Dianat Khan, 307
Dikas Banu, 7*n*
Dilawwar, 35, 106
Dilir Khan, 67, 69, 77, 100–2, 149, 164, 166– 167, 172, 174–75, 178, 179, 181, 185, 192, 194, 201–4, 214, 230, 232, 234, 241, 340, 342
  invaded Bijapur, 202
  invaded Golkonda (1677), 199–200
  disgraced and recalled, 204
Dilras Banu Begum, 11, 13
Dindori, 176–77
diplomatic relations, 25
Dowager Sultan, 217
Durgadas. *See* Rathor, Durgadas

E

East India Company, 2, 242, 323, 326, 328, 330–32, 335, 363, 382–83
economic drain of Aurangzib's ceaseless warfare, 352–53
English trade, traders
  with Bengal, 320–21; Mughal officials, friction, 321–23
English war
  with Aurangzib in Bengal (1686–89), 323–26
  with the Mughals on the West Coast, 326–27
European pirates in Indian seas, Seventeenth century, 327–29
exertion (*jihad*), 117, 120, 371

F

Fahimullah, Shaikh, 211
Fakhr-ul-Islam, 332
fanatics, 37, 329, 350, 375
Farhad Khan, 106–7
Fatawa-i-Alamgiri, 367
Fathullah Khan, 177, 290, 291
faujdars, 387
Fazil Khan, 243, 346
Fazl Khan, 159
Feringi pirates, 104–6
Fidai Khan, 114, 346–47
Firuz Jang, Ghazi-ud-din Khan Bahadur, 57, 208, 210, 221, 222–23, 241, 242, 257, 275, 289, 295, 338–39, 341
Fulad Khan, 170–71

G

Gadadhar Singh, 104
Gangaram, rising in Bihar, 319–20

Garha, 341–42
Garnock, Job, 323
Gauhar-ara Begam, 302
Gaur, Arjun Singh, 49
Gaur, Bhagwant Singh, 318–19
Gaur, Bhim Singh, 55
Gaur, Devi Singh, 319
Gaur, Gopal Singh, 319
Gaur, Pahar Singh, 318–19
Gaur, Shivram, 55
Gaurs, 145
Gayer, John, 329, 331–32
Ghairat Khan, Sayyid, 61, 222
Ghalib, 159
Ghazni, 379
Ghazzali, Imam Muhammad, 7
Ghilzais, 114
Ghorpare, Hindu Rao, 296, 303
Ghorpare, Ranuji, 277, 282, 289–90
Ghorpare, Santa, 148, 251, 255–59, 264–67, 270–76, 282–83, 296
Goa, invasion of Shambhuji (1683), 236–37
Gohain, Bar, 102
Gohain, Burha, 102, 104
Gokla, 127
Golkonda, 25, 26–27, 44, 116, 147–48, 171, 179, 182, 193–94, 199, 206–8, 212, 215–17, 233, 240, 242, 244, 249, 250, 255, 260–61, 268, 320, 356, 384
  invasion by Aurangzib, 21, 29–31; besieges, 3, 5, 26, 217–21, 245, 353; wrangles with Shah Jahan over booty, 31–35
  Dilir Khan and Bahlol Khan invaded, 199–200
  Mughal policy towards king, 213–14
  Shivaji's alliance, 182–84
  surrendered by treachery, 224–25
Gond chiefs, kingdom of Deogarh, 9, 11, 25
  and their relations with Mughals, 341–43
Gond, Bakht Buland, 338, 342, 343–44
Gondwana, 171
Govind Rai, tenth Sikh guru, 131–33
Gray, Henry, 242
Gujarat, 11, 15, 39, 44, 62, 64, 82, 123–25, 143, 171, 175, 178, 290, 302–3, 307, 348, 378
  governors under Aurangzib, 349
  Murad Bakhsh crowns himself, 40–42
Gul Muhammad, 65
Gulrukh Banu, 75
Gwalior, 51–52

H

Hadas of Bundi, 145, 312–13
Hada, Rao Anurudh Singh, 233, 313, 318
Hada, Chhatra Sal, Rao of Bundi, 34, 54–57, 83
Hada, Durjan Sal, 313, 341
Hada, Mukund Singh, 49–50
Hada, Ram Singh, 270
Hadi, Muhammad, 336
Hafiz Ambar, 284
Haidar, Qazi, 239
Haidarabad, 26, 29–30, 223–24, 299
Hambir Rao, 187
Hamid-ud-din Khan, 258, 274, 284, 290, 307
Hanumant Rao, 251, 277, 289
Har Govind, sixth Sikh guru, 130–31
Har Kishan, seventh Sikh guru, 131
Harris, Benjamin, 326
Harshvardhan, 1
Hasan, Abdal, 113, 114, 181

Hasan Ali Khan, Sayyid, 127, 232
Hasan Ali Khan, 128, 137
Hashim, Mir Muhammad of Gilan, 6
Hassan Hamidan, 330
Hastings, Warren, 355
Hayat Bakhsh Begam, 212
hereditary succession, 370
heretics, persecution, 88–89
Himmat Khan, 252, 257, 259, 274
Hindu Rai, 248
Hindus, 48, 78, 105, 120–21, 125, 132, 243, 348, 355, 358, 361–62, 364
  of Kashmir, 131
  of Mathura district oppressed, peasant uprisings, 127–28
  and Muhammadans, difference, 370–71; occasional union, 374–75
  politically depressed and degraded under Aurangzib, 371–72
  repressive measures against, 126–27
  society, deterioration and inherent weakness, 374
Hinduism, 92, 96–97, 119, 123, 127, 149
Hira Bai Zainabadi, 12–13
Hiraji Farzand, 170–71, 230
Hizbar Khan, 114
Humayun, 67, 91, 308
Husain Shah, 10

I

Ibn Husain, 101, 106–7
Ibrahim Khan, 325, 335–36, 346–47
Ibrahim, Muhammad, 213, 260, 329
idolatory, 92, 127
Iftikhar Khan, 50, 174
Ikhlas Khan Miana, 176, 178
Imam-ud-din, Sayyid, 350
imperial dominions harassed by Marathas (1706–7), 302–303
Inayet Khan, 142, 162
Indian civilization, decay in Aurangzib's reign, causes and signs, 358–59
Indian Ocean, 18, 150, 327–28, 330
Indramani, Rajah of Dhamdhera, 45
Indus, 65, 110
Inu Mand, 303
Iradat Khan, 5
Ishwardas, 313–14
Islam Khan (governor of Malwa), 54, 75, 198, 334
Islam, Islamic, 92, 146
  ordinances of Aurangzib, 85–88
  rigidity, 376
  theocracy, 117, 122
Islampuri, 250, 252, 277, 286, 292, 314
Ismail, 160
Ismailia sect, 348, 350
Itibar Khan, 332
Itimad Khan, 329, 331, 346
Itiqad Khan, 247, 343
Izid Bakhsh, 302

J

Jadav Rao of Kaliani, 179, 192
Jadav, Dhana Singh, 251, 255–56, 258–59, 264–65, 266, 268, 270, 275–76, 277, 282, 283, 287, 290, 296, 303, 349
Jafar Jatali, 359
Jafar Khan, 44, 363
Jafar Quli, 316
jagirdars, jagirs, 22, 24, 173, 380
Jahanara, 14, 37, 59, 94, 95, 305
Jahangir, 6, 8, 9, 18, 104, 109, 130, 334, 363

Jahanzeb Banu, 233–34
Jai Singh, Mirza Rajah, 8, 39, 63–65, 67–68, 74, 103, 134, 140, 144, 149, 168–72, 214, 291, 340, 363
 failure and death, 194–95
 invasion of Bijapur (1665–66), 191–93
 forced retreat from Bijapur, 1666, 193–94
 against Shivaji, capture of Purandar, 164–67
Jalal Khan, 72
Jan Muhammad, Sayyid, 186
Jani Sahiba, 217
Jaswant Singh, Maharajah of Marwar, 39, 46, 47–48, 62–63, 80, 83, 112, 134, 160, 162, 169, 172, 174–75, 195, 243, 314
 battle of Dharmat, 48–51
 death, 134–35
 treachery, 70–71
Jat disturbances near Agra, 316–18
Jat uprisings, 127–28
Jauhar, Siddi. *See* Salabat Khan
Jawhar, 26, 179
Jayadhwaj, Rajah of Kuch Bihar, 99, 101
jaziya, 186, 355, 322, 382
Jhala, Dayal Singh, 49
Jhujhar Singh, 8
Jija Bai, 151, 152, 168
Jinji, 27, 153, 183, 184, 187, 248, 250–52, 257–69, 275–76, 281–82, 338
 Siege, 263–64, 270–71
Jiv Mahala, 158
Jiwan, Malik, 65, 67

K

Kabir, 130
Kachhwa, Bishun Singh, Rajah of Amber, 317–18
Kali Kumari, Rani, 83
Kalian, 156, 159–60, 174, 179, 279
Kaliani, 34–35, 43, 192, 194, 199
Kam Bakhsh, Muhammad, 12, 14, 251, 264, 265, 266, 268, 284, 286, 296, 302, 303–4, 305, 306–7, 361
Kamal Afghan, Khwajah, 74
Kamil Khan, 110
Kamrup, Mughals lost (1667–81), 103–4
Kar Talb Khan, 160, 336
Karan, Rao of Bhutiya clan, 82
Karan, Rao of Bikaner, 45
Karani-dan, 313
Karnatak
 Eastern, 379; its division and history, 259–60; Mughal penetration (1687), 260–61
 Mughal-Maratha struggle (1690–98), 353
 operations during (1693–94), 268–69
Kasari Singh, Gond Rajah, 25
Kashgar, 91
Kashmir, 378
 Aurangzib's viceroys and their doings, 346–47 condition under the Mughals, 344–46
Kavi-Kalash, 230–32, 236, 238–39, 245–47
Keigwin, Richard, 242
Kesari Singh, 186, 342
Keshav Rai temple, Mathura, 123, 127
Khafi Khan, 5, 128, 189, 283, 300, 359
Khajwa battle, 71–73, 83
Khajwa, Jaswant Singh's treachery, 70–71
Khalilullah Khan, 53, 56*n*, 58, 61, 65, 215
Khalji, Ala-ud-din, 118

Khan Bakhsh, 265–66
Khan Muhammad, 32–34, 156, 183
Khanazad Khan (Lord High Steward), 272–74
Khandesh, 171, 177, 179, 181, 187, 229, 239, 242, 279, 303, 307, 338, 348, 378; annexed by Akbar, 9
Khan-i-Alam, 302
Khan-i-Dauran, 11, 25, 61
Khan-i-Zaman, 45
Khatak(s), 108, 116
  risings (1672), 111–14
Khatak, Khus-hal Khan, 115
Khawas Khan, 192, 197–98
Khelna, siege, 290–92
Khichi, Lal Singh, 318
Khizr Khan Pani, 198
Khojas, 350
Khushhal Khan, 111–12
Khusrau, 130
Khwaja Khan, 258
Khwajah Anwar, 336
Khwajah Nuruddin, 347
Kidd, William, 330
Kishan Singh, Rajah of Chanda, 343
Koli, occupied by Marathas, 179
Kondana (Singhgarh), Rajgarh and Torna, siege, 292–93
Kondana fort, 173
Kond-dev, Dadaji, 152, 153
Konkan, 26
  war (1689–1704), 278
Korde, Raghunath Balla, 154
Krishna Ram, 335–36
Kuch Bihar, 5, 82, 84, 102, 383
  Mir Jumla conquers, 98–99
  Mughal relations before (1658), 96–97
  recovered, 104
Kuch Hajo, 96–97
Ḳuk Singh, Rajah of Deogarh, 342
Kulbarga, 34, 35, 146, 199–201, 249, 258, 294

L

Lahor, 6, 61–62, 65–66, 81, 85, 88, 130–31, 378
Lakhi, Jadav Rao, 285
Lakshmi Narayan, 96
Lal Tikri, 295–96
lawlessness in Aurangzib's reign, 82–83
Lodi, Sher Khan, 184
Lodi, Sher Shah, 183–84
Ludi Khan, 174
Luso-Maratha war, 238
Lutfullah Khan, 257

M

Madan Singh, 284
Madanna Pandit, 182–84, 199, 208, 213–14, 216–17
Madhu Singh, 284
Mahab Khan, 260
Mahabat Khan, 34, 39, 112–13, 178, 260, 317, 349
Mahadev Anant, 230
Mahadik, Harji, 244, 255, 259–60, 262
Maharashtra, 10–11, 121, 171, 187, 230, 238, 252, 256, 258–59, 268, 270, 276, 281–83, 292, 311, 313, 379
  the land and its people, 150–51. *See also* Marathas
Mahdavi sect, 196, 348
Maka, Ismail Khan, 261–62, 264–65, 268
Makaji, 176
Makhdum, Sayyid, 205
Malhar, Dado, 277
Malhar, Krishna, 290
Malhar, Shankaraji, 255, 256–57, 282
Malik Ambar, 9–10, 151–52

Maloji, 151
Malwa, 171, 348, 378
  importance in Mughal times, 337–38
  Maratha incursions, 338–39
  rising of Gopal Singh Chandrawat, 319–20, 339
Mane, Nagoji, 257, 285
Manji Malar, Rajah of Chanda, 342
mansabdars, 86, 266, 380, 385
Manucci, Nicholas, 6, 12 56*n*, 62, 87, 105, 125, 225, 254, 269*n*, 293, 298, 300, 317, 352, 361, 368
manufacturers and trade. *See* trade and industry
Maqbul, Khwajah, 64
Maratha(s), 150–51, 176, 177, 207, 227–30, 233, 270, 279, 294–99
  activities during (1673), 179–81
  and Aurangzib's struggle up to (1700), 249*ff*
  confederacy, 1
  government policy (1689–99), 281–82
  invasion of Gujarat (1706), 349–50
  kingdom, internal condition and Shambhji's doings (1685–87), 244–45
  occupation of the Koli country and demand of *chauth* from Surat, 179
  light cavalry, 10
  military operations against, 149
  navy and wars with Siddis (1680–82), 234–85
  power, rise of, 146*ff*
  recovery (1690–95), 250, 256–58
  systems of spoliation and warfare, 299–300
Marhamat Khan, 243
Marwar
  seized by Aurangzib, 134–35
  thirty years' warfare, 311–13
Masaud, Siddi, 185–86, 193, 200–2, 205–7, 243
Masir-i-Alamgir, 4
Masulipatam, 26, 320, 379, 384
Masum Aqil Khan, 5
Matabar Khan, 279–80
Mathura, 123, 127–28, 171
Mathurapur, 100–1
Matlab Khan, 258
Medini Singh, 68
Melgiri Pandit, 206
Mian Mir, 37, 66, 88
Mihr-un-nisa, 14, 302
military arrangements of imperialists during 1696, 274–75
Minhaj, Shaikh, 200, 216–17
Mir Atish, 243
Mir Husain, 347
Mir Ibrahim of Haidarabad *See* Mahabat Khan
Mir Ibrahim, Sayyid, 89
Mir Jumla, 31–35, 38–39, 43, 44, 45, 53, 70, 73–78, 88, 98, 100, 102–4, 334
  greatness of character, 102–3
  history and position, 26–28
  conquest of Kuch Bihar and Assam, 98–99, 105
  resumes the offensive, 101
Mir Khalil, 12
Mir Muhammad Ibrahim, 216
Mir Murtaza, 99
Mir, Shaikh, 45, 49, 54, 55, 62, 64
Mirza Mohammad Amin, 183
Mirza Tafakhkhur, 360
Mohite, Hambir Rao, 228–29
Mongoloid chiefs of Arrakan, 104
moral degeneration of the Mughal aristocracy, 359–61
Moro Pant, 160, 178, 228
Mavles, 153
Muazzam, Muhammad. *See* Shah Alam

Mughal Empire, Mughal government, Mughals
- and Afghans, relations, 108–10
- bankruptcy, 355–57
- Bijapur, 208; conquest of provinces, 242–43; and Shivaji (1678–79), 184–86
- conquest of Chatgaon, 106–8
- disintegration, 1–2
- penetration into Eastern Karnatak, 260–61
- failure, emperor's distraction and suspicion, 233–34
- famine and pestilence, 223–24
- generals, campaigns (1671–72), 178
- and Gond kingdom, relations, 341–43
- policy towards the Golkonda king, 213–14
- lost Kamrup (1667–81), 103–4
- Maratha struggle (1690–98), 353–54
- true character and aim, 369–70
- war with Chhatra Sal Bundela, 340–41
- war with Maharana of Udaipur, 137–39

Mughis-ud-din, Qazi, 118
Muhakam Singh, 178, 316
Muhammad Said. *See* Mir Jumla
Muhammad Shah, 109
Muhammad Sultan, Prince, 12, 29–31, 56, 58, 70, 71, 73, 75, 77, 92
Muhammad, Sayyid of Qanauj, 94
Muhtasib, 386
Muizz-ud-din, 232, 251, 257
Mukarram Khan, 114
Mukhlis Khan, 45, 243, 330
Mulhir, 176, 178
Mulla Ahmad, 156
Mulla Chalak, 110
Mullah Salih, 6
Multan, 18, 62, 378
Muluk Chand, Rai, 318
Mumtaz Mahal, 6, 95
Munawwar Khan, 107
Muqarrab Khan, 245
Murad Bakhsh, Muhammad, 16, 39, 40–42, 44, 47, 50, 54–55, 58, 78, 94, 153, 290, 302
- captivity and death, 59–60

Murshid Quli Khan, 22–24, 45, 49, 254, 336–37
Musa Khan, 213
Muslims, decline in India, its causes, 372–73
Mustafa Khan, 153, 224
Mutamand, 92
Muzaffar, Sayyid, 212–13

N

Nadir Shah, 1, 378
Nadira Banu, 65–66
Nagar, Ishwarda; *Futuhat-i-Alamgiri*, 5
Nagoji Mane, 275
Nanak, Guru (first Sikh guru), 129–30
Napoleon I, 248, 368
Nara Narayan, Raja of Kuch Bihar, 96
Narnol, 128–29
Nasir Muhammad Khan, 183
Nasiri Afghan, 339
Nasiri Khan, 155
Nasrat Jang, 285–286, 289–90, 291, 292, 297, 303
Navarro, Abraham, 327
Nawal Shah, 344
Nayak, Barmappa, 272, 273, 274
Nayak, Dulva, 239
Nayak, Pam, 203, 205, 208, 242, 294

Nayak, Pedda Pidia, 289, 294–95, 296–97
Nayak, Som Singh, 296–97
Nayak, Yachapa, 261, 262, 268–69
Nazar Ali Khan, 303, 349
Nazar Muhammad Khan, 16, 17, 91
Nejabat Khan, 332
Neknam Khan, 177
Netaji Palkar, 158, 160, 169, 192, 230
Nila Prabhu, 186
Nima, 338
Nimbalkar, Amrit Rao, 275
Nimbalkar, Shidhoji, 186
Niraji Raoji, 171, 173, 182, 255
Nizam Shahi dynasty, Nizam Shah, 9, 11, 146, 151–52
Nizam, Shaikh, 245
Norris, William, 331
Nur Jahan, 363
Nur-ud-din Khawas, 60
Nur-ul-Haq, 332
Nurullah Khan, 335

O

official bribery, life and character of the official world, 363–64
official peerage, 379–81
Oudh, 307, 357, 374, 378, 383
over-centralization: its disastrous effect on the administration, 368–69

P

Padishahnamah, 4
Palamau, 82
  conquest of, 83–84
Pandhre, Baharji, 285
Pandhre, Mankholi, 257
Panhala, 158–60, 180–81, 184, 186, 203, 227–28, 292, 331
  siege, 245, 256–58, 289–90
Panipat battle, second, 351
Parashuram Trimbak, 255, 256, 278, 282–83, 287–88, 291
Parekh, Keshav, 332
Parenda, 43, 44, 174, 193
Parli fort captured, 288–89
Pasha, Boutros, 120*n*
Pasha, Ghazi Mustafa Kamal, 376–77
Path Jang Khan, 193
peasant uprisings, 127–28
Penu-konda, 303
Persian Gulf, 18, 328, 331, 383
Persian war, 57
Phukan, Baduli, 101–2
Phukan, Bar Patra, 102, 104
Pingle, Kesho Trimbak, 260, 261
Pingle, Moro Trimbak, 158, 177, 179, 230
Pingle, Nilkanth Moreshwar, 230, 255, 262
Pishin, 18
political disabilities of non-Muslims, 118–20
poll-tax (*jiziya*) on non-Muslims, 118, 124–25, 135, 137, 144, 338
polytheism, 117
Portuguese, 104, 239, 280
  pirates of Chatgaon, 334
  Shambhuji war (1683), 235–36
Prahlad Niraji, 182, 245, 255, 262
Pran Narayan, Rajah of Kuch Bihar, 97, 104
Pratap Chero, 84
Pratap Rao, 173, 176–77, 180
Pratap Rudra, Rajah of Warangal, 268
Pratapgarh fort, 154, 157, 158
Prithwi Singh, Rajah of Srinagar, 67–68
Puna, 165

occupied by Shaista Khan, 159–60
Purandar, 154
captured by Jai Singh, 164–67
Treaty (1665), 167–68, 173, 191
Purhunar Banu, 94

Q

Qabil Khan, 363
Qalich Khan, 19, 219
Qandahar, 17, 21, 37, 65, 112, 164, 378
besieged by Aurangzib, 18–20
Qasim Khan, 39, 48–51, 206, 252, 257, 259, 268, 272–74
Qasim, Siddi, 242
Qasimbhai, 332
Qattal, Sayyid Raju, 212
Qazi-ul-quzat, 386
Quli Uzbak, Sayyid, 77
Quran, 6–7, 41, 85, 94–95, 209, 314, 366, 373
political ideals, influence on Muslim population and the subject creeds, 120–22
Qutb Khan, 216
Qutb Shahi dynasty/Sultans of Golkonda, 10, 26, 32, 147–48, 192, 199, 200, 208
Abdullah Qutb Shah, sixth king, 27–29, 31–32, 44, 212, 217–18
Abul Hasan Qutb Shah, 182–83, 185, 215, 217, 219, 220, 222, 225; accession, 212–13
decline and fall, 212*ff*
rupture with the Mughals (1655), 28–29
rupture with Shivaji, 184
war with the Mughals and capture of Haidarabad, 215–16
Qutb-ud-din, Sayyid, 89
Qutb-ul-mulk, 30–31

R

Rabia, Saint, 11
Radandaz Khan, 129
Radha Bai, 275
Raghudev, 96
Raghu-mitra, 171
Raghunath Narayan Hanumante, 259
Raghunath Pant, 155
Raghunath, Bahtti noble, 136
rahdari, 322–23
Rahim Khan, 335–36
Rahmat-un-nisa (Nawab Bai), 12, 14
Raibhan, 284–85
Raigarh, 154
capture and Shambhuji's family, 247–48
Raj Singh, Maharana, 136, 137, 140, 349
Rajaram, 128, 227–28, 230–31, 247–48, 250, 252, 261–65, 267–71, 275–78, 281, 283, 285, 287–88, 317–18, 338, 343
at Jinji, 261–63
leading Maratha ministers and generals at accession, 254–57
return home and activities (1698–99), 276–77
Rajas Bai, 278, 285
Rajputana, Rajasthan, 80, 249
partial peace, 144–45
war in, rebellion of Akbar, 134*ff*
Rajputs, 52, 54–55, 57, 62, 64, 71, 114, 133, 137–43, 164, 174, 230, 233, 297, 358, 375
clans, divided, 47–48
battle of Dharmat, 48–51
tribal system, 108
Rajrup, Rajah, 63, 68
Raju, Rajah of Rajauri, Kashmir, 12
Ram Singh, Rajah of Chanda, 343
Ram Singh, son of Jai Singh 74, 103–4, 169–70, 171

Ramaji Pandit, 278
Ramchandra Nilkantha. *See* Bavdekar, Ramchandra Nilkantha
Ramdas Swami, 288
Ranchordas Jodha, 136
Randaula Khan, 11, 34
Ranga, Kasturi, 157
Ranjit Singh, Maharaja of Punjab, 133
Ranmast Khan, 186, 232–33, 235, 294
Ratan Singh, 319
Rathors, 50, 62, 113, 136, 137, 139–41, 311–15
Rathor, Durgadas, 135–37, 140, 142, 143, 144, 230, 231, 311–12, 315–16
  in Marwar (1687–98), 313–15. *See also* Ajit Singh
Rathor, Indra Singh, 135, 136
Rathor, Raja Ram Singh, 54–55
Rathor, Raja Rup Singh, 55
Rathor, Ratan Singh, 49, 51
Raushanara, 66
Razi, Aqil Khan, 45
religious persecution of the Bothra and Khoja sects, 350
religious policy of Aurangzib, 117*ff*
revenue system
  of Malik Amber, 10
  Murshid Quli Khan, 22–25
Ruhullah Khan, 206, 224, 232–33, 247, 260, 294
Rustam Khan, 19, 54, 55, 57, 213, 217, 223, 250, 256–58, 261, 338–39
ryots, 23

S

Sadiq, Muhammad, 261, 262
Sadullah Khan, Wazir, 18–19, 31, 359
Saif Shikan Khan, 49, 50, 54, 62, 210, 220
Safdar Khan, 319, 349
Safi Khan, 313, 317
Safiyat-un-nisa, 313–14
Said, Muhammad. *See* Mir Jumla
Saif Khan, 346
Salabat Khan (Jauhar, Siddi), 158–59, 220
Samudragupta, 1
Samugarh battle (1658), 53–55, 57–58, 67
Saqi Mustad Khan, 7
Sarbarah Khan, 222
Sardar Khan, 186, 224
Sarfaraz Khan, 192
Sarmad, 37, 88–89
Satara, 288
  siege by Aurangzib, 286–87
Satnami sect, risings (1672), 128–29
sauda-i-khas, 322
Savant, Khem, 239
Savant, Krishna, 277, 338–39
Sayyid Sultan, 212
Sayyids of Barha, 67, 78, 89, 196, 309
Senapati, 281
Shah Abbas, 18
Shah Abbas II, 89–91
Shah Alam (Muazzam, Muhammad), 12, 14, 45, 139, 142, 143, 149, 162, 172, 173, 174, 178, 195, 203–4, 207, 208, 209, 215, 216–17, 237, 265, 303, 305, 361
  and Dilir Khan, quarrel, 174–75
  imprisoned, 219–20
  invades South Konkan, 240–41
Shah Ismail I Safavi, 11
Shah Jahan, 3, 4, 6, 7, 8, 9, 10, 11, 15, 16, 17, 18, 22, 26, 29, 35, 52, 65, 69, 70, 80, 82, 88, 104, 130, 153, 285, 302, 309, 358–59, 363, 380

and Aurangzib, conflict over Golkonda booty, 31–32
captivity (1658), 57–59; life in captivity at Agra fort, 91–94
illness and the rebellion of his sons, 36ff; consequent disorder in the Empire, 38–40
last days, 94–95
Shah Nawaz Khan, 11, 46, 62–64
Shah of Persia, 41
Shah Quli, 208
Shahar Banu Begam, 200–1, 204
Shahbaz Khan, 40–41
Shahbazgarhi, 114
Shahji. *See* Bhonsle, Shahji
Shahji II, 268–69
Shahji, Sayyid, 350
Shahu, son of Shambhuji (Shivaji II), 228, 247–48, 283, 284–85
Shaikh-ul-Islam, 5
Shaista Khan, 39, 44, 58, 66, 104–6, 149, 164, 170, 321–22, 324–25, 334–35
Shivaji's night attack, 160–62
occupies Puna and Chakan, 159–60
Shambhuji, 143, 144, 147–48, 149–50, 158, 168, 172, 173, 185–87, 191, 203–7, 209, 215, 250–51, 254, 259–60, 275, 279, 284–85, 300
capture and execution, 245–47
conspiracy against, 230–32
doings after (1683), 241–42
invades Goa (1683), 236–37
rebellions against, Mughal operations from (1683), 239–40
reign 1680–89, 227*ff*
renewed war with Mughals, 228–30
war with Portuguese (1683), 235–36
Shambhuji II, 278, 283
Shams-ud-din Mukhtar Khan, 45
Shankara, 287
Shankardev, 97, 365
Sharf Yahia, Shaikh of Munir, 7
Sharza Khan, 185, 192–93, 198, 201, 204–6, 207–8, 210
Sher Afkan Khan, 341
Shias, 27, 89–90, 220, 308, 345–48, 375. *See also* Sunnis
Shihab-ud-din Khan, 141, 232, 241
Shinwaris, 108
Shirazi, Mir Lutfullah, 97
Shirazi, Shaikh Zain-ud-din Qutb Muhi, 7
Shirke, Kanhoji, 285
Shirkes, 231
Shivaji, 104, 116, 147–49, 178, 180, 191–92, 197, 200, 201, 203, 245, 251, 260, 268, 279, 285, 288, 351
(1670–1680), 173*ff*
slays Afzal Khan of Bijapur, 156–58
escape from Agra, 170–72
visits Aurangzib at Agra, 168–70
last campaign, 186–87
central administration, 188–89
character and place in history, 189–90
childhood, education and character, 152–53 early conquests, 153–54
defeats Daud Khan at Dindori (1670) and raids Berar, 176–77
alliance with Golkonda and conquest of Karnatak, 182–84
Jai Singh against, 164–67
Karnatak Expedition, 182
kingdom, army and revenue, 187–88
first war with Mughals (1657), 154–56

rupture with Mughals and recovery of forts, 173–74
besieged in Panhala, 158–60
night attack on Shaista Khan, 160–62
Surat, first sack of, 162–64; second loot, 175–76
Shivaji III, son of Tarabai, 278, 283
Sholapur, 10, 180
Shova Singh, 335–36
Shuja Shah, 8, 39, 52, 62–63, 67, 82, 83, 91, 105, 244, 321
battle of Bahadurpur, 69–70
abandons Bengal, his end, 78
pursuit of and war in Bihar, 73–76
battle of Khajwa, 71–73
Shujaet Khan, 112–13, 312, 313, 349
Siadat Khan, 303
Siddi Halal, 179
Siddi Marjan, 33–34
Siddi of Janjira, 327
Siddis, 172, 234–35, 279
Sikandar, 193
Sikh religion, changes, 129–32
Sikhs, 1, 361
Sindhia, Nima, 251, 257
Sipihr Shukoh, 14, 54, 64, 66, 67
Sisodia, Rajah Rai Singh, 34, 50
Sisodia, Sujan Singh, 49
Sisodias, 137, 140, 144
Siwistan, 65
slavery, 118, 362
Somaji, 230
Somnath temple, Benares, 123
Sonaji, 154
Sorya Bai, 230–31
Subhan Quli, 17
Subh-Karn, 179
Sudhakar (elephant), 7–8
Sufism, 37, 375
Sulaiman Shukoh, 39, 52–53, 69, 94; end of, 67–68
Sultan Abil Hasan, 213
Sultan Husain (Mir Malang), 304
Sunnis, 201, 220, 345–47, 350, 373, 375
superstitions, 361–62
Surat, 7, 41, 62, 187, 228, 234, 238, 244, 277–79, 316, 321–23, 325–32, 348, 353, 379
English factors, 175
first sack by Shivaji, 162–64
Maraths' demand for chauth, 179
second loot, 175–76

T

Tagore, Rabindranath, 129
Tahawwur Khan, 136, 139–41
murder and failure of Akbar, 142–43
Tahir Wahid, Mirza, 90
Tahir, Muhammad, 45, 89
Talish, Shihab-ud-din, 5
Talmud, 37
Tanaji Malusare, 173
Tantric worship and animism, 365
taqavvi loans, 23
Tara Bai, 277–78, 283
Tarbiyat Khan, 90, 287, 290, 303
Tartars, 175
Tatta, 62, 378
tax for land (*kharaj*), 118
taxations for non-Muslims, 118. *See also jaziya*
Tegh Bahadur, eighth Sikh guru, 131
Telinga dynasty, 353
Telingana, 179, 291, 378
temples, destroyed in Auranzib's reign, 120, 123–24, 375
theologians, persecution, 88–89
Timur, 16, 40, 289
Tipam rajah, 101
Todar Mal, 23
trade and industry, under Aurangzib's reign, 381–84

injury by war, disorder, and official exactions, 354–57
Tuka bai, 152
Tulsidas, 365
Turks, 18, 114, 164, 372

U

Udai-bhan, 173
Udaipur, 134; Mughal war with Maharana, 137–39
Udipuri Mahal, 12, 286, 302, 306
Umar Pathan, 339
Ummed Khan, 106
Uzbeks, 16, 17, 41, 57

V

Vaishnavism, 334, 365
Vajragarh (Rudramal) fort, 165–66
Vansittart, 355
Vellore, 183–84, 187, 259, 263, 268, 270–71
Venkatadri Murari, 185
Versailles, 80, 351
Vijaynagar Empire, 27, 183, 320
Vikram Shah, Koli Rajah, 179
village communities, 387
Vishwa Singh, 97
Vishwanath temple, Benares, 123
Vyankoji Datto. *See* Bhonsle, Vyankoji Datto

W

Wagingera, 205, 253, 264, 293–94, 303; captured by Aurangzib (1705), 295–98, 300
Waite, Nicholas, 331
Wandiwash, 250, 261, 267–71
war of succession, 24, 42–44, 85, 89, 191; Auragzib's triumph, 47*ff*; end of Dara and Shuja, 61*ff*
Wardhangarh, 290, 291
Wazir Khan, 45
Weldon, G., 327
Wellesley, Lord, 355
Western Ghats, 278–80
Wilkins, Thomas, 242

Y

Yesu Bai, 185, 284
Yuan Chwang, 150
Yusuf, Muhammad, 346
Yusufzais, 108, 111–12, 114–15; risings of 1667, 109–10, 172

Z

Zabardast Khan, 336
Zain-ud-din, Shaikh, 305
Zain-ul-abidin, 77
zakat, 379
Zeb-un-nisa, 13, 143, 302
Zia-ud-din Muhammad, 244
zimmi (non-Muslim), 118–19
Zinat-un-nisa, 13–14, 268, 286, 305
Zubdat-un-nisa, 14
Zulfiqar Khan, 54, 73, 75–76, 248, 255, 262, 263–65, 266, 267–68, 286; operations during 1696, 270–71; movements and difficulties, 1695, 269–70